Living with Christ — Subscription Order Form

Receive Christ's message every day!

This monthly missalette brings the [...] in a way that is truly breathtaking. [...] tiful daily devotional for [...]

YES! Please [...] t's 14 issues (1 per mon[...] and Easter 2017) or 14 [...] nd Sacred Journey as specified

☐ *PLUS* Edition
$43.50/yr (+tax)

☐ Essential Edition
$38.50/yr (+tax)

PLUS Edition: With tax, in QC, NS: $50.01, ON, NB, NL, MB: $49.16 Rest of Canada: $45.68
Essential Edition: With tax, in QC, NS: $44.26, ON, NB, NL, MB: $43.51 Rest of Canada: $40.43

Name _____ Client # _____

Apt _____ Address _____

City _____ Prov/State _____

Postal Code _____ Telephone _____

Email _____

☐ I would like to receive special offers, promotions, newsletters, contest and event information from Novalis and Bayard Press Canada.

☐ Enclosed is my cheque/money order (do not send cash)

Charge my: ☐ VISA ☐ MASTERCARD

Card # _____ Exp _____

Signature _____

Subscription to be paid in CDN $ in Canada. Outside of Canada please call for prices.
Special offer expires June 30, 2017.

P.O. Box 11050, Centre-Ville Stn, Montreal, QC, H3C 4Y6
Tel: 1-800-387-7164 (US & Canada)
Email: living@novalis.ca

SMAD17

Living with Christ

SUNDAY MISSAL

2016-2017

with Prayers and Hymns

Approved for use in Canada

NOVALIS

©2016 Novalis Publishing Inc.

Novalis Publishing Inc.
10 Lower Spadina Ave., Suite 400
Toronto, ON M5V 2Z2
Canada

Telephone: 1-800-387-7164
Fax: 1-800-204-4140
Email: books@novalis.ca

www.novalis.ca

Since 1936 Novalis has dedicated itself to the development
of pastoral resources which assist the People of God in
preparing for and participating in the liturgy.

Please write, phone, or visit us for further information on
our publications, or visit our website at www.novalis.ca.

For more suggested intentions for the Prayer of the Faithful,
please visit: www.livingwithchrist.ca.

Editor-in-chief: Natalia Kononenko, email: LWC@novalis.ca

Associate editor: Nancy Keyes

Music: All credits accompany the music texts.

Cover design & layout: Jessica AuCoin

ISBN: 978-2-89688-273-1

ISSN: 0832-5324

Printed in Canada

We acknowledge the financial support of the Government of
Canada through the Book Publishing Industry Development
Program (BPIDP) for our publishing activities.

Contents

*As two pieces of wax
fused together make one,
so they who receive
Holy Communion
are so united with Christ
that Christ is in them
and they are in Christ.*

St. Cyril of Alexandria

Introductory Rites

ENTRANCE CHANT
(or Entrance Antiphon — ▶ The appropriate day)

GREETING
In the name of the Father, and of the Son, and of the Holy Spirit. **Amen.**

1 The grace of our Lord Jesus Christ, and the love of God, and the communion of the Holy Spirit be with you all.

2 Grace to you and peace from God our Father and the Lord Jesus Christ.

3 The Lord be with you.

And with your spirit.

PENITENTIAL ACT
(or Rite for the Blessing and Sprinkling of Water, p. 7)

Brothers and sisters, let us acknowledge our sins, and so prepare ourselves to celebrate the sacred mysteries. *(Pause)*

1 **I confess to almighty God
   and to you, my brothers and sisters,
   that I have greatly sinned,
   in my thoughts and in my words,
   in what I have done and in what I have
   failed to do,
   through my fault, through my fault,
   through my most grievous fault;
   therefore I ask blessed Mary ever-Virgin,
   all the Angels and Saints,**

and you, my brothers and sisters,
to pray for me to the Lord our God.

May almighty God have mercy on us, forgive
us our sins, and bring us to everlasting life.
Amen.

Lord, have mercy.	**Lord, have mercy.**
or Kyrie, eleison.	**Kyrie, eleison.**
Christ, have mercy.	**Christ, have mercy.**
or Christe, eleison.	**Christe, eleison.**
Lord, have mercy.	**Lord, have mercy.**
or Kyrie, eleison.	**Kyrie, eleison.**

2 Have mercy on us, O Lord.
   For we have sinned against you.

   Show us, O Lord, your mercy.
   And grant us your salvation.

   May almighty God have mercy on us, forgive
   us our sins, and bring us to everlasting life.
   Amen.

Lord, have mercy.	**Lord, have mercy.**
or Kyrie, eleison.	**Kyrie, eleison.**
Christ, have mercy.	**Christ, have mercy.**
or Christe, eleison.	**Christe, eleison.**
Lord, have mercy.	**Lord, have mercy.**
or Kyrie, eleison.	**Kyrie, eleison.**

3 You were sent to heal the contrite of heart:

Lord, have mercy.	**Lord, have mercy.**
or Kyrie, eleison.	**Kyrie, eleison.**

You came to call sinners:

Christ, have mercy. **Christ, have mercy.**
or Christe, eleison. **Christe, eleison.**

You are seated at the right hand of the Father
to intercede for us:

Lord, have mercy. **Lord, have mercy.**
or Kyrie, eleison. **Kyrie, eleison.**

May almighty God have mercy on us, forgive
us our sins, and bring us to everlasting life.
Amen.

(▶ *Glory to God, p. 10*)

RITE FOR THE BLESSING AND SPRINKLING OF WATER

Dear brothers and sisters, let us humbly beseech
the Lord our God to bless this water he has created, which will be sprinkled on us as a memorial of our Baptism. May he help us by his grace
to remain faithful to the Spirit we have received.
(Pause)

1 Almighty ever-living God, who willed that
   through water, the fountain of life and the source
   of purification, even souls should be cleansed
   and receive the gift of eternal life; be pleased,
   we pray, to bless this water, by which we seek
   protection on this your day, O Lord. Renew the
   living spring of your grace within us and grant
   that by this water we may be defended from all
   ills of spirit and body, and so approach you with
   hearts made clean and worthily receive your
   salvation. Through Christ our Lord. **Amen.**

2 Almighty Lord and God, who are the source and origin of all life, whether of body or soul, we ask you to bless this water, which we use in confidence to implore forgiveness for our sins and to obtain the protection of your grace against all illness and every snare of the enemy. Grant, O Lord, in your mercy, that living waters may always spring up for our salvation, and so may we approach you with a pure heart and avoid all danger to body and soul. Through Christ our Lord. **Amen.**

3 *During Easter Time:*
Lord our God, in your mercy be present to your people's prayers, and, for us who recall the wondrous work of our creation and the still greater work of our redemption, graciously bless this water. For you created water to make the fields fruitful and to refresh and cleanse our bodies. You also made water the instrument of your mercy: for through water you freed your people from slavery and quenched their thirst in the desert; through water the Prophets proclaimed the new covenant you were to enter upon with the human race; and last of all, through water, which Christ made holy in the Jordan, you have renewed our corrupted nature in the bath of regeneration. Therefore, may this water be for us a memorial of the Baptism we have received, and grant that we may share in the gladness of our brothers and sisters who at Easter have received their Baptism. Through Christ our Lord. **Amen.**

Where it is customary to bless salt also, add:

We humbly ask you, almighty God: be pleased in your faithful love to bless this salt you have created, for it was you who commanded the prophet Elisha to cast salt into water, that impure water might be purified. Grant, O Lord, we pray, that, wherever this mixture of salt and water is sprinkled, every attack of the enemy may be repulsed and your Holy Spirit may be present to keep us safe at all times. Through Christ our Lord. **Amen.**

During the sprinkling, an appropriate song may be sung.

May almighty God cleanse us of our sins, and through the celebration of this Eucharist make us worthy to share at the table of his Kingdom. **Amen.**

GLORY TO GOD
Omitted during Advent and Lent.

Glory to God in the highest,
and on earth peace to people of good will.

We praise you,
we bless you,
we adore you,
we glorify you,
we give you thanks for your great glory,
Lord God, heavenly King,
O God, almighty Father.

Lord Jesus Christ, Only Begotten Son,
Lord God, Lamb of God, Son of the Father,
you take away the sins of the world,
    have mercy on us;
you take away the sins of the world,
    receive our prayer;
you are seated at the right hand of the Father,
    have mercy on us.

For you alone are the Holy One,
you alone are the Lord,
you alone are the Most High,
Jesus Christ,
with the Holy Spirit,
in the glory of God the Father.
Amen.

COLLECT (▶ *The appropriate day*)

Liturgy of the Word

READINGS (▶ *The appropriate day*)

HOMILY

PROFESSION OF FAITH

1 Nicene Creed
All bow at the words in italics.

I believe in one God,
the Father almighty,
maker of heaven and earth,
of all things visible and invisible.

I believe in one Lord Jesus Christ,
the Only Begotten Son of God,
born of the Father before all ages.
God from God, Light from Light,
true God from true God,
begotten, not made,
consubstantial with the Father;
through him all things were made.
For us men and for our salvation
he came down from heaven,
and by the Holy Spirit was incarnate
of the Virgin Mary,
and became man.
For our sake he was crucified under
Pontius Pilate,
he suffered death and was buried,
and rose again on the third day
in accordance with the Scriptures.
He ascended into heaven

11

and is seated at the right hand of the Father.
He will come again in glory
to judge the living and the dead
and his kingdom will have no end.

I believe in the Holy Spirit, the Lord,
    the giver of life,
who proceeds from the Father and the Son,
who with the Father and the Son is adored
    and glorified,
who has spoken through the prophets.

I believe in one, holy, catholic and
    apostolic Church.
I confess one Baptism for the forgiveness
    of sins
and I look forward to the resurrection of
    the dead
and the life of the world to come. Amen.

2 Apostles' Creed
All bow at the words in italics.

I believe in God,
the Father almighty,
Creator of heaven and earth,
and in Jesus Christ, his only Son, our Lord,
who was conceived by the Holy Spirit,
born of the Virgin Mary,
suffered under Pontius Pilate,
was crucified, died and was buried;
he descended into hell;
on the third day he rose again from the dead;
he ascended into heaven,
and is seated at the right hand of God
    the Father almighty;
from there he will come to judge
    the living and the dead.

I believe in the Holy Spirit,
the holy catholic Church,
the communion of saints,
the forgiveness of sins,
the resurrection of the body,
and life everlasting. Amen.

PRAYER OF THE FAITHFUL (▶ *The appropriate day*)

Liturgy of the Eucharist

PREPARATION OF THE GIFTS

Blessed are you, Lord God of all creation, for through your goodness we have received the bread we offer you: fruit of the earth and work of human hands, it will become for us the bread of life. **Blessed be God for ever.**

> By the mystery of this water and wine may we come to share in the divinity of Christ who humbled himself to share in our humanity.

Blessed are you, Lord God of all creation, for through your goodness we have received the wine we offer you: fruit of the vine and work of human hands, it will become our spiritual drink. **Blessed be God for ever.**

> With humble spirit and contrite heart may we be accepted by you, O Lord, and may our sacrifice in your sight this day be pleasing to you, Lord God.
>
> Wash me, O Lord, from my iniquity and cleanse me from my sin.

Pray, brothers and sisters, that my sacrifice and yours may be acceptable to God, the almighty Father.
May the Lord accept the sacrifice at your hands for the praise and glory of his name, for our good and the good of all his holy Church.

PRAYER OVER THE OFFERINGS
(The appropriate day)

THE EUCHARISTIC PRAYER

The Lord be with you. **And with your spirit.**
Lift up your hearts. **We lift them up to the Lord.**
Let us give thanks to the Lord our God.
It is right and just.

*The Priest selects an appropriate Preface, which
concludes with the* Holy, Holy.

PREFACE I OF ADVENT

It is truly right and just, our duty and our salvation, always and everywhere to give you thanks,
Lord, holy Father, almighty and eternal God,
through Christ our Lord.

For he assumed at his first coming the lowliness of human flesh, and so fulfilled the design
you formed long ago, and opened for us the way
to eternal salvation, that, when he comes again in
glory and majesty and all is at last made manifest,
we who watch for that day may inherit the great
promise in which now we dare to hope.

And so, with Angels and Archangels, with
Thrones and Dominions, and with all the hosts
and Powers of heaven, we sing the hymn of your
glory, as without end we acclaim: **Holy, Holy**
(p. 37)

PREFACE II OF ADVENT

It is truly right and just, our duty and our salvation, always and everywhere to give you thanks,
Lord, holy Father, almighty and eternal God,
through Christ our Lord.

15

For all the oracles of the prophets foretold him, the Virgin Mother longed for him with love beyond all telling, John the Baptist sang of his coming and proclaimed his presence when he came.

It is by his gift that already we rejoice at the mystery of his Nativity, so that he may find us watchful in prayer and exultant in his praise.

And so, with Angels and Archangels, with Thrones and Dominions, and with all the hosts and Powers of heaven, we sing the hymn of your glory, as without end we acclaim: **Holy, Holy** *(p. 37)*

PREFACE I OF THE NATIVITY OF THE LORD

It is truly right and just, our duty and our salvation, always and everywhere to give you thanks, Lord, holy Father, almighty and eternal God.

For in the mystery of the Word made flesh a new light of your glory has shone upon the eyes of our mind, so that, as we recognize in him God made visible, we may be caught up through him in love of things invisible.

And so, with Angels and Archangels, with Thrones and Dominions, and with all the hosts and Powers of heaven, we sing the hymn of your glory, as without end we acclaim: **Holy, Holy** *(p. 37)*

PREFACE II OF THE NATIVITY OF THE LORD

It is truly right and just, our duty and our salvation, always and everywhere to give you thanks, Lord, holy Father, almighty and eternal God, through Christ our Lord.

For on the feast of this awe-filled mystery, though invisible in his own divine nature, he has appeared visibly in ours; and begotten before all ages, he has begun to exist in time; so that, raising up in himself all that was cast down, he might restore unity to all creation and call straying humanity back to the heavenly Kingdom.

And so, with all the Angels, we praise you, as in joyful celebration we acclaim: **Holy, Holy** *(p. 37)*

PREFACE III OF THE NATIVITY OF THE LORD

It is truly right and just, our duty and our salvation, always and everywhere to give you thanks, Lord, holy Father, almighty and eternal God, through Christ our Lord.

For through him the holy exchange that restores our life has shone forth today in splendour: when our frailty is assumed by your Word not only does human mortality receive unending honour but by this wondrous union we, too, are made eternal.

And so, in company with the choirs of Angels, we praise you, and with joy we proclaim: **Holy, Holy** *(p. 37)*

PREFACE I OF THE BLESSED VIRGIN MARY

It is truly right and just, our duty and our salvation, always and everywhere to give you thanks, Lord, holy Father, almighty and eternal God, and to praise, bless, and glorify your name on the Solemnity of the Motherhood of the Blessed ever-Virgin Mary.

For by the overshadowing of the Holy Spirit she conceived your Only Begotten Son, and without losing the glory of virginity, brought forth into the world the eternal Light, Jesus Christ our Lord.

Through him the Angels praise your majesty, Dominions adore and Powers tremble before you. Heaven and the Virtues of heaven and the blessed Seraphim worship together with exultation. May our voices, we pray, join with theirs in humble praise, as we acclaim: **Holy, Holy** *(p. 37)*

PREFACE OF THE EPIPHANY OF THE LORD

It is truly right and just, our duty and our salvation, always and everywhere to give you thanks, Lord, holy Father, almighty and eternal God.

For today you have revealed the mystery of our salvation in Christ as a light for the nations, and, when he appeared in our mortal nature, you made us new by the glory of his immortal nature.

And so, with Angels and Archangels, with Thrones and Dominions, and with all the hosts and Powers of heaven, we sing the hymn of your glory, as without end we acclaim: **Holy, Holy** *(p. 37)*

PREFACE I OF LENT

It is truly right and just, our duty and our salvation, always and everywhere to give you thanks, Lord, holy Father, almighty and eternal God, through Christ our Lord.

For by your gracious gift each year your faithful await the sacred paschal feasts with the joy of minds made pure, so that, more eagerly intent on prayer and on the works of charity, and participating in the mysteries by which they have been reborn, they may be led to the fullness of grace that you bestow on your sons and daughters.

And so, with Angels and Archangels, with Thrones and Dominions, and with all the hosts and

Powers of heaven, we sing the hymn of your glory, as without end we acclaim: **Holy, Holy** *(p. 37)*

PREFACE II OF LENT

It is truly right and just, our duty and our salvation, always and everywhere to give you thanks, Lord, holy Father, almighty and eternal God.

For you have given your children a sacred time for the renewing and purifying of their hearts, that, freed from disordered affections, they may so deal with the things of this passing world as to hold rather to the things that eternally endure.

And so, with all the Angels and Saints, we praise you, as without end we acclaim: **Holy, Holy** *(p. 37)*

PREFACE III OF LENT

It is truly right and just, our duty and our salvation, always and everywhere to give you thanks, Lord, holy Father, almighty and eternal God.

For you will that our self-denial should give you thanks, humble our sinful pride, contribute to the feeding of the poor, and so help us imitate you in your kindness.

And so we glorify you with countless Angels, as with one voice of praise we acclaim: **Holy, Holy** *(p.37)*

PREFACE IV OF LENT

It is truly right and just, our duty and our salvation, always and everywhere to give you thanks, Lord, holy Father, almighty and eternal God.

19

For through bodily fasting you restrain our faults, raise up our minds, and bestow both virtue and its rewards, through Christ our Lord.

Through him the Angels praise your majesty, Dominions adore and Powers tremble before you. Heaven and the Virtues of heaven and the blessed Seraphim worship together with exultation. May our voices, we pray, join with theirs in humble praise, as we acclaim: **Holy, Holy** *(p. 37)*

PREFACE OF 1ST SUNDAY OF LENT

It is truly right and just, our duty and our salvation, always and everywhere to give you thanks, Lord, holy Father, almighty and eternal God, through Christ our Lord.

By abstaining forty long days from earthly food, he consecrated through his fast the pattern of our Lenten observance and, by overturning all the snares of the ancient serpent, taught us to cast out the leaven of malice, so that, celebrating worthily the Paschal Mystery, we might pass over at last to the eternal paschal feast.

And so, with the company of Angels and Saints, we sing the hymn of your praise, as without end we acclaim: **Holy, Holy** *(p. 37)*

PREFACE OF 2ND SUNDAY OF LENT

It is truly right and just, our duty and our salvation, always and everywhere to give you thanks, Lord, holy Father, almighty and eternal God, through Christ our Lord.

For after he had told the disciples of his coming Death, on the holy mountain he manifested to them his glory, to show, even by the testimony of the law and the prophets, that the Passion leads to the glory of the Resurrection.

And so, with the Powers of heaven, we worship you constantly on earth, and before your majesty without end we acclaim: **Holy, Holy** *(p. 37)*

PREFACE OF 3RD SUNDAY OF LENT

It is truly right and just, our duty and our salvation, always and everywhere to give you thanks, Lord, holy Father, almighty and eternal God, through Christ our Lord.

For when he asked the Samaritan woman for water to drink, he had already created the gift of faith within her and so ardently did he thirst for her faith, that he kindled in her the fire of divine love.

And so we, too, give you thanks and with the Angels praise your mighty deeds, as we acclaim: **Holy, Holy** *(p. 37)*

PREFACE OF 4TH SUNDAY OF LENT

It is truly right and just, our duty and our salvation, always and everywhere to give you thanks, Lord, holy Father, almighty and eternal God, through Christ our Lord.

By the mystery of the Incarnation, he has led the human race that walked in darkness into the radiance of the faith and has brought those born in slavery to ancient sin through the waters of regeneration to make them your adopted children.

Therefore, all creatures of heaven and earth sing a new song in adoration, and we, with all the host of Angels, cry out, and without end acclaim: **Holy, Holy** *(p. 37)*

21

PREFACE OF 5TH SUNDAY OF LENT

It is truly right and just, our duty and our salvations, always and everywhere to give you thanks, Lord, holy Father, almighty and eternal God, through Christ our Lord.

For as true man he wept for Lazarus his friend and as eternal God raised him from the tomb, just as, taking pity on the human race, he leads us by sacred mysteries to new life.

Through him the host of Angels adores your majesty and rejoices in your presence for ever. May our voices, we pray, join with theirs in one chorus of exultant praise, as we acclaim: **Holy, Holy** (p. 37)

PREFACE OF THE PASSION OF THE LORD
(Palm Sunday)

It is truly right and just, our duty and our salvation, always and everywhere to give you thanks, Lord, holy Father, almighty and eternal God, through Christ our Lord.

For, though innocent, he suffered willingly for sinners and accepted unjust condemnation to save the guilty. His Death has washed away our sins, and his Resurrection has purchased our justification.

And so, with all the Angels, we praise you, as in joyful celebration we acclaim: **Holy, Holy** (p. 37)

PREFACE I OF EASTER

It is truly right and just, our duty and our salvation, at all times to acclaim you, O Lord, but

> *Easter Vigil:* on this night
> *Easter Sunday and Octave:* on this day
> *rest of Easter Time:* in this time

above all to laud you yet more gloriously, when Christ our Passover has been sacrificed.

For he is the true Lamb who has taken away the sins of the world; by dying he has destroyed our death, and by rising, restored our life.

Therefore, overcome with paschal joy, every land, every people exults in your praise and even the heavenly Powers, with the angelic hosts, sing together the unending hymn of your glory, as they acclaim: **Holy, Holy** *(p. 37)*

PREFACE II OF EASTER

It is truly right and just, our duty and our salvation, at all times to acclaim you, O Lord, but in this time above all to laud you yet more gloriously, when Christ our Passover has been sacrificed.

Through him the children of light rise to eternal life and the halls of the heavenly Kingdom are thrown open to the faithful; for his Death is our ransom from death, and in his rising the life of all has risen.

Therefore, overcome with paschal joy, every land, every people exults in your praise and even the heavenly Powers, with the angelic hosts, sing together the unending hymn of your glory, as they acclaim: **Holy, Holy** *(p. 37)*

PREFACE III OF EASTER

It is truly right and just, our duty and our salvation, at all times to acclaim you, O Lord, but in this time above all to laud you yet more gloriously, when Christ our Passover has been sacrificed.

He never ceases to offer himself for us but defends us and ever pleads our cause before you:

he is the sacrificial Victim who dies no more, the Lamb, once slain, who lives for ever.

Therefore, overcome with paschal joy, every land, every people exults in your praise and even the heavenly Powers, with the angelic hosts, sing together the unending hymn of your glory, as they acclaim: **Holy, Holy** *(p. 37)*

PREFACE IV OF EASTER

It is truly right and just, our duty and our salvation, at all times to acclaim you, O Lord, but in this time above all to laud you yet more gloriously, when Christ our Passover has been sacrificed.

For, with the old order destroyed, a universe cast down is renewed, and integrity of life is restored to us in Christ.

Therefore, overcome with paschal joy, every land, every people exults in your praise and even the heavenly Powers, with the angelic hosts, sing together the unending hymn of your glory, as they acclaim: **Holy, Holy** *(p. 37)*

PREFACE V OF EASTER

It is truly right and just, our duty and our salvation, at all times to acclaim you, O Lord, but in this time above all to laud you yet more gloriously, when Christ our Passover has been sacrificed.

By the oblation of his Body, he brought the sacrifices of old to fulfillment in the reality of the Cross and, by commending himself to you for our salvation, showed himself the Priest, the Altar, and the Lamb of sacrifice.

Therefore, overcome with paschal joy, every land, every people exults in your praise and even the heavenly Powers, with the angelic hosts, sing together the unending hymn of your glory, as they acclaim: **Holy, Holy** *(p. 37)*

PREFACE I OF THE ASCENSION OF THE LORD

It is truly right and just, our duty and our salvation, always and everywhere to give you thanks, Lord, holy Father, almighty and eternal God.

For the Lord Jesus, the King of glory, conqueror of sin and death, ascended (today) to the highest heavens, as the Angels gazed in wonder.

Mediator between God and man, judge of the world and Lord of hosts, he ascended, not to distance himself from our lowly state but that we, his members, might be confident of following where he, our Head and Founder, has gone before.

Therefore, overcome with paschal joy, every land, every people exults in your praise and even the heavenly Powers, with the angelic hosts, sing together the unending hymn of your glory, as they acclaim: **Holy, Holy** *(p. 37)*

PREFACE II OF THE ASCENSION OF THE LORD

It is truly right and just, our duty and our salvation, always and everywhere to give you thanks, Lord, holy Father, almighty and eternal God, through Christ our Lord.

For after his Resurrection he plainly appeared to all his disciples and was taken up to heaven in their sight, that he might make us sharers in his divinity.

Therefore, overcome with paschal joy, every land, every people exults in your praise and even the heavenly Powers, with the angelic hosts, sing

together the unending hymn of your glory, as they
acclaim: **Holy, Holy** *(p. 37)*

PREFACE OF PENTECOST

It is truly right and just, our duty and our salvation, always and everywhere to give you thanks,
Lord, holy Father, almighty and eternal God.

For, bringing your Paschal Mystery to completion, you bestowed the Holy Spirit today on those
you made your adopted children by uniting them
to your Only Begotten Son.

This same Spirit, as the Church came to birth,
opened to all peoples the knowledge of God and
brought together the many languages of the earth
in profession of the one faith.

Therefore, overcome with paschal joy, every
land, every people exults in your praise and even
the heavenly Powers, with the angelic hosts, sing
together the unending hymn of your glory, as they
acclaim: **Holy, Holy** *(p. 37)*

PREFACE OF HOLY TRINITY

It is truly right and just, our duty and our salvation, always and everywhere to give you thanks,
Lord, holy Father, almighty and eternal God.

For with your Only Begotten Son and the Holy
Spirit you are one God, one Lord: not in the unity
of a single person, but in a Trinity of one substance.

For what you have revealed to us of your glory
we believe equally of your Son and of the Holy
Spirit, so that, in the confessing of the true and
eternal Godhead, you might be adored in what is
proper to each Person, their unity in substance,
and their equality in majesty.

For this is praised by Angels and Archangels, Cherubim, too, and Seraphim, who never cease to cry out each day, as with one voice they acclaim: **Holy, Holy** *(p. 37)*

PREFACE I OF THE MOST HOLY EUCHARIST

It is truly right and just, our duty and our salvation, always and everywhere to give you thanks, Lord, holy Father, almighty and eternal God, through Christ our Lord.

For he is the true and eternal Priest, who instituted the pattern of an everlasting sacrifice and was the first to offer himself as the saving Victim, commanding us to make this offering as his memorial.

As we eat his flesh that was sacrificed for us, we are made strong, and, as we drink his Blood that was poured out for us, we are washed clean.

And so, with Angels and Archangels, with Thrones and Dominions, and with all the hosts and Powers of heaven, we sing the hymn of your glory, as without end we acclaim: **Holy, Holy** *(p. 37)*

PREFACE II OF THE MOST HOLY EUCHARIST

It is truly right and just, our duty and our salvation, always and everywhere to give you thanks, Lord, holy Father, almighty and eternal God, through Christ our Lord.

For at the Last Supper with his Apostles, establishing for the ages to come the saving memorial of the Cross, he offered himself to you as the unblemished Lamb, the acceptable gift of perfect praise.

Nourishing your faithful by this sacred mystery, you make them holy, so that the human race,

27

bounded by one world, may be enlightened by one faith and united by one bond of charity.

And so, we approach the table of this wondrous Sacrament, so that, bathed in the sweetness of your grace, we may pass over to the heavenly realities here foreshadowed.

Therefore, all creatures of heaven and earth sing a new song in adoration, and we, with all the host of Angels, cry out, and without end we acclaim: **Holy, Holy** *(p. 37)*

PREFACE OF THE TRANSFIGURATION OF THE LORD

It is truly right and just, our duty and our salvation, always and everywhere to give you thanks, Lord, holy Father, almighty and eternal God, through Christ our Lord.

For he revealed his glory in the presence of chosen witnesses and filled with the greatest splendour that bodily form which he shares with all humanity, that the scandal of the Cross might be removed from the hearts of his disciples and that he might show how in the Body of the whole Church is to be fulfilled what so wonderfully shone forth first in its Head.

And so, with the Powers of heaven, we worship you constantly on earth, and before your majesty without end we acclaim: **Holy, Holy** *(p. 37)*

PREFACE I OF SUNDAYS IN ORDINARY TIME

It is truly right and just, our duty and our salvation, always and everywhere to give you thanks, Lord, holy Father, almighty and eternal God, through Christ our Lord.

For through his Paschal Mystery, he accomplished the marvellous deed, by which he has freed us from the yoke of sin and death, summoning us to the glory of being now called a chosen race, a royal priesthood, a holy nation, a people for your own possession, to proclaim everywhere your mighty works, for you have called us out of darkness into your own wonderful light.

And so, with Angels and Archangels, with Thrones and Dominions, and with all the hosts and Powers of heaven, we sing the hymn of your glory, as without end we acclaim: **Holy, Holy** *(p.37)*

PREFACE II OF SUNDAYS IN ORDINARY TIME
It is truly right and just, our duty and our salvation, always and everywhere to give you thanks, Lord, holy Father, almighty and eternal God, through Christ our Lord.

For out of compassion for the waywardness that is ours, he humbled himself and was born of the Virgin; by the passion of the Cross he freed us from unending death, and by rising from the dead he gave us life eternal.

And so, with Angels and Archangels, with Thrones and Dominions, and with all the hosts and Powers of heaven, we sing the hymn of your glory, as without end we acclaim: **Holy, Holy** *(p.37)*

PREFACE III OF SUNDAYS IN ORDINARY TIME
It is truly right and just, our duty and our salvation, always and everywhere to give you thanks, Lord, holy Father, almighty and eternal God.

For we know it belongs to your boundless glory, that you came to the aid of mortal beings

29

with your divinity and even fashioned for us a remedy out of mortality itself, that the cause of our downfall might become the means of our salvation, through Christ our Lord.

Through him the host of Angels adores your majesty and rejoices in your presence for ever. May our voices, we pray, join with theirs in one chorus of exultant praise, as we acclaim: **Holy, Holy** *(p. 37)*

PREFACE IV OF SUNDAYS IN ORDINARY TIME

It is truly right and just, our duty and our salvation, always and everywhere to give you thanks, Lord, holy Father, almighty and eternal God, through Christ our Lord.

For by his birth he brought renewal to humanity's fallen state, and by his suffering, cancelled out our sins; by his rising from the dead he has opened the way to eternal life, and by ascending to you, O Father, he has unlocked the gates of heaven.

And so, with the company of Angels and Saints, we sing the hymn of your praise, as without end we acclaim: **Holy, Holy** *(p. 37)*

PREFACE V OF SUNDAYS IN ORDINARY TIME

It is truly right and just, our duty and our salvation, always and everywhere to give you thanks, Lord, holy Father, almighty and eternal God.

For you laid the foundations of the world and have arranged the changing of times and seasons; you formed man in your own image and set humanity over the whole world in all its wonder, to rule in your name over all you have made and for ever praise you in your mighty works, through Christ our Lord.

And so, with all the Angels, we praise you, as in joyful celebration we acclaim: **Holy, Holy** *(p. 37)*

PREFACE VI OF SUNDAYS IN ORDINARY TIME

It is truly right and just, our duty and our salvation, always and everywhere to give you thanks, Lord, holy Father, almighty and eternal God.

For in you we live and move and have our being, and while in this body we not only experience the daily effects of your care, but even now possess the pledge of life eternal.

For, having received the first fruits of the Spirit, through whom you raised up Jesus from the dead, we hope for an everlasting share in the Paschal Mystery.

And so, with all the Angels, we praise you, as in joyful celebration we acclaim: **Holy, Holy** *(p. 37)*

PREFACE VII OF SUNDAYS IN ORDINARY TIME

It is truly right and just, our duty and our salvation, always and everywhere to give you thanks, Lord, holy Father, almighty and eternal God.

For you so loved the world that in your mercy you sent us the Redeemer, to live like us in all things but sin, so that you might love in us what you loved in your Son, by whose obedience we have been restored to those gifts of yours that, by sinning, we had lost in disobedience.

And so, Lord, with all the Angels and Saints, we, too, give you thanks, as in exultation we acclaim: **Holy, Holy** *(p. 37)*

PREFACE VIII OF SUNDAYS IN ORDINARY TIME

It is truly right and just, our duty and our salvation, always and everywhere to give you thanks, Lord, holy Father, almighty and eternal God.

For, when your children were scattered afar by sin, through the Blood of your Son and the power of the Spirit, you gathered them again to yourself, that a people, formed as one by the unity of the Trinity, made the body of Christ and the temple of the Holy Spirit, might, to the praise of your manifold wisdom, be manifest as the Church.

And so, in company with the choirs of Angels, we praise you, and with joy we proclaim: **Holy, Holy** (p. 37)

PREFACE OF OUR LORD JESUS CHRIST, KING OF THE UNIVERSE

It is truly right and just, our duty and our salvation, always and everywhere to give you thanks, Lord, holy Father, almighty and eternal God.

For you anointed your Only Begotten Son, our Lord Jesus Christ, with the oil of gladness as eternal Priest and King of all creation, so that, by offering himself on the altar of the Cross as a spotless sacrifice to bring us peace, he might accomplish the mysteries of human redemption and, making all created things subject to his rule, he might present to the immensity of your majesty an eternal and universal kingdom, a kingdom of truth and life, a kingdom of holiness and grace, a kingdom of justice, love and peace.

And so, with Angels and Archangels, with Thrones and Dominions, and with all the hosts and

Powers of heaven, we sing the hymn of your glory, as without end we acclaim: **Holy, Holy** *(p. 37)*

PREFACE OF RECONCILIATION I

It is truly right and just that we should always give you thanks, Lord, holy Father, almighty and eternal God.

For you do not cease to spur us on to possess a more abundant life and, being rich in mercy, you constantly offer pardon and call on sinners to trust in your forgiveness alone.

Never did you turn away from us, and, though time and again we have broken your covenant, you have bound the human family to yourself through Jesus your Son, our Redeemer, with a new bond of love so tight that it can never be undone.

Even now you set before your people a time of grace and reconciliation, and, as they turn back to you in spirit, you grant them hope in Christ Jesus and a desire to be of service to all, while they entrust themselves more fully to the Holy Spirit.

And so, filled with wonder, we extol the power of your love, and, proclaiming our joy at the salvation that comes from you, we join in the heavenly hymn of countless hosts, as without end we acclaim: **Holy, Holy** *(p. 37)*

PREFACE OF RECONCILIATION II

It is truly right and just that we should give you thanks and praise, O God, almighty Father, for all you do in this world, through our Lord Jesus Christ.

For though the human race is divided by dissension and discord, yet we know that by testing us you change our hearts to prepare them for reconciliation.

33

Even more, by your Spirit you move human hearts that enemies may speak to each other again, adversaries join hands, and peoples seek to meet together.

By the working of your power it comes about, O Lord, that hatred is overcome by love, revenge gives way to forgiveness, and discord is changed to mutual respect.

Therefore, as we give you ceaseless thanks with the choirs of heaven, we cry out to your majesty on earth, and without end we acclaim: **Holy, Holy** *(p.37)*

PREFACE OF VARIOUS NEEDS I

It is truly right and just to give you thanks and raise to you a hymn of glory and praise, O Lord, Father of infinite goodness.

For by the word of your Son's Gospel you have brought together one Church from every people, tongue, and nation, and, having filled her with life by the power of your Spirit, you never cease through her to gather the whole human race into one.

Manifesting the covenant of your love, she dispenses without ceasing the blessed hope of your Kingdom and shines bright as the sign of your faithfulness, which in Christ Jesus our Lord you promised would last for eternity.

And so, with all the Powers of heaven, we worship you constantly on earth, while, with all the Church, as one voice we acclaim: **Holy, Holy** *(p.37)*

PREFACE OF VARIOUS NEEDS II

It is truly right and just, our duty and our salvation, always and everywhere to give you thanks, Lord, holy Father, creator of the world and source of all life.

For you never forsake the works of your wisdom, but by your providence are even now at work in our midst. With mighty hand and outstretched arm you led your people Israel through the desert. Now, as your Church makes her pilgrim journey in the world, you always accompany her by the power of the Holy Spirit and lead her along the paths of time to the eternal joy of your Kingdom, through Christ our Lord.

And so, with the Angels and Saints, we, too, sing the hymn of your glory, as without end we acclaim: **Holy, Holy** *(p. 37)*

PREFACE OF VARIOUS NEEDS III

It is truly right and just, our duty and our salvation, always and everywhere to give you thanks, holy Father, Lord of heaven and earth, through Christ our Lord.

For by your Word you created the world and you govern all things in harmony. You gave us the same Word made flesh as Mediator, and he has spoken your words to us and called us to follow him. He is the way that leads us to you, the truth that sets us free, the life that fills us with gladness.

Through your Son you gather men and women, whom you made for the glory of your name, into one family, redeemed by the Blood of his Cross and signed with the seal of the Spirit.

35

Therefore, now and for ages unending, with all the Angels, we proclaim your glory, as in joyful celebration we acclaim: **Holy, Holy** *(p. 37)*

PREFACE OF VARIOUS NEEDS IV

It is truly right and just, our duty and our salvation, always and everywhere to give you thanks, Father of mercies and faithful God.

For you have given us Jesus Christ, your Son, as our Lord and Redeemer.

He always showed compassion for children and for the poor, for the sick and for sinners, and he became a neighbour to the oppressed and the afflicted.

By word and deed he announced to the world that you are our Father and that you care for all your sons and daughters.

And so, with all the Angels and Saints, we exalt and bless your name and sing the hymn of your glory, as without end we acclaim: **Holy, Holy** *(p. 37)*

PREFACE OF EUCHARISTIC PRAYER II

It is truly right and just, our duty and our salvation, always and everywhere to give you thanks, Father most holy, through your beloved Son, Jesus Christ, your Word through whom you made all things, whom you sent as our Saviour and Redeemer, incarnate by the Holy Spirit and born of the Virgin.

Fulfilling your will and gaining for you a holy people, he stretched out his hands as he endured his Passion, so as to break the bonds of death and manifest the resurrection.

And so, with the Angels and all the Saints we declare your glory, as with one voice we acclaim: **Holy, Holy** *(p. 37)*

PREFACE OF EUCHARISTIC PRAYER IV

It is truly right to give you thanks, truly just to give you glory, Father most holy, for you are the one God living and true, existing before all ages and abiding for all eternity, dwelling in unapproachable light; yet you, who alone are good, the source of life, have made all that is, so that you might fill your creatures with blessings and bring joy to many of them by the glory of your light.

And so, in your presence are countless hosts of Angels, who serve you day and night and, gazing upon the glory of your face, glorify you without ceasing.

With them we, too, confess your name in exultation, giving voice to every creature under heaven, as we acclaim:

HOLY, HOLY

Holy, Holy, Holy Lord God of hosts.
Heaven and earth are full of your glory.
Hosanna in the highest.
Blessed is he who comes in the name of the Lord.
Hosanna in the highest.

The Eucharistic Prayer continues:

EUCHARISTIC PRAYER I

To you, therefore, most merciful Father, we make humble prayer and petition through Jesus Christ, your Son, our Lord: that you accept and bless these gifts, these offerings, these holy and unblemished sacrifices, which we offer you firstly for your holy catholic Church. Be pleased to grant her peace, to guard, unite and govern her throughout the whole world, together with your servant N. our Pope and N. our Bishop, and all those who, holding to the truth, hand on the catholic and apostolic faith.

Remember, Lord, your servants

Christian Initiation (Scrutinies):
who are to present your chosen ones for the holy grace of your Baptism,

N. and N. and all gathered here, whose faith and devotion are known to you. For them, we offer you this sacrifice of praise or they offer it for themselves and all who are dear to them: for the redemption of their souls, in hope of health and well-being, and paying their homage to you, the eternal God, living and true.

Nativity of the Lord and Octave of the Nativity:
Celebrating the most sacred night (day) on which blessed Mary the immaculate Virgin brought forth the Saviour for this world, and

Epiphany of the Lord:
Celebrating the most sacred day on which your Only Begotten Son, eternal with you in your glory, appeared in a human body, truly sharing our flesh, and

39

Holy Thursday:
Celebrating the most sacred day on which our Lord Jesus Christ was handed over for our sake, and

Easter Vigil to Second Sunday of Easter:
Celebrating the most sacred night (day) of the Resurrection of our Lord Jesus Christ in the flesh, and

Ascension of the Lord:
Celebrating the most sacred day on which your Only Begotten Son, our Lord, placed at the right hand of your glory our weak human nature, which he had united to himself, and

Pentecost Sunday:
Celebrating the most sacred day of Pentecost, on which the Holy Spirit appeared to the Apostles in tongues of fire, and

In communion with those whose memory we venerate, especially the glorious ever-Virgin Mary, Mother of our God and Lord, Jesus Christ, and blessed Joseph, her Spouse, your blessed Apostles and Martyrs, Peter and Paul, Andrew,

James, John, Thomas, James, Philip, Bartholomew, Matthew, Simon and Jude; Linus, Cletus, Clement, Sixtus, Cornelius, Cyprian, Lawrence, Chrysogonus, John and Paul, Cosmas and Damian

and all your Saints; we ask that through their merits and prayers, in all things we may be defended by your protecting help. (Through Christ our Lord. Amen.)

Therefore, Lord, we pray: graciously accept this oblation of our service, that of your whole family;

Christian Initiation (Scrutinies):
which we make to you for your servants, whom you have been pleased to enroll, choose and call for eternal life and for the blessed gift of your grace. (Through Christ our Lord. Amen.)

Holy Thursday:
which we make to you as we observe the day on which our Lord Jesus Christ handed on the mysteries of his Body and Blood for his disciples to celebrate;

Easter Vigil to Second Sunday of Easter:
which we make to you also for those to whom you have been pleased to give the new birth of water and the Holy Spirit, granting them forgiveness of all their sins;

order our days in your peace, and command that we be delivered from eternal damnation and counted among the flock of those you have chosen. (Through Christ our Lord. Amen.)

Be pleased, O God, we pray, to bless, acknowledge, and approve this offering in every respect; make it spiritual and acceptable, so that it may become for us the Body and Blood of your most beloved Son, our Lord Jesus Christ.

On the day before he was to suffer,

Holy Thursday:
for our salvation and the salvation of all, that is today,

he took bread in his holy and venerable hands, and with eyes raised to heaven to you, O God, his almighty Father, giving you thanks, he said the blessing, broke the bread and gave it to his disciples, saying:

Take this, all of you, and eat of it,
for this is my Body
which will be given up for you.

In a similar way, when supper was ended, he took this precious chalice in his holy and venerable hands, and once more giving you thanks, he said the blessing and gave the chalice to his disciples, saying:

Take this, all of you, and drink from it,
for this is the chalice of my Blood,
the Blood of the new and eternal covenant,
which will be poured out for you and for many
for the forgiveness of sins.
Do this in memory of me.

The mystery of faith.

1 **We proclaim your Death, O Lord, and profess your Resurrection until you come again.**

2 **When we eat this Bread and drink this Cup, we proclaim your Death, O Lord, until you come again.**

3 **Save us, Saviour of the world, for by your Cross and Resurrection you have set us free.**

Therefore, O Lord, as we celebrate the memorial of the blessed Passion, the Resurrection from the dead, and the glorious Ascension into heaven of Christ, your Son, our Lord, we, your servants and your holy people, offer to your glorious majesty from the gifts that you have given us, this pure victim, this holy victim, this spotless victim, the holy Bread of eternal life and the Chalice of everlasting salvation.

Be pleased to look upon these offerings with a serene and kindly countenance, and to accept them, as once you were pleased to accept the gifts of your servant Abel the just, the sacrifice of Abraham, our father in faith, and the offering of your high priest Melchizedek, a holy sacrifice, a spotless victim.

In humble prayer we ask you, almighty God: command that these gifts be borne by the hands of your holy Angel to your altar on high in the sight of your divine majesty, so that all of us, who through this participation at the altar receive the most holy Body and Blood of your Son, may be filled with every grace and heavenly blessing. (Through Christ our Lord. Amen.)

Remember also, Lord, your servants N. and N., who have gone before us with the sign of faith and rest in the sleep of peace. *(Pause)* Grant them, O Lord, we pray, and all who sleep in Christ, a place of refreshment, light and peace. (Through Christ our Lord. Amen.)

To us, also, your servants, who, though sinners, hope in your abundant mercies, graciously grant some share and fellowship with your holy Apostles and Martyrs: with John the Baptist, Stephen, Matthias, Barnabas,

Ignatius, Alexander, Marcellinus, Peter, Felicity, Perpetua, Agatha, Lucy, Agnes, Cecilia, Anastasia

and all your Saints; admit us, we beseech you, into their company, not weighing our merits, but granting us your pardon, through Christ our Lord.

Through whom you continue to make all these good things, O Lord; you sanctify them, fill them with life, bless them, and bestow them upon us.

Through him, and with him, and in him, O God, almighty Father, in the unity of the Holy Spirit, all glory and honour is yours, for ever and ever. **Amen.**

(▶ *Communion Rite, p. 68*)

EUCHARISTIC PRAYER II

You are indeed Holy, O Lord, the fount of all holiness. Make holy, therefore, these gifts, we pray, by sending down your Spirit upon them like the dewfall, so that they may become for us the Body and Blood of our Lord Jesus Christ.

At the time he was betrayed and entered willingly into his Passion, he took bread and, giving thanks, broke it, and gave it to his disciples, saying:

Take this, all of you, and eat of it,
for this is my Body
which will be given up for you.

In a similar way, when supper was ended, he took the chalice and, once more giving thanks, he gave it to his disciples, saying:

Take this, all of you, and drink from it,
for this is the chalice of my Blood,
the Blood of the new and eternal covenant,
which will be poured out for you and for many
for the forgiveness of sins.
Do this in memory of me.

The mystery of faith.

1 **We proclaim your Death, O Lord, and profess your Resurrection until you come again.**

2 **When we eat this Bread and drink this Cup, we proclaim your Death, O Lord, until you come again.**

3 **Save us, Saviour of the world, for by your Cross and Resurrection you have set us free.**

Therefore, as we celebrate the memorial of his Death and Resurrection, we offer you, Lord, the Bread of life and the Chalice of salvation, giving thanks that you have held us worthy to be in your presence and minister to you.

Humbly we pray that, partaking of the Body and Blood of Christ, we may be gathered into one by the Holy Spirit.

Remember, Lord, your Church, spread throughout the world, and bring her to the fullness of charity, together with N. our Pope and N. our Bishop and all the clergy.

Christian Initiation (Scrutinies):
Remember also, Lord, your servants who are to present these chosen ones at the font of rebirth.

Remember also our brothers and sisters who have fallen asleep in the hope of the resurrection, and all who have died in your mercy: welcome them into the light of your face. Have mercy on us all, we pray, that with the Blessed Virgin Mary, Mother of God, with blessed Joseph, her Spouse, with the blessed Apostles, and all the Saints who have pleased you throughout the ages, we may merit to be co-heirs to eternal life, and may praise and glorify you through your Son, Jesus Christ.

Through him, and with him, and in him, O God, almighty Father, in the unity of the Holy Spirit, all glory and honour is yours, for ever and ever. **Amen.**

(▶ *Communion Rite, p. 68*)

EUCHARISTIC PRAYER III

You are indeed Holy, O Lord, and all you have created rightly gives you praise, for through your Son our Lord Jesus Christ, by the power and working of the Holy Spirit, you give life to all things and make them holy, and you never cease to gather a people to yourself, so that from the rising of the sun to its setting a pure sacrifice may be offered to your name.

Therefore, O Lord, we humbly implore you: by the same Spirit graciously make holy these gifts we have brought to you for consecration, that they may become the Body and Blood of your Son our Lord Jesus Christ, at whose command we celebrate these mysteries.

For on the night he was betrayed he himself took bread, and, giving you thanks, he said the blessing, broke the bread and gave it to his disciples, saying:

Take this, all of you, and eat of it,
for this is my Body
which will be given up for you.

In a similar way, when supper was ended, he took the chalice, and, giving you thanks, he said the blessing, and gave the chalice to his disciples, saying:

Take this, all of you, and drink from it,
for this is the chalice of my Blood,
the Blood of the new and eternal covenant,
which will be poured out for you and for many
for the forgiveness of sins.
Do this in memory of me.

The mystery of faith.

1   **We proclaim your Death, O Lord, and profess
    your Resurrection until you come again.**

2   **When we eat this Bread and drink this Cup,
    we proclaim your Death, O Lord, until you
    come again.**

3   **Save us, Saviour of the world, for by your
    Cross and Resurrection you have set us free.**

Therefore, O Lord, as we celebrate the memorial of the saving Passion of your Son, his wondrous Resurrection and Ascension into heaven, and as we look forward to his second coming, we offer you in thanksgiving this holy and living sacrifice.

Look, we pray, upon the oblation of your Church and, recognizing the sacrificial Victim by whose death you willed to reconcile us to yourself, grant that we, who are nourished by the Body and Blood of your Son and filled with his Holy Spirit, may become one body, one spirit in Christ.

May he make of us an eternal offering to you, so that we may obtain an inheritance with your elect, especially with the most Blessed Virgin Mary, Mother of God, with blessed Joseph, her

Spouse, with your blessed Apostles and glorious Martyrs, (with Saint N.) and with all the Saints, on whose constant intercession in your presence we rely for unfailing help.

May this Sacrifice of our reconciliation, we pray, O Lord, advance the peace and salvation of all the world. Be pleased to confirm in faith and charity your pilgrim Church on earth, with your servant N. our Pope and N. our Bishop, the Order of Bishops, all the clergy, and the entire people you have gained for your own.

Christian Initiation (Scrutinies):
Assist your servants with your grace, O Lord, we pray, that they may lead these chosen ones by word and example to new life in Christ, our Lord.

Listen graciously to the prayers of this family, whom you have summoned before you: in your compassion, O merciful Father, gather to yourself all your children scattered throughout the world. To our departed brothers and sisters and to all who were pleasing to you at their passing from this life, give kind admittance to your kingdom. There we hope to enjoy for ever the fullness of your glory through Christ our Lord, through whom you bestow on the world all that is good.

Through him, and with him, and in him, O God, almighty Father, in the unity of the Holy Spirit, all glory and honour is yours, for ever and ever. **Amen.**

(▶ *Communion Rite, p. 68*)

EUCHARISTIC PRAYER IV

We give you praise, Father most holy, for you are great and you have fashioned all your works in wisdom and in love. You formed man in your own image and entrusted the whole world to his care, so that in serving you alone, the Creator, he might have dominion over all creatures. And when through disobedience he had lost your friendship, you did not abandon him to the domain of death. For you came in mercy to the aid of all, so that those who seek might find you. Time and again you offered them covenants and through the prophets taught them to look forward to salvation.

And you so loved the world, Father most holy, that in the fullness of time you sent your Only Begotten Son to be our Saviour. Made incarnate by the Holy Spirit and born of the Virgin Mary, he shared our human nature in all things but sin. To the poor he proclaimed the good news of salvation, to prisoners, freedom, and to the sorrowful of heart, joy. To accomplish your plan, he gave himself up to death, and, rising from the dead, he destroyed death and restored life.

And that we might live no longer for ourselves but for him who died and rose again for us, he sent the Holy Spirit from you, Father, as the first fruits for those who believe, so that, bringing to perfection his work in the world, he might sanctify creation to the full.

Therefore, O Lord, we pray: may this same Holy Spirit graciously sanctify these offerings, that they may become the Body and Blood of our Lord Jesus

Christ for the celebration of this great mystery, which he himself left us as an eternal covenant.

For when the hour had come for him to be glorified by you, Father most holy, having loved his own who were in the world, he loved them to the end: and while they were at supper, he took bread, blessed and broke it, and gave it to his disciples, saying:

Take this, all of you, and eat of it,
for this is my Body
which will be given up for you.

In a similar way, taking the chalice filled with the fruit of the vine, he gave thanks, and gave the chalice to his disciples, saying:

Take this, all of you, and drink from it,
for this is the chalice of my Blood,
the Blood of the new and eternal covenant,
which will be poured out for you and for many
for the forgiveness of sins.
Do this in memory of me.

The mystery of faith.

1   **We proclaim your Death, O Lord, and profess your Resurrection until you come again.**

2   **When we eat this Bread and drink this Cup, we proclaim your Death, O Lord, until you come again.**

3   **Save us, Saviour of the world, for by your Cross and Resurrection you have set us free.**

Therefore, O Lord, as we now celebrate the memorial of our redemption, we remember Christ's Death and his descent to the realm of the dead, we proclaim his

Resurrection and his Ascension to your right hand, and, as we await his coming in glory, we offer you his Body and Blood, the sacrifice acceptable to you which brings salvation to the whole world.

Look, O Lord, upon the Sacrifice which you yourself have provided for your Church, and grant in your loving kindness to all who partake of this one Bread and one Chalice that, gathered into one body by the Holy Spirit, they may truly become a living sacrifice in Christ to the praise of your glory.

Therefore, Lord, remember now all for whom we offer this sacrifice: especially your servant N. our Pope, N. our Bishop, and the whole Order of Bishops, all the clergy, those who take part in this offering, those gathered here before you, your entire people, and all who seek you with a sincere heart.

Remember also those who have died in the peace of your Christ and all the dead, whose faith you alone have known.

To all of us, your children, grant, O merciful Father, that we may enter into a heavenly inheritance with the Blessed Virgin Mary, Mother of God, with blessed Joseph, her Spouse, and with your Apostles and Saints in your kingdom. There, with the whole of creation, freed from the corruption of sin and death, may we glorify you through Christ our Lord, through whom you bestow on the world all that is good.

Through him, and with him, and in him, O God, almighty Father, in the unity of the Holy Spirit, all glory and honour is yours, for ever and ever. **Amen.**

(▶ Communion Rite, p. 68)

EUCHARISTIC PRAYER
FOR RECONCILIATION I

You are indeed Holy, O Lord, and from the world's beginning are ceaselessly at work, so that the human race may become holy, just as you yourself are holy.

Look, we pray, upon your people's offerings and pour out on them the power of your Spirit, that they may become the Body and Blood of your beloved Son, Jesus Christ, in whom we, too, are your sons and daughters. Indeed, though we once were lost and could not approach you, you loved us with the greatest love: for your Son, who alone is just, handed himself over to death, and did not disdain to be nailed for our sake to the wood of the Cross.

But before his arms were outstretched between heaven and earth, to become the lasting sign of your covenant, he desired to celebrate the Passover with his disciples.

As he ate with them, he took bread and, giving you thanks, he said the blessing, broke the bread and gave it to them, saying:

Take this, all of you, and eat of it,
for this is my Body
which will be given up for you.

In a similar way, when supper was ended, knowing that he was about to reconcile all things in himself through his Blood to be shed on the Cross, he took the chalice, filled with the fruit of the vine, and once more giving you thanks, handed the chalice to his disciples, saying:

Take this, all of you, and drink from it,
for this is the chalice of my Blood,
the Blood of the new and eternal covenant,
which will be poured out for you and for many
for the forgiveness of sins.
Do this in memory of me.

The mystery of faith.

1 **We proclaim your Death, O Lord, and profess your Resurrection until you come again.**

2 **When we eat this Bread and drink this Cup, we proclaim your Death, O Lord, until you come again.**

3 **Save us, Saviour of the world, for by your Cross and Resurrection you have set us free.**

Therefore, as we celebrate the memorial of your Son Jesus Christ, who is our Passover and our surest peace, we celebrate his Death and Resurrection from the dead, and looking forward to his blessed Coming, we offer you, who are our faithful and merciful God, this sacrificial Victim who reconciles to you the human race.

Look kindly, most compassionate Father, on those you unite to yourself by the Sacrifice of your Son, and grant that, by the power of the Holy Spirit, as they partake of this one Bread and one Chalice, they may be gathered into one Body in Christ, who heals every division.

Be pleased to keep us always in communion of mind and heart, together with N. our Pope and N. our Bishop. Help us to work together for the coming of your Kingdom, until the hour when we stand before you, Saints among the Saints in the halls of heaven, with the Blessed Virgin Mary, Mother of God, the blessed Apostles and all the Saints, and with our deceased brothers and sisters, whom we humbly commend to your mercy.

Then, freed at last from the wound of corruption and made fully into a new creation, we shall sing to you with gladness the thanksgiving of Christ, who lives for all eternity.

Through him, and with him, and in him, O God, almighty Father, in the unity of the Holy Spirit, all glory and honour is yours, for ever and ever. **Amen.**

(▶ Communion Rite, p. 68)

EUCHARISTIC PRAYER FOR RECONCILIATION II

You, therefore, almighty Father, we bless through Jesus Christ your Son, who comes in your name. He himself is the Word that brings salvation, the hand you extend to sinners, the way by which your peace is offered to us. When we ourselves had turned away from you on account of our sins, you brought us back to be reconciled, O Lord, so that, converted at last to you, we might love one another through your Son, whom for our sake you handed over to death.

And now, celebrating the reconciliation Christ has brought us, we entreat you: sanctify these gifts by the outpouring of your Spirit, that they may become the Body and Blood of your Son, whose command we fulfill when we celebrate these mysteries.

For when about to give his life to set us free, as he reclined at supper, he himself took bread into his hands, and, giving you thanks, he said the blessing, broke the bread and gave it to his disciples, saying:

Take this, all of you, and eat of it,
for this is my Body
which will be given up for you.

In a similar way, on that same evening, he took the chalice of blessing in his hands, confessing your mercy, and gave the chalice to his disciples, saying:

Take this, all of you, and drink from it,
for this is the chalice of my Blood,
the Blood of the new and eternal covenant,
which will be poured out for you and for many
for the forgiveness of sins.
Do this in memory of me.

The mystery of faith.

1 We proclaim your Death, O Lord, and profess your Resurrection until you come again.

2 When we eat this Bread and drink this Cup, we proclaim your Death, O Lord, until you come again.

3 Save us, Saviour of the world, for by your Cross and Resurrection you have set us free.

Celebrating, therefore, the memorial of the Death and Resurrection of your Son, who left us this pledge of his love, we offer you what you have bestowed on us, the Sacrifice of perfect reconciliation.

Holy Father, we humbly beseech you to accept us also, together with your Son, and in this saving banquet graciously to endow us with his very Spirit, who takes away everything that estranges us from one another.

May he make your Church a sign of unity and an instrument of your peace among all people and may he keep us in communion with N. our Pope and N. our Bishop and all the Bishops and your entire people.

Just as you have gathered us now at the table of your Son, so also bring us together, with the glorious Virgin Mary, Mother of God, with your blessed Apostles and all the Saints, with our brothers and sisters and those of every race and tongue who have died in your friendship. Bring us to share with them the unending banquet of unity in a new heaven and a new earth, where the fullness of your peace will shine forth in Christ Jesus our Lord.

Through him, and with him, and in him, O God, almighty Father, in the unity of the Holy Spirit, all glory and honour is yours, for ever and ever. **Amen.**

(► *Communion Rite, p. 68*)

EUCHARISTIC PRAYER FOR MASS FOR VARIOUS NEEDS I
The Church on the Path of Unity

You are indeed Holy and to be glorified, O God, who love the human race and who always walk with us on the journey of life. Blessed indeed is your Son, present in our midst when we are gathered by his love, and when, as once for the disciples, so now for us, he opens the Scriptures and breaks the bread.

Therefore, Father most merciful, we ask that you send forth your Holy Spirit to sanctify these gifts of bread and wine, that they may become for us the Body and Blood of our Lord Jesus Christ.

On the day before he was to suffer, on the night of the Last Supper, he took bread and said the blessing, broke the bread and gave it to his disciples, saying:

Take this, all of you, and eat of it,
for this is my Body
which will be given up for you.

In a similar way, when supper was ended, he took the chalice, gave you thanks and gave the chalice to his disciples, saying:

Take this, all of you, and drink from it,
for this is the chalice of my Blood,
the Blood of the new and eternal covenant,
which will be poured out for you and for many
for the forgiveness of sins.
Do this in memory of me.

The mystery of faith.

1   **We proclaim your Death, O Lord, and profess your Resurrection until you come again.**

2   **When we eat this Bread and drink this Cup, we proclaim your Death, O Lord, until you come again.**

3   **Save us, Saviour of the world, for by your Cross and Resurrection you have set us free.**

Therefore, holy Father, as we celebrate the memorial of Christ your Son, our Saviour, whom you led through his Passion and Death on the Cross to the glory of the Resurrection, and whom you have seated at your right hand, we proclaim the work of your love until he comes again and we offer you the Bread of life and the Chalice of blessing.

Look with favour on the oblation of your Church, in which we show forth the paschal Sacrifice of Christ that has been handed on to us, and grant that, by the power of the Spirit of your love, we may be counted now and until the day of eternity among the members of your Son, in whose Body and Blood we have communion.

Lord, renew your Church (which is in N.) by the light of the Gospel. Strengthen the bond of unity between the faithful and the pastors of your people, together with N. our Pope, N. our Bishop, and the whole Order of Bishops, that in a world torn by strife your people may shine forth as a prophetic sign of unity and concord.

Remember our brothers and sisters (N. and N.), who have fallen asleep in the peace of your Christ, and all the dead, whose faith you alone have known. Admit them to rejoice in the light of your face, and in the resurrection give them the fullness of life.

Grant also to us, when our earthly pilgrimage is done, that we may come to an eternal dwelling place and live with you for ever; there, in communion with the Blessed Virgin Mary, Mother of God, with the Apostles and Martyrs, (with Saint N.) and with all the Saints, we shall praise and exalt you through Jesus Christ, your Son.

Through him, and with him, and in him, O God, almighty Father, in the unity of the Holy Spirit, all glory and honour is yours, for ever and ever. **Amen.**

(▶ Communion Rite, p. 68)

EUCHARISTIC PRAYER FOR MASS FOR VARIOUS NEEDS II
God Guides His Church along the Way of Salvation

You are indeed Holy and to be glorified, O God, who love the human race and who always walk with us on the journey of life. Blessed indeed is your Son, present in our midst when we are gathered by his love and when, as once for the disciples, so now for us, he opens the Scriptures and breaks the bread.

Therefore, Father most merciful, we ask that you send forth your Holy Spirit to sanctify these gifts of bread and wine, that they may become for us the Body and Blood of our Lord Jesus Christ.

On the day before he was to suffer, on the night of the Last Supper, he took bread and said the blessing, broke the bread and gave it to his disciples, saying:

Take this, all of you, and eat of it,
for this is my Body
which will be given up for you.

In a similar way, when supper was ended, he took the chalice, gave you thanks and gave the chalice to his disciples, saying:

Take this, all of you, and drink from it,
for this is the chalice of my Blood,
the Blood of the new and eternal covenant,
which will be poured out for you and for many
for the forgiveness of sins.
Do this in memory of me.

The mystery of faith.

1 **We proclaim your Death, O Lord, and profess your Resurrection until you come again.**

2 **When we eat this Bread and drink this Cup, we proclaim your Death, O Lord, until you come again.**

3 **Save us, Saviour of the world, for by your Cross and Resurrection you have set us free.**

Therefore, holy Father, as we celebrate the memorial of Christ your Son, our Saviour, whom you led through his Passion and Death on the Cross to the glory of the Resurrection, and whom you have seated at your right hand, we proclaim the work of your love until he comes again and we offer you the Bread of life and the Chalice of blessing.

Look with favour on the oblation of your Church, in which we show forth the paschal Sacrifice of Christ that has been handed on to us, and grant that, by the power of the Spirit of your love, we may be counted now and until the day of eternity among the members of your Son, in whose Body and Blood we have communion.

And so, having called us to your table, Lord, confirm us in unity, so that, together with N. our Pope and N. our Bishop, with all Bishops, Priests and Deacons, and your entire people, as we walk your ways with faith and hope, we may strive to bring joy and trust into the world.

Remember our brothers and sisters (N. and N.), who have fallen asleep in the peace of your Christ, and all the dead, whose faith you alone have known. Admit them to rejoice in the light of your face, and in the resurrection give them the fullness of life.

Grant also to us, when our earthly pilgrimage is done, that we may come to an eternal dwelling place and live with you for ever; there, in communion with the Blessed Virgin Mary, Mother of God, with the Apostles and Martyrs, (with Saint N.) and with all the Saints, we shall praise and exalt you through Jesus Christ, your Son.

Through him, and with him, and in him, O God, almighty Father, in the unity of the Holy Spirit, all glory and honour is yours, for ever and ever. **Amen.**

(▶ Communion Rite, p. 68)

EUCHARISTIC PRAYER FOR MASS FOR VARIOUS NEEDS III

Jesus, the Way to the Father

You are indeed Holy and to be glorified, O God, who love the human race and who always walk with us on the journey of life. Blessed indeed is your Son, present in our midst when we are gathered by his love and when, as once for the disciples, so now for us, he opens the Scriptures and breaks the bread.

Therefore, Father most merciful, we ask that you send forth your Holy Spirit to sanctify these gifts of bread and wine, that they may become for us the Body and Blood of our Lord Jesus Christ.

On the day before he was to suffer, on the night of the Last Supper, he took bread and said the blessing, broke the bread and gave it to his disciples, saying:

Take this, all of you, and eat of it,
for this is my Body
which will be given up for you.

In a similar way, when supper was ended, he took the chalice, gave you thanks and gave the chalice to his disciples, saying:

Take this, all of you, and drink from it,
for this is the chalice of my Blood,
the Blood of the new and eternal covenant,
which will be poured out for you and for many
for the forgiveness of sins.
Do this in memory of me.

The mystery of faith.

1 **We proclaim your Death, O Lord, and profess your Resurrection until you come again.**

2 **When we eat this Bread and drink this Cup, we proclaim your Death, O Lord, until you come again.**

3 **Save us, Saviour of the world, for by your Cross and Resurrection you have set us free.**

Therefore, holy Father, as we celebrate the memorial of Christ your Son, our Saviour, whom you led through his Passion and Death on the Cross to the glory of the Resurrection, and whom you have seated at your right hand, we proclaim the work of your love until he comes again and we offer you the Bread of life and the Chalice of blessing.

Look with favour on the oblation of your Church, in which we show forth the paschal Sacrifice of Christ that has been handed on to us, and grant that, by the power of the Spirit of your love, we may be counted now and until the day of eternity among the members of your Son, in whose Body and Blood we have communion.

By our partaking of this mystery, almighty Father, give us life through your Spirit, grant that we may be conformed to the image of your Son, and confirm us in the bond of communion, together with N. our Pope and N. our Bishop, with all other Bishops, with Priests and Deacons, and with your entire people.

Grant that all the faithful of the Church, looking into the signs of the times by the light of faith, may constantly devote themselves to the service of the Gospel.

Keep us attentive to the needs of all that, sharing their grief and pain, their joy and hope, we may faithfully bring them the good news of salvation and go forward with them along the way of your Kingdom.

Remember our brothers and sisters (N. and N.), who have fallen asleep in the peace of your Christ, and all the dead, whose faith you alone have known. Admit them to rejoice in the light of your face, and in the resurrection give them the fullness of life.

Grant also to us, when our earthly pilgrimage is done, that we may come to an eternal dwelling place and live with you for ever; there, in communion with the Blessed Virgin Mary, Mother of God, with the Apostles and Martyrs, (with Saint N.) and with all the Saints, we shall praise and exalt you through Jesus Christ, your Son.

Through him, and with him, and in him, O God, almighty Father, in the unity of the Holy Spirit, all glory and honour is yours, for ever and ever. **Amen.**

(▶ *Communion Rite, p. 68*)

EUCHARISTIC PRAYER FOR
MASS FOR VARIOUS NEEDS IV
Jesus, Who Went About Doing Good

You are indeed Holy and to be glorified, O God, who love the human race and who always walk with us on the journey of life. Blessed indeed is your Son, present in our midst when we are gathered by his love and when, as once for the disciples, so now for us, he opens the Scriptures and breaks the bread.

Therefore, Father most merciful, we ask that you send forth your Holy Spirit to sanctify these gifts of bread and wine, that they may become for us the Body and Blood of our Lord Jesus Christ.

On the day before he was to suffer, on the night of the Last Supper, he took bread and said the blessing, broke the bread and gave it to his disciples, saying:

Take this, all of you, and eat of it,
for this is my Body
which will be given up for you.

In a similar way, when supper was ended, he took the chalice, gave you thanks and gave the chalice to his disciples, saying:

Take this, all of you, and drink from it,
for this is the chalice of my Blood,
the Blood of the new and eternal covenant,
which will be poured out for you and for many
for the forgiveness of sins.
Do this in memory of me.

The mystery of faith.

1 **We proclaim your Death, O Lord, and profess your Resurrection until you come again.**

2 **When we eat this Bread and drink this Cup, we proclaim your Death, O Lord, until you come again.**

3 **Save us, Saviour of the world, for by your Cross and Resurrection you have set us free.**

Therefore, holy Father, as we celebrate the memorial of Christ your Son, our Saviour, whom you led through his Passion and Death on the Cross to the glory of the Resurrection, and whom you have seated at your right hand, we proclaim the work of your love until he comes again and we offer you the Bread of life and the Chalice of blessing.

Look with favour on the oblation of your Church, in which we show forth the paschal Sacrifice of Christ that has been handed on to us, and grant that, by the power of the Spirit of your love, we may be counted now and until the day of eternity among the members of your Son, in whose Body and Blood we have communion.

Bring your Church, O Lord, to perfect faith and charity, together with N. our Pope and N. our Bishop, with all Bishops, Priests and Deacons, and the entire people you have made your own.

Open our eyes to the needs of our brothers and sisters; inspire in us words and actions to comfort those who labour and are burdened. Make us serve them truly, after the example of Christ and at his command. And may your Church stand as a living witness to truth and freedom, to peace and justice, that all people may be raised up to a new hope.

Remember our brothers and sisters (N. and N.), who have fallen asleep in the peace of your Christ, and all the dead, whose faith you alone have known. Admit them to rejoice in the light of your face, and in the resurrection give them the fullness of life.

Grant also to us, when our earthly pilgrimage is done, that we may come to an eternal dwelling place and live with you for ever; there, in communion with the Blessed Virgin Mary, Mother of God, with the Apostles and Martyrs, (with Saint N.) and with all the Saints, we shall praise and exalt you through Jesus Christ, your Son.

Through him, and with him, and in him, O God, almighty Father, in the unity of the Holy Spirit, all glory and honour is yours, for ever and ever. **Amen.**

The Communion Rite

At the Saviour's command and formed by divine teaching, we dare to say:

**Our Father, who art in heaven,
hallowed be thy name;
thy kingdom come,
thy will be done
on earth as it is in heaven.
Give us this day our daily bread,
and forgive us our trespasses,
as we forgive those who trespass against us;
and lead us not into temptation,
but deliver us from evil.**

Deliver us, Lord, we pray, from every evil, graciously grant peace in our days, that, by the help of your mercy, we may be always free from sin and safe from all distress, as we await the blessed hope and the coming of our Saviour, Jesus Christ.

**For the kingdom,
the power and the glory are yours
now and for ever.**

Lord Jesus Christ, who said to your Apostles: Peace I leave you, my peace I give you, look not on our sins, but on the faith of your Church, and graciously grant her peace and unity in accordance with your will. Who live and reign for ever and ever. **Amen.**

The peace of the Lord be with you always. **And with your spirit.**

Let us offer each other the sign of peace.

May this mingling of the Body and Blood of our Lord
Jesus Christ bring eternal life to us who receive it.

**Lamb of God, you take away the sins of the world,
have mercy on us.**

**Lamb of God, you take away the sins of the world,
have mercy on us.**

**Lamb of God, you take away the sins of the world,
grant us peace.**

1   Lord Jesus Christ, Son of the living God, who, by the
    will of the Father and the work of the Holy Spirit,
    through your Death gave life to the world, free me by
    this, your most holy Body and Blood, from all my sins
    and from every evil; keep me always faithful to your
    commandments, and never let me be parted from you.

2   May the receiving of your Body and Blood, Lord
    Jesus Christ, not bring me to judgment and condem-
    nation, but through your loving mercy be for me
    protection in mind and body and a healing remedy.

Behold the Lamb of God, behold him who takes
away the sins of the world. Blessed are those
called to the supper of the Lamb.

**Lord, I am not worthy that you should enter
under my roof, but only say the word and my
soul shall be healed.**

May the Body (Blood) of Christ keep me safe for
eternal life.

COMMUNION CHANT
(or Communion Antiphon — ▶ The appropriate day)

PRAYER AFTER COMMUNION
(▶ The appropriate day)   69

Concluding Rites

ANNOUNCEMENTS *(Optional)*

BLESSING *(or Solemn Blessing — Optional)*

The Lord be with you. **And with your spirit.**
May almighty God bless you, the Father, and the
Son, and the Holy Spirit. **Amen.**

DISMISSAL
During Easter Octave, add the double alleluia.

1   Go forth, the Mass is ended.

2   Go and announce the Gospel of the Lord.

3   Go in peace, glorifying the Lord by your life.

4   Go in peace.

Thanks be to God.

November 27

A new beginning! Exciting words — a chance to start over with a clean slate. Who wouldn't relish the possibility of starting over and getting it right?

The First Sunday of Advent is the Church's way of announcing the beginning of a new liturgical year — and this Sunday the beginning of the three-year cycle of readings. Today's readings give us a recipe for how to "get it right," not just for ourselves but for the whole world.

Advent is a time of expectant preparation for the celebration of Christmas. We observe it as a season of prayer, fasting and repentance — the ways Christians "start over."

In a sense it is also the beginning of the rest of our life. The readings give us the key for how to live in this moment and for all time in peace and harmony.

The words of the prophet Isaiah tell of the coming of a judge who will help people from all nations to surrender their weapons and make peace. And in that peace, we are told to choose light over darkness. That light is the coming of Christ, for whom we "must be ready, for the Son of Man is coming at an unexpected hour."

Exciting? Indeed — a message of hope — the coming of a Saviour and the key to preparing for eternity.

Patrick M. Doyle, Carleton Place, ON

ENTRANCE ANTIPHON (Cf. Psalm 24.1-3)
To you, I lift up my soul, O my God. In you, I have trusted; let me not be put to shame. Nor let my enemies exult over me; and let none who hope in you be put to shame.

INTRODUCTORY RITES (p. 5)

COLLECT
Grant your faithful, we pray, almighty God, the resolve to run forth to meet your Christ with righteous deeds at his coming, so that, gathered at his right hand, they may be worthy to possess the heavenly Kingdom. Through our Lord Jesus Christ, your Son, who lives and reigns with you in the unity of the Holy Spirit, one God, for ever and ever. **Amen.**

FIRST READING (Isaiah 2.1-5)
The word that Isaiah son of Amoz saw concerning Judah and Jerusalem. In days to come the mountain of the Lord's house shall be established as the highest of the mountains, and shall be raised above the hills; all the nations shall stream to it.

Many peoples shall come and say, "Come, let us go up to the mountain of the Lord, to the house of the God of Jacob; that he may teach us his ways and that we may walk in his paths."

For out of Zion shall go forth instruction, and the word of the Lord from Jerusalem. He shall judge between the nations, and shall arbitrate for many peoples; they shall beat their swords into ploughshares, and their spears into pruning hooks; nation shall not lift up sword against nation, neither shall they learn war any more.

O house of Jacob, come, let us walk in the light
of the Lord!

The word of the Lord. **Thanks be to God.**

RESPONSORIAL PSALM *(Psalm 122)*

Let us go re-joic-ing to the house of the

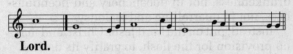

Lord.

℟. **Let us go rejoicing to the house of the Lord.**

I was glad when they said · **to** me,
"Let us go to the house of · **the** Lord!"
Our feet · **are** standing
within your gates, O · **Je**-rusalem. ℟.

To it the tribes go up, the tribes · **of_the** Lord,
as it was decreed for Israel,
    to give thanks to the name of · **the** Lord.
For there the thrones for judgment · **were_set** up,
the thrones of the · **house_of** David. ℟.

Pray for the peace of · **Je**-rusalem:
"May they prosper · **who** love_you.
Peace be within · **your** walls,
and security within · **your** towers." ℟.

For the sake of my relatives · **and** friends
I will say, "Peace be · **with**-in_you."
For the sake of the house of the Lord · **our** God,
I will seek · **your** good. ℟.

©2010 Gordon Johnston/Novalis

SECOND READING *(Romans 13.11-14)*
Brothers and sisters, you know what time it is,
how it is now the moment for you to wake from
sleep. For salvation is nearer to us now than
when we became believers; the night is far gone,
the day is near. Let us then lay aside the works
of darkness and put on the armour of light; let us
live honourably as in the day, not in revelling and
drunkenness, not in debauchery and licentious-
ness, not in quarrelling and jealousy.

Instead, put on the Lord Jesus Christ, and make
no provision for the flesh, to gratify its desires.

The word of the Lord. **Thanks be to God.**

GOSPEL ACCLAMATION *(Psalm 85.7)*
Alleluia. Alleluia. Show us your steadfast love, O
Lord, and grant us your salvation. **Alleluia.**

GOSPEL *(Matthew 24.37-44)*
The Lord be with you. **And with your spirit.**
A reading from the holy Gospel according to Mat-
thew. **Glory to you, O Lord.**

Jesus spoke to his disciples: "As the days of
Noah were, so will be the coming of the Son of Man.
For as in those days before the flood they were eating and drinking, marrying and giving in marriage,
until the day Noah entered the ark, and they knew
nothing until the flood came and swept them all
away, so too will be the coming of the Son of Man.
Then two will be in the field; one will be taken and
one will be left. Two women will be grinding meal
together; one will be taken and one will be left.

"Keep awake, therefore, for you do not know
on what day your Lord is coming. But understand

this: if the owner of the house had known in what part of the night the thief was coming, he would have stayed awake and would not have let his house be broken into. Therefore you also must be ready, for the Son of Man is coming at an unexpected hour."

The Gospel of the Lord. **Praise to you, Lord Jesus Christ.**

PROFESSION OF FAITH *(p. 11)*

PRAYER OF THE FAITHFUL

The following intentions are suggestions only. There are more suggestions at www.livingwithchrist.ca

℟. **Lord, hear our prayer.**

For the Church, witness to God's word in the world, we pray to the Lord: ℟.

For government leaders guided by principles of justice and mercy, we pray to the Lord: ℟.

For those who search for hope amidst despair, we pray to the Lord: ℟.

For this community, called to welcome those who have lost hope, we pray to the Lord: ℟.

PREPARATION OF THE GIFTS *(p. 14)*

PRAYER OVER THE OFFERINGS

Accept, we pray, O Lord, these offerings we make, gathered from among your gifts to us, and may what you grant us to celebrate devoutly here below gain for us the prize of eternal redemption. Through Christ our Lord. **Amen.**

PREFACE *(Advent I, p. 15)*

COMMUNION ANTIPHON *(Psalm 84.13)*
The Lord will bestow his bounty, and our earth shall yield its increase.

PRAYER AFTER COMMUNION
May these mysteries, O Lord, in which we have participated, profit us, we pray, for even now, as we walk amid passing things, you teach us by them to love the things of heaven and hold fast to what endures. Through Christ our Lord. **Amen.**

SOLEMN BLESSING — ADVENT *(Optional)*
Bow down for the blessing.

May the almighty and merciful God, by whose grace you have placed your faith in the First Coming of his Only Begotten Son and yearn for his coming again, sanctify you by the radiance of Christ's Advent and enrich you with his blessing. **Amen.**

As you run the race of this present life, may he make you firm in faith, joyful in hope and active in charity. **Amen.**

So that, rejoicing now with devotion at the Redeemer's coming in the flesh, you may be endowed with the rich reward of eternal life when he comes again in majesty. **Amen.**

And may the blessing of almighty God, the Father, and the Son, and the Holy Spirit, come down on you and remain with you for ever. **Amen.**

DISMISSAL *(p. 70)*

December Saints' Days

The following saints are traditionally remembered in December in Canada.

3   Saint Francis Xavier

4   Saint John Damascene

6   Saint Nicholas

7   Saint Ambrose

9   Saint Juan Diego Cuauhtlatoatzin

11   Saint Damasus I

12   Our Lady of Guadalupe,
Patroness of the Americas

13   Saint Lucy

14   Saint John of the Cross

21   Saint Peter Canisius

23   Saint John of Kanty

26   Saint Stephen

27   Saint John

28   The Holy Innocents

29   Saint Thomas Becket

31   Saint Sylvester I

December 4

What would it feel like to stand before John the Baptist admonishing you to confess your sins? It sounds scary, but is there not a longing in us for the healing and wholeness he is offering?

John is preparing the way for God's definitive Word who will come into our midst. His call to repentance is a call to stand before Almighty God, the All-Good, the All-Holy, and to recognize ourselves as sinners. Recall Isaiah seeing God in the Temple and exclaiming, "Woe is me... I am a man of unclean lips... among a people of unclean lips!" (Isa 6.5) Or Peter's awareness, after Jesus directs him to the abundant catch of fish: "Go away from me, Lord, for I am a sinful man!" (Lk 5.8)

Seeing ourselves as sinners before God, and confessing during this Advent/Preparation season, is not meant to make us feel bad. Rather, we acknowledge who we are in order to open ourselves to what God wants to do for us. Through gentle mercy and graciousness, God frees us from sin and its consequences, inviting us into the kingdom of heaven announced by John and Jesus.

And what is this kingdom of heaven? In today's readings Isaiah describes a kingdom of peace and justice. Then Paul says it is where we find "encouragement... to live in harmony with one another." This is the purpose of repentance.

Fr. Mark Miller, CSsR, Toronto, ON

ENTRANCE ANTIPHON (Cf. Isaiah 30.19, 30)
O people of Sion, behold, the Lord will come
to save the nations, and the Lord will make the
glory of his voice heard in the joy of your heart.

INTRODUCTORY RITES (p. 5)

COLLECT
Almighty and merciful God, may no earthly un-
dertaking hinder those who set out in haste to
meet your Son, but may our learning of heavenly
wisdom gain us admittance to his company. Who
lives and reigns with you in the unity of the Holy
Spirit, one God, for ever and ever. **Amen.**

FIRST READING (Isaiah 11.1-10)
On that day:
A shoot shall come out from the stump of Jesse,
and a branch shall grow out of his roots.
The spirit of the Lord shall rest on him,
the spirit of wisdom and understanding,
the spirit of counsel and might,
the spirit of knowledge and the fear of the Lord.
His delight shall be in the fear of the Lord.

He shall not judge by what his eyes see,
or decide by what his ears hear;
but with righteousness he shall judge the poor,
and decide with equity for the meek of the earth;
he shall strike the earth with the rod of his mouth,
and with the breath of his lips
    he shall kill the wicked.
Righteousness shall be the belt around his waist,
and faithfulness the belt around his loins.

The wolf shall live with the lamb,
the leopard shall lie down with the kid,
the calf and the lion and the fatling together,
and a little child shall lead them.
The cow and the bear shall graze,
their young shall lie down together;
and the lion shall eat straw like the ox.
The nursing child shall play over the hole
    of the asp,
and the weaned child shall put its hand
    on the adder's den.
They will not hurt or destroy
on all my holy mountain;
for the earth will be full of the knowledge
    of the Lord
as the waters cover the sea.

On that day the root of Jesse shall stand
as a signal to the peoples;
the nations shall inquire of him,
and his dwelling shall be glorious.

The word of the Lord. **Thanks be to God.**

RESPONSORIAL PSALM *(Psalm 72)*

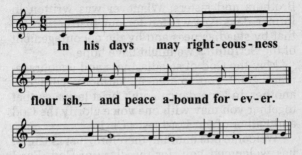

In his days may right-eous-ness flour ish,— and peace a-bound for-ev-er.

℟. **In his days may righteousness flourish,
and peace abound forever.**

Give the king your justice, O · **God,**
and your righteousness to a king's · **son.**
May he judge your · **people** with
righteousness,
and your · **poor** with justice. ℟.

In his days may righteousness · **flourish**
and peace abound, until the moon is no · **more.**
May he have dominion from · **sea** to sea,
and from the River to the · **ends_of** the earth. ℟.

For he delivers the needy one who · **calls,**
the poor and the one who has no · **helper.**
He has pity on the · **weak_and** the needy,
and saves the · **lives_of** the needy. ℟.

May his name endure for-·**ever,**
his fame continue as long as the · **sun.**
May all nations be · **blessed** in him;
may they pro-·**nounce** him happy. ℟.

©2010 Gordon Johnston/Novalis

SECOND READING *(Romans 15.4-9)*

Brothers and sisters: Whatever was written in former days was written for our instruction, so that by steadfastness and by the encouragement of the Scriptures we might have hope.

May the God of steadfastness and encouragement grant you to live in harmony with one another, in accordance with Christ Jesus, so that together you may with one voice glorify the God and Father of our Lord Jesus Christ.

Welcome one another, therefore, just as Christ has welcomed you, for the glory of God. For I tell you that Christ has become a servant of the circumcised on behalf of the truth of God in order that he might confirm the promises given to the patriarchs, and in order that the Gentiles might glorify God for his mercy. As it is written, "Therefore I will confess you among the Gentiles, and sing praises to your name."

The word of the Lord. **Thanks be to God.**

GOSPEL ACCLAMATION *(See Luke 3.4, 6)*

Alleluia. Alleluia. Prepare the way of the Lord, make straight his paths: all flesh shall see the salvation of God. **Alleluia.**

GOSPEL *(Matthew 3.1-12)*

The Lord be with you. **And with your spirit.**
A reading from the holy Gospel according to Matthew. **Glory to you, O Lord.**

In those days John the Baptist appeared in the wilderness of Judea, proclaiming, "Repent, for the kingdom of heaven has come near." This is the one of whom the Prophet Isaiah spoke when he said, "The voice of one crying out in the wilderness: 'Prepare the way of the Lord, make his paths straight.'"

Now John wore clothing of camel's hair with a leather belt around his waist, and his food was locusts and wild honey. Then the people of Jerusalem and all Judea were going out to him, and all the region along the Jordan, and they were baptized by him in the river Jordan, confessing their sins.

But when he saw many Pharisees and Sadducees coming for baptism, John said to them, "You brood of vipers! Who warned you to flee from the wrath to come? Bear fruit worthy of repentance. Do not presume to say to yourselves, 'We have Abraham as our father'; for I tell you, God is able from these stones to raise up children to Abraham. Even now the axe is lying at the root of the trees; every tree therefore that does not bear good fruit is cut down and thrown into the fire.

"I baptize you with water for repentance, but one who is more powerful than I is coming after me; I am not worthy to carry his sandals. He will baptize you with the Holy Spirit and fire. His winnowing fork is in his hand, and he will clear his threshing floor and will gather his wheat into the granary; but the chaff he will burn with unquenchable fire."

The Gospel of the Lord. **Praise to you, Lord Jesus Christ.**

PROFESSION OF FAITH *(p. 11)*

PRAYER OF THE FAITHFUL

The following intentions are suggestions only. There are more suggestions at www.livingwithchrist.ca

R℣. **Lord, hear our prayer.**

For all Christians, called to work together to prepare the Lord's way, we pray to the Lord: R℣.

For an end to persecution and wars, we pray to the Lord: R℣.

For those caught up in turmoil and uncertainty, and for all who assist them, we pray to the Lord: R℣.

For God's people gathered here, called to walk the path of new life, we pray to the Lord: R℣.

PREPARATION OF THE GIFTS *(p. 14)*

PRAYER OVER THE OFFERINGS

Be pleased, O Lord, with our humble prayers and offerings, and, since we have no merits to plead our cause, come, we pray, to our rescue with the protection of your mercy. Through Christ our Lord. **Amen.**

PREFACE *(Advent I, p. 15)*

COMMUNION ANTIPHON *(Baruch 5.5; 4.36)*
Jerusalem, arise and stand upon the heights, and behold the joy which comes to you from God.

PRAYER AFTER COMMUNION
Replenished by the food of spiritual nourishment, we humbly beseech you, O Lord, that, through our partaking in this mystery, you may teach us to judge wisely the things of earth and hold firm to the things of heaven. Through Christ our Lord. **Amen.**

SOLEMN BLESSING AND DISMISSAL *(p. 76)*

December 11

'Tis the season for runaway anticipation. Expending seemingly unlimited time and energy on preparing for the big day, it's easy to lose sight of what Christmas is all about. Then, when it's come and gone, we are left to wonder what all the bustling, buying and baking were for. What a letdown!

That empty, disquieting feeling must have plagued John the Baptist as he languished in Herod's prison awaiting his execution. The Baptist sent word by the disciples to Jesus, asking him, "Are you the one who is to come, or are we to wait for another?"

John the Baptist had been sent to prepare the way for Jesus, the Saviour. John anticipated the coming of a messiah and he was confident that Jesus was that messiah. So, why the lingering doubts? Jesus didn't really fit with John's preconceived notion of a messiah who would come breathing fire and brimstone and take the unsuspecting and unrepentant world by storm.

Jesus sent a return message: "The blind receive their sight, the lame walk, the lepers are cleansed, the deaf hear, the dead are raised, and the poor have good news brought to them." Certainly not fire and brimstone — rather a genuine Christmas story of love and salvation. It's time that we too shifted our focus from unrealistic expectation to embrace the promise of Jesus as the true meaning of Christmas.

Frank Campbell, Enfield, NS

ENTRANCE ANTIPHON *(Philippians 4.4-5)*
**Rejoice in the Lord always; again I say, rejoice.
Indeed, the Lord is near.**

INTRODUCTORY RITES *(p. 5)*

COLLECT
O God, who see how your people faithfully await
the feast of the Lord's Nativity, enable us, we pray,
to attain the joys of so great a salvation and to
celebrate them always with solemn worship and
glad rejoicing. Through our Lord Jesus Christ,
your Son, who lives and reigns with you in the
unity of the Holy Spirit, one God, for ever and
ever. **Amen.**

FIRST READING *(Isaiah 35.1-6a, 10)*
The wilderness and the dry land shall be glad,
the desert shall rejoice and blossom;
like the crocus it shall blossom abundantly,
and rejoice with joy and singing.
The glory of Lebanon shall be given to it,
the majesty of Carmel and Sharon.
They shall see the glory of the Lord,
the majesty of our God.

Strengthen the weak hands,
and make firm the feeble knees.
Say to those who are of a fearful heart,
"Be strong, do not fear!
Here is your God.
He will come with vengeance,
with terrible recompense.
He will come and save you."

Then the eyes of the blind shall be opened,
and the ears of the deaf unstopped;
then the lame shall leap like a deer,
and the tongue of the mute sing for joy.

And the ransomed of the Lord shall return,
and come to Zion with singing;
everlasting joy shall be upon their heads;
they shall obtain joy and gladness,
and sorrow and sighing shall flee away.

The word of the Lord. **Thanks be to God.**

RESPONSORIAL PSALM *(Psalm 146)*

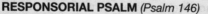

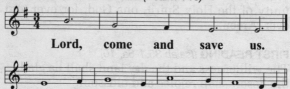

R̶. **Lord, come and save us.**
or **Alleluia!**

It is the Lord who keeps faith for-·**ever**,
who executes justice for the op-·**pressed**;
who gives food to the · **hungry**.
The Lord sets the · **prisoners** free. R̶.

The Lord opens the eyes of the · **blind**
and lifts up those who are bowed · **down**;
the Lord loves the · **righteous**
and watches over · **the** strangers. R̶.

The Lord upholds the orphan and the · **widow**,
but the way of the wicked he brings to · **ruin**.

The Lord will reign for·-**ever,**
your God, O Zion, for all · **gener**-ations. R.

©2010 Gordon Johnston/Novalis
To hear the Sunday Psalms, visit www.livingwithchrist.ca.

SECOND READING *(James 5.7-10)*
Be patient, brothers and sisters, until the coming of the Lord. The farmer waits for the precious crop from the earth, being patient with it until it receives the early and the late rains. You also must be patient. Strengthen your hearts, for the coming of the Lord is near.

Brothers and sisters, do not grumble against one another, so that you may not be judged. See, the Judge is standing at the doors! As an example of suffering and patience, brothers and sisters, take the Prophets who spoke in the name of the Lord.

The word of the Lord. **Thanks be to God.**

GOSPEL ACCLAMATION *(Luke 4.18 [see Isaiah 61.1])*
Alleluia. Alleluia. The Spirit of the Lord is upon me; he has sent me to bring good news to the poor. **Alleluia.**

GOSPEL *(Matthew 11.2-11)*
The Lord be with you. **And with your spirit.**
A reading from the holy Gospel according to Matthew. **Glory to you, O Lord.**

When John the Baptist heard in prison about the deeds of the Christ, he sent word by his disciples who said to Jesus, "Are you the one who is to come, or are we to wait for another?"

Jesus answered them, "Go and tell John what you hear and see: the blind receive their sight, the lame walk, the lepers are cleansed, the deaf hear, the dead are raised, and the poor have good news brought to them. And blessed is anyone who takes no offence at me."

As they went away, Jesus began to speak to the crowds about John: "What did you go out into the wilderness to look at? A reed shaken by the wind? What then did you go out to see? Someone dressed in soft robes? Look, those who wear soft robes are in royal palaces. What then did you go out to see? A Prophet? Yes, I tell you, and more than a Prophet. This is the one about whom it is written, 'See, I am sending my messenger ahead of you, who will prepare your way before you.'

"Truly I tell you, among those born of women no one has arisen greater than John the Baptist; yet the least in the kingdom of heaven is greater than he."

The Gospel of the Lord. **Praise to you, Lord Jesus Christ.**

PROFESSION OF FAITH (p. 11)

PRAYER OF THE FAITHFUL

The following intentions are suggestions only. There are more suggestions at www.livingwithchrist.ca

℟. **Lord, hear our prayer.**

For Christians everywhere, called to witness to God's love by joyful and practical service in the world, we pray to the Lord: ℟.

For the swift coming of God's rule of peace and justice among all nations, we pray to the Lord: R.

For people among us who are lonely or separated from family and friends, we pray to the Lord: R.

For all who work to help families experience true peace and joy, we pray to the Lord: R.

PREPARATION OF THE GIFTS (p. 14)

PRAYER OVER THE OFFERINGS
May the sacrifice of our worship, Lord, we pray, be offered to you unceasingly, to complete what was begun in sacred mystery and powerfully accomplish for us your saving work. Through Christ our Lord. **Amen.**

PREFACE (Advent I, p. 15)

COMMUNION ANTIPHON (Cf. Isaiah 35.4)
Say to the faint of heart: Be strong and do not fear. Behold, our God will come, and he will save us.

PRAYER AFTER COMMUNION
We implore your mercy, Lord, that this divine sustenance may cleanse us of our faults and prepare us for the coming feasts. Through Christ our Lord. **Amen.**

SOLEMN BLESSING AND DISMISSAL (p. 76)

December 18

By far, the best way to celebrate Christmas is to be with children. And we are so close to Christmas now that our children can barely contain their excitement!

Yet, before his marriage, poor Joseph could not have been very excited to hear that Mary was with child. Sure, most fathers, when they learn their wife is expecting, can get a little bewildered, too. But Joseph felt that this was not the expected way to bring children into the world, and so he planned to dismiss Mary quietly from his life.

And then the unexpected happened to this bewildered man who was just looking to do the right thing. Divine intervention arrived in the form of a dream — complete with talking angels. This convinced Joseph that his plans had to change. Will the unexpected presence of God awaken us this Advent, and really change our lives as a result?

Advent is all about deeply living this exciting time of expectation, a precious time to prepare to change ourselves, our homes, and our hearts, for sharing. We have to remember that it was the Divine who initiated this sharing in that first Feast of the Incarnation, sending his Son to be the Saviour that our lives yearn for most. Emmanuel — "God with us!" Can we open our hearts to see the signs that "God is with us" today?

Joe Gunn, Ottawa, ON

ENTRANCE ANTIPHON (Cf. Isaiah 45.8)
Drop down dew from above, you heavens, and let
the clouds rain down the Just One; let the earth
be opened and bring forth a Saviour.

INTRODUCTORY RITES (p. 5)

COLLECT
Pour forth, we beseech you, O Lord, your grace
into our hearts, that we, to whom the Incarnation
of Christ your Son was made known by the message of an Angel, may by his Passion and Cross
be brought to the glory of his Resurrection. Who
lives and reigns with you in the unity of the Holy
Spirit, one God, for ever and ever. **Amen.**

FIRST READING (Isaiah 7.10-14)
The Lord spoke to Ahaz, saying, "Ask a sign of
the Lord your God; let it be deep as Sheol or high
as heaven." But Ahaz said, "I will not ask, and I
will not put the Lord to the test."

Then Isaiah said: "Hear then, O house of David! Is it too little for you to weary the people,
that you weary my God also? Therefore the Lord
himself will give you a sign. Look, the young
woman is with child and shall bear a son, and
shall name him Emmanuel."

The word of the Lord. **Thanks be to God.**

RESPONSORIAL PSALM *(Psalm 24)*

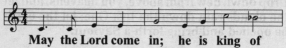

May the Lord come in; he is king of

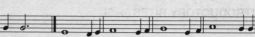

glo-ry.

℞. **May the Lord come in; he is king of glory.**

The earth is the Lord's and all that · **is** in_it,
the world, and those · **who** live_in_it;
for he has founded it · **on_the** seas,
and established it · **on_the** rivers. ℞.

Who shall ascend the hill · **of_the** Lord?
And who shall stand in his · **holy** place?
Someone who has clean hands and
a · **pure** heart,
who does not lift up their soul
to · **what_is** false. ℞.

That person will receive blessing
· **from_the** Lord,
and vindication from the God of their
· **sal**-vation.
Such is the company of those · **who** seek_him,
who seek the face of the God · **of** Jacob. ℞.

©2010 Gordon Johnston/Novalis
To hear the Sunday Psalms, visit www.livingwithchrist.ca.

SECOND READING *(Romans 1.1-7)*
From Paul, a servant of Jesus Christ, called to be
an Apostle, set apart for the Gospel of God, which

God promised beforehand through his Prophets in the holy Scriptures: the Gospel concerning his Son, who was descended from David according to the flesh and was declared to be Son of God with power according to the spirit of holiness by resurrection from the dead, Jesus Christ our Lord.

Through Christ we have received grace and apostleship to bring about the obedience of faith among all the Gentiles for the sake of his name, including yourselves who are called to belong to Jesus Christ.

To all God's beloved in Rome, who are called to be saints: Grace to you and peace from God our Father and the Lord Jesus Christ.

The word of the Lord. **Thanks be to God.**

GOSPEL ACCLAMATION *(Matthew 1.23)*

Alleluia. Alleluia. The virgin shall be with child and bear a son; and they shall name him Emmanuel: God is with us. **Alleluia.**

GOSPEL *(Matthew 1.18-24)*

The Lord be with you. **And with your spirit.**
A reading from the holy Gospel according to Matthew. **Glory to you, O Lord.**

The birth of Jesus the Christ took place in this way. When his mother Mary had been engaged to Joseph, but before they lived together, she was found to be with child from the Holy Spirit. Her husband Joseph, being a righteous man and unwilling to expose her to public disgrace, planned to dismiss her quietly.

But just when he had resolved to do this, an Angel of the Lord appeared to him in a dream and said, "Joseph, son of David, do not be afraid to take Mary as your wife, for the child conceived in her is from the Holy Spirit. She will bear a son, and you are to name him Jesus, for he will save his people from their sins."

All this took place to fulfill what had been spoken by the Lord through the Prophet: "Look, the virgin shall conceive and bear a son, and they shall name him Emmanuel," which means, "God is with us." When Joseph awoke from sleep, he did as the Angel of the Lord commanded him; he took her as his wife.

The Gospel of the Lord. **Praise to you, Lord Jesus Christ.**

PROFESSION OF FAITH *(p. 11)*

PRAYER OF THE FAITHFUL

The following intentions are suggestions only. There are more suggestions at www.livingwithchrist.ca

R. **Lord, hear our prayer.**

For the Church, called as Mary was, to give Christ to the world, we pray to the Lord: R.

For all the world's children, born and unborn, signs of God's gift of life, we pray to the Lord: R.

For people in our midst who reach out for love and hope, we pray to the Lord: R.

For us, God's people gathered here, called to bring the presence of Christ to each other, we pray to the Lord: R.

PREPARATION OF THE GIFTS (p. 14)

PRAYER OVER THE OFFERINGS
May the Holy Spirit, O Lord, sanctify these gifts laid upon your altar, just as he filled with his power the womb of the Blessed Virgin Mary. Through Christ our Lord. **Amen.**

PREFACE (Advent II, p. 15)

COMMUNION ANTIPHON (Isaiah 7.14)
Behold, a Virgin shall conceive and bear a son; and his name will be called Emmanuel.

PRAYER AFTER COMMUNION
Having received this pledge of eternal redemption, we pray, almighty God, that, as the feast day of our salvation draws ever nearer, so we may press forward all the more eagerly to the worthy celebration of the mystery of your Son's Nativity. Who lives and reigns for ever and ever. **Amen.**

SOLEMN BLESSING AND DISMISSAL (p. 76)

December 25

Christmas day is truly an amazing grace for all humankind. It's a day that has been eagerly awaited by generations of believers and entertained through the many and hopeful oracles of biblical prophets. Today, the promises of God are now fulfilled through the amazing birth of a child in the night of Bethlehem and in the chillness of a manger. First, Mary and Joseph are the only witnesses of such a marvel. But soon, the good news is proclaimed twice to humble shepherds "keeping watch over their flock by night," by "an Angel of the Lord," joined later by "a multitude of the heavenly host."

This was only the beginning of the greatest good news ever proclaimed on earth. In Luke's narrative, it's not only the number of heavenly messengers that increases, but also that of the human recipients: "on earth peace among those whom [God] favours." Born in the city of David, this child is not only the Saviour and Messiah awaited by Israel: he is no less, as the Letter to Titus puts it, "the grace of God... bringing salvation to all." Let us rejoice then — both as people who believe in this Saviour and Messiah, and together with all nations on earth whom God favours.

Jean-Pierre Prévost, Chénéville, QC

MASS DURING THE NIGHT

ENTRANCE ANTIPHON *(Psalm 2.7)*
The Lord said to me: You are my Son. It is I who have begotten you this day.

or

Let us all rejoice in the Lord, for our Saviour has been born in the world. Today true peace has come down to us from heaven.

INTRODUCTORY RITES *(p. 5)*

COLLECT
O God, who have made this most sacred night radiant with the splendour of the true light, grant, we pray, that we, who have known the mysteries of his light on earth, may also delight in his gladness in heaven. Who lives and reigns with you in the unity of the Holy Spirit, one God, for ever and ever. **Amen.**

FIRST READING *(Isaiah 9.2-4, 6-7)*
The people who walked in darkness have seen
    a great light;
those who lived in a land of deep darkness —
on them light has shone.
You have multiplied the nation,
you have increased its joy;
they rejoice before you
as with joy at the harvest,
as people exult when dividing plunder.

For the yoke of their burden,
and the bar across their shoulders,
the rod of their oppressor,
you have broken as on the day of Midian.

For a child has been born for us,
a son given to us;
authority rests upon his shoulders;
and he is named
Wonderful Counsellor, Mighty God,
Everlasting Father, Prince of Peace.

His authority shall grow continually,
and there shall be endless peace
for the throne of David and his kingdom.
He will establish and uphold it
with justice and with righteousness
from this time onward and forevermore.
The zeal of the Lord of hosts will do this.

The word of the Lord. **Thanks be to God.**

RESPONSORIAL PSALM *(Psalm 96)*

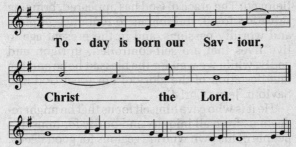

To - day is born our Sav - iour,

Christ_____ the Lord.

℟. **Today is born our Saviour, Christ the Lord.**

O sing to the Lord a · **new** song;
sing to the Lord, · **all_the** earth.
Sing to the Lord, · **bless_his** name;
tell of his salvation from day · **to** day. ℟.

Declare his glory among · **the** nations,
his marvellous works among all · **the** peoples.
For great is the Lord, and greatly · **to_be** praised;
he is to be revered above · **all** gods. ℟.

Let the heavens be glad, and let the earth
· **re**-joice;
let the sea roar, and all · **that** fills_it;
let the field exult, and every-·**thing** in_it.
Then shall all the trees of the forest sing
· **for** joy. ℟.

Rejoice before the Lord; for · **he_is** coming,
for he is coming to judge · **the** earth.
He will judge the world · **with** righteousness,
and the peoples · **with_his** truth. ℟.

SECOND READING (Titus 2.11-14)

Beloved: The grace of God has appeared, bringing salvation to all, training us to renounce impiety and worldly passions, and in the present age to live lives that are self-controlled, upright, and godly, while we wait for the blessed hope and the manifestation of the glory of our great God and Saviour, Jesus Christ.

He it is who gave himself for us that he might redeem us from all iniquity and purify for himself a people of his own who are zealous for good deeds.

The word of the Lord. **Thanks be to God.**

GOSPEL ACCLAMATION (Luke 2.10-11)

Alleluia. Alleluia. Good news and great joy to all the world: today is born our Saviour, Christ the Lord. **Alleluia.**

GOSPEL (Luke 2.1-16)

The Lord be with you. **And with your spirit.** A reading from the holy Gospel according to Luke. **Glory to you, O Lord.**

In those days a decree went out from Caesar Augustus that all the world should be registered. This was the first registration and was taken while Quirinius was governor of Syria. All went to their own towns to be registered. Joseph also went from the town of Nazareth in Galilee to Judea, to the city of David called Bethlehem, because he was descended from the house and family of David. He went to be registered with Mary, to whom he was engaged and who was expecting a child.

While they were there, the time came for her to deliver her child. And she gave birth to her firstborn son and wrapped him in swaddling clothes, and laid him in a manger, because there was no place for them in the inn.

In that region there were shepherds living in the fields, keeping watch over their flock by night. Then an Angel of the Lord stood before them, and the glory of the Lord shone around them, and they were terrified. But the Angel said to them, "Do not be afraid; for see — I am bringing you good news of great joy for all the people: to you is born this day in the city of David a Saviour, who is the Christ, the Lord. This will be a sign for you: you will find a child wrapped in swaddling clothes and lying in a manger."

And suddenly there was with the Angel a multitude of the heavenly host, praising God and saying, "Glory to God in the highest heaven, and on earth peace among those whom he favours!"

When the Angels had left them and gone into heaven, the shepherds said to one another, "Let us go now to Bethlehem and see this thing that has taken place, which the Lord has made known to us." So they went with haste and found Mary and Joseph, and the child lying in the manger.

The Gospel of the Lord. **Praise to you, Lord Jesus Christ.**

PROFESSION OF FAITH *(p. 11. All kneel at the words "and by the Holy Spirit was incarnate.")*

PRAYER OF THE FAITHFUL

The following intentions are suggestions only. There are more suggestions at www.livingwithchrist.ca

R. **Lord, hear our prayer.**

For the Church, called to see with the eyes of faith God's living presence in our midst, we pray to the Lord: R.

For all the world's children, gracious sacraments of God's gift of life, we pray to the Lord: R.

For people in our midst who, in this season of joyful light, walk in darkness, loneliness and despair, we pray to the Lord: R.

For us, the family of God, called to recognize God's presence in all things, we pray to the Lord: R.

PREPARATION OF THE GIFTS *(p. 14)*

PRAYER OVER THE OFFERINGS

May the oblation of this day's feast be pleasing to you, O Lord, we pray, that through this most holy exchange we may be found in the likeness of Christ, in whom our nature is united to you. Who lives and reigns for ever and ever. **Amen.**

PREFACE *(Nativity, p. 16)*

COMMUNION ANTIPHON *(John 1.14)*

The Word became flesh, and we have seen his glory.

PRAYER AFTER COMMUNION

Grant us, we pray, O Lord our God, that we, who are gladdened by participation in the feast of our Redeemer's Nativity, may through an honourable way of life become worthy of union with him. Who lives and reigns for ever and ever. **Amen.**

SOLEMN BLESSING — NATIVITY (Optional)

Bow down for the blessing.

May the God of infinite goodness, who by the Incarnation of his Son has driven darkness from the world and by that glorious Birth has illumined this most holy night (day), drive far from you the darkness of vice and illumine your hearts with the light of virtue. **Amen.**

May God, who willed that the great joy of his Son's saving Birth be announced to shepherds by the Angel, fill your minds with the gladness he gives and make you heralds of his Gospel. **Amen.**

And may God, who by the Incarnation brought together the earthly and heavenly realm, fill you with the gift of his peace and favour and make you sharers with the Church in heaven. **Amen.**

And may the blessing of almighty God, the Father, and the Son, and the Holy Spirit, come down on you and remain with you for ever. **Amen.**

DISMISSAL (p. 70)

MASS AT DAWN

ENTRANCE ANTIPHON *(Cf. Isaiah 9.1, 5; Luke 1.33)*
Today a light will shine upon us, for the Lord is born for us; and he will be called Wondrous God, Prince of peace, Father of future ages: and his reign will be without end.

INTRODUCTORY RITES *(p. 5)*

COLLECT
Grant, we pray, almighty God, that, as we are bathed in the new radiance of your incarnate Word, the light of faith, which illumines our minds, may also shine through in our deeds. Through our Lord Jesus Christ, your Son, who lives and reigns with you in the unity of the Holy Spirit, one God, for ever and ever. **Amen.**

FIRST READING *(Isaiah 62.11-12)*
The Lord has proclaimed to the end of the earth:
"Say to daughter Zion,
See, your salvation comes;
his reward is with him,
and his recompense before him.

"They shall be called 'The Holy People,'
'The Redeemed of the Lord';
and you shall be called 'Sought Out,'
'A City Not Forsaken.'"

The word of the Lord. **Thanks be to God.**

RESPONSORIAL PSALM *(Psalm 97)*

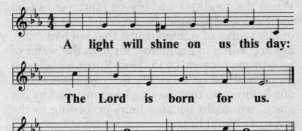

A light will shine on us this day:

The Lord is born for us.

℟. **A light will shine on us this day:**
The Lord is born for us.

The Lord is king! Let the earth re-**joice;**
let the many coastlands be · **glad!**
Clouds and thick darkness are all a-**round_him;**
righteousness and justice are the foundation
of his · **throne.** ℟.

The mountains melt like wax before the · **Lord,**
before the Lord of all the · **earth.**
The heavens proclaim his · **righteousness;**
and all the peoples behold his · **glory.** ℟.

Light dawns for the · **righteous,**
and joy for the upright in · **heart.**
Rejoice in the Lord, O you · **righteous,**
and give thanks to his holy · **name!** ℟.

©2009 Gordon Johnston/Novalis
To hear the Sunday Psalms, visit www.livingwithchrist.ca.

SECOND READING *(Titus 3.4-7)*

When the goodness and loving kindness of God our Saviour appeared, he saved us, not because of any works of righteousness that we had done, but according to his mercy, through the water of rebirth and renewal by the Holy Spirit. This Spirit he poured out on us richly through Jesus Christ our Saviour, so that, having been justified by his grace, we might become heirs according to the hope of eternal life.

The word of the Lord. **Thanks be to God.**

GOSPEL ACCLAMATION *(Luke 2.14)*

Alleluia. Alleluia. Glory to God in the highest heaven; peace on earth to people of good will. **Alleluia.**

GOSPEL *(Luke 2.15-20)*

The Lord be with you. **And with your spirit.** A reading from the holy Gospel according to Luke. **Glory to you, O Lord.**

When the Angels had left them and gone into heaven, the shepherds said to one another, "Let us go now to Bethlehem and see this thing that has taken place, which the Lord has made known to us."

So they went with haste and found Mary and Joseph, and the child lying in the manger. When they saw this, they made known what had been told them about this child; and all who heard it were amazed at what the shepherds told them.

But Mary treasured all these words and pondered them in her heart. The shepherds returned, glorifying and praising God for all they had heard and seen, as it had been told them.

The Gospel of the Lord. **Praise to you, Lord Jesus Christ.**

PROFESSION OF FAITH (p. 11. All kneel at the words "and by the Holy Spirit was incarnate.")

PRAYER OF THE FAITHFUL (p. 104)

PREPARATION OF THE GIFTS (p. 14)

PRAYER OVER THE OFFERINGS
May our offerings be worthy, we pray, O Lord, of the mysteries of the Nativity this day, that, just as Christ was born a man and also shone forth as God, so these earthly gifts may confer on us what is divine. Through Christ our Lord. **Amen.**

PREFACE (Nativity, p. 16)

COMMUNION ANTIPHON (Cf. Zechariah 9.9)
Rejoice, O Daughter Sion; lift up praise, Daughter Jerusalem: Behold, your King will come, the Holy One and Saviour of the world.

PRAYER AFTER COMMUNION
Grant us, Lord, as we honour with joyful devotion the Nativity of your Son, that we may come to know with fullness of faith the hidden depths of this mystery and to love them ever more and more. Through Christ our Lord. **Amen.**

SOLEMN BLESSING AND DISMISSAL (p. 105)

MASS DURING THE DAY

ENTRANCE ANTIPHON *(Cf. Isaiah 9.5)*
A child is born for us, and a son is given to us; his sceptre of power rests upon his shoulder, and his name will be called Messenger of great counsel.

INTRODUCTORY RITES *(p. 5)*

COLLECT
O God, who wonderfully created the dignity of human nature and still more wonderfully restored it, grant, we pray, that we may share in the divinity of Christ, who humbled himself to share in our humanity. Who lives and reigns with you in the unity of the Holy Spirit, one God, for ever and ever. **Amen.**

FIRST READING *(Isaiah 52.7-10)*
How beautiful upon the mountains are the feet of the messenger who announces peace, who brings good news, who announces salvation, who says to Zion, "Your God reigns."

Listen! Your watchmen lift up their voices, together they sing for joy; for in plain sight they see the return of the Lord to Zion.

Break forth together into singing, you ruins of Jerusalem; for the Lord has comforted his people, he has redeemed Jerusalem. The Lord has bared his holy arm before the eyes of all the nations; and all the ends of the earth shall see the salvation of our God.

The word of the Lord. **Thanks be to God.**

RESPONSORIAL PSALM (*Psalm 98*)

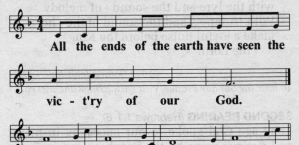

All the ends of the earth have seen the
vic - t'ry of our God.

R. **All the ends of the earth have seen
the victory of our God.**

O sing to the Lord a · **new** song,
for he has done · **marvellous** things.
His right hand and his holy · **arm**
have brought · **him** victory. R.

The Lord has made known · **his** victory;
he has revealed his vindication in the sight
of · **the** nations.
He has remembered his steadfast love and
· **faithfulness**
to the house · **of** Israel. R.

All the ends of the earth · **have** seen
the victory of · **our** God.
Make a joyful noise to the Lord, all the · **earth;**
break forth into joyous song and · **sing**
praises. R.

Sing praises to the Lord with · **the** lyre,
with the lyre and the sound · **of** melody.
With trumpets and the sound of the · **horn**
make a joyful noise before the King,
· **the** Lord. R.

©2009 Gordon Johnston/Novalis

To hear the Sunday Psalms, visit www.livingwithchrist.ca.

SECOND READING *(Hebrews 1.1-6)*

Long ago God spoke to our ancestors in many and various ways by the Prophets, but in these last days he has spoken to us by the Son, whom he appointed heir of all things, through whom he also created the ages.

He is the reflection of God's glory and the exact imprint of God's very being, and he sustains all things by his powerful word. When he had made purification for sins, he sat down at the right hand of the Majesty on high, having become as much superior to Angels as the name he has inherited is more excellent than theirs.

For to which of the Angels did God ever say, "You are my Son; today I have begotten you"? Or again, "I will be his Father, and he will be my Son"? And again, when he brings the firstborn into the world, he says, "Let all God's Angels worship him."

The word of the Lord. **Thanks be to God.**

GOSPEL ACCLAMATION

Alleluia. Alleluia. A holy day has dawned upon us. Come you nations and adore the Lord. Today a great light has come down upon the earth. **Alleluia.**

GOSPEL *(John 1.1-18)*

For the shorter version, omit the indented parts.

The Lord be with you. **And with your spirit.**
A reading from the holy Gospel according to John.
Glory to you, O Lord.

In the beginning was the Word, and the Word was with God, and the Word was God. He was in the beginning with God. All things came into being through him, and without him not one thing came into being. What has come into being in him was life, and the life was the light of the human race.

The light shines in the darkness, and the darkness did not overcome it.

There was a man sent from God, whose name was John. He came as a witness to testify to the light, so that all might believe through him. He himself was not the light, but he came to testify to the light. The true light, which enlightens everyone, was coming into the world. He was in the world, and the world came into being through him; yet the world did not know him. He came to what was his own, and his own people did not accept him. But to all who received him, who believed in his name, he gave power to become children of God, who were born, not of blood or of the will of the flesh or of the will of man, but of God.

And the Word became flesh and lived among us, and we have seen his glory, the glory as of a father's only-begotten son, full of grace and truth.

John testified to him and cried out, "This was he of whom I said, 'He who comes after me ranks ahead of me because he was before me.'" From his fullness we have all received, grace upon grace. The law indeed was given through Moses; grace and truth came through Jesus Christ. No one has ever seen God. It is God the only-begotten Son, who is close to the Father's heart, who has made him known. The Gospel of the Lord. **Praise to you, Lord Jesus Christ.**

PROFESSION OF FAITH (p. 11. All kneel at the words "and by the Holy Spirit was incarnate.")

PRAYER OF THE FAITHFUL (p. 104)

PREPARATION OF THE GIFTS (p. 14)

PRAYER OVER THE OFFERINGS
Make acceptable, O Lord, our oblation on this solemn day, when you manifested the reconciliation that makes us wholly pleasing in your sight and inaugurated for us the fullness of divine worship. Through Christ our Lord. **Amen.**

PREFACE (Nativity, p. 16)

COMMUNION ANTIPHON (Cf. Psalm 97.3)
All the ends of the earth have seen the salvation of our God.

PRAYER AFTER COMMUNION
Grant, O merciful God, that, just as the Saviour of the world, born this day, is the author of divine generation for us, so he may be the giver even of immortality. Who lives and reigns for ever and ever. **Amen.**

SOLEMN BLESSING AND DISMISSAL (p. 105)

January Saints' Days

The following saints are traditionally remembered in January in Canada.

1	Solemnity of Mary, the Holy Mother of God
2	Saints Basil the Great and Gregory Nazianzen
7	Saint André Bessette
8	Saint Raymond of Penyafort
12	Saint Marguerite Bourgeoys
13	Saint Hilary
17	Saint Anthony
20	Saint Fabian
	Saint Sebastian
21	Saint Agnes
22	Saint Vincent
24	Saint Francis de Sales
26	Saints Timothy and Titus
27	Saint Angela Merici
28	Saint Thomas Aquinas
31	Saint John Bosco

January 1
World Day of Peace

"God sent his Son, born of a woman." This mysterious encounter, where a vulnerable girl finds the strength to say yes, brings about our adoption into the family of God. That fragile young woman becomes our holy mother, to whom we turn in our own moments of fragility. And God becomes our "Abba," whom we cry out to like a small child calling for their daddy.

From that "born of a woman" miracle, we are welcomed into an economy of grace that turns the power structures of this world on their heads. You want to see tough? Meet this unmarried girl face to face with a terrifying angel. You want to see a powerful king? Here is Christ crucified.

The encounter with the living God turns this broken world, full of oppression and abuses of power, onto its head. Mary embraced the encounter, and through that embrace Christ enters our world to "bring good news to the poor." The world-transformation we long for isn't subtle. Jesus promises captives released, blindness reversed, the oppressed going free: no half measures.

The encounter with the face of God is an encounter with a terrifying, purifying light. That light transforms with burning heat and renders the darkness unrecognizable. From vulnerability, strength. From the darkness, light. May the Lord make his face to shine upon us.

Kate McGee, Toronto, ON

ENTRANCE ANTIPHON
Hail, Holy Mother, who gave birth to the King
who rules heaven and earth for ever.
or (Cf. Isaiah 9.1, 5; Luke 1.33)
Today a light will shine upon us, for the Lord
is born for us; and he will be called Wondrous
God, Prince of peace, Father of future ages: and
his reign will be without end.

INTRODUCTORY RITES *(p. 5)*

COLLECT
O God, who through the fruitful virginity of
Blessed Mary bestowed on the human race the
grace of eternal salvation, grant, we pray, that we
may experience the intercession of her, through
whom we were found worthy to receive the author of life, our Lord Jesus Christ, your Son. Who
lives and reigns with you in the unity of the Holy
Spirit, one God, for ever and ever. **Amen.**

FIRST READING *(Numbers 6.22-27)*
The Lord spoke to Moses: Speak to Aaron and his
sons, saying, Thus you shall bless the children of
Israel: You shall say to them,
  The Lord bless you and keep you;
  the Lord make his face to shine upon you,
  and be gracious to you;
  the Lord lift up his countenance upon you,
  and give you peace.
So they shall put my name on the children of
Israel, and I will bless them.
  The word of the Lord. **Thanks be to God.**

117

RESPONSORIAL PSALM *(Psalm 67)*

May God be gra-cious to us and bless us.

R̥. **May God be gracious to us and bless us.**

May God be gracious to us · **and** bless_us
and make his face to shine · **up**-on_us,
that your way may be known up--**on** earth,
your saving power a--**mong** all nations. R̥.

Let the nations be glad and sing · **for** joy,
for you judge the peoples with equity
    and guide the nations up--**on** earth.
Let the peoples praise you, · **O** God;
let all the · **peo**-ples praise_you. R̥.

The earth has yielded · **its** increase;
God, our God, · **has** blessed_us.
May God continue · **to** bless_us;
let all the ends of the · **earth** re-vere_him. R̥.

©2009 Gordon Johnston/Novalis

SECOND READING *(Galatians 4.4-7)*

Brothers and sisters: When the fullness of time had come, God sent his Son, born of a woman, born under the law, in order to redeem those who were under the law, so that we might receive adoption to sonship.

And because you are sons and daughters, God has sent the Spirit of his Son into our hearts, crying, "Abba! Father!" So you are no longer slave but son, and if son then also heir, through God.

The word of the Lord. **Thanks be to God.**

GOSPEL ACCLAMATION (Hebrews 1.1-2)
Alleluia. Alleluia. Long ago God spoke to our ancestors by the Prophets; in these last days he has spoken to us by the Son. **Alleluia.**

GOSPEL (Luke 2.16-21)
The Lord be with you. **And with your spirit.**
A reading from the holy Gospel according to Luke. **Glory to you, O Lord.**

The shepherds went with haste to Bethlehem and found Mary and Joseph, and the child lying in the manger. When they saw this, they made known what had been told them about this child; and all who heard it were amazed at what the shepherds told them.

But Mary treasured all these words and pondered them in her heart.

The shepherds returned, glorifying and praising God for all they had heard and seen, as it had been told them.

After eight days had passed, it was time to circumcise the child; and he was called Jesus, the name given by the Angel before he was conceived in the womb.

The Gospel of the Lord. **Praise to you, Lord Jesus Christ.**

PROFESSION OF FAITH *(p. 11)*

PRAYER OF THE FAITHFUL

The following intentions are suggestions only. There are more suggestions at www.livingwithchrist.ca

℞. **Lord, hear our prayer.**

For all Christians, called to be a sign of unity as we work together for justice, we pray to the Lord: ℞.

For peace in a world broken by violence, abuse and the misuse of the world's resources, we pray to the Lord: ℞.

For all who hunger and thirst for freedom from poverty, unemployment and prejudice, we pray to the Lord: ℞.

For all those who, like Mary, display strength, courage and perseverance, we pray to the Lord: ℞.

PREPARATION OF THE GIFTS *(p. 14)*

PRAYER OVER THE OFFERINGS
O God, who in your kindness begin all good things and bring them to fulfillment, grant to us, who find joy in the Solemnity of the holy Mother of God, that, just as we glory in the beginnings of your grace, so one day we may rejoice in its completion. Through Christ our Lord. **Amen.**

PREFACE *(BVM, p. 17)*

COMMUNION ANTIPHON *(Hebrews 13.8)*
Jesus Christ is the same yesterday, today, and for ever.

PRAYER AFTER COMMUNION
We have received this heavenly Sacrament with joy, O Lord: grant, we pray, that it may lead us to eternal life, for we rejoice to proclaim the blessed ever-Virgin Mary Mother of your Son and Mother of the Church. Through Christ our Lord. **Amen.**

SOLEMN BLESSING — NEW YEAR (Optional)
Bow down for the blessing.

May God, the source and origin of all blessing, grant you grace, pour out his blessing in abundance, and keep you safe from harm throughout the year. **Amen.**

May he give you integrity in the faith, endurance in hope, and perseverance in charity with holy patience to the end. **Amen.**

May he order your days and your deeds in his peace, grant your prayers in this and in every place, and lead you happily to eternal life. **Amen.**

And may the blessing of almighty God, the Father, and the Son, and the Holy Spirit, come down on you and remain with you for ever. **Amen.**

DISMISSAL (p. 70)

January 8

It is very clear that the Jewish people are the chosen people of God. Yet in the Old and New Testaments there are indications that the message of the God of all creation is to be offered to all nations.

The early Christians, after Jesus's death, held that The Way of Jesus was intended for Jewish Christians but not for Gentiles, even though Jesus was open to them in his lifetime. Paul's conversion turned all that upside down. "In former generations this mystery was not made known to humankind."

Paul had a tough time convincing some of the apostles that Jesus and his message were to be shared with Gentiles. Eventually, Peter recognized Paul's approach and missionary efforts to the Gentiles. Paul went out to "all nations" and the word of God spread. He took the light of Christ to everyone he met and wherever he went.

The feast of the Epiphany, the feast of "opening" our doors to others, speaks to our day. Mary opened the door of her house to the Wise Men from the East. Pope Francis opens his arms to all. The promise of a Messiah for all is fulfilled.

This Epiphany, let us advance the fulfillment of the promise by inviting and welcoming all who want to praise Jesus Christ, the Son of God.

Friar Ed Debono, OFM Conv, Kingston, ON

ENTRANCE ANTIPHON
(Cf. Malachi 3.1; 1 Chronicles 29.12)
Behold, the Lord, the Mighty One, has come; and kingship is in his grasp, and power and dominion.

INTRODUCTORY RITES *(p. 5)*

COLLECT
O God, who on this day revealed your Only Begotten Son to the nations by the guidance of a star, grant in your mercy that we, who know you already by faith, may be brought to behold the beauty of your sublime glory. Through our Lord Jesus Christ, your Son, who lives and reigns with you in the unity of the Holy Spirit, one God, for ever and ever. **Amen.**

FIRST READING *(Isaiah 60.1-6)*
Arise, shine, for your light has come,
and the glory of the Lord has risen upon you!
For darkness shall cover the earth,
and thick darkness the peoples;
but the Lord will arise upon you,
and his glory will appear over you.
Nations shall come to your light,
and kings to the brightness of your dawn.
Lift up your eyes and look around;
they all gather together, they come to you;
your sons shall come from far away,
and your daughters shall be carried on their
    nurses' arms.

Then you shall see and be radiant;
your heart shall thrill and rejoice,

because the abundance of the sea shall be
    brought to you,
the wealth of the nations shall come to you.
A multitude of camels shall cover you,
the young camels of Midian and Ephah;
all those from Sheba shall come.
They shall bring gold and frankincense,
and shall proclaim the praise of the Lord.

The word of the Lord. **Thanks be to God.**

RESPONSORIAL PSALM (*Psalm 72*)

Lord, eve - ry na - tion on earth will a - dore you.

℟. **Lord, every nation on earth will adore you.**

Give the king your justice, O · **God,**
and your righteousness to a king's · **son.**
May he judge your · **people** with
    righteousness,
and your · **poor** with justice. ℟.

In his days may righteousness · **flourish**
and peace abound, until the moon is
    no · **more.**
May he have dominion from · **sea** to sea,
and from the River to the · **ends_of**
    the earth. ℟.

May the kings of Tarshish and of the isles
   render him · **tribute,**
may the kings of Sheba and Seba bring · **gifts.**
May all kings fall · **down** be-fore_him,
all nations · **give** him service. R.

For he delivers the needy one who · **calls,**
the poor and the one who has no · **helper.**
He has pity on the · **weak_and** the needy,
and saves the · **lives_of** the needy. R.

©2009 Gordon Johnston/Novalis
To hear the Sunday Psalms, visit www.livingwithchrist.ca.

SECOND READING *(Ephesians 3.2-3a, 5-6)*
Brothers and sisters: Surely you have already
heard of the commission of God's grace that was
given me for you, and how the mystery was made
known to me by revelation.

In former generations this mystery was not
made known to humankind as it has now been
revealed to his holy Apostles and Prophets by the
Spirit: that is, the Gentiles have become fellow
heirs, members of the same body, and sharers in
the promise in Christ Jesus through the Gospel.

The word of the Lord. **Thanks be to God.**

GOSPEL ACCLAMATION *(See Matthew 2.2)*
Alleluia. Alleluia. We observed his star at its rising,
and have come to pay homage to the Lord. **Alleluia.**

GOSPEL *(Matthew 2.1-12)*
The Lord be with you. **And with your spirit.**
A reading from the holy Gospel according to Mat-
thew. **Glory to you, O Lord.**

In the time of King Herod, after Jesus was born in Bethlehem of Judea, wise men from the East came to Jerusalem, asking, "Where is the child who has been born king of the Jews? For we observed his star at its rising, and have come to pay him homage."

When King Herod heard this, he was frightened, and all Jerusalem with him; and calling together all the chief priests and scribes of the people, he inquired of them where the Messiah was to be born. They told him, "In Bethlehem of Judea; for so it has been written by the Prophet: 'And you, Bethlehem, in the land of Judah, are by no means least among the rulers of Judah; for from you shall come a ruler who is to shepherd my people Israel.'"

Then Herod secretly called for the wise men and learned from them the exact time when the star had appeared. Then he sent them to Bethlehem, saying, "Go and search diligently for the child; and when you have found him, bring me word so that I may also go and pay him homage."

When they had heard the king, they set out; and there, ahead of them, went the star that they had seen at its rising, until it stopped over the place where the child was. When they saw that the star had stopped, they were overwhelmed with joy.

On entering the house, they saw the child with Mary his mother; and they knelt down and paid him homage. Then, opening their treasure chests, they offered him gifts of gold, frankincense, and myrrh.

And having been warned in a dream not to return to Herod, they left for their own country by another road.

The Gospel of the Lord. **Praise to you, Lord Jesus Christ.**

PROFESSION OF FAITH *(p. 11)*

PRAYER OF THE FAITHFUL

The following intentions are suggestions only. There are more suggestions at www.livingwithchrist.ca

℟. **Lord, hear our prayer.**

For the Church, light of the nations, witness to the message of Jesus, we pray to the Lord: ℟.

For a deep and mutual respect for all faith traditions among all leaders and teachers, we pray to the Lord: ℟.

For those who seek a welcome at our table and a place in our communities, we pray to the Lord: ℟.

For us, God's people, yearning for fresh hope as we seek the Light, we pray to the Lord: ℟.

PREPARATION OF THE GIFTS *(p. 14)*

PRAYER OVER THE OFFERINGS

Look with favour, Lord, we pray, on these gifts of your Church, in which are offered now not gold or frankincense or myrrh, but he who by them is proclaimed, sacrificed and received, Jesus Christ. Who lives and reigns for ever and ever. **Amen.**

PREFACE *(Epiphany, p. 18)*

COMMUNION ANTIPHON (Cf. Matthew 2.2)
We have seen his star in the East, and have come with gifts to adore the Lord.

PRAYER AFTER COMMUNION
Go before us with heavenly light, O Lord, always and everywhere, that we may perceive with clear sight and revere with true affection the mystery in which you have willed us to participate. Through Christ our Lord. **Amen.**

SOLEMN BLESSING — EPIPHANY (Optional)
Bow down for the blessing.

May God, who has called you out of darkness into his wonderful light, pour out in kindness his blessing upon you and make your hearts firm in faith, hope and charity. **Amen.**

And since in all confidence you follow Christ, who today appeared in the world as a light shining in darkness, may God make you, too, a light for your brothers and sisters. **Amen.**

And so when your pilgrimage is ended, may you come to him whom the Magi sought as they followed the star and whom they found with great joy, the Light from Light, who is Christ the Lord. **Amen.**

And may the blessing of almighty God, the Father, and the Son, and the Holy Spirit, come down on you and remain with you for ever. **Amen.**

DISMISSAL (p. 70)

January 15
World Day of Migrants and Refugees

What is a purpose-driven life? Sometimes, the meaning only becomes clear after an experience makes us look back at seemingly unrelated decisions that made us who we are. It's that "ah-ha" moment.

The gospel today describes John the Baptist's "ah-ha" moment. Until that day, John had been following a path he couldn't quite see clearly, wandering the wilderness, preaching of the Son of God whom he might never even meet in the flesh.

John was a recluse who attracted a huge following. These followers believed his wrath-inflicting Messiah would be the political ruler they had been waiting for. But the meaning of John's life decisions became clear in his meeting with Jesus. The heavens literally opened and God spoke to him! Jesus' ministry would be non-political and characterized by love. Jesus was the one for whom John was preparing the way, and John's future was forever changed by Jesus.

The purpose of our lives may not always be as dramatically revealed to us as John's was by God. Some of us may feel lost, wandering in our own wilderness. But recognizing the need to search is the first brave step toward finding that purpose. In that search we, like John, may meet Jesus by our own river bank. It is an encounter that will radically change our future.

Saskia Sivananthan, Vancouver, BC

ENTRANCE ANTIPHON *(Psalm 65.4)*
All the earth shall bow down before you, O God, and shall sing to you, shall sing to your name, O Most High!

INTRODUCTORY RITES *(p. 5)*

COLLECT
Almighty ever-living God, who govern all things, both in heaven and on earth, mercifully hear the pleading of your people and bestow your peace on our times. Through our Lord Jesus Christ, your Son, who lives and reigns with you in the unity of the Holy Spirit, one God, for ever and ever. **Amen.**

FIRST READING *(Isaiah 49.3, 5-6)*
The Lord said to me, "You are my servant,
Israel, in whom I will be glorified."

And now the Lord says,
who formed me in the womb to be his servant,
to bring Jacob back to him,
and that Israel might be gathered to him,
for I am honoured in the sight of the Lord,
and my God has become my strength.

He says,
"It is too small a thing that you should be
    my servant
to raise up the tribes of Jacob
and to restore the survivors of Israel;
I will give you as a light to the nations,
that my salvation may reach to the end of the earth."

The word of the Lord. **Thanks be to God.**

RESPONSORIAL PSALM (Psalm 40)

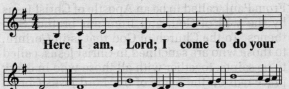

Here I am, Lord; I come to do your will.

℟. **Here I am, Lord; I come to do your will.**

I waited patiently for the · **Lord;**
he inclined to me and · **heard** my cry.
He put a new song in · **my** mouth,
a song of praise · **to** our God. ℟.

Sacrifice and offering you do not de-·**sire,**
but you have given me an · **o**-pen ear.
Burnt offering · **and** sin_offering
you have · **not** re-quired. ℟.

Then I said, "Here I · **am;**
in the scroll of the book it is · **written** of me.
I delight to do your will, O · **my** God;
your law is with-·**in** my heart." ℟.

I have told the glad news of de-·**liverance**
in the great · **con**-gre-gation;
see, I have not restrained · **my** lips,
as you · know, **O** Lord. ℟.

©2010 Gordon Johnston/Novalis
To hear the Sunday Psalms, visit www.livingwithchrist.ca.

SECOND READING *(1 Corinthians 1.1-3)*
From Paul, called to be an Apostle of Christ Jesus
by the will of God, and from our brother Sos-
thenes. To the Church of God that is in Corinth,
to those who are sanctified in Christ Jesus, called
to be saints, together with all those who in every
place call on the name of our Lord Jesus Christ,
both their Lord and ours:

Grace to you and peace from God our Father
and the Lord Jesus Christ.

The word of the Lord. **Thanks be to God.**

GOSPEL ACCLAMATION *(John 1.14, 12)*
Alleluia. Alleluia. The Word became flesh and
lived among us. To all who received him, he gave
the power to become children of God. **Alleluia.**

GOSPEL *(John 1.29-34)*
The Lord be with you. **And with your spirit.**
A reading from the holy Gospel according to John.
Glory to you, O Lord.

John the Baptist saw Jesus coming toward him
and declared, "Here is the Lamb of God who takes
away the sin of the world! This is he of whom I
said, 'After me comes a man who ranks ahead of
me because he was before me.' I myself did not
know him; but I came baptizing with water for
this reason, that he might be revealed to Israel."

And John testified, "I saw the Spirit descending from heaven like a dove, and remain on him.
I myself did not know him, but the one who sent
me to baptize with water said to me, 'He on whom
you see the Spirit descend and remain is the one
who baptizes with the Holy Spirit.' And I myself

have seen and have testified that this is the Son of God."

The Gospel of the Lord. **Praise to you, Lord Jesus Christ.**

PROFESSION OF FAITH *(p. 11)*

PRAYER OF THE FAITHFUL

The following intentions are suggestions only. There are more suggestions at www.livingwithchrist.ca

R. **Lord, hear our prayer.**

For the Church, called to faithfully proclaim the mission of Jesus, we pray to the Lord: R.

For leaders of nations and peoples, from whom is expected prudent, just and wise action, we pray to the Lord: R.

For the elderly among us who are lonely, shut-in or ignored, we pray to the Lord: R.

For all refugees, searching for welcome, peace and security in their new homeland, we pray to the Lord: R.

For us, God's people gathered here, seeking healing and renewal in this celebration of the Lord's death and resurrection, we pray to the Lord: R.

PREPARATION OF THE GIFTS *(p. 14)*

PRAYER OVER THE OFFERINGS

Grant us, O Lord, we pray, that we may participate worthily in these mysteries, for whenever the memorial of this sacrifice is celebrated the work of our redemption is accomplished. Through Christ our Lord. **Amen.**

PREFACE *(Sundays in Ordinary Time, p. 28)*

COMMUNION ANTIPHON *(Cf. Psalm 22.5)*
You have prepared a table before me, and how precious is the chalice that quenches my thirst.
or (1 John 4.16)
We have come to know and to believe in the love that God has for us.

PRAYER AFTER COMMUNION
Pour on us, O Lord, the Spirit of your love, and in your kindness make those you have nourished by this one heavenly Bread one in mind and heart. Through Christ our Lord. **Amen.**

BLESSING AND DISMISSAL *(p. 70)*

January 22

Week of Prayer for Christian Unity
"Reconciliation — the love of Christ compels us"

Does it not strike you as amazing that Jesus calls on ordinary people to become his first disciples? Jesus wants them to join him in a new kind of community and to experience intimately a loving and faithful relationship with him and with each other. It is a call to proclaim "the good news of the kingdom" to all people they will encounter and minister to.

What would so profoundly influence their decision to become Jesus' first disciples? I believe it was their faith in and desire for the love of God that inspired them to bring love and hope to a dark world. They were being given the opportunity through God's gift of grace to change their ways and participate as a community in God's plan of love and salvation.

During this Week of Prayer for Christian Unity, let this gospel serve as a reminder that Jesus summons all of us to be in real relationship with him and with those around us. As Christians in community, let us listen to Paul who reminds us we are "united in the same mind and for the same purpose," to serve and care for those around us, especially for the poor. It is in communion with Jesus that our hope and promise of God's abundant grace are to be found — a pure gift for all of us.

Julie Cachia, Toronto, ON

ENTRANCE ANTIPHON *(Cf. Psalm 95.1, 6)*
O sing a new song to the Lord; sing to the Lord, all the earth. In his presence are majesty and splendour, strength and honour in his holy place.

INTRODUCTORY RITES *(p. 5)*

COLLECT
Almighty ever-living God, direct our actions according to your good pleasure, that in the name of your beloved Son we may abound in good works. Through our Lord Jesus Christ, your Son, who lives and reigns with you in the unity of the Holy Spirit, one God, for ever and ever. **Amen.**

FIRST READING *(Isaiah 9.1-4)*
There will be no gloom for those who were in anguish. In the former time the Lord brought into contempt the land of Zebulun and the land of Naphtali, but in the latter time he will make glorious the way of the sea, the land beyond the Jordan, Galilee of the nations.

The people who walked in darkness have seen a great light; those who lived in a land of deep darkness — on them light has shone. You have multiplied the nation, you have increased its joy; they rejoice before you as with joy at the harvest, as people exult when dividing plunder.

For the yoke of their burden, and the bar across their shoulders, the rod of their oppressor, you have broken as on the day of Midian.

The word of the Lord. **Thanks be to God.**

RESPONSORIAL PSALM *(Psalm 27)*

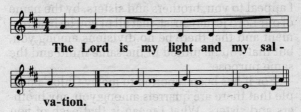

The Lord is my light and my sal-

va-tion.

R. **The Lord is my light and my salvation.**

The Lord is my light and my sal--**vation;**
whom shall · I fear?
The Lord is the stronghold of my · **life;**
of whom shall I be · **a-**fraid? R.

One thing I asked of the Lord, that will
    I · **seek_after:**
to live in the house of the Lord all the days
    of · **my** life,
to behold the beauty of the · **Lord,**
and to inquire in · **his** temple. R.

I believe that I shall see the goodness
    of the · **Lord**
in the land of · **the** living.
Wait for the Lord; be · **strong,**
and let your heart take courage; wait
    · **for_the** Lord! R.

©2010 Gordon Johnston/Novalis

To hear the Sunday Psalms, visit www.livingwithchrist.ca.

SECOND READING *(1 Corinthians 1.10-13, 17-18)*
I appeal to you, brothers and sisters, by the name of our Lord Jesus Christ, that all of you be in agreement and that there be no divisions among you, but that you be united in the same mind and the same purpose.

For it has been reported to me by Chloe's people that there are quarrels among you, my brothers and sisters. What I mean is that each of you says, "I belong to Paul," or "I belong to Apollos," or "I belong to Cephas," or "I belong to Christ."

Has Christ been divided? Was Paul crucified for you? Or were you baptized in the name of Paul?

For Christ did not send me to baptize but to proclaim the Gospel, and not with eloquent wisdom so that the Cross of Christ might not be emptied of its power.

For the message about the Cross is foolishness to those who are perishing, but to us who are being saved it is the power of God.

The word of the Lord. **Thanks be to God.**

GOSPEL ACCLAMATION *(See Matthew 4.23)*
Alleluia. Alleluia. Jesus proclaimed the good news of the kingdom curing every sickness among the people. **Alleluia.**

GOSPEL *(Matthew 4.12-23)*
The shorter version ends at the asterisks.
The Lord be with you. **And with your spirit.**
A reading from the holy Gospel according to Matthew. **Glory to you, O Lord.**

When Jesus heard that John had been arrested, he withdrew to Galilee. He left Nazareth and made his home in Capernaum by the sea, in the territory of Zebulun and Naphtali, so that what had been spoken through the Prophet Isaiah might be fulfilled: "Land of Zebulun, land of Naphtali, on the road by the sea, across the Jordan, Galilee of the Gentiles — the people who sat in darkness have seen a great light, and for those who sat in the region and shadow of death light has dawned."

From that time Jesus began to proclaim, "Repent, for the kingdom of heaven has come near."

* * *

As he walked by the Sea of Galilee, he saw two brothers, Simon, who is called Peter, and Andrew his brother, casting a net into the sea, for they were fishermen. And he said to them, "Come, follow me, and I will make you fishers of people." Immediately they left their nets and followed him.

As he went from there, he saw two other brothers, James son of Zebedee and his brother John, in the boat with their father Zebedee, mending their nets, and he called them. Immediately they left the boat and their father, and followed him.

Jesus went throughout Galilee, teaching in their synagogues and proclaiming the good news of the kingdom and curing every disease and every sickness among the people.

The Gospel of the Lord. **Praise to you, Lord Jesus Christ.**

PROFESSION OF FAITH *(p. 11)*

PRAYER OF THE FAITHFUL

The following intentions are suggestions only. There are more suggestions at www.livingwithchrist.ca

R. **Lord, hear our prayer.**

For dialogue, reconciliation and the unity of Christians throughout the world, we pray to the Lord: R.

For leaders of nations, entrusted with the political and economic futures of their peoples, we pray to the Lord: R.

For those in our global community who, poor, unemployed and oppressed, seek justice, we pray to the Lord: R.

For our parish community, called in baptism to be responsible for one another, we pray to the Lord: R.

PREPARATION OF THE GIFTS *(p. 14)*

PRAYER OVER THE OFFERINGS
Accept our offerings, O Lord, we pray, and in sanctifying them grant that they may profit us for salvation. Through Christ our Lord. **Amen.**

PREFACE *(Sundays in Ordinary Time, p. 28)*

COMMUNION ANTIPHON *(Cf. Psalm 33.6)*
Look toward the Lord and be radiant; let your faces not be abashed.

or (John 8.12)

I am the light of the world, says the Lord; whoever follows me will not walk in darkness, but will have the light of life.

PRAYER AFTER COMMUNION

Grant, we pray, almighty God, that, receiving the grace by which you bring us to new life, we may always glory in your gift. Through Christ our Lord. **Amen.**

BLESSING AND DISMISSAL *(p. 70)*

January 29

We seek glory because it is our human nature to do so. Self-seeking glory is all around us. God challenges us to recognize that God-in-us will lead to great things. God in our small, weak selves leads to holiness, a different glory. And though our culture shapes us, we shape our culture; the culture changes only when God shapes us. When Jesus taught The Beatitudes, he was challenging the culture, too.

Each one of Jesus' exhortations — *Blessed are...* — is a profound witness of faith and trust in someone greater than ourselves. Suffering the cost of living The Beatitudes shows the world a new way to live, one rooted in Christ. Can we be surprised that it will be exceedingly difficult to live this way? How shall we?

Here is how. God's love for us compels him to share his divine nature with us through Christ. Does he need us to accomplish his plan? Not really. Does he invite us? Every day. Let us say *yes*.

Rejoice then, that Jesus can use us to teach the strong and, at times, humble them. Even in this, no one can boast, because we all share the same self-glorifying human nature. We are only our best selves when God's divine nature is at work in us. There is no glory for us when living The Beatitudes. All glory belongs to God.

Johanne Brownrigg, Orleans, ON

ENTRANCE ANTIPHON *(Psalm 105.47)*
**Save us, O Lord our God! And gather us from the
nations, to give thanks to your holy name, and
make it our glory to praise you.**

INTRODUCTORY RITES *(p. 5)*

COLLECT
Grant us, Lord our God, that we may honour you
with all our mind, and love everyone in truth of
heart. Through our Lord Jesus Christ, your Son,
who lives and reigns with you in the unity of the
Holy Spirit, one God, for ever and ever. **Amen.**

FIRST READING *(Zephaniah 2.3; 3.12-13)*
Seek the Lord, all you humble of the land,
who do his commands;
seek righteousness, seek humility;
perhaps you may be hidden on the day
    of the Lord's wrath.

For I will leave in the midst of you
a people humble and lowly.
They shall seek refuge in the name
    of the Lord —
the remnant of Israel;
they shall do no wrong and utter no lies,
nor shall a deceitful tongue be found
    in their mouths.
Then they will pasture and lie down,
and no one shall make them afraid.

The word of the Lord. **Thanks be to God.**

RESPONSORIAL PSALM *(Psalm 146)*

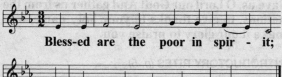

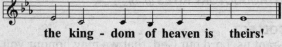

℟. **Blessed are the poor in spirit;**
the kingdom of heaven is theirs!
or **Alleluia!**

It is the Lord who keeps faith for-·**ever,**
who executes justice for the op-·**pressed;**
who gives food to the · **hungry.**
The Lord sets the · **prisoners** free. ℟.

The Lord opens the eyes of the · **blind**
and lifts up those who are bowed · **down;**
the Lord loves the · **righteous**
and watches over · **the** strangers. ℟.

The Lord upholds the orphan and the · **widow,**
but the way of the wicked he brings to · **ruin.**
The Lord will reign for-·**ever,**
your God, O Zion, for all · **gener**-ations. ℟.

©2010 Gordon Johnston/Novalis

SECOND READING *(1 Corinthians 1.26-31)*
Consider your own call, brothers and sisters: not
many of you were wise by human standards, not

many were powerful, not many were of noble birth. But God chose what is foolish in the world to shame the wise; God chose what is weak in the world to shame the strong; God chose what is low and despised in the world, things that are not, to reduce to nothing things that are, so that no one might boast in the presence of God.

God is the source of your life in Christ Jesus, who became for us wisdom from God, and righteousness and sanctification and redemption, in order that, as it is written, "Let the one who boasts, boast in the Lord."

The word of the Lord. **Thanks be to God.**

GOSPEL ACCLAMATION *(Matthew 5.12)*
Alleluia. Alleluia. Rejoice and be glad, for your reward is great in heaven. **Alleluia.**

GOSPEL *(Matthew 5.1-12)*
The Lord be with you. **And with your spirit.** A reading from the holy Gospel according to Matthew. **Glory to you, O Lord.**

When Jesus saw the crowds, he went up the mountain; and after he sat down, his disciples came to him. Then he began to speak, and taught them, saying:

"Blessed are the poor in spirit, for theirs is the kingdom of heaven. Blessed are those who mourn, for they will be comforted. Blessed are the meek, for they will inherit the earth. Blessed are those who hunger and thirst for righteousness, for they will be filled.

"Blessed are the merciful, for they will receive mercy. Blessed are the pure in heart, for they will see God. Blessed are the peacemakers, for they will be called children of God. Blessed are those who are persecuted for righteousness' sake, for theirs is the kingdom of heaven.

"Blessed are you when people revile you and persecute you and utter all kinds of evil against you falsely on my account. Rejoice and be glad, for your reward is great in heaven, for in the same way they persecuted the Prophets who were before you."

The Gospel of the Lord. **Praise to you, Lord Jesus Christ.**

PROFESSION OF FAITH (p. 11)

PRAYER OF THE FAITHFUL

The following intentions are suggestions only. There are more suggestions at www.livingwithchrist.ca

R. **Lord, hear our prayer.**

For the Church, called to serve all nations, we pray to the Lord: R.

For open and ongoing dialogue between nations, we pray to the Lord: R.

For those who suffer persecution and loneliness, we pray to the Lord: R.

For us, called in baptism to be prophets of God's word, we pray to the Lord: R.

PREPARATION OF THE GIFTS (p. 14)

PRAYER OVER THE OFFERINGS

O Lord, we bring to your altar these offerings of our service: be pleased to receive them, we pray, and transform them into the Sacrament of our redemption. Through Christ our Lord. **Amen.**

PREFACE *(Sundays in Ordinary Time, p. 28)*

COMMUNION ANTIPHON *(Cf. Psalm 30.17-18)*
Let your face shine on your servant. Save me in your merciful love. O Lord, let me never be put to shame, for I call on you.
or (Matthew 5.3-4)
Blessed are the poor in spirit, for theirs is the Kingdom of Heaven. Blessed are the meek, for they shall possess the land.

PRAYER AFTER COMMUNION

Nourished by these redeeming gifts, we pray, O Lord, that through this help to eternal salvation true faith may ever increase. Through Christ our Lord. **Amen.**

BLESSING AND DISMISSAL *(p. 70)*

February Saints' Days

The following saints are traditionally remembered in February in Canada.

3 Saint Blaise
   Saint Ansgar

5 Saint Agatha

6 Saint Paul Miki and Companions

8 Saint Jerome Emiliani
   Saint Josephine Bakhita

10 Saint Scholastica

11 Our Lady of Lourdes

14 Saints Cyril and Methodius

17 The Seven Holy Founders of the Servite Order

21 Saint Peter Damian

23 Saint Polycarp

February 5

As Christians, we are the salt of the earth and the light of the world. We must keep our fervour in spreading the good news of the gospel. Unfortunately, there are many forces trying to suppress our faith. Our own culture would prefer that we hush up about it. Sadly, there is even a growing attitude among Christians that we should keep our faith to ourselves.

What could be further from our vocation? A relationship with Jesus Christ, the Son of God, is our source of happiness and fulfillment. It is the only path to eternal life. In a world starved of true joy, how can we not spread the message of God's love? If you found the cure for cancer, would you keep it to yourself?

Let us not shy away from proclaiming our faith. This does not mean shouting on street corners, but rather witnessing within the context of a relationship. Pray for the opportunity, and always be an example of holiness. When the right time comes, have that crucial conversation with your friend, co-worker or family member. Remind them that Jesus loves them and wants a relationship with them more than anything. Be not afraid; the Holy Spirit is with you. May we go forward as faithful Christians to enlighten the world with our faith!

Connor Brownrigg, Ottawa, ON

ENTRANCE ANTIPHON *(Psalm 94.6-7)*
O come, let us worship God and bow low before
the God who made us, for he is the Lord our God.

INTRODUCTORY RITES *(p. 5)*

COLLECT
Keep your family safe, O Lord, with unfailing
care, that, relying solely on the hope of heavenly
grace, they may be defended always by your protection. Through our Lord Jesus Christ, your Son,
who lives and reigns with you in the unity of the
Holy Spirit, one God, for ever and ever. **Amen.**

FIRST READING *(Isaiah 58.6-10)*
Thus says the Lord:
Is this not the fast that I choose:
to loose the bonds of injustice,
to undo the thongs of the yoke,
to let the oppressed go free,
and to break every yoke?
Is it not to share your bread with the hungry,
and bring the homeless poor into your house;
when you see the naked, to cover them,
and not to hide yourself from your own kin?

Then your light shall break forth like the dawn,
and your healing shall spring up quickly;
your vindicator shall go before you,
the glory of the Lord shall be your rear guard.
Then you shall call, and the Lord will answer;
you shall cry for help, and he will say, Here I am.

If you remove the yoke from among you,
the pointing of the finger, the speaking of evil,

if you offer your food to the hungry
and satisfy the needs of the afflicted,
then your light shall rise in the darkness
and your gloom be like the noonday.

The word of the Lord. **Thanks be to God.**

RESPONSORIAL PSALM *(Psalm 112)*

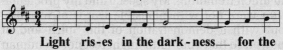

R̷. **Light rises in the darkness for the upright.**
or **Alleluia!**

Light rises in the darkness · **for_the** upright:
gracious, merciful · **and** righteous.
It is well with the person who deals generously
· **and** lends,
who conducts their af--**fairs** with justice. R̷.

For the righteous person will never · **be** moved;
they will be remembered · **for**-ever.
Unafraid of · **evil** tidings;
their heart is firm, secure · **in** the Lord. R̷.

That person's heart is steady and will not
· **be_a**-fraid.
One who has distributed freely, who has given
· **to_the** poor,
their righteousness endures · **for**-ever:
their name is ex--**alted** in honour. R̷.

©2010 Gordon Johnston/Novalis

SECOND READING *(1 Corinthians 2.1-5)*
When I came to you, brothers and sisters, I did not come proclaiming the mystery of God to you in lofty words or wisdom. For I decided to know nothing among you except Jesus Christ, and him crucified.

And I came to you in weakness and in fear and in much trembling. My speech and my proclamation were not with plausible words of wisdom, but with a demonstration of the Spirit and of power, so that your faith might rest not on human wisdom but on the power of God.

The word of the Lord. **Thanks be to God.**

GOSPEL ACCLAMATION *(See John 8.12)*
Alleluia. Alleluia. I am the light of the world, says the Lord; whoever follows me will have the light of life. **Alleluia.**

GOSPEL *(Matthew 5.13-16)*
The Lord be with you. **And with your spirit.** A reading from the holy Gospel according to Matthew. **Glory to you, O Lord.**

Jesus said to his disciples: "You are the salt of the earth; but if salt has lost its taste, how can its saltiness be restored? It is no longer good for anything, but is thrown out and trampled under foot.

"You are the light of the world. A city built on a hill cannot be hidden. No one after lighting a lamp puts it under the bushel basket, but on the lampstand, and it gives light to all in the house. In the same way, let your light shine before human beings, so that they may see your good works and give glory to your Father in heaven."

The Gospel of the Lord. **Praise to you, Lord Jesus Christ.**

PROFESSION OF FAITH *(p. 11)*

PRAYER OF THE FAITHFUL

The following intentions are suggestions only. There are more suggestions at www.livingwithchrist.ca

R. **Lord, hear our prayer.**

For the Church, community of disciples, called to follow Jesus in all things, we pray to the Lord: R.

For nations and peoples as they struggle to build a world of peace and justice, we pray to the Lord: R.

For those among us who seek healing, sustenance and peace, we pray to the Lord: R.

For us, God's people, invited to discover God in the routine of our lives, we pray to the Lord: R.

PREPARATION OF THE GIFTS *(p. 14)*

PRAYER OVER THE OFFERINGS

O Lord our God, who once established these created things to sustain us in our frailty, grant, we pray, that they may become for us now the Sacrament of eternal life. Through Christ our Lord. **Amen.**

PREFACE *(Sundays in Ordinary Time, p. 28)*

COMMUNION ANTIPHON *(Cf. Psalm 106.8-9)*
Let them thank the Lord for his mercy, his wonders for the children of men, for he satisfies the thirsty soul, and the hungry he fills with good things.

or (Matthew 5.5-6)
Blessed are those who mourn, for they shall be consoled. Blessed are those who hunger and thirst for righteousness, for they shall have their fill.

PRAYER AFTER COMMUNION
O God, who have willed that we be partakers in the one Bread and the one Chalice, grant us, we pray, so to live that, made one in Christ, we may joyfully bear fruit for the salvation of the world. Through Christ our Lord. **Amen.**

BLESSING AND DISMISSAL *(p. 70)*

February 12

Today's Scripture passages echo and re-echo the same essential concept. The verses of Psalm 119 will guide our response. "Give me understanding, that I may keep your law and observe it with my whole heart."

The reading from Matthew's Gospel is packed with potential actions, optional responses and possible consequences. "But I say to you" signals that the stakes are being raised to a whole new level. We find the same approach in the reading from Sirach: fire and water, life and death, good and evil. The Lord is not interested in half measures or lukewarm responses. Pick one or the other; there is no room here to sit on the fence. The message is unchanging: come to the Lord completely.

This should not surprise us, for it is from the One who chose to empty himself completely and become one of us to show us the way to God. It comes from the One who lived among us and then gave himself up to pain and death for us. It comes from the One who fully and absolutely understands what it is to be human.

And it comes with the promise that we can spend our whole life in a constant and profound relationship with divine grace and love, immersed in God forever.

Marilyn J. Sweet, Falmouth, NS

ENTRANCE ANTIPHON *(Cf. Psalm 30.3-4)*
Be my protector, O God, a mighty stronghold to
save me. For you are my rock, my stronghold!
Lead me, guide me, for the sake of your name.

INTRODUCTORY RITES *(p. 5)*

COLLECT
O God, who teach us that you abide in hearts
that are just and true, grant that we may be so
fashioned by your grace as to become a dwelling
pleasing to you. Through our Lord Jesus Christ,
your Son, who lives and reigns with you in the
unity of the Holy Spirit, one God, for ever and
ever. **Amen.**

FIRST READING *(Sirach 15.15-20)*
If you choose, you can keep the commandments,
and they will save you. If you trust in God, you
too shall live, and to act faithfully is a matter of
your own choice.

The Lord has placed before you fire and water;
stretch out your hand for whichever you choose.
Before each person are life and death, good and evil
and whichever one chooses, that shall be given.

For great is the wisdom of the Lord; he is
mighty in power and sees everything; his eyes
are on those who fear him, and he knows every
human action. He has not commanded anyone to
be wicked, and he has not given anyone permission to sin.

The word of the Lord. **Thanks be to God.**

RESPONSORIAL PSALM *(Psalm 119)*

Bless-ed are those who walk in the law of the

Lord!

R. **Blessed are those who walk in the law of the Lord!**

Blessed are those whose way · **is** blameless,
who walk in the law of · **the** Lord.
Blessed are those who · **keep_his** de-crees,
who seek him · **with** their whole heart. R.

You have commanded · **your** precepts
to be · **kept** diligently.
O that my ways · **may** be steadfast
in · **keep**-ing your statutes! R.

Deal bountifully with · **your** servant,
so that I may live and observe · **your** word.
Open my eyes, so that I · **may** be-hold
wondrous things · **out** of your law. R.

Teach me, O Lord, the way of · **your** statutes,
and I will observe it · **to_the** end.
Give me understanding, that I may
· **keep** your law
and observe it · **with** my whole heart. R.

©2010 Gordon Johnston/Novalis
To hear the Sunday Psalms, visit www.livingwithchrist.ca.

SECOND READING *(1 Corinthians 2.6-10)*
Brothers and sisters: Among the mature we do speak wisdom, though it is not a wisdom of this age or of the rulers of this age, who are doomed to perish. But we speak God's wisdom, secret and hidden, which God decreed before the ages for our glory. None of the rulers of this age understood this; for if they had, they would not have crucified the Lord of glory.

As it is written, "What no eye has seen, nor ear heard, nor the human heart conceived, what God has prepared for those who love him." These things God has revealed to us through the Spirit; for the Spirit searches everything, even the depths of God.

The word of the Lord. **Thanks be to God.**

GOSPEL ACCLAMATION *(See Matthew 11.25)*
Alleluia. Alleluia. Blessed are you, Father, Lord of heaven and earth; you have revealed to little ones the mysteries of the kingdom. **Alleluia.**

GOSPEL *(Matthew 5.17-37)*
For the shorter version, omit the indented parts.
The Lord be with you. **And with your spirit.** A reading from the holy Gospel according to Matthew. **Glory to you, O Lord.**

Jesus said to his disciples: "Do not think that I have come to abolish the Law or the Prophets; I have come not to abolish but to fulfill.

For truly I tell you, until heaven and earth pass away, not one letter, not one stroke of a letter, will pass from the Law until all is accomplished. Therefore, whoever breaks one of the least of these commandments, and teaches others to do the same, will be called least in the kingdom of heaven; but whoever does them and teaches them will be called great in the kingdom of heaven.

"For I tell you, unless your righteousness exceeds that of the scribes and Pharisees, you will never enter the kingdom of heaven.

"You have heard that it was said to those of ancient times, 'You shall not murder'; and 'whoever murders shall be liable to judgment.' But I say to you that the one who is angry with their brother or sister, will be liable to judgment; and whoever insults their brother or sister, will be liable to the council; and whoever says, 'You fool,' will be liable to the hell of fire.

"So when you are offering your gift at the altar, if you remember that your brother or sister has something against you, leave your gift there before the altar and go; first be reconciled to your brother or sister, and then come and offer your gift.

"Come to terms quickly with your accuser while the two of you are on the way to court, or your accuser may hand you over to the judge, and the judge to the guard, and you will be thrown into prison. Truly I tell you, you will never get out until you have paid the last penny.

"You have heard that it was said, 'You shall not commit adultery.' But I say to you that everyone who looks at a woman with lust has already committed adultery with her in his heart.

"If your right eye causes you to sin, tear it out and throw it away; it is better for you to lose one of your members than for your whole body to be thrown into hell. And if your right hand causes you to sin, cut it off and throw it away;

it is better for you to lose one of your members than for your whole body to go into hell.

"It was also said, 'Whoever divorces his wife, let him give her a certificate of divorce.' But I say to you that anyone who divorces his wife, except on the ground of unchastity, causes her to commit adultery; and whoever marries a divorced woman commits adultery.

"Again, you have heard that it was said to those of ancient times, 'You shall not swear falsely, but carry out the vows you have made to the Lord.' But I say to you: Do not swear at all.

either by heaven, for it is the throne of God, or by the earth, for it is his footstool, or by Jerusalem, for it is the city of the great King. And do not swear by your head, for you cannot make one hair white or black.

"Let your word be 'Yes,' if 'Yes,' or 'No,' if 'No'; anything more than this comes from the evil one."

The Gospel of the Lord. **Praise to you, Lord Jesus Christ.**

PROFESSION OF FAITH (p. 11)

PRAYER OF THE FAITHFUL

The following intentions are suggestions only. There are more suggestions at www.livingwithchrist.ca

R. **Lord, hear our prayer.**

For the Church, called to trust in the Lord, who alone brings salvation, we pray to the Lord: R.

For those who shoulder the burden of public service and the challenge of promoting the good of all, we pray to the Lord: R.

For those whose riches, power and success have left them unsatisfied, we pray to the Lord: R.

For us, baptized into discipleship, called to stand with the poor, the hungry and the unemployed in their search for justice, we pray to the Lord: R.

PREPARATION OF THE GIFTS *(p. 14)*

PRAYER OVER THE OFFERINGS
May this oblation, O Lord, we pray, cleanse and renew us and may it become for those who do your will the source of eternal reward. Through Christ our Lord. **Amen.**

PREFACE *(Sundays in Ordinary Time, p. 28)*

COMMUNION ANTIPHON *(Cf. Psalm 77.29-30)*
They ate and had their fill, and what they craved the Lord gave them; they were not disappointed in what they craved.
  or (John 3.16)
God so loved the world that he gave his Only Begotten Son, so that all who believe in him may not perish, but may have eternal life.

PRAYER AFTER COMMUNION
Having fed upon these heavenly delights, we pray, O Lord, that we may always long for that food by which we truly live. Through Christ our Lord. **Amen.**

BLESSING AND DISMISSAL *(p. 70)*

161

February 19

I have never really been put to the test when it comes to the set of expectations that Jesus places before us in today's gospel. I really don't know what I would do in the heat of the moment, if someone struck my cheek or demanded my coat. I do know that my instinctive responses seldom follow the path of the "WWJD – what would Jesus do?" movement.

I think Jesus knew we would have a problem with this set of instructions. So instead of beating myself up about where my instincts lead me, I look to see if Jesus had some additional purpose in mind. Did he have an additional message that he hid among all those expectations? As I look more deeply I find a message about our "heavenly Father." I see that Jesus has actually painted for us a picture of the rich merciful love that God showers on us every day. All these extravagant behaviours are modelled on the extravagant behaviour of God toward us.

The extravagance of God is precisely why we gather today and every Sunday: to celebrate God's abundant love revealed to us in our very own lives. God's style of love is a hard act to follow, but nourished by the Body and Blood of Christ, we take up the challenge to show God's love to those who most need to experience it.

Margaret Bick, Toronto, ON

ENTRANCE ANTIPHON *(Psalm 12.6)*
O Lord, I trust in your merciful love. My heart
will rejoice in your salvation. I will sing to the
Lord who has been bountiful with me.

INTRODUCTORY RITES *(p. 5)*

COLLECT
Grant, we pray, almighty God, that, always pon-
dering spiritual things, we may carry out in both
word and deed that which is pleasing to you.
Through our Lord Jesus Christ, your Son, who
lives and reigns with you in the unity of the Holy
Spirit, one God, for ever and ever. **Amen.**

FIRST READING *(Leviticus 19.1-2, 17-18)*
The Lord spoke to Moses:
"Speak to all the congregation of the children
    of Israel
and say to them:
'You shall be holy, for I the Lord your God
    am holy.
You shall not hate in your heart anyone
    of your kin;
you shall reprove your neighbour,
or you will incur guilt yourself.
You shall not take vengeance
or bear a grudge against any of your people,
but you shall love your neighbour as yourself:
I am the Lord.'"

The word of the Lord. **Thanks be to God.**

RESPONSORIAL PSALM *(Psalm 103)*

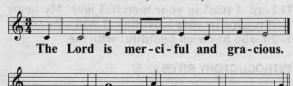

The Lord is mer-ci-ful and gra-cious.

R. **The Lord is merciful and gracious.**

Bless the Lord, O my · **soul,**
and all that is within me, bless his · **holy** name.
Bless the Lord, O my · **soul,**
and do not forget all · **his** benefits. R.

It is the Lord who forgives all your in-·**iquity,**
who heals all your · **dis**-eases,
who redeems your life from the · **Pit,**
who crowns you with steadfast love
· **and** mercy. R.

The Lord is merciful and · **gracious,**
slow to anger and abounding in stead-·**fast** love.
He does not deal with us according
to our · **sins,**
nor repay us according to our · **in**-iquities. R.

As far as the east is from the · **west,**
so far he removes our transgressions · **from** us.
As a father has compassion for his · **children,**
so the Lord has compassion for those
· **who** fear_him. R.

©2010 Gordon Johnston/Novalis
To hear the Sunday Psalms, visit www.livingwithchrist.ca.

SECOND READING *(1 Corinthians 3.16-23)*

Brothers and sisters: Do you not know that you are God's temple and that God's Spirit dwells in you? If anyone destroys God's temple, God will destroy that person. For God's temple is holy, and you are that temple.

Do not deceive yourselves. If you think that you are wise in this age, you should become fools so that you may become wise. For the wisdom of this world is foolishness with God. For it is written, "He catches the wise in their craftiness," and again, "The Lord knows the thoughts of the wise, that they are futile."

So let no one boast about human beings. For all things are yours — whether Paul or Apollos or Cephas, or the world or life or death, or the present or the future — all belong to you, and you belong to Christ, and Christ belongs to God.

The word of the Lord. **Thanks be to God.**

GOSPEL ACCLAMATION *(See 1 John 2.5)*

Alleluia. Alleluia. Whoever obeys the word of Christ, grows perfect in the love of God. **Alleluia.**

GOSPEL *(Matthew 5.38-48)*

The Lord be with you. **And with your spirit.** A reading from the holy Gospel according to Matthew. **Glory to you, O Lord.**

Jesus said to his disciples, "You have heard that it was said, 'An eye for an eye and a tooth for a tooth.' But I say to you, Do not resist an evildoer. But if anyone strikes you on the right cheek, turn the other also; and if anyone wants to sue you and take your coat, give your cloak as well; and if anyone forces you to go one mile, go with them also the second mile. Give to everyone who begs from you, and do not refuse anyone who wants to borrow from you.

"You have heard that it was said, 'You shall love your neighbour and hate your enemy.' But I say to you, Love your enemies and pray for those who persecute you, so that you may be children of your Father in heaven; for he makes his sun rise on the evil and on the good, and sends rain on the righteous and on the unrighteous.

"For if you love those who love you, what reward do you have? Do not even the tax collectors do the same? And if you greet only your brothers and sisters, what more are you doing than others? Do not even the Gentiles do the same? Be perfect, therefore, as your heavenly Father is perfect."

The Gospel of the Lord. **Praise to you, Lord Jesus Christ.**

PROFESSION OF FAITH (p. 11)

PRAYER OF THE FAITHFUL

The following intentions are suggestions only. There are more suggestions at www.livingwithchrist.ca

R. **Lord, hear our prayer.**

For the Church and its leaders, called to stand in solidarity with victims of oppression and abuse, we pray to the Lord: R.

For world peace built on non-violence, we pray to the Lord: R.

For the healing and empowerment of victims of violence and oppression, we pray to the Lord: R.

For us, God's holy people, challenged to love our enemies, we pray to the Lord: R.

PREPARATION OF THE GIFTS *(p. 14)*

PRAYER OVER THE OFFERINGS
As we celebrate your mysteries, O Lord, with the observance that is your due, we humbly ask you, that what we offer to the honour of your majesty may profit us for salvation. Through Christ our Lord. **Amen.**

PREFACE *(Sundays in Ordinary Time, p. 28)*

COMMUNION ANTIPHON *(Psalm 9.2-3)*
I will recount all your wonders, I will rejoice in you and be glad, and sing psalms to your name, O Most High.

or (John 11.27)
Lord, I have come to believe that you are the Christ, the Son of the living God, who is coming into this world.

PRAYER AFTER COMMUNION
Grant, we pray, almighty God, that we may experience the effects of the salvation which is pledged to us by these mysteries. Through Christ our Lord. **Amen.**

BLESSING AND DISMISSAL *(p. 70)*

February 26

Anxiety can be debilitating. Fear can not only hold our mind hostage, but can manifest itself through all sorts of physical symptoms. In today's readings — especially in the gospel — God reveals that he wants humanity to be free from the shackles of fear that can keep us from experiencing the fullness of life.

In the gospel, just before Jesus implores his listeners not to worry, he states that we cannot serve two masters. Who is Jesus referring to? The one master is God, but who is the other? Evil? Satan? In a way yes, but in another way, Jesus may be referring to a more specific manifestation of evil. Evil can hold our hopes, fears and expectations hostage by crippling us with anxiety. Instead of looking towards God, we can look to fear. We cannot therefore serve God, who is Love, and evil, which brings despair and uncertainty. The other master opposed to God is one of ill-will and misery.

In the first reading, God reassures Zion's people. They have not been abandoned to evil. God's love is beyond worldly limits and therefore cannot be depleted.

In today's world, the media, financial concerns, success all give reason to worry. Some worrying is normal. However, to let anxiety master us, is to give up hope that God is greater than all worldly obstacles.

Andrew Hume, Toronto, ON

ENTRANCE ANTIPHON *(Cf. Psalm 17.19-20)*
The Lord became my protector. He brought me out to a place of freedom; he saved me because he delighted in me.

INTRODUCTORY RITES *(p. 5)*

COLLECT
Grant us, O Lord, we pray, that the course of our world may be directed by your peaceful rule and that your Church may rejoice, untroubled in her devotion. Through our Lord Jesus Christ, your Son, who lives and reigns with you in the unity of the Holy Spirit, one God, for ever and ever. **Amen.**

FIRST READING *(Isaiah 49.14-15)*
Zion said, "The Lord has forsaken me,
my Lord has forgotten me."
Can a woman forget her nursing child,
or show no compassion for the child of her womb?
Even these may forget,
yet I will not forget you.

The word of the Lord. **Thanks be to God.**

RESPONSORIAL PSALM *(Psalm 62)*

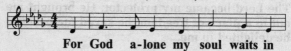

For God a-lone my soul waits in si-lence.

R̂. **For God alone my soul waits in silence.**

For God alone my soul waits in · **silence;**
from him comes my sal-·**vation.**
He alone is my rock and my salvation,
  my · **fortress;**
I shall never · **be** shaken. R̂.

For God alone my soul waits in · **silence,**
for my hope is from · **him.**
He alone is my rock and my salvation,
  my · **fortress;**
I shall not · **be** shaken. R̂.

On God rests my deliverance and my · **honour;**
my mighty rock, my refuge is in · **God.**
Trust in him at all times, O · **people;**
pour out your heart · **be-**fore_him. R̂.

©2010 Gordon Johnston/Novalis
To hear the Sunday Psalms, visit www.livingwithchrist.ca.

SECOND READING *(1 Corinthians 4.1-5)*
Brothers and sisters: Think of us in this way, as servants of Christ and stewards of God's mysteries. Moreover, it is required of stewards that they be found trustworthy.

But with me it is a very small thing that I should be judged by you or by any human court. I do not even judge myself. I am not aware of anything against myself, but I am not thereby acquitted. It is the Lord who judges me.

Therefore do not pronounce judgment before the time, before the Lord comes, who will bring to light the things now hidden in darkness and will disclose the purposes of the heart. Then each one will receive commendation from God.

The word of the Lord. **Thanks be to God.**

GOSPEL ACCLAMATION *(See Hebrews 4.12)*
Alleluia. Alleluia. The word of God is living and active; it judges the thoughts and intentions of the heart. **Alleluia.**

GOSPEL *(Matthew 6.24-34)*
The Lord be with you. **And with your spirit.**
A reading from the holy Gospel according to Matthew. **Glory to you, O Lord.**

Jesus taught his disciples, saying. "No one can serve two masters; for a slave will either hate the one and love the other, or be devoted to the one and despise the other. You cannot serve God and wealth.

"Therefore I tell you, do not worry about your life, what you will eat or what you will drink, or about your body, what you will wear. Is not life more than food, and the body more than clothing?

"Look at the birds of the air; they neither sow nor reap nor gather into barns, and yet your heavenly Father feeds them. Are you not of more value than they? And can any one of you by worrying add a single hour to their span of life?

"And why do you worry about clothing? Consider the lilies of the field, how they grow; they neither toil nor spin, yet I tell you, even Solomon in all his glory was not clothed like one of these. But if God so clothes the grass of the field, which is alive today and tomorrow is thrown into the oven, will he not much more clothe you — you of little faith?

"Therefore do not worry, saying, 'What will we eat?' or 'What will we drink?' or 'What will we wear?' For it is the Gentiles who strive for all these things; and indeed your heavenly Father knows that you need all these things. But strive first for the kingdom of God and his righteousness, and all these things will be given to you as well.

"So do not worry about tomorrow, for tomorrow will bring worries of its own. Today's trouble is enough for today."

The Gospel of the Lord. **Praise to you, Lord Jesus Christ.**

PROFESSION OF FAITH (p. 11)

PRAYER OF THE FAITHFUL

The following intentions are suggestions only. There are more suggestions at www.livingwithchrist.ca

R. **Lord, hear our prayer.**

For the Church, a community called to integrity of speech and action, we pray to the Lord: R.

For peace and justice among nations, built on mutual assistance, we pray to the Lord: R.

For the healing of those who suffer harsh and unfair criticism, we pray to the Lord: R.

For us, God's people gathered here, called to speak words of goodness and love, we pray to the Lord: R.

PREPARATION OF THE GIFTS (p. 14)

PRAYER OVER THE OFFERINGS
O God, who provide gifts to be offered to your name and count our oblations as signs of our desire to serve you with devotion, we ask of your mercy that what you grant as the source of merit may also help us to attain merit's reward. Through Christ our Lord. **Amen.**

PREFACE (Sundays in Ordinary Time, p. 28)

COMMUNION ANTIPHON (Cf. Psalm 12.6)
I will sing to the Lord who has been bountiful with me, sing psalms to the name of the Lord Most High.
or (Matthew 28.20)
Behold, I am with you always, even to the end of the age, says the Lord.

PRAYER AFTER COMMUNION
Nourished by your saving gifts, we beseech your mercy, Lord, that by this same Sacrament with which you feed us in the present age, you may make us partakers of life eternal. Through Christ our Lord. **Amen.**

BLESSING AND DISMISSAL (p. 70)

March Saints' Days

The following saints are traditionally remembered in March in Canada.

4 Saint Casimir

7 Saints Perpetua and Felicity

8 Saint John of God

9 Saint Frances of Rome

17 Saint Patrick

18 Saint Cyril of Jerusalem

19 Saint Joseph, Principal Patron of Canada

23 Saint Turibius of Mogrovejo

March 1

The Jubilee Year of Mercy finished in November — and now, just three months later, God's mercy is front and centre again in the Entrance Antiphon: "You are merciful to all, O Lord, and despise nothing that you have made." Lest we forget God's mercy, each Lent offers a mini-jubilee that calls us to remember God's mercy to us, to open ourselves to that mercy, and to pass it on to our sisters and brothers.

Far from being a time of penance imposed, Lent is a time of receiving God's gift: "You have given your children a sacred time for the renewing and purifying of their hearts" (Preface II of Lent). Yes, that is the remarkable thing about God's mercy. We don't earn it: it arises from the womb of God, suggesting God's profound attachment to us, God's instinctive tenderness to us. In short, the compassionate divine presence.

Praying, "Have mercy, O Lord, for we have sinned," we evoke God's attachment to us and let God renew intimacy with us. That renewal "works" only if it also renews our bonds with others. Today's liturgy cautions us that the only display of renewal that matters is being merciful as the Father is merciful. To help us become ambassadors of reconciliation, the season asks us to fast from food and fury; share ourselves and our riches; and pray for our world.

Bernadette Gasslein, Edmonton, AB

ENTRANCE ANTIPHON *(Wisdom 11.24, 25, 27)*
You are merciful to all, O Lord, and despise nothing that you have made. You overlook people's sins, to bring them to repentance, and you spare them, for you are the Lord our God.

GREETING *(p. 5)*
The Penitential Act *and the* Glory to God *are omitted today.*

COLLECT
Grant, O Lord, that we may begin with holy fasting this campaign of Christian service, so that, as we take up battle against spiritual evils, we may be armed with weapons of self-restraint. Through our Lord Jesus Christ, your Son, who lives and reigns with you in the unity of the Holy Spirit, one God, for ever and ever. **Amen.**

FIRST READING *(Joel 2.12-18)*
Even now, says the Lord, return to me with all your heart, with fasting, with weeping, and with mourning; rend your hearts and not your clothing.

Return to the Lord, your God, for he is gracious and merciful, slow to anger, and abounding in steadfast love, and relents from punishing.

Who knows whether the Lord will not turn and relent, and leave a blessing behind him: a grain offering and a drink offering to be presented to the Lord, your God?

Blow the trumpet in Zion; sanctify a fast; call a solemn assembly; gather the people. Sanctify the congregation; assemble the aged; gather the children, even infants at the breast. Let the bridegroom leave his room, and the bride her canopy.

Between the vestibule and the altar let the priests, the ministers of the Lord, weep. Let them say, "Spare your people, O Lord, and do not make your heritage a mockery, a byword among the nations. Why should it be said among the peoples, 'Where is their God?'"

Then the Lord became jealous for his land, and had pity on his people.

The word of the Lord. **Thanks be to God.**

RESPONSORIAL PSALM (*Psalm 51*)

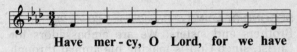

Have mer-cy, O Lord, for we have

sinned.

℟. **Have mercy, O Lord, for we have sinned.**

Have mercy on me, O God, according
    to your steadfast · **love;**
according to your abundant mercy blot out
    my trans-·**gressions.**
Wash me thoroughly from my in-·**iquity,**
and cleanse me from my · **sin.** ℟.

For I know my trans-·**gressions,**
and my sin is ever be-·**fore_me.**
Against you, you alone, have I · **sinned,**
and done what is evil in your · **sight.** ℟.

Create in me a clean heart, O · **God,**
and put a new and right spirit with·-in_me.
Do not cast me away from your · **presence,**
and do not take your holy spirit from · **me.** ℟

Restore to me the joy of your sal·-**vation,**
and sustain in me a willing · **spirit.**
O Lord, open my · **lips,**
and my mouth will declare your · **praise.** ℟

©2009 Gordon Johnston/Novalis
To hear the Sunday Psalms, visit www.livingwithchrist.ca.

SECOND READING *(2 Corinthians 5.20 – 6.2)*
Brothers and sisters: We are ambassadors for
Christ, since God is making his appeal through
us; we entreat you on behalf of Christ, be reconciled to God. For our sake God made Christ to be
sin who knew no sin, so that in Christ we might
become the righteousness of God. As we work
together with him, we urge you also not to accept
the grace of God in vain. For the Lord says, "At
an acceptable time I have listened to you, and
on a day of salvation I have helped you." See,
now is the acceptable time; see, now is the day
of salvation!

The word of the Lord. **Thanks be to God.**

GOSPEL ACCLAMATION *(Psalm 95.7-8)*
Praise to you, Lord, king of eternal glory! Today,
do not harden your hearts, but listen to the voice
of the Lord. **Praise to you, Lord, king of eternal
glory!**

GOSPEL *(Matthew 6.1-6, 16-18)*

The Lord be with you. **And with your spirit.**
A reading from the holy Gospel according to Matthew. **Glory to you, O Lord.**

Jesus said to the disciples: "Beware of practising your piety before people in order to be seen by them; for then you have no reward from your Father in heaven.

"So whenever you give alms, do not sound a trumpet before you, as the hypocrites do in the synagogues and in the streets, so that they may be praised by others. Truly I tell you, they have received their reward. But when you give alms, do not let your left hand know what your right hand is doing, so that your alms may be done in secret; and your Father who sees in secret will reward you.

"And whenever you pray, do not be like the hypocrites; for they love to stand and pray in the synagogues and at the street corners, so that they may be seen by others. Truly I tell you, they have received their reward. But whenever you pray, go into your room and shut the door and pray to your Father who is in secret; and your Father who sees in secret will reward you.

"And whenever you fast, do not look dismal, like the hypocrites, for they disfigure their faces so as to show others that they are fasting. Truly I tell you, they have received their reward. But when you fast, put oil on your head and wash your face, so that your fasting may be seen not by others but by your Father who is in secret; and your Father who sees in secret will reward you."

179

The Gospel of the Lord. **Praise to you, Lord Jesus Christ.**

BLESSING AND DISTRIBUTION OF ASHES

Dear brothers and sisters, let us humbly ask God our Father that he be pleased to bless with the abundance of his grace these ashes, which we will put on our heads in penitence. *(Pause)*

1 O God, who are moved by acts of humility and respond with forgiveness to works of penance, lend your merciful ear to our prayers and in your kindness pour out the grace of your blessing on your servants who are marked with these ashes, that, as they follow the Lenten observances, they may be worthy to come with minds made pure to celebrate the Paschal Mystery of your Son. Through Christ our Lord. **Amen.**

2 O God, who desire not the death of sinners, but their conversion, mercifully hear our prayers and in your kindness be pleased to bless these ashes, which we intend to receive upon our heads, that we, who acknowledge we are but ashes and shall return to dust, may, through a steadfast observance of Lent, gain pardon for sins and newness of life after the likeness of your Risen Son. Who lives and reigns for ever and ever. **Amen.**

While the faithful come forward to receive ashes, an appropriate song may be sung.

1 Repent, and believe in the Gospel.
2 Remember that you are dust, and to dust you shall return.

PRAYER OF THE FAITHFUL

The following intentions are suggestions only. More suggestions are available at www.livingwithchrist.ca

R. **Lord, hear our prayer.**

For the Church, called in this season of Lent to open our hearts to God's kingdom among us, we pray to the Lord: R.

For renewed generosity among nations for the sake of our brothers and sisters who are poor and dispossessed, we pray to the Lord: R.

For all who suffer loneliness and loss, we pray to the Lord: R.

For all of us gathered here, called to care for each other as God cares for us, we pray to the Lord: R.

* Ash Wednesday Service: When ashes are blessed outside Mass, the ceremony concludes with the Prayer over the People *and the* Blessing *(p. 182).*

PREPARATION OF THE GIFTS *(p. 14)*

PRAYER OVER THE OFFERINGS

As we solemnly offer the annual sacrifice for the beginning of Lent, we entreat you, O Lord, that, through works of penance and charity, we may turn away from harmful pleasures and, cleansed from our sins, may become worthy to celebrate devoutly the Passion of your Son. Who lives and reigns for ever and ever. **Amen.**

PREFACE *(Lent III-IV, p. 19)*

COMMUNION ANTIPHON *(Cf. Psalm 1.2-3)*
He who ponders the law of the Lord day and night will yield fruit in due season.

PRAYER AFTER COMMUNION
May the Sacrament we have received sustain us, O Lord, that our Lenten fast may be pleasing to you and be for us a healing remedy. Through Christ our Lord. **Amen.**

PRAYER OVER THE PEOPLE
Pour out a spirit of compunction, O God, on those who bow before your majesty, and by your mercy may they merit the rewards you promise to those who do penance. Through Christ our Lord. **Amen.**

BLESSING AND DISMISSAL *(p. 70)*

March 5

At the beginning of his ministry, Jesus responded to the Holy Spirit's direction and went into the desert to be tempted by the devil. Through his willingness to enter a weakened state, Jesus showed his love for us and the ways in which we can find strength. Through him, in him and with him, we can find renewal, freedom and the joy we seek.

Who has not been in a weakened state — emotionally wrought, spiritually tired, or physically suffering? Who has not been just plain worn down? Do you have your own launch sequence when seeking comfort? Do you deliberately walk by the bakery on your way to work? Or that bar? Do you flirt with the stranger at the coffee shop? Does the pressure let up a bit? Does the relief from your discontent last?

Yet here is our God, who loves us, knowing our dark ways, showing us the way to lasting comfort and freedom: serving only the Lord. On our own? No. In our weakness, God is strong for us. This Lenten season is *our* 40 days. Let us embrace the eucharistic love that will create a clean heart in us and renew in us a steadfast spirit. May we allow the Holy Spirit to restore the gladness of our salvation. Let us allow God to lead us out of our desert.

Johanne Brownrigg, Orleans, ON

Parishes engaged in the Rite of Christian Initiation of Adults (RCIA) *may celebrate the* Rite of Election *today.*

ENTRANCE ANTIPHON *(Cf. Psalm 90.15-16)*

When he calls on me, I will answer him; I will deliver him and give him glory, I will grant him length of days.

Rite of Election (Cf. Ps 104.3-4):

Let the hearts that seek the Lord rejoice; turn to the Lord and his strength; constantly seek his face.

INTRODUCTORY RITES *(p. 5)*

COLLECT

Grant, almighty God, through the yearly observances of holy Lent, that we may grow in understanding of the riches hidden in Christ and by worthy conduct pursue their effects. Through our Lord Jesus Christ, your Son, who lives and reigns with you in the unity of the Holy Spirit, one God, for ever and ever. **Amen.**

Rite of Election:

O God, who though you are ever the cause of the salvation of the human race now gladden your people with grace in still greater measure, look mercifully, we pray, upon your chosen ones, that your compassionate and protecting help may defend both those yet to be born anew and those already reborn. Through our Lord Jesus Christ, your Son, who lives and reigns with you in the unity of the Holy Spirit, one God, for ever and ever. **Amen.**

FIRST READING *(Genesis 2.7-9, 16-18, 25; 3.1-7)*
The Lord God formed man from the dust of the ground, and breathed into his nostrils the breath of life; and the man became a living being. And the Lord God planted a garden in Eden, in the east; and there he put the man whom he had formed. Out of the ground the Lord God made to grow every tree that is pleasant to the sight and good for food, the tree of life also in the midst of the garden, and the tree of the knowledge of good and evil.

And the Lord God commanded the man, "You may freely eat of every tree of the garden; but of the tree of the knowledge of good and evil you shall not eat, for in the day that you eat of it you shall die."

Then the Lord God said, "It is not good that the man should be alone; I will make him a helper as his partner." And the man and his wife were both naked, and were not ashamed.

Now the serpent was more crafty than any other wild animal that the Lord God had made. He said to the woman, "Did God say, 'You shall not eat from any tree in the garden'?" The woman said to the serpent, "We may eat of the fruit of the trees in the garden; but God said, 'You shall not eat of the fruit of the tree that is in the middle of the garden, nor shall you touch it, or you shall die.'" But the serpent said to the woman, "You will not die; for God knows that when you eat of it your eyes will be opened, and you will be like God, knowing good and evil." So when the woman saw that the tree was good for food, and that it was a delight to the eyes, and that the tree

was to be desired to make one wise, she took of
its fruit and ate; and she also gave some to her
husband, who was with her, and he ate.

Then the eyes of both were opened, and they
knew that they were naked; and they sewed fig
leaves together and made loincloths for themselves.

The word of the Lord. **Thanks be to God.**

RESPONSORIAL PSALM (*Psalm 51*)

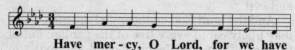

sinned.

℞. **Have mercy, O Lord, for we have sinned.**

Have mercy on me, O God, according
    to your steadfast · **love;**
according to your abundant mercy blot out
    my trans-·**gressions.**
Wash me thoroughly from my in-·**iquity,**
and cleanse me from my · **sin.** ℞.

For I know my trans-·**gressions,**
and my sin is ever be-·**fore_me.**
Against you, you alone, have I · **sinned,**
and done what is evil in your · **sight.** ℞.

Create in me a clean heart, O · **God,**
and put a new and right spirit with-·**in_me.**
Do not cast me away from your · **presence,**
and do not take your holy spirit from · **me.** ℞.

Restore to me the joy of your sal·-**vation,**
and sustain in me a willing · **spirit.**
O Lord, open my · **lips,**
and my mouth will declare your · **praise.** R.

To hear the Sunday Psalms, visit www.livingwithchrist.ca.

SECOND READING *(Romans 5.12-19)*

For the shorter version, omit the indented parts.

Brothers and sisters: Just as sin came into the world through one man, and death came through sin, so death spread to all people, because all have sinned.

Sin was indeed in the world before the law, but sin is not reckoned when there is no law. Yet death exercised dominion from Adam to Moses, even over those whose sins were not like the transgression of Adam, who is a type of the one who was to come.

But the free gift is not like the trespass. For if the many died through the one man's trespass, much more surely have the grace of God and the free gift in the grace of the one man, Jesus Christ, abounded for the many. And the free gift is not like the effect of the one man's sin. For the judgment following one trespass brought condemnation, but the free gift following many trespasses brings justification.

If, because of the one man's trespass, death exercised dominion through that one, much more surely will those who receive the abundance of grace and the free gift of righteousness exercise dominion in life through the one man, Jesus Christ.

Therefore just as one man's trespass led to condemnation for all people, so one man's act of righteousness leads to justification and life for all people. For just as by the one man's disobedience the many were made sinners, so by the one man's obedience the many will be made righteous.

The word of the Lord. **Thanks be to God.**

GOSPEL ACCLAMATION (Matthew 4.4)

Praise to you, Lord, king of eternal glory! Man does not live by bread alone, but by every word that comes from the mouth of God. **Praise to you, Lord, king of eternal glory!**

GOSPEL (Matthew 4.1-11)

The Lord be with you. **And with your spirit.** A reading from the holy Gospel according to Matthew. **Glory to you, O Lord.**

Jesus was led up by the Spirit into the wilderness to be tempted by the devil. He fasted forty days and forty nights, and afterwards he was famished. The tempter came and said to him, "If you are the Son of God, command these stones to become loaves of bread." But he answered, "It is written, 'Man does not live by bread alone, but by every word that comes from the mouth of God.'"

Then the devil took him to the holy city and placed him on the pinnacle of the temple, saying to him, "If you are the Son of God, throw yourself down; for it is written, 'He will command his Angels concerning you,' and 'On their hands they will bear you up, so that you will not dash your foot against a stone.'" Jesus said to him, "Again it is written, 'Do not put the Lord your God to the test.'"

Again, the devil took him to a very high mountain and showed him all the kingdoms of the world and their splendour; and he said to him, "All these I will give you, if you will fall down and worship me." Jesus said to him, "Away with you, Satan! for it is written, 'Worship the Lord your God, and serve only him.'"

Then the devil left him, and suddenly Angels came and waited on him.

The Gospel of the Lord. **Praise to you, Lord Jesus Christ.**

For parishes engaged in the RCIA, *the* Rite of Election *takes place now.*

PROFESSION OF FAITH *(p. 11)*

PRAYER OF THE FAITHFUL

The following intentions are suggestions only. More suggestions are available at www.livingwithchrist.ca

R. **Lord, hear our prayer.**

For the Church, cherished community to whom the Lord speaks, we pray to the Lord: R.

For leaders of nations, entrusted with the political and economic futures of their peoples, we pray to the Lord: R.

For those who are discouraged by temptation, we pray to the Lord: R.

For us, God's people gathered here, called to conversion at the start of our Lenten journey, we pray to the Lord: **R̲.**

PREPARATION OF THE GIFTS *(p. 14)*

PRAYER OVER THE OFFERINGS
Give us the right dispositions, O Lord, we pray, to make these offerings, for with them we celebrate the beginning of this venerable and sacred time. Through Christ our Lord. **Amen.**

Rite of Election:
Almighty ever-living God, who restore us by the Sacrament of Baptism to eternal life as we confess your name, receive, we beseech you, the offerings and prayers of your servants and command that those who hope in you may have their desires fulfilled and their sins cancelled out. Through Christ our Lord. **Amen.**

PREFACE *(1st Sunday of Lent, p. 20)*

COMMUNION ANTIPHON *(Matthew 4.4)*
One does not live by bread alone, but by every word that comes forth from the mouth of God.
or (Cf. Psalm 90.4)
The Lord will conceal you with his pinions, and under his wings you will trust.
Rite of Election (Ephesians 1.7):
In Christ, we have redemption by his Blood and forgiveness of our sins, in accord with the riches of his grace.

PRAYER AFTER COMMUNION

Renewed now with heavenly bread, by which faith is nourished, hope increased, and charity strengthened, we pray, O Lord, that we may learn to hunger for Christ, the true and living Bread, and strive to live by every word which proceeds from your mouth. Through Christ our Lord. **Amen.**

Rite of Election:

May this Sacrament we have received purify us, we pray, O Lord, and grant your servants freedom from all blame, that those bound by a guilty conscience may glory in the fullness of heavenly remedy. Through Christ our Lord. **Amen.**

PRAYER OVER THE PEOPLE

May bountiful blessing, O Lord, we pray, come down upon your people, that hope may grow in tribulation, virtue be strengthened in temptation, and eternal redemption be assured. Through Christ our Lord. **Amen.**

BLESSING AND DISMISSAL *(p. 70)*

March 12

Lulled by the repetition of my days, I often miss what matters most. Moments pass me like news-feeds as I blindly scroll... scroll... scroll from one duty to the next. No wonder I grow jaded. Or rather: No *wonder*, I grow jaded.

Without even realizing — or perhaps because of it — I have grown bored, weary and indifferent. A sure sign it's time to take a hike.

Come on, Jesus says, tapping our shoulders, drawing us away to be alone with him on a mountaintop. Answer that invitation to rise above it all; to be still and breathe deep; to see Jesus with new eyes. Because no matter how well we think we know him, and no doubt his three closest disciples thought they did, Jesus always has more to reveal about himself, about his father, and about the world and our place in it.

When those men returned from the mountain that day, fish needed catching, buckets needed filling and fires needed stoking. Their world, duties and lives had not changed and yet, surely everything had. Now they knew; they'd seen; and they were filled with wonder. Time with Jesus does that.

Today as we celebrate Jesus' presence in the Eucharist, spend time with Jesus on that mountain. Feel the wonder. Listen to him. For even just a glimpse of his glory changes everything.

Caroline Pignat, Kanata, ON

ENTRANCE ANTIPHON *(Cf. Psalm 26.8-9)*
Of you my heart has spoken: Seek his face. It is your face, O Lord, that I seek; hide not your face from me.

or (Cf. Psalm 24.6, 2, 22)
Remember your compassion, O Lord, and your merciful love, for they are from of old. Let not our enemies exult over us. Redeem us, O God of Israel, from all our distress.

INTRODUCTORY RITES *(p. 5)*

COLLECT
O God, who have commanded us to listen to your beloved Son, be pleased, we pray, to nourish us inwardly by your word, that, with spiritual sight made pure, we may rejoice to behold your glory. Through our Lord Jesus Christ, your Son, who lives and reigns with you in the unity of the Holy Spirit, one God, for ever and ever. **Amen.**

FIRST READING *(Genesis 12.1-4)*
The Lord said to Abram, "Go from your country and your kindred and your father's house to the land that I will show you. I will make of you a great nation, and I will bless you, and make your name great, so that you will be a blessing. I will bless those who bless you, and the one who curses you I will curse; and in you all the families of the earth shall be blessed."

So Abram went, as the Lord had told him.
The word of the Lord. **Thanks be to God.**

RESPONSORIAL PSALM (Psalm 33)

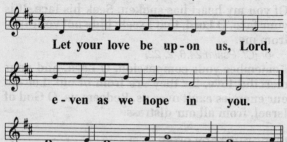

Let your love be up-on us, Lord,
e-ven as we hope in you.

R. **Let your love be upon us, Lord,
even as we hope in you.**

The word of the Lord is · **upright,**
and all his work is done in · **faithfulness.**
He loves righteousness and · **justice;**
the earth is full of the steadfast love
of the · **Lord.** R.

Truly the eye of the Lord is on those
who · **fear_him,**
on those who hope in his steadfast · **love,**
to deliver their soul from · **death,**
and to keep them alive in · **famine.** R.

Our soul waits for the · **Lord;**
he is our help and · **shield.**
Let your steadfast love, O Lord, be up-·**on_us,**
even as we hope in · **you.** R.

©2010 Gordon Johnston/Novalis
To hear the Sunday Psalms, visit www.livingwithchrist.ca.

SECOND READING *(2 Timothy 1.8b-10)*
Brothers and sisters: Join with me in suffering
for the Gospel, relying on the power of God, who
saved us and called us with a holy calling, not
according to our works but according to his own
purpose and grace.

This grace was given to us in Christ Jesus before the ages began, but it has now been revealed
through the appearing of our Saviour Christ Jesus,
who abolished death and brought life and immortality to light through the Gospel.

The word of the Lord. **Thanks be to God.**

GOSPEL ACCLAMATION *(See Luke 9.35)*
Praise to you, Lord, king of eternal glory! From
the bright cloud the Father's voice is heard: This
is my Son, the Beloved; listen to him. **Praise to
you, Lord, king of eternal glory!**

GOSPEL *(Matthew 17.1-9)*
The Lord be with you. **And with your spirit.**
A reading from the holy Gospel according to Mat-
thew. **Glory to you, O Lord.**

Jesus took with him Peter and James and his
brother John and led them up a high mountain, by
themselves. And he was transfigured before them,
and his face shone like the sun, and his clothes
became dazzling white. Suddenly there appeared
to them Moses and Elijah, talking with him.

Then Peter said to Jesus, "Lord, it is good
for us to be here; if you wish, I will make three
dwellings here, one for you, one for Moses, and
one for Elijah."

While he was still speaking, suddenly a bright cloud overshadowed them, and from the cloud a voice said, "This is my Son, the Beloved; with him I am well pleased; listen to him!"

When the disciples heard this, they fell to the ground and were overcome by fear. But Jesus came and touched them, saying, "Get up and do not be afraid." And when they looked up, they saw no one except Jesus himself alone.

As they were coming down the mountain, Jesus ordered them, "Tell no one about the vision until after the Son of Man has been raised from the dead."

The Gospel of the Lord. **Praise to you, Lord Jesus Christ.**

PROFESSION OF FAITH (p. 11)

PRAYER OF THE FAITHFUL

The following intentions are suggestions only. More suggestions are available at www.livingwithchrist.ca

R̥. **Lord, hear our prayer.**

For the Church, journeying toward Easter rebirth through fasting and prayer, we pray to the Lord: R̥.

For the liberation of those who suffer poverty and political and economic oppression, we pray to the Lord: R̥.

For those among us who are sick, lonely, unemployed, we pray to the Lord: R̥.

For us, God's people gathered here, called to be a transforming presence to our neighbours, we pray to the Lord: R̥.

PREPARATION OF THE GIFTS *(p. 14)*

PRAYER OVER THE OFFERINGS

May this sacrifice, O Lord, we pray, cleanse us of our faults and sanctify your faithful in body and mind for the celebration of the paschal festivities. Through Christ our Lord. **Amen.**

PREFACE *(2nd Sunday of Lent, p. 20)*

COMMUNION ANTIPHON *(Matthew 17.5)*

This is my beloved Son, with whom I am well pleased; listen to him.

PRAYER AFTER COMMUNION

As we receive these glorious mysteries, we make thanksgiving to you, O Lord, for allowing us while still on earth to be partakers even now of the things of heaven. Through Christ our Lord. **Amen.**

PRAYER OVER THE PEOPLE

Bless your faithful, we pray, O Lord, with a blessing that endures for ever, and keep them faithful to the Gospel of your Only Begotten Son, so that they may always desire and at last attain that glory whose beauty he showed in his own Body, to the amazement of his Apostles. Through Christ our Lord. **Amen.**

BLESSING AND DISMISSAL *(p. 70)*

March 19

Given that I try to drink eight glasses of water a day, I cannot truly relate to the thirst expressed in two of today's readings. Literally, I don't know the desert and I don't go to the well for water. Yet today's gospel is one of my favourites. I hear the back and forth of the conversation between the woman and Jesus. And I laugh as I picture them splashing water, living water gushing up to eternal life!

A line in the first reading that does resonate with my experience is the complaining of the Israelites in the desert. When I do not see God's hand concretely and explicitly visible in my life, I cry out as if it is God's fault. When my bucket is empty, I cry! Lent can be a tough season of prayer, fasting and giving alms.

The challenges only make sense as a path to Easter. My thirst must lead me to others and to Jesus. When I thirst, will others share from their bucket? When I meet others who thirst, will I share from mine? Only then will Paul's image in the Letter to the Romans make sense — "God's love has been poured into our hearts."

Sr. Susan Kidd, CND, Charlottetown, PE

Parishes engaged in the Rite of Christian Initiation of Adults (RCIA) *may celebrate the* 1st Scrutiny *today.*

ENTRANCE ANTIPHON *(Cf. Psalm 24.15-16)*
My eyes are always on the Lord, for he rescues my feet from the snare. Turn to me and have mercy on me, for I am alone and poor.

or (Cf. Ezekiel 36.23-26)
When I prove my holiness among you, I will gather you from all the foreign lands; and I will pour clean water upon you and cleanse you from all your impurities, and I will give you a new spirit, says the Lord.

1st Scrutiny: (Ezekiel 36.23-26, above)
or (Cf. Isaiah 55.1)
Come to the waters, you who are thirsty, says the Lord; you who have no money, come and drink joyfully.

INTRODUCTORY RITES *(p. 5)*

COLLECT
O God, author of every mercy and of all goodness, who in fasting, prayer and almsgiving have shown us a remedy for sin, look graciously on this confession of our lowliness, that we, who are bowed down by our conscience, may always be lifted up by your mercy. Through our Lord Jesus Christ, your Son, who lives and reigns with you in the unity of the Holy Spirit, one God, for ever and ever. **Amen.**

1st Scrutiny:
Grant, we pray, O Lord, that these chosen ones may come worthily and wisely to the confes-

sion of your praise, so that in accordance with that first dignity which they lost by original sin they may be fashioned anew through your glory. Through our Lord Jesus Christ, your Son, who lives and reigns with you in the unity of the Holy Spirit, one God, for ever and ever. **Amen.**

FIRST READING (*Exodus 17.3-7*)

In the wilderness the people thirsted for water; and the people complained against Moses and said, "Why did you bring us out of Egypt, to kill us and our children and livestock with thirst?" So Moses cried out to the Lord, "What shall I do with this people? They are almost ready to stone me."

The Lord said to Moses, "Go on ahead of the people, and take some of the elders of Israel with you; take in your hand the staff with which you struck the Nile, and go. I will be standing there in front of you on the rock at Horeb. Strike the rock, and water will come out of it, so that the people may drink." Moses did so, in the sight of the elders of Israel.

He called the place Massah and Meribah, because the children of Israel quarrelled and tested the Lord, saying, "Is the Lord among us or not?"

The word of the Lord. **Thanks be to God.**

RESPONSORIAL PSALM *(Psalm 95)*

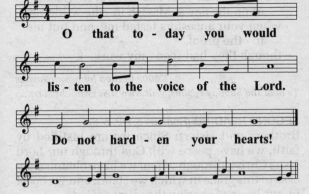

O that to-day you would lis-ten to the voice of the Lord. Do not hard-en your hearts!

℟. **O that today you would listen
to the voice of the Lord.
Do not harden your hearts!**

O come, let us sing to · **the** Lord;
let us make a joyful noise to the rock
    of our · **sal**-vation!
Let us come into his presence with
    · **thanks**-giving;
let us make a joyful noise to him with
    songs · **of** praise! ℟.

O come, let us worship and · **bow** down,
let us kneel before the Lord, · **our** Maker!
For he is our God, and we are the people
    of · **his** pasture,
and the sheep of · **his** hand. ℟.

201

O that today you would listen to · **his** voice!
Do not harden your hearts, as at Meribah,
　　as on the day at Massah in · **the** wilderness,
when your ancestors tested me, and put me
　　to · **the** proof,
though they had seen · **my** work. R.

©2009 Gordon Johnston/Novalis
To hear the Sunday Psalms, visit www.livingwithchrist.ca.

SECOND READING *(Romans 5.1-2, 5-8)*
Brothers and sisters: Since we are justified by
faith, we have peace with God through our Lord
Jesus Christ, through whom we have obtained ac-
cess to this grace in which we stand; and we boast
in our hope of sharing the glory of God.

　　And hope does not disappoint us, because
God's love has been poured into our hearts
through the Holy Spirit that has been given to
us. For while we were still weak, at the right
time Christ died for the ungodly. Indeed, rarely
will anyone die for a righteous person — though
perhaps for a good person someone might actually dare to die. But God proves his love for us in
that while we still were sinners Christ died for us.

　　The word of the Lord. **Thanks be to God.**

GOSPEL ACCLAMATION *(John 4.42, 15)*
Praise to you, Lord, king of eternal glory! Lord,
you are truly the Saviour of the world; give me
living water, that I may never be thirsty. **Praise to
you, Lord, king of eternal glory!**

GOSPEL *(John 4.5-42)*

For the shorter reading, omit the indented parts.

The Lord be with you. **And with your spirit.**
A reading from the holy Gospel according to John.
Glory to you, O Lord.

Jesus came to a Samaritan city called Sychar,
near the plot of ground that Jacob had given to
his son Joseph. Jacob's well was there, and Jesus,
tired out by his journey, was sitting by the well.
It was about noon.

A Samaritan woman came to draw water, and
Jesus said to her, "Give me a drink." (His disciples
had gone to the city to buy food.)

The Samaritan woman said to him, "How is
it that you, a Jew, ask a drink of me, a woman of
Samaria?" (Jews do not share things in common
with Samaritans.) Jesus answered her, "If you
knew the gift of God, and who it is that is saying
to you, 'Give me a drink,' you would have asked
him, and he would have given you living water."

The woman said to him, "Sir, you have no
bucket, and the well is deep. Where do you get
that living water? Are you greater than our father
Jacob, who gave us the well, and with his children and his flocks drank from it?" Jesus said to
her, "Everyone who drinks of this water will be
thirsty again, but the one who drinks of the water
that I will give will never be thirsty. The water
that I will give him will become in him a spring
of water gushing up to eternal life." The woman
said to him, "Sir, give me this water, so that I may
never be thirsty or have to keep coming here to
draw water."

Jesus said to her, "Go, call your husband, and come back." The woman answered him, "I have no husband." Jesus said to her, "You are right in saying, 'I have no husband'; for you have had five husbands, and the one you have now is not your husband. What you have said is true!" The woman said to him, "Sir, "I see that you are a Prophet. Our ancestors worshipped on this mountain, but you say that the place where people must worship is in Jerusalem."

Jesus said to her, "Woman, believe me, the hour is coming when you will worship the Father neither on this mountain nor in Jerusalem. You worship what you do not know; we worship what we know, for salvation is from the Jews. But the hour is coming, and is now here, when the true worshippers will worship the Father in spirit and truth, for the Father seeks such as these to worship him. God is spirit, and those who worship him must worship in spirit and truth."

The woman said to him, "I know that the Messiah is coming" (who is called the Christ). "When he comes, he will proclaim all things to us." Jesus said to her, "I am he, the one who is speaking to you."

Just then his disciples came. They were astonished that he was speaking with a woman, but no one said, "What do you want?" or, "Why are you speaking with her?" Then the woman left her water jar and went back to the city. She said to the people, "Come and see a man who told me everything I have ever done! He cannot be the Messiah, can he?" They left the city and were on their way to him. Meanwhile the disciples were urging him, "Rabbi, eat something." But he said to them, "I have food to eat that you do not know about." So the disciples said to one another, "Surely no one has brought him something to eat?"

Jesus said to them, "My food is to do the will of him who sent me and to complete his work. Do you not say, 'Four months more, then comes the harvest'? But I tell you, look around you, and see how the fields are ripe for harvesting. The reaper is already receiving wages and is gathering fruit for eternal life, so that sower and reaper may rejoice together. For here the saying holds true, 'One sows and another reaps.' I sent you to reap that for which you did not labour. Others have laboured, and you have entered into their labour."

Many Samaritans from that city believed in Jesus. because of the woman's testimony, "He told me everything I have ever done."

So when they [the Samaritans] came to him, they asked him to stay with them; and he stayed there two days. And many more believed because of his word. They said to the woman, "It is no longer because of what you said that we believe, for we have heard for ourselves, and we know that this is truly the Saviour of the world."

The Gospel of the Lord. **Praise to you, Lord Jesus Christ.**

PROFESSION OF FAITH (p. 11)

PRAYER OF THE FAITHFUL

The following intentions are suggestions only. More suggestions are available at www.livingwithchrist.ca

℟. **Lord, hear our prayer.**

For the Church, herald of the Good News of God's love for all creation, we pray to the Lord: ℟.

For the world's peoples who seek safe haven, and for our own country, strong in its tradition of welcoming strangers, we pray to the Lord: ℟.

For God's beloved sons and daughters who are in pain and distress, or enslaved by fear or depression, we pray to the Lord: ℟.

For God's people gathered here, invited to grow in caring and fidelity to our families and our Christian communities, we pray to the Lord: ℟.

PREPARATION OF THE GIFTS *(p. 14)*

PRAYER OVER THE OFFERINGS

Be pleased, O Lord, with these sacrificial offerings, and grant that we who beseech pardon for our own sins may take care to forgive our neighbour. Through Christ our Lord. **Amen.**

1st Scrutiny:

May your merciful grace prepare your servants, O Lord, for the worthy celebration of these mysteries and lead them to it by a devout way of life. Through Christ our Lord. **Amen.**

PREFACE *(3rd Sunday of Lent, p. 21)*

COMMUNION ANTIPHON *(John 4.13-14)*
For anyone who drinks it, says the Lord, the water I shall give will become in him a spring welling up to eternal life.

PRAYER AFTER COMMUNION
As we receive the pledge of things yet hidden in heaven and are nourished while still on earth with the Bread that comes from on high, we humbly entreat you, O Lord, that what is being brought about in us in mystery may come to true completion. Through Christ our Lord. **Amen.**

1st Scrutiny:
Give help, O Lord, we pray, by the grace of your redemption and be pleased to protect and prepare those you are to initiate through the Sacraments of eternal life. Through Christ our Lord. **Amen.**

PRAYER OVER THE PEOPLE
Direct, O Lord, we pray, the hearts of your faithful, and in your kindness grant your servants this grace: that, abiding in the love of you and their neighbour, they may fulfill the whole of your commands. Through Christ our Lord. **Amen.**

BLESSING AND DISMISSAL *(p. 70)*

March 26

Samuel has been commissioned by God to choose a successor to Saul. Like us, Samuel frequently judges by appearances, while God judges by the heart. Samuel's selection of David and Jesus' healing the blind man in today's gospel speak to us of God's choices. Jesus sees in the blind man someone with great potential who moves from a world of darkness to collaborate with Jesus. He will be the one to display the work of God and reveal Jesus to others.

The readings call us to move from our blindness to the revelation of God in Jesus. To believe is to come to the light, while to disbelieve is to be spiritually blind and walk in the darkness. Paul reminds us that when we are committed to Christ, we become children of the light, and earlier in his letter to the Ephesians he prays that his community might have "the eyes of your heart enlightened" (1.18).

"I once was blind but now I see." John Newton composed *Amazing Grace* and based it on his own conversion experience, after which he began a life-long ministry of reconciliation. The blind man received not only the gift of sight but also the gift of faith. May we like him experience this Lent as a true conversion of heart.

Fr. Jack Lynch, SFM, Scarborough, ON

Parishes engaged in the Rite of Christian Initiation of Adults (RCIA) *may celebrate the* 2nd Scrutiny *today.*

ENTRANCE ANTIPHON *(Cf. Isaiah 66.10-11)*

Rejoice, Jerusalem, and all who love her. Be joyful, all who were in mourning; exult and be satisfied at her consoling breast.

2nd Scrutiny (Cf. Psalm 24.15-16):

My eyes are always on the Lord, for he rescues my feet from the snare. Turn to me and have mercy on me, for I am alone and poor.

INTRODUCTORY RITES *(p. 5)*

COLLECT

O God, who through your Word reconcile the human race to yourself in a wonderful way, grant, we pray, that with prompt devotion and eager faith the Christian people may hasten toward the solemn celebrations to come. Through our Lord Jesus Christ, your Son, who lives and reigns with you in the unity of the Holy Spirit, one God, for ever and ever. **Amen.**

2nd Scrutiny:

Almighty ever-living God, give to your Church an increase in spiritual joy, so that those once born of earth may be reborn as citizens of heaven. Through our Lord Jesus Christ, your Son, who lives and reigns with you in the unity of the Holy Spirit, one God, for ever and ever. **Amen.**

FIRST READING *(1 Samuel 16.1b, 6-7, 10-13)*

The Lord said to Samuel, "Fill your horn with oil and set out; I will send you to Jesse of Bethlehem, for I have provided for myself a king among his sons."

When the sons of Jesse came, Samuel looked on Eliab and thought, "Surely the Lord's anointed is now before the Lord." But the Lord said to Samuel, "Do not look on his appearance or on the height of his stature, because I have rejected him; for the Lord does not see as the human sees; the human looks on the outward appearance, but the Lord looks on the heart."

Jesse made seven of his sons pass before Samuel, and Samuel said to Jesse, "The Lord has not chosen any of these." Samuel said to Jesse, "Are all your sons here?" And he said, "There remains yet the youngest, but he is keeping the sheep." And Samuel said to Jesse, "Send and bring him; for we will not sit down until he comes here." Jesse sent and brought David in. Now he was ruddy, and had beautiful eyes, and was handsome. The Lord said, "Rise and anoint him; for this is the one."

Then Samuel took the horn of oil, and anointed him in the presence of his brothers; and the spirit of the Lord came mightily upon David from that day forward.

The word of the Lord. **Thanks be to God.**

RESPONSORIAL PSALM (*Psalm 23*)

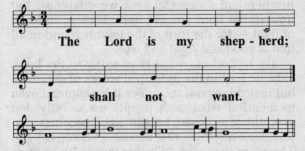

The Lord is my shep - herd; I shall not want.

R. **The Lord is my shepherd; I shall not want.**

The Lord is my shepherd, I shall · **not** want.
He makes me lie down in · **green** pastures;
he leads me be-·-**side** still waters;
he re-·-**stores** my soul. R.

He leads me in right paths for his · **name's** sake.
Even though I walk through the darkest valley,
    I fear · **no** evil;
for · **you** are with_me;
your rod and your · **staff** — they comfort_me. R.

You prepare a table · **be**-fore_me
in the presence · **of_my** enemies;
you anoint my · **head** with oil;
my · **cup** over-flows. R.

Surely goodness and mercy · **shall** follow_me
all the days of · **my** life,
and I shall dwell in the · **house_of** the Lord
my · **whole** life long. R.

©*2009 Gordon Johnston/Novalis*
To hear the Sunday Psalms, visit www.livingwithchrist.ca.

SECOND READING *(Ephesians 5.8-14)*
Brothers and sisters: Once you were darkness, but now in the Lord you are light. Live as children of light — for the fruit of the light is found in all that is good and right and true.

Try to find out what is pleasing to the Lord. Take no part in the unfruitful works of darkness, but instead expose them. For it is shameful even to mention what such people do secretly; but everything exposed by the light becomes visible, for everything that becomes visible is light. Therefore it is said, "Sleeper, awake! Rise from the dead, and Christ will shine on you."

The word of the Lord. **Thanks be to God.**

GOSPEL ACCLAMATION *(John 8.12)*
Praise to you, Lord, king of eternal glory! I am the light of the world, says the Lord; whoever follows me will have the light of life. **Praise to you, Lord, king of eternal glory!**

GOSPEL *(John 9.1-41)*
For the shorter version, omit the indented parts.
The Lord be with you. **And with your spirit.**
A reading from the holy Gospel according to John. **Glory to you, O Lord.**

As Jesus walked along, he saw a man blind from birth.

His disciples asked him, "Rabbi, who sinned, this man or his parents, that he was born blind?"

Jesus answered, "Neither this man nor his parents sinned; he was born blind so that God's works might be revealed in him. We must work the works of him who sent me while it is day; night is coming when no one can work. As long as I am in the world, I am the light of the world." When he had said this, He spat on the ground and made mud with the saliva and spread the mud on the man's eyes, saying to him, "Go, wash in the pool of Siloam" (which means Sent).

Then the man who was blind went and washed, and came back able to see. The neighbours and those who had seen him before as a beggar began to ask, "Is this not the man who used to sit and beg?" Some were saying, "It is he." Others were saying, "No, but it is someone like him." He kept saying, "I am the man."

But they kept asking him, "Then how were your eyes opened?" He answered, "The man called Jesus made mud, spread it on my eyes, and said to me, 'Go to Siloam and wash.' Then I went and washed and received my sight." They said to him, "Where is he?" He said, "I do not know."

They brought to the Pharisees the man who had formerly been blind. Now it was a Sabbath day when Jesus made the mud and opened his eyes. Then the Pharisees also began to ask him how he had received his sight. He said to them, "He put mud on my eyes. Then I washed, and now I see." Some of the Pharisees said, "This man is not from God, for he does not observe the Sabbath." But others said, "How can a man who is a sinner perform such signs?" And they were divided. So they said again to the blind man, "What do you say about him? It was your eyes he opened." He said, "He is a Prophet."

They did not believe that he had been blind and had received his sight until they called the parents of the man who had received his sight and asked them, "Is this your son, who you say was born blind? How then does he now see?" His parents answered, "We know that this is our son, and that he was born blind; but we do not know how it is that now he sees, nor do we know who opened his eyes. Ask him; he is of age. He will speak for himself." His parents said this because they were afraid of the Jewish authorities, who had already agreed that anyone who confessed Jesus to be the Messiah would be put out of the synagogue. Therefore his parents said, "He is of age; ask him."

So for the second time they called the man who had been blind, and they said to him, "Give glory to God! We know that this man is a sinner." He answered, "I do not know whether he is a sinner. One thing I do know, that though I was blind, now I see." They said to him, "What did he do to you? How did he open your eyes?" He answered them, "I have told you already, and you would not listen. Why do you want to hear it again? Do you also want to become his disciples?" Then they reviled him, saying, "You are his disciple, but we are disciples of Moses. We know that God has spoken to Moses, but as for this man, we do not know where he comes from."

The man answered, "Here is an astonishing thing! You do not know where he comes from, and yet he opened my eyes. We know that God does not listen to sinners, but he does listen to one who worships him and obeys his will. Never since the world began has it been heard that anyone opened the eyes of a person born blind. If this man were not from God, he could do nothing."

They answered him, "You were born entirely in sins, and are you trying to teach us?" And they drove him out.

Jesus heard that they had driven him out, and when he found him, he said, "Do you believe in the Son of Man?" He answered, "And who is he, sir? Tell me, so that I may believe in him." Jesus said to him, "You have seen him, and the one speaking with you is he." He said, "Lord, I believe." And he worshipped him.

Jesus said, "I came into this world for judgment so that those who do not see may see, and those who do see may become blind." Some of the Pharisees near him heard this and said to him, "Surely we are not blind, are we?" Jesus said to them, "If you were blind, you would have no sin. But now that you say, 'We see,' your sin remains."

The Gospel of the Lord. **Praise to you, Lord Jesus Christ.**

PROFESSION OF FAITH (*p. 11*)

PRAYER OF THE FAITHFUL

The following intentions are suggestions only. There are more suggestions at www.livingwithchrist.ca

R. **Lord, hear our prayer.**

For the Church, broken yet strong, healing yet seeking wholeness, we pray to the Lord: R.

For leaders of nations, struggling to witness to love and compassion in a world of suffering and loneliness, we pray to the Lord: R.

For those who are searching for a word of hope, we pray to the Lord: R.

For those seeking initiation into the Christian community and the outstretched arms of God's love and forgiveness, we pray to the Lord: R.

PREPARATION OF THE GIFTS *(p. 14)*

PRAYER OVER THE OFFERINGS
We place before you with joy these offerings, which bring eternal remedy, O Lord, praying that we may both faithfully revere them and present them to you, as is fitting, for the salvation of all the world. Through Christ our Lord. **Amen.**

2nd Scrutiny:
We place before you with joy these offerings, which bring eternal remedy, O Lord, praying that we may both faithfully revere them and present them to you, as is fitting, for those who seek salvation. Through Christ our Lord. **Amen.**

PREFACE *(4th Sunday of Lent, p. 21)*

COMMUNION ANTIPHON *(Cf. John 9.11, 38)*
The Lord anointed my eyes: I went, I washed, I saw and I believed in God.

PRAYER AFTER COMMUNION
O God, who enlighten everyone who comes into this world, illuminate our hearts, we pray, with the splendour of your grace, that we may always ponder what is worthy and pleasing to your majesty and love you in all sincerity. Through Christ our Lord. **Amen.**

2nd Scrutiny:
Sustain your family always in your kindness, O Lord, we pray, correct them, set them in order, graciously protect them under your rule, and in your unfailing goodness direct them along the way of salvation. Through Christ our Lord. **Amen.**

PRAYER OVER THE PEOPLE
Look upon those who call to you, O Lord, and sustain the weak; give life by your unfailing light to those who walk in the shadow of death, and bring those rescued by your mercy from every evil to reach the highest good. Through Christ our Lord. **Amen.**

BLESSING AND DISMISSAL *(p. 70)*

April Saints' Days

The following saints are traditionally remembered in April in Canada.

2   Saint Francis of Paola

4   Saint Isidore

5   Saint Vincent Ferrer

7   Saint John Baptist de la Salle

11 Saint Stanislaus

13 Saint Martin I

17 Saint Kateri Tekakwitha

18 Blessed Marie-Anne Blondin

21 Saint Anselm

23 Saint George
     Saint Adalbert

24 Saint Fidelis of Sigmaringen

25 Saint Mark

26 Our Lady of Good Counsel

28 Saint Peter Chanel
     Saint Louis Grignion de Montfort

29 Saint Catherine of Siena

30 Saint Marie of the Incarnation

April 2

Resurrection is a central tenet of the Christian faith. When he rose after three days in the tomb, Jesus showed that he had defeated death once and for all. His resurrection is also the basis for our belief that we too shall overcome death and rise again. Moreover, as Paul tells us in the second reading, Christ's resurrection transforms our life today, empowering us to reject sin and live in righteousness.

The story of Lazarus demonstrates that resurrection is not restricted to Jesus alone. In order to make this clear, Jesus delayed going to see his sick friend, with the result that by the time Jesus arrived, Lazarus had been dead for four days. This reminds us of Jesus' own resurrection after three days.

In the Bible, three days often symbolizes the time span during which things are within human control, but beyond three days only God can act. By delaying his arrival, Jesus made sure that he would not be healing a sick man but rather raising a dead man. He also reinforced that this was the result of God's intervention.

Every time we gather, we celebrate Jesus' death and resurrection in the Eucharist. We also proclaim it aloud when we recite the Mystery of Faith, affirming his death, his resurrection and his return in glory, when we too shall rise from the dead.

John L. McLaughlin, Toronto, ON

National Collection for Development and Peace

Parishes engaged in the Rite of Christian Initiation of Adults (RCIA) *may celebrate the* 3rd Scrutiny *today.*

ENTRANCE ANTIPHON *(Cf. Psalm 42.1-2)*
Give me justice, O God, and plead my cause against a nation that is faithless. From the deceitful and cunning rescue me, for you, O God, are my strength.

3rd Scrutiny (Cf. Psalm 17.5-7):
The waves of death rose about me; the pains of the netherworld surrounded me. In my anguish I called to the Lord; and from his holy temple he heard my voice.

INTRODUCTORY RITES *(p. 5)*

COLLECT
By your help, we beseech you, Lord our God, may we walk eagerly in that same charity with which, out of love for the world, your Son handed himself over to death. Through our Lord Jesus Christ, your Son, who lives and reigns with you in the unity of the Holy Spirit, one God, for ever and ever. **Amen.**

3rd Scrutiny:
Grant, O Lord, to these chosen ones that, instructed in the holy mysteries, they may receive new life at the font of Baptism and be numbered among the members of your Church. Through our Lord Jesus Christ, your Son, who lives and reigns with you in the unity of the Holy Spirit, one God, for ever and ever. **Amen.**

FIRST READING *(Ezekiel 37.12-14)*

Thus says the Lord God: "I am going to open your graves, and bring you up from your graves, O my people; and I will bring you back to the land of Israel. And you shall know that I am the Lord, when I open your graves, and bring you up from your graves, O my people.

"I will put my spirit within you, and you shall live, and I will place you on your own soil; then you shall know that I, the Lord, have spoken and will act," says the Lord.

The word of the Lord. **Thanks be to God.**

RESPONSORIAL PSALM *(Psalm 130)*

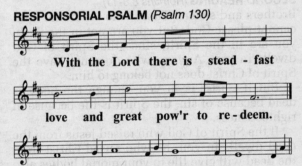

With the Lord there is stead - fast

love and great pow'r to re - deem.

R. **With the Lord there is steadfast love and great power to redeem.**

Out of the depths I cry to you, O · **Lord.**
Lord, hear · **my** voice!
Let your ears be at--**tentive**
to the voice of my sup--**pli**-cations! R.

If you, O Lord, should mark in--**iquities,**
Lord, who · **could** stand?
But there is forgiveness with · **you,**
so that you may be · **re**-vered. R.

I wait for the · **Lord,**
my soul waits, and in his word · **I** hope;
my soul waits for the · **Lord**
more than watchmen for · **the** morning. ℞

For with the Lord there is steadfast · **love,**
and with him is great power to · **re**-deem.
It is he who will redeem · **Israel**
from all its · **in**-iquities. ℞

©2009 Gordon Johnston/Novalis
To hear the Sunday Psalms, visit www.livingwithchrist.ca.

SECOND READING *(Romans 8.8-11)*

Brothers and sisters: Those who are in the flesh
cannot please God. But you are not in the flesh;
you are in the Spirit, since the Spirit of God
dwells in you. Anyone who does not have the
Spirit of Christ does not belong to him.

But if Christ is in you, though the body is
dead because of sin, the Spirit is life because of
righteousness.

If the Spirit of God who raised Jesus from the
dead dwells in you, he who raised Christ from
the dead will give life to your mortal bodies also
through his Spirit that dwells in you.

The word of the Lord. **Thanks be to God.**

GOSPEL ACCLAMATION *(John 11.25, 26)*

Praise to you, Lord, king of eternal glory! I am the
resurrection and the life, says the Lord; whoever
believes in me will never die. **Praise to you, Lord,
king of eternal glory!**

GOSPEL *(John 11.1-45)*

For the shorter version, omit the indented parts.

The Lord be with you. **And with your spirit.**
A reading from the holy Gospel according to John.
Glory to you, O Lord.

Now a certain man, Lazarus, was ill. He was
from Bethany, the village of Mary and her sister Martha. Mary was the one who anointed
the Lord with perfume and wiped his feet
with her hair; her brother Lazarus was ill. So
The sisters [of Lazarus] sent a message to Jesus,
"Lord, he whom you love is ill." But when Jesus
heard this, he said, "This illness does not lead to
death; rather it is for God's glory, so that the Son
of God may be glorified through it." Accordingly,
though Jesus loved Martha and her sister and
Lazarus, after having heard that Lazarus was ill,
he stayed two days longer in the place where he
was. Then after this he said to the disciples, "Let
us go to Judea again."

The disciples said to him, "Rabbi, the people
there were just now trying to stone you, and
are you going there again?" Jesus answered,
"Are there not twelve hours of daylight?
Those who walk during the day do not stumble, because they see the light of this world.
But those who walk at night stumble, because
the light is not in them."

After saying this, he told them, "Our friend
Lazarus has fallen asleep, but I am going there
to awaken him." The disciples said to him,
"Lord, if he has fallen asleep, he will be all
right." Jesus, however, had been speaking
about his death, but they thought that he was

223

referring merely to sleep. Then Jesus told them plainly, "Lazarus is dead. For your sake I am glad I was not there, so that you may believe. But let us go to him." Thomas, who was called the Twin, said to his fellow disciples, "Let us also go, that we may die with him." When Jesus arrived, he found that Lazarus had already been in the tomb four days.

Now Bethany was near Jerusalem, some two miles away, and many Jews had come to Martha and Mary to console them about their brother.

When Martha heard that Jesus was coming, she went and met him, while Mary stayed at home. Martha said to Jesus, "Lord, if you had been here, my brother would not have died. But even now I know that God will give you whatever you ask of him." Jesus said to her, "Your brother will rise again." Martha said to him, "I know that he will rise again in the resurrection on the last day." Jesus said to her, "I am the resurrection and the life. Whoever believes in me, even though they die, will live, and everyone who lives and believes in me will never die. Do you believe this?" She said to him, "Yes, Lord, I believe that you are the Christ, the Son of God, the one coming into the world."

When she had said this, she went back and called her sister Mary, and told her privately, "The Teacher is here and is calling for you." And when Mary heard it, she got up quickly and went to him. Now Jesus had not yet come to the village, but was still at the place where Martha had met him. The Jews who were with her in the house, consoling her, saw Mary get up quickly and go out. They followed her because they thought that she was going to the tomb to weep there.

When Mary came where Jesus was and saw him, she knelt at his feet and said to him, "Lord, if you had been here, my brother would not have died." When Jesus saw her weeping, and the Jews who came with her also weeping, he

[Jesus] was greatly disturbed in spirit and deeply moved. He said, "Where have you laid him?" They said to him, "Lord, come and see." Jesus began to weep. So the Jews said, "See how he loved him!" But some of them said, "Could not he who opened the eyes of the blind man have kept this man from dying?"

Then Jesus, again greatly disturbed, came to the tomb. It was a cave, and a stone was lying against it. Jesus said, "Take away the stone." Martha, the sister of the dead man, said to him, "Lord, already there is a stench because he has been dead four days." Jesus said to her, "Did I not tell you that if you believed, you would see the glory of God?" So they took away the stone. And Jesus looked upward and said, "Father, I thank you for having heard me. I knew that you always hear me, but I have said this for the sake of the crowd standing here, so that they may believe that you sent me."

When he had said this, he cried with a loud voice, "Lazarus, come out!" The dead man came out, his hands and feet bound with strips of cloth, and his face wrapped in a cloth. Jesus said to them, "Unbind him, and let him go."

Many of the Jews therefore, who had come with Mary and had seen what Jesus did, believed in him.

The Gospel of the Lord. **Praise to you, Lord Jesus Christ.**

PROFESSION OF FAITH *(p. 11)*

PRAYER OF THE FAITHFUL

The following intentions are suggestions only. There are more suggestions at www.livingwithchrist.ca

R. **Lord, hear our prayer.**

For the Church, called to be a community of solidarity with those who are oppressed, we pray to the Lord: R.

For leaders of nations, entrusted with the task of building a just world, we pray to the Lord: R.

For our brothers and sisters in Asia, Africa and Latin America, as they teach us how we can support their efforts to improve their lives, we pray to the Lord: R.

For us, God's holy people, witnesses to the dignity and respect owed each human person, we pray to the Lord: R.

PREPARATION OF THE GIFTS *(p. 14)*

PRAYER OVER THE OFFERINGS

Hear us, almighty God, and, having instilled in your servants the teachings of the Christian faith, graciously purify them by the working of this sacrifice. Through Christ our Lord. **Amen.**

3rd Scrutiny:
Hear us, almighty God, and, having instilled in your servants the first fruits of the Christian faith, graciously purify them by the working of this sacrifice. Through Christ our Lord. **Amen.**

PREFACE *(5th Sunday of Lent, p. 22)*

COMMUNION ANTIPHON *(Cf. John 11.26)*
Everyone who lives and believes in me will not die for ever, says the Lord.

PRAYER AFTER COMMUNION
We pray, almighty God, that we may always be counted among the members of Christ, in whose Body and Blood we have communion. Who lives and reigns for ever and ever. **Amen.**
3rd Scrutiny:
May your people be at one, O Lord, we pray, and in wholehearted submission to you may they obtain this grace: that, safe from all distress, they may readily live out their joy at being saved and remember in loving prayer those to be reborn. Through Christ our Lord. **Amen.**

PRAYER OVER THE PEOPLE
Bless, O Lord, your people, who long for the gift of your mercy, and grant that what, at your prompting, they desire they may receive by your generous gift. Through Christ our Lord. **Amen.**

BLESSING AND DISMISSAL *(p. 70)*

April 9

World Day of Youth

What did Jesus cling to? Not to the fleeting glory of crowds shouting, "Hosanna!" Paul says Jesus didn't even cling to his divine position: he "did not regard equality with God as something to be exploited, but emptied himself," becoming human. He accepted the suffering and pain of human life. He lived in vulnerability, God's Suffering Servant, not hiding his face "from insult and spitting."

But he did not cling to suffering... he did not let it become the final word. Not even on the cross. He clung, instead, to his identity as God's beloved. He clung to his relationship with the Father. Even in his agony, he remembered who he was. His final, heartbroken, cry was, nonetheless, a cry of faith, a prayer from Psalm 22: "My God, my God, why have you forsaken me?" He clung to what he knew best: he was God's beloved; he trusted in God. And God did not let him down. Paul assures us, "God highly exalted him."

We need to be reminded that evil, hatred, suffering and death don't have the final word. Jesus gives us this gift. He shows us that life is stronger than death; love is stronger than hatred; faith and hope are stronger than fear and suffering. He shows us that we, too, are God's beloved. Let us cling to this love.

Dinah Simmons, Halifax, NS

Commemoration of the Lord's Entrance into Jerusalem

FIRST FORM: The Procession

INTRODUCTION

The people, carrying palm branches, gather in a suitable place distinct from the church to which the procession will move. The assembly may sing Hosanna! *or another suitable hymn.*

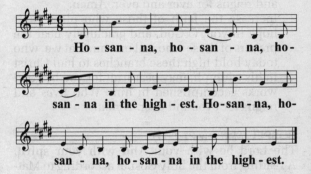

Ho - san - na, ho - san - na, ho - san - na in the high - est. Ho - san - na, ho - san - na, ho - san - na in the high - est.

© Michel Guimont

GREETING (p. 5)

Dear brothers and sisters, since the beginning of Lent until now we have prepared our hearts by penance and charitable works. Today we gather together to herald with the whole Church the beginning of the celebration of our Lord's Paschal Mystery, that is to say, of his Passion and Resurrection. For it was to accomplish this mystery that he entered his own city of Jerusalem. Therefore,

229

with all faith and devotion, let us commemorate the Lord's entry into the city for our salvation, following in his footsteps, so that, being made by his grace partakers of the Cross, we may have a share also in his Resurrection and in his life.

Let us pray.

1   Almighty ever-living God, sanctify these branches with your blessing, that we, who follow Christ the King in exultation, may reach the eternal Jerusalem through him. Who lives and reigns for ever and ever. **Amen.**

2   Increase the faith of those who place their hope in you, O God, and graciously hear the prayers of those who call on you, that we, who today hold high these branches to hail Christ in his triumph, may bear fruit for you by good works accomplished in him. Who lives and reigns for ever and ever. **Amen.**

GOSPEL *(Matthew 21.1-11)*

The Lord be with you. **And with your spirit.** A reading from the holy Gospel according to Matthew. **Glory to you, O Lord.**

When they had come near Jerusalem and had reached Bethphage, at the Mount of Olives, Jesus sent two disciples, saying to them, "Go into the village ahead of you, and immediately you will find a donkey tied, and a colt with her; untie them and bring them to me. If anyone says anything to you, just say this, 'The Lord needs them.' And he will send them immediately."

This took place to fulfill what had been spoken through the Prophet, saying, "Tell the daughter of Zion, Look, your king is coming to you, humble, and mounted on a donkey, and on a colt, the foal of a donkey."

The disciples went and did as Jesus had directed them; they brought the donkey and the colt, and put their cloaks on them, and he sat on them. A very large crowd spread their cloaks on the road, and others cut branches from the trees and spread them on the road. The crowds that went ahead of him and that followed were shouting, "Hosanna to the Son of David! Blessed is the one who comes in the name of the Lord! Hosanna in the highest heaven!"

When Jesus entered Jerusalem, the whole city was in turmoil, asking, "Who is this?" The crowds were saying, "This is the Prophet Jesus from Nazareth in Galilee."

The Gospel of the Lord. **Praise to you, Lord Jesus Christ.**

PROCESSION

1 Dear brothers and sisters, like the crowds who acclaimed Jesus in Jerusalem, let us go forth in peace.

2 Let us go forth in peace. **In the name of Christ. Amen.**

All process to the church singing a hymn in honour of Christ the King. Mass continues with the Collect *(p. 233).*

231

SECOND FORM: The Solemn Entrance

The blessing of branches and proclamation of the Gospel take place, as above, but in the church. After the Gospel, the priest moves solemnly through the church to the sanctuary, while all sing. Mass continues with the Collect *(p. 233).*

THIRD FORM: The Simple Entrance

The people gather in the church as usual. While the priest goes to the altar, the following Entrance Antiphon *or a suitable hymn is sung.*

ENTRANCE ANTIPHON

(Cf. John 12.1, 12-13; Psalm 23.9-10)

Six days before the Passover, when the Lord came into the city of Jerusalem, the children ran to meet him; in their hands they carried palm branches and with a loud voice cried out:

Hosanna in the highest!
Blessed are you, who have come
    in your abundant mercy!

O gates, lift high your heads;
grow higher, ancient doors.
Let him enter, the king of glory!
Who is this king of glory?
He, the Lord of hosts, he is the king of glory.

Hosanna in the highest!
Blessed are you, who have come
    in your abundant mercy!

INTRODUCTORY RITES *(p. 5)*

COLLECT

Almighty ever-living God, who as an example of humility for the human race to follow caused our Saviour to take flesh and submit to the Cross, graciously grant that we may heed his lesson of patient suffering and so merit a share in his Resurrection. Who lives and reigns with you in the unity of the Holy Spirit, one God, for ever and ever. **Amen.**

FIRST READING *(Isaiah 50.4-7)*

The servant of the Lord said: "The Lord God has given me the tongue of a teacher, that I may know how to sustain the weary with a word. Morning by morning he wakens — wakens my ear to listen as those who are taught. The Lord God has opened my ear, and I was not rebellious, I did not turn backward.

"I gave my back to those who struck me, and my cheeks to those who pulled out the beard; I did not hide my face from insult and spitting.

"The Lord God helps me; therefore I have not been disgraced; therefore I have set my face like flint, and I know that I shall not be put to shame."

The word of the Lord. **Thanks be to God.**

RESPONSORIAL PSALM *(Psalm 22)*

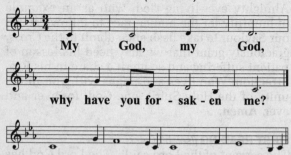

My God, my God, why have you for-sak-en me?

℟. **My God, my God, why have you forsaken me?**

All who see me · **mock_at_me;**
they make mouths at me,
    they shake · **their** heads;
"Commit your cause to the Lord;
    let him de·-**liver;**
let him rescue the one in whom
    he · **de**-lights!" ℟.

For dogs are all a·-**round_me;**
a company of evildoers · **en**-circles_me.
My hands and feet have · **shrivelled;**
I can count all · **my** bones. ℟.

They divide my clothes a·-**mong_themselves,**
and for my clothing they · **cast** lots.
But you, O Lord, do not be far a·-**way!**
O my help, come quickly · **to_my** aid! ℟.

I will tell of your name to my brothers and
   sisters; in the midst of the congregation
   I will · **praise_you:**
You who fear the · **Lord,** praise_him!
All you offspring of Jacob, · **glorify_him;**
stand in awe of him, all you offspring
   · **of** Israel! R.

To hear the Sunday Psalms, visit www.livingwithchrist.ca.

SECOND READING *(Philippians 2.6-11)*
Christ Jesus, though he was in the form of God,
did not regard equality with God as something
to be exploited, but emptied himself, taking the
form of a slave, being born in human likeness.
And being found in human form, he humbled
himself and became obedient to the point of death
— even death on a cross.

Therefore God highly exalted him and gave
him the name that is above every name, so that
at the name of Jesus every knee should bend, in
heaven and on earth and under the earth, and
every tongue should confess that Jesus Christ is
Lord, to the glory of God the Father.

The word of the Lord. **Thanks be to God.**

GOSPEL ACCLAMATION *(Philippians 2.8-9)*
Praise to you, Lord, king of eternal glory! Christ
became obedient for us to death, even death on a
Cross. Therefore God exalted him and gave him
the name above every name. **Praise to you, Lord,
king of eternal glory!**

GOSPEL *(Matthew 26.14 – 27.66)*

Several readers may proclaim the passion narrative today. N indicates the narrator, J the words of Jesus, and S the words of other speakers.

N The Passion of our Lord Jesus Christ according to Matthew.

One of the twelve, who was called Judas Iscariot, went to the chief priests and said,

S *What will you give me if I betray him to you?*

N They paid him thirty pieces of silver. And from that moment he began to look for an opportunity to betray him.

On the first day of Unleavened Bread the disciples came to Jesus, saying,

S *Where do you want us to make the preparations for you to eat the Passover?*

J **Go into the city to a certain man, and say to him, "The Teacher says, My time is near; I will keep the Passover at your house with my disciples."**

N So the disciples did as Jesus had directed them, and they prepared the Passover meal.

When it was evening, he took his place with the twelve; and while they were eating, he said,

J **Truly I tell you, one of you will betray me.**

N And they became greatly distressed and began to say to him one after another,

S *Surely not I, Lord?*

J **The one who has dipped his hand into the bowl with me will betray me. The Son of Man goes as it is written of him, but woe to that one by whom the Son of Man is betrayed! It**

N would have been better for that one not to
have been born.

N Judas, who betrayed him, said,

S *Surely not I, Rabbi?*

J You have said so.

N While they were eating, Jesus took a loaf of
bread, and after blessing it he broke it, gave it
to the disciples, and said,

J **Take, eat; this is my Body.**

N Then he took a cup, and after giving thanks he
gave it to them, saying,

J **Drink from it, all of you; for this is my Blood
of the covenant, which is poured out for
many for the forgiveness of sins. I tell you, I
will never again drink of this fruit of the vine
until that day when I drink it new with you
in my Father's kingdom.**

N When they had sung the hymn, they went
out to the Mount of Olives. Then Jesus said to
them,

J **You will all become deserters because of me
this night; for it is written, "I will strike the
shepherd, and the sheep of the flock will be
scattered." But after I am raised up, I will go
ahead of you to Galilee.**

N Peter said to him,

S *Though all become deserters because of
you, I will never desert you.*

J **Truly I tell you, this very night, before the
cock crows, you will deny me three times.**

N Peter said to him,

S *Even though I must die with you, I will not
deny you.*

N And so said all the disciples.

*At this point all may join in singing
an appropriate acclamation.*

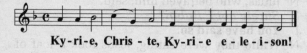

Ky - ri - e, Chris - te, Ky - ri - e e - le - i - son!

Text: Didier Rimaud, © *CNPL.* **Music:** Jacques Berthier
Source: © *Éditions Musicales Studio SM,* 060794-2

N Then Jesus went with them to a place called
Gethsemane; and he said to his disciples,

J **Sit here while I go over there and pray.**

N He took with him Peter and the two sons of
Zebedee, and began to be grieved and agitated. Then he said to them,

J **I am deeply grieved, even to death; remain
here, and stay awake with me.**

N And going a little farther, he threw himself on
the ground and prayed,

J **My Father, if it is possible, let this cup pass
from me; yet not what I want, but what you
want.**

N Then he came to the disciples and found them
sleeping; and he said to Peter,

J **So, could you not stay awake with me one
hour? Stay awake and pray that you may not
come into temptation; for the spirit indeed is
willing, but the flesh is weak.**

N Again he went away for the second time and
prayed,

J **My Father, if this cannot pass unless I drink
it, your will be done.**

N Again he came and found them sleeping, for their eyes were heavy. So leaving them again, he went away and prayed for the third time, saying the same words. Then he came to the disciples and said to them,

J **Are you still sleeping and taking your rest? See, the hour is at hand, and the Son of Man is betrayed into the hands of sinners. Get up, let us be going. See, my betrayer is at hand.**

N While he was still speaking, Judas, one of the twelve, arrived; with him was a large crowd with swords and clubs, from the chief priests and the elders of the people. Now the betrayer had given them a sign, saying,

S *The one I will kiss is the man; arrest him.*

N At once he came up to Jesus and said,

S *Greetings, Rabbi!*

N and kissed him. Jesus said to him,

J **Friend, do what you are here to do.**

N Then they came and laid hands on Jesus and arrested him.

    Suddenly, one of those with Jesus put his hand on his sword, drew it, and struck the slave of the high priest, cutting off his ear. Then Jesus said to him,

J **Put your sword back into its place; for all who take the sword will perish by the sword. Do you think that I cannot appeal to my Father, and he will at once send me more than twelve legions of Angels? But how then would the Scriptures be fulfilled, which say it must happen in this way?**

N At that hour Jesus said to the crowds,

J   **Have you come out with swords and clubs to arrest me as though I were a bandit? Day after day I sat in the temple teaching, and you did not arrest me. But all this has taken place so that the Scriptures of the Prophets may be fulfilled.**

N   Then all the disciples deserted him and fled.

Those who had arrested Jesus took him to Caiaphas the high priest, in whose house the scribes and the elders had gathered.

But Peter was following him at a distance, as far as the courtyard of the high priest; and going inside, he sat with the guards in order to see how this would end.

Now the chief priests and the whole council were looking for false testimony against Jesus so that they might put him to death, but they found none, though many false witnesses came forward. At last two came forward and said,

S   *This fellow said, "I am able to destroy the temple of God and to build it in three days."*

N   The high priest stood up and said,

S   *Have you no answer? What is it that they testify against you?*

N   But Jesus was silent.

Then the high priest said to him,

S   *I put you under oath before the living God, tell us if you are the Christ, the Son of God.*

N   Jesus said to him,

J   **You have said so. But I tell you, from now on you will see the Son of Man seated at the right hand of Power and coming on the clouds of heaven.**

N Then the high priest tore his clothes and said,

S *He has blasphemed! Why do we still need witnesses? You have now heard his blasphemy. What is your verdict?*

N They answered,

S *He deserves death.*

N Then they spat in his face and struck him; and some slapped him, saying,

S *Prophesy to us, Christ! Who is it that struck you?*

N Now Peter was sitting outside in the courtyard. A servant girl came to him and said,

S *You also were with Jesus the Galilean.*

N But he denied it before all of them, saying,

S *I do not know what you are talking about.*

N When Peter went out to the porch, another servant girl saw him, and she said to the bystanders,

S *This man was with Jesus of Nazareth.*

N Again he denied it with an oath,

S *I do not know the man.*

N After a little while the bystanders came up and said to Peter,

S *Certainly you are also one of them, for your accent betrays you.*

N Then he began to curse, and he swore an oath,

S *I do not know the man!*

N At that moment the cock crowed. Then Peter remembered what Jesus had said: "Before the cock crows, you will deny me three times." And he went out and wept bitterly.

*At this point all may join in singing
an appropriate acclamation.*

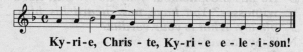

Ky - ri - e, Chris - te, Ky - ri - e e - le - i - son!

Text: Didier Rimaud, © *CNPL.* **Music:** Jacques Berthier
Source: © *Éditions Musicales Studio SM,* 060794-2

N When morning came, all the chief priests and
the elders of the people conferred together
against Jesus in order to bring about his death.
They bound him, led him away, and handed
him over to Pilate the governor.

When Judas, his betrayer, saw that Jesus
was condemned, he repented and brought
back the thirty pieces of silver to the chief
priests and the elders.

S *I have sinned by betraying innocent blood.*

N But they said,

S *What is that to us? See to it yourself.*

N Throwing down the pieces of silver in the
temple, he departed; and he went and hanged
himself.

But the chief priests, taking the pieces of
silver, said,

S *It is not lawful to put them into the treasury,
since they are blood money.*

N After conferring together, they used them to
buy the potter's field as a place to bury foreigners. For this reason that field has been
called the Field of Blood to this day. Then was
fulfilled what had been spoken through the
Prophet Jeremiah, "And they took the thirty

pieces of silver, the price of the one on whom a price had been set, on whom some of the people of Israel had set a price, and they gave them for the potter's field, as the Lord commanded me."

Now Jesus stood before the governor; and the governor asked him,

S *Are you the King of the Jews?*

J **You say so.**

N But when he was accused by the chief priests and elders, he did not answer. Then Pilate said to him,

S *Do you not hear how many accusations they make against you?*

N But Jesus gave him no answer, not even to a single charge, so that the governor was greatly amazed.

Now at the festival the governor was accustomed to release a prisoner for the crowd, anyone they wanted. At that time they had a notorious prisoner, called Barabbas. So after they had gathered, Pilate said to them,

S *Whom do you want me to release for you, Barabbas or Jesus who is called the Christ?*

N For he realized that it was out of jealousy that they had handed him over.

While he was sitting on the judgment seat, his wife sent word to him,

S *Have nothing to do with that innocent man, for today I have suffered a great deal because of a dream about him.*

N Now the chief priests and the elders persuaded the crowds to ask for Barabbas and to have Jesus killed. The governor again said to them,

S *Which of the two do you want me to release for you?*

N And they said,

S *Barabbas.*

N Pilate said to them,

S *Then what should I do with Jesus who is called the Christ?*

N All of them said,

S *Let him be crucified!*

N Then he asked,

S *Why, what evil has he done?*

N But they shouted all the more,

S *Let him be crucified!*

N So when Pilate saw that he could do nothing, but rather that a riot was beginning, he took some water and washed his hands before the crowd, saying,

S *I am innocent of this man's blood; see to it yourselves.*

N Then the people as a whole answered,

S *"His blood be on us and on our children!"*

N So he released Barabbas for them; and after flogging Jesus, he handed him over to be crucified.

Then the soldiers of the governor took Jesus into the governor's headquarters, and they gathered the whole cohort around him. They stripped him and put a scarlet robe on him, and after twisting some thorns into a crown, they put it on his head. They put a reed in his right hand and knelt before him and mocked him, saying,

S *Hail, King of the Jews!*

N They spat on him, and took the reed and struck him on the head. After mocking him, they stripped him of the robe and put his own clothes on him. Then they led him away to crucify him.

As they went out, they came upon a man from Cyrene named Simon; they compelled this man to carry his Cross.

At this point all may join in singing an appropriate acclamation.

Ky - ri - e, Chris - te, Ky - ri - e e - le - i - son!

Text: Didier Rimaud, © *CNPL*. **Music:** Jacques Berthier
Source: © *Éditions Musicales Studio SM*, 060794-2

N   And when they came to a place called Golgotha which means Place of a Skull, they offered him wine to drink, mixed with gall; but when he tasted it, he would not drink it.

And when they had crucified him, they divided his clothes among themselves by casting lots; then they sat down there and kept watch over him.

Over his head they put the charge against him, which read, "This is Jesus, the King of the Jews."

Then two bandits were crucified with him, one on his right and one on his left. Those who passed by derided him, shaking their heads and saying,

S   *You who would destroy the temple and build it in three days, save yourself! If you are the Son of God, come down from the Cross.*

N   In the same way the chief priests also, along with the scribes and elders, were mocking him, saying,

S   *He saved others; he cannot save himself. He is the King of Israel; let him come down from the Cross now, and we will believe in him. He trusts in God; let God deliver him now, if he wants to; for he said, "I am God's Son."*

N   The bandits who were crucified with him also taunted him in the same way.

   From noon on, darkness came over the whole land until three in the afternoon. And about three o'clock Jesus cried with a loud voice,

J   **Eli, Eli, lema sabachthani?**

N   that is, "My God, my God, why have you forsaken me?" When some of the bystanders heard it, they said,

S   *This man is calling for Elijah.*

N   At once one of them ran and got a sponge, filled it with sour wine, put it on a stick, and gave it to him to drink. But the others said,

S   *Wait, let us see whether Elijah will come to save him.*

N   Then Jesus cried again with a loud voice and breathed his last.

Here all kneel and pause for a short time.

N   At that moment the curtain of the temple was torn in two, from top to bottom. The earth shook, and the rocks were split. The tombs also were opened, and many bodies of the saints who had fallen asleep were raised.

After his resurrection they came out of the tombs and entered the holy city and appeared to many.

Now when the centurion and those with him, who were keeping watch over Jesus, saw the earthquake and what took place, they were terrified and said,

S *Truly this man was God's Son!*

N Many women were also there, looking on from a distance; they had followed Jesus from Galilee and had provided for him. Among them were Mary Magdalene, and Mary the mother of James and Joseph, and the mother of the sons of Zebedee.

When it was evening, there came a rich man from Arimathea, named Joseph, who was also a disciple of Jesus. He went to Pilate and asked for the body of Jesus; then Pilate ordered it to be given to him. So Joseph took the body and wrapped it in a clean linen cloth and laid it in his own new tomb, which he had hewn in the rock. He then rolled a great stone to the door of the tomb and went away.

Mary Magdalene and the other Mary were there, sitting opposite the tomb. The next day, that is, after the day of Preparation, the chief priests and the Pharisees gathered before Pilate and said,

S *Sir, we remember what that impostor said while he was still alive, "After three days I will rise again." Therefore command the tomb to be made secure until the third day; otherwise his disciples may go and steal him away, and tell the people, "He has been*

N   *raised from the dead," and the last decep-*
     tion would be worse than the first.

N   Pilate said to them,

S   *You have a guard of soldiers; go, make it as*
     secure as you can.

N   So they went with the guard and made the
     tomb secure by sealing the stone.

The readers return to their places in silence.

PROFESSION OF FAITH *(p. 11)*

PRAYER OF THE FAITHFUL

*The following intentions are suggestions only. There are
more suggestions at www.livingwithchrist.ca*

R. **Lord, hear our prayer.**

For the Church, community of the crucified
Christ, manifesting solidarity with the poor and
oppressed, we pray to the Lord: R.

For leaders of peoples and nations, struggling to
implement policies that promote development,
justice and peace, we pray to the Lord: R.

For those whom we, as a Church or a society, have
rejected, we pray to the Lord: R.

For us, God's people, striving to see the world
through the eyes of the crucified Christ, we pray
to the Lord: R.

PREPARATION OF THE GIFTS *(p. 14)*

PRAYER OVER THE OFFERINGS
Through the Passion of your Only Begotten Son,
O Lord, may our reconciliation with you be near
at hand, so that, though we do not merit it by our
own deeds, yet by this sacrifice made once for
all, we may feel already the effects of your mercy.
Through Christ our Lord. **Amen.**

PREFACE *(Passion Sunday, p. 22)*

COMMUNION ANTIPHON *(Matthew 26.42)*
**Father, if this chalice cannot pass without my
drinking it, your will be done.**

PRAYER AFTER COMMUNION
Nourished with these sacred gifts, we humbly
beseech you, O Lord, that, just as through the
death of your Son you have brought us to hope
for what we believe, so by his Resurrection you
may lead us to where you call. Through Christ
our Lord. **Amen.**

PRAYER OVER THE PEOPLE
Look, we pray, O Lord, on this your family, for
whom our Lord Jesus Christ did not hesitate to
be delivered into the hands of the wicked and
submit to the agony of the Cross. Who lives and
reigns for ever and ever. **Amen.**

SOLEMN BLESSING — PASSION OF THE LORD
(Optional)
Bow down for the blessing.
    May God, the Father of mercies, who has given
you an example of love in the Passion of his Only

Begotten Son, grant that, by serving God and your neighbour, you may lay hold of the wondrous gift of his blessing. **Amen.**

So that you may receive the reward of everlasting life from him, through whose earthly Death you believe that you escape eternal death. **Amen.**

And by following the example of his self-abasement, may you possess a share in his Resurrection. **Amen.**

And may the blessing of almighty God, the Father, and the Son, and the Holy Spirit, come down on you and remain with you for ever. **Amen.**

DISMISSAL *(p. 70)*

April 13
Mass of the Lord's Supper

There is a perfect little full circle knit into today's gospel. Jesus knew "that he had come from God and was going to God." Completion was nearing for Jesus at the Last Supper, and with it fulfillment of the Scriptures and of his human life. This perfect circle is there for each of us, at every ordinary moment. We came from God; we are headed for God. This is no ordinary fact but an astounding mystery, a truth that undergirds our lives and majestically eclipses them at the same time. How are we to respond? How do we respond to the gift of life and our ultimate homecoming?

Jesus shows us how to respond. In the same sentence, Jesus "took off his outer robe, and tied a towel around himself." There's a gentleness in this sacrifice and the foot-washing gesture is confounding to his companions. Jesus' response to the gift of life is to serve.

Paul writes that Jesus said of the bread, "This is my body that is for you." This is Jesus' response and he teaches us so that it can be ours: be *for* one another. Your life is a gift and the only appropriate response is to give. The message of the Last Supper, and of every eucharistic celebration, is tender and insistent: be for one another and for the whole world.

Kate McGee, Toronto, ON

ENTRANCE ANTIPHON *(Cf. Galatians 6.14)*
We should glory in the Cross of our Lord Jesus Christ, in whom is our salvation, life and resurrection, through whom we are saved and delivered.

INTRODUCTORY RITES *(p. 5)*

COLLECT
O God, who have called us to participate in this most sacred Supper, in which your Only Begotten Son, when about to hand himself over to death, entrusted to the Church a sacrifice new for all eternity, the banquet of his love, grant, we pray, that we may draw from so great a mystery, the fullness of charity and of life. Through our Lord Jesus Christ, your Son, who lives and reigns with you in the unity of the Holy Spirit, one God, for ever and ever. **Amen.**

FIRST READING *(Exodus 12.1-8, 11-14)*
The Lord said to Moses and Aaron in the land of Egypt: This month shall mark for you the beginning of months; it shall be the first month of the year for you. Tell the whole congregation of Israel that on the tenth of this month they are to take a lamb for each family, a lamb for each household. If a household is too small for a whole lamb, it shall join its closest neighbour in obtaining one; the lamb shall be divided in proportion to the number of people who eat of it.

Your lamb shall be without blemish, a year-old male; you may take it from the sheep or from the goats. You shall keep it until the fourteenth day of this month; then the whole assembled congregation of Israel shall slaughter it at twilight. They shall take some of the blood and put it on the two doorposts and the lintel of the houses in which they eat it. They shall eat the lamb that same night; they shall eat it roasted over the fire with unleavened bread and bitter herbs.

This is how you shall eat it: your loins girded, your sandals on your feet, and your staff in your hand; and you shall eat it hurriedly. It is the Passover of the Lord. For I will pass through the land of Egypt that night, and I will strike down every firstborn in the land of Egypt, both human beings and animals; on all the gods of Egypt I will execute judgments: I am the Lord.

The blood shall be a sign for you on the houses where you live: when I see the blood, I will pass over you, and no plague shall destroy you when I strike the land of Egypt.

This day shall be a day of remembrance for you. You shall celebrate it as a festival to the Lord; throughout your generations you shall observe it as a perpetual ordinance.

The word of the Lord. **Thanks be to God.**

RESPONSORIAL PSALM *(Psalm 116)*

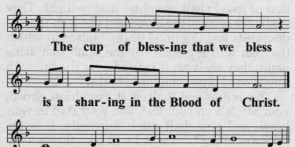

The cup of bless-ing that we bless

is a shar-ing in the Blood of Christ.

R. **The cup of blessing that we bless
is a sharing in the Blood of Christ.**

What shall I return to the · **Lord**
for all his bounty to · **me?**
I will lift up the cup of sal--**vation**
and call on the name · **of_the** Lord. R.

Precious in the sight of the · **Lord**
is the death of his · **faithful_ones.**
I am your servant, the son
of your · **serving_girl.**
You have loosed · **my** bonds. R.

I will offer to you a thanksgiving · **sacrifice**
and call on the name of the · **Lord.**
I will pay my vows to the · **Lord**
in the presence of all · **his** people. R.

©2009 Gordon Johnston/Novalis
To hear the Sunday Psalms, visit www.livingwithchrist.ca.

SECOND READING *(1 Corinthians 11.23-26)*
Brothers and sisters: I received from the Lord what I also handed on to you, that the Lord Jesus on the night when he was betrayed took a loaf of bread, and when he had given thanks, he broke it and said, "This is my Body that is for you. Do this in remembrance of me."

In the same way he took the cup also, after supper, saying, "This cup is the new covenant in my Blood. Do this, as often as you drink it, in remembrance of me." For as often as you eat this bread and drink the cup, you proclaim the Lord's death until he comes.

The word of the Lord. **Thanks be to God.**

GOSPEL ACCLAMATION *(John 13.34)*
Praise to you, Lord, king of eternal glory! I give you a new commandment: love one another as I have loved you. **Praise to you, Lord, king of eternal glory!**

GOSPEL *(John 13.1-15)*
The Lord be with you. **And with your spirit.**
A reading from the holy Gospel according to John.
Glory to you, O Lord.

Before the festival of the Passover, Jesus knew that his hour had come to depart from this world and go to the Father. Having loved his own who were in the world, he loved them to the end.

The devil had already put it into the heart of Judas, son of Simon Iscariot, to betray him. And during supper Jesus, knowing that the Father had given all things into his hands, and that he had come from God and was going to God, got up from the table, took off his outer robe, and tied a towel around himself. Then he poured water into a basin and began to wash the disciples' feet and to wipe them with the towel that was tied around him.

He came to Simon Peter, who said to him, "Lord, are you going to wash my feet?" Jesus answered, "You do not know now what I am doing, but later you will understand." Peter said to him, "You will never wash my feet." Jesus answered, "Unless I wash you, you have no share with me." Simon Peter said to him, "Lord, not my feet only but also my hands and my head!" Jesus said to him, "One who has bathed does not need to wash, except for the feet, but is entirely clean. And you are clean, though not all of you." For he knew who was to betray him; for this reason he said, "Not all of you are clean."

After he had washed their feet, put on his robe, and returned to the table, Jesus said to them, "Do you know what I have done to you? You call me Teacher and Lord — and you are right, for that is what I am. So if I, your Lord and Teacher, have washed your feet, you also ought to wash one another's feet. For I have set you an example, that you also should do as I have done to you."

The Gospel of the Lord. **Praise to you, Lord Jesus Christ.**

The Profession of Faith *is omitted.*

THE WASHING OF FEET (Optional)
During the washing of feet, an appropriate song may be sung.

PRAYER OF THE FAITHFUL

The following intentions are suggestions only. There are more suggestions at www.livingwithchrist.ca

R. **Lord, hear our prayer.**

For the Church, witness to true love and service in Christ, we pray to the Lord: R.

For world leaders, trusted by their people to promote justice and human dignity through true service, we pray to the Lord: R.

For all who suffer from our greed and selfishness, we pray to the Lord: R.

For us, the Body of Christ, called to pour out our lives for others as Jesus did for us, we pray to the Lord: R.

PREPARATION OF THE GIFTS *(p. 14)*

PRAYER OVER THE OFFERINGS

Grant us, O Lord, we pray, that we may participate worthily in these mysteries, for whenever the memorial of this sacrifice is celebrated, the work of our redemption is accomplished. Through Christ our Lord. **Amen.**

PREFACE *(Holy Eucharist I, p. 27)*

COMMUNION ANTIPHON *(1 Corinthians 11.24-25)*
This is the Body that will be given up for you; this is the Chalice of the new covenant in my Blood, says the Lord; do this, whenever you receive it, in memory of me.

PRAYER AFTER COMMUNION

Grant, almighty God, that, just as we are renewed
by the Supper of your Son in this present age, so
we may enjoy his banquet for all eternity. Who
lives and reigns for ever and ever. **Amen.**

The Blessing and Dismissal are omitted tonight.

TRANSFER OF THE HOLY EUCHARIST

*The Blessed Sacrament is carried through the church to the
place of repose. During the procession, the hymn* Pange
Lingua *(p. 259, stanzas 1-4) or another eucharistic song
is sung. At the place of repose, the presider incenses the
Blessed Sacrament, while* Tantum ergo Sacramentum *(Pange
Lingua, stanzas 5-6) or another eucharistic song is sung.
The tabernacle of repose is then closed.*

*After a period of silent adoration, the priests and ministers
of the altar retire. The faithful are encouraged to continue
adoration before the Blessed Sacrament for a suitable period
of time. There should be no solemn adoration after midnight.*

HAIL OUR SAVIOUR'S GLORIOUS BODY
(Pange Lingua)

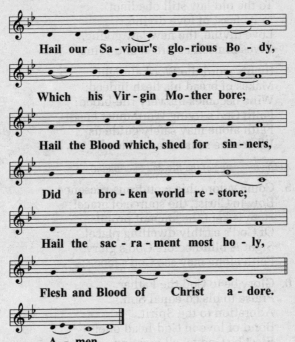

Hail our Saviour's glorious Body,
Which his Virgin Mother bore;
Hail the Blood which, shed for sinners,
Did a broken world restore;
Hail the sacrament most holy,
Flesh and Blood of Christ adore.

A - men.

2. To the Virgin, for our healing,
   His own Son the Father sends;
   From the Father's love proceeding
   Sower, seed and word descends;
   Wondrous life of Word incarnate
   With his greatest wonder ends.

3. On that paschal evening see him
   With the chosen twelve recline,
   To the old law still obedient
   In its feast of love divine;
   Love divine, the new law giving,
   Gives himself as Bread and Wine.

4. By his word the Word almighty
   Makes of bread his flesh indeed;
   Wine becomes his very life-blood;
   Faith God's living Word must heed!
   Faith alone may safely guide us
   Where the senses cannot lead!

At the incensing of the Blessed Sacrament:

5. Come, adore this wondrous presence;
   Bow to Christ, the source of grace!
   Here is kept the ancient promise
   Of God's earthly dwelling place!
   Sight is blind before God's glory,
   Faith alone may see God's face.

6. Glory be to God the Father,
   Praise to his co-equal Son,
   Adoration to the Spirit,
   Bond of love in God-head one!
   Blest be God by all creation
   Joyously while ages run! Amen.

Text: *Pange Lingua,* Thomas Aquinas, 1227-74; tr. James Quinn, SJ (1919-2010). Used by permission of Oregon Catholic Press. **Tune:** PANGE LINGUA, 87.87.87. **Music:** CBW II 583; CBW III 381

April 14
Celebration of the Passion of the Lord

Today we are called to walk a hard road with Jesus. The worst of Jesus' suffering may not be the physical torture he endures but his knowledge that he is abandoned by many of his closest friends. Like Jesus, most of the hurts in our lives are experienced through our relationships, often with those we love the most.

As we listen to the Passion story today, let us try to move beyond the witnessing of an historic moment and seek a change of heart. During Jesus' life he loved those who were different. In his death he forgave those who persecuted and abandoned him. As we stand at the foot of the cross today, let us imagine looking up into his eyes and asking him, "How can I love more? How can I be more merciful and less judgmental?" If we are honest, we might not want to hear what Jesus tells us! What we hear will likely be very hard to do. We will certainly fail in our best attempts.

Naked and vulnerable on the cross, Jesus is not judging us for not loving well. He wants us to know that loving is often hard and demands our full attention. He wants us to be certain that forgiveness is indispensable when we are in relationship — and to believe that love and mercy lead to resurrection.

Joseph Vorstermans, Toronto, ON

National Collection for the Church in the Holy Land

PRAYER

1 Remember your mercies, O Lord, and with your eternal protection sanctify your servants, for whom Christ your Son, by the shedding of his Blood, established the Paschal Mystery. Who lives and reigns for ever and ever. **Amen.**

2 O God, who by the Passion of Christ your Son, our Lord, abolished the death inherited from ancient sin by every succeeding generation, grant that just as, being conformed to him, we have borne by the law of nature the image of the man of earth, so by the sanctification of grace we may bear the image of the Man of heaven. Through Christ our Lord. **Amen.**

LITURGY OF THE WORD

FIRST READING *(Isaiah 52.13 – 53.12)*

See, my servant shall prosper; he shall be exalted and lifted up, and shall be very high.

Just as there were many who were astonished at him — so marred was his appearance, beyond human semblance, and his form beyond that of the sons of man — so he shall startle many nations; kings shall shut their mouths because of him; for that which had not been told them they shall see, and that which they had not heard they shall contemplate. Who has believed what we have heard? And to whom has the arm of the Lord been revealed?

For he grew up before the Lord like a young plant, and like a root out of dry ground; he had no form or majesty that we should look at him, nothing in his appearance that we should desire him. He was despised and rejected by men; a man of suffering and acquainted with infirmity; and as one from whom others hide their faces he was despised, and we held him of no account.

Surely he has borne our infirmities and carried our diseases; yet we accounted him stricken, struck down by God, and afflicted. But he was wounded for our transgressions, crushed for our iniquities; upon him was the punishment that made us whole, and by his bruises we are healed.

All we like sheep have gone astray; each has turned to their own way and the Lord has laid on him the iniquity of us all.

He was oppressed, and he was afflicted, yet he did not open his mouth; like a lamb that is led to the slaughter, and like a sheep that before its shearers is silent, so he did not open his mouth.

By a perversion of justice he was taken away. Who could have imagined his future? For he was cut off from the land of the living, stricken for the transgression of my people. They made his grave with the wicked and his tomb with the rich, although he had done no violence, and there was no deceit in his mouth.

Yet it was the will of the Lord to crush him with pain. When you make his life an offering for sin, he shall see his offspring, and shall prolong his days; through him the will of the Lord shall prosper. Out of his anguish he shall see light; he shall find satisfaction through his knowledge. The righteous one, my servant, shall make many righteous, and he shall bear their iniquities.

Therefore I will allot him a portion with the great, and he shall divide the spoil with the strong; because he poured out himself to death, and was numbered with the transgressors; yet he bore the sin of many, and made intercession for the transgressors.

The word of the Lord. **Thanks be to God.**

RESPONSORIAL PSALM *(Psalm 31)*

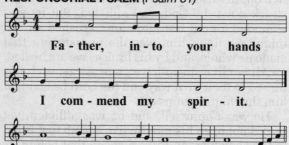

Fa - ther, in - to your hands I com - mend my spir - it.

R. **Father, into your hands I commend my spirit.**

In you, O Lord, I seek refuge;
  do not let me ever be put · **to** shame;
in your righteousness · **de-**liver_me.
Into your hand I commit · **my** spirit;
  you have redeemed me,
    O Lord, · **faith-**ful God. R.

I am the scorn of all my adversaries,
  a horror to my neighbours,
    an object of dread to my · **ac-**quaintances.
Those who see me in the · **street** flee_from_me.
I have passed out of mind like one
  who · **is** dead;
I have become like a · **bro-**ken vessel. R.

But I trust in you, · **O** Lord;
I say, "You are · **my** God."
My times are in · **your** hand;
deliver me from the hand
    of my · **enemies** and persecutors. ℟

Let your face shine upon · **your** servant;
save me in your stead-**fast** love.
Be strong, and let your heart · **take** courage,
all you who wait · **for** the Lord. ℟

©2009 Gordon Johnston/Novalis
To hear the Sunday Psalms, visit www.livingwithchrist.ca.

SECOND READING *(Hebrews 4.14-16; 5.7-9)*
Brothers and sisters: Since we have a great high priest who has passed through the heavens, Jesus, the Son of God, let us hold fast to our confession. For we do not have a high priest who is unable to sympathize with our weaknesses, but we have one who in every respect has been tested as we are, yet without sin. Let us therefore approach the throne of grace with boldness, so that we may receive mercy and find grace to help in time of need.

In the days of his flesh, Jesus offered up prayers and supplications, with loud cries and tears, to the one who was able to save him from death, and he was heard because of his reverent submission. Although he was a Son, he learned obedience through what he suffered; and having been made perfect, he became the source of eternal salvation for all who obey him.

The word of the Lord. **Thanks be to God.**

GOSPEL ACCLAMATION *(Philippians 2.8-9)*

Praise to you, Lord, king of eternal glory! Christ became obedient for us to death, even death on a Cross. Therefore God exalted him and gave him the name above every name. **Praise to you, Lord, king of eternal glory!**

GOSPEL *(John 18.1 – 19.42)*

Several readers may proclaim the passion narrative today. N indicates the narrator, J the words of Jesus, and S the words of other speakers.

N The Passion of our Lord Jesus Christ according to John.

After they had eaten the supper, Jesus went out with his disciples across the Kidron valley to a place where there was a garden, which he and his disciples entered. Now Judas, who betrayed him, also knew the place, because Jesus often met there with his disciples. So Judas brought a detachment of soldiers together with police from the chief priests and the Pharisees, and they came there with lanterns and torches and weapons.

Then Jesus, knowing all that was to happen to him, came forward and asked them,

J **Whom are you looking for?**

N They answered,

S *Jesus of Nazareth.*

J **I am he.**

N Judas, who betrayed him, was standing with them. When Jesus said to them, "I am he," they stepped back and fell to the ground. Again he asked them,

J **Whom are you looking for?**

S *Jesus of Nazareth.*

J **I told you that I am he. So if you are looking for me, let these men go.**

N This was to fulfill the word that he had spoken, "I did not lose a single one of those whom you gave me."

Then Simon Peter, who had a sword, drew it, struck the high priest's slave, and cut off his right ear. The slave's name was Malchus. Jesus said to Peter,

J **Put your sword back into its sheath. Am I not to drink the cup that the Father has given me?**

N So the soldiers, their officer, and the Jewish police arrested Jesus and bound him. First they took him to Annas, who was the father-in-law of Caiaphas, the high priest that year. Caiaphas was the one who had advised the Jews that it was better to have one person die for the people.

Simon Peter and another disciple followed Jesus. Since that disciple was known to the high priest, he went with Jesus into the court-yard of the high priest, but Peter was standing outside at the gate. So the other disciple, who was known to the high priest, went out, spoke to the woman who guarded the gate, and brought Peter in. The woman said to Peter,

S *You are not also one of this man's disciples, are you?*

N Peter said,

S *I am not.*

N Now the slaves and the police had made a charcoal fire because it was cold, and they were standing around it and warming themselves. Peter also was standing with them and warming himself.

Then the high priest questioned Jesus about his disciples and about his teaching. Jesus answered,

J **I have spoken openly to the world; I have always taught in synagogues and in the temple, where all the Jews come together. I have said nothing in secret. Why do you ask me? Ask those who heard what I said to them; they know what I said.**

N When he had said this, one of the police standing nearby struck Jesus on the face, saying,

S *Is that how you answer the high priest?*

J **If I have spoken wrongly, testify to the wrong. But if I have spoken rightly, why do you strike me?**

N Then Annas sent him bound to Caiaphas the high priest.

Now Simon Peter was standing and warming himself. They asked him,

S *You are not also one of his disciples, are you?*

N He denied it and said,

S *I am not.*

N One of the slaves of the high priest, a relative of the man whose ear Peter had cut off, asked,

S *Did I not see you in the garden with him?*

N Again Peter denied it, and at that moment the cock crowed.

At this point all may join in singing
an appropriate acclamation.

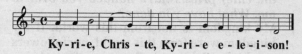

Ky - ri - e, Chris - te, Ky - ri - e e - le - i - son!

Text: Didier Rimaud, © *CNPL.* **Music:** Jacques Berthier
Source: © *Éditions Musicales Studio SM,* 060794-2

N Then they took Jesus from Caiaphas to Pilate's headquarters. It was early in the morning. They themselves did not enter the headquarters, so as to avoid ritual defilement and to be able to eat the Passover. So Pilate went out to them and said,

S *What accusation do you bring against this man?*

N They answered,

S *If this man were not a criminal, we would not have handed him over to you.*

N Pilate said to them,

S *Take him yourselves and judge him according to your law.*

N They replied,

S *We are not permitted to put anyone to death.*

N This was to fulfill what Jesus had said when he indicated the kind of death he was to die. Then Pilate entered the headquarters again, summoned Jesus, and asked him,

S *Are you the King of the Jews?*

J **Do you ask this on your own, or did others tell you about me?**

269

S *I am not a Jew, am I? Your own nation and the chief priests have handed you over to me. What have you done?*

J My kingdom is not from this world. If my kingdom were from this world, my followers would be fighting to keep me from being handed over to the Jews. But as it is, my kingdom is not from here.

S *So you are a king?*

J You say that I am a king. For this I was born, and for this I came into the world, to testify to the truth. Everyone who belongs to the truth listens to my voice.

S *What is truth?*

N After he had said this, Pilate went out to the Jews again and told them,

S *I find no case against him. But you have a custom that I release someone for you at the Passover. Do you want me to release for you the King of the Jews?*

N They shouted in reply,

S *Not this man, but Barabbas!*

N Now Barabbas was a bandit. Then Pilate took Jesus and had him flogged. And the soldiers wove a crown of thorns and put it on his head, and they dressed him in a purple robe. They kept coming up to him, saying,

S *"Hail, King of the Jews!"*

N and they struck him on the face. Pilate went out again and said to them,

S *Look, I am bringing him out to you to let you know that I find no case against him.*

N So Jesus came out, wearing the crown of thorns and the purple robe. Pilate said to them,

S *Here is the man!*

N When the chief priests and the police saw him, they shouted,

S *Crucify him! Crucify him!*

N Pilate said to them,

S *Take him yourselves and crucify him; I find no case against him.*

N They answered him,

S *We have a law, and according to that law he ought to die because he has claimed to be the Son of God.*

N Now when Pilate heard this, he was more afraid than ever. He entered his headquarters again and asked Jesus,

S *Where are you from?*

N But Jesus gave him no answer. Pilate therefore said to him,

S *Do you refuse to speak to me? Do you not know that I have power to release you, and power to crucify you?*

J **You would have no power over me unless it had been given you from above; therefore the one who handed me over to you is guilty of a greater sin.**

N From then on Pilate tried to release him, but the Jews cried out,

S *If you release this man, you are no friend of the emperor. Everyone who claims to be a king sets himself against the emperor.*

N When Pilate heard these words, he brought Jesus outside and sat on the judge's bench at a place called "The Stone Pavement," or in Hebrew "Gabbatha."

Now it was the day of Preparation for the Passover; and it was about noon. Pilate said to the Jews,

S *Here is your King!*

N They cried out,

S *Away with him! Away with him! Crucify him!*

N Pilate asked them,

S *Shall I crucify your King?*

N The chief priests answered,

S *We have no king but the emperor.*

At this point all may join in singing an appropriate acclamation.

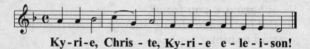

Ky - ri - e, Chris - te, Ky - ri - e e - le - i - son!

Text: Didier Rimaud, © *CNPL*. **Music:** Jacques Berthier
Source: © *Éditions Musicales Studio SM,* 060794-2

N Then Pilate handed Jesus over to them to be crucified. So they took Jesus; and carrying the Cross by himself, he went out to what is called The Place of the Skull, which in Hebrew is called Golgotha. There they crucified him, and with him two others, one on either side, with Jesus between them.

Pilate also had an inscription written and put on the Cross. It read, "Jesus of Nazareth, the King of the Jews." Many of the people read this inscription, because the place where Jesus was crucified was near the city; and it was written in Hebrew, in Latin, and in

Greek. Then the chief priests of the Jews said to Pilate,

S *Do not write, "The King of the Jews," but, "This man said, I am King of the Jews."*

N Pilate answered,

S *What I have written I have written.*

N When the soldiers had crucified Jesus, they took his clothes and divided them into four parts, one for each soldier. They also took his tunic; now the tunic was seamless, woven in one piece from the top. So they said to one another,

S *Let us not tear it, but cast lots for it to see who will get it.*

N This was to fulfill what the Scripture says, "They divided my clothes among themselves, and for my clothing they cast lots." And that is what the soldiers did.

Meanwhile, standing near the Cross of Jesus were his mother, and his mother's sister, Mary the wife of Clopas, and Mary Magdalene. When Jesus saw his mother and the disciple whom he loved standing beside her, he said to his mother,

J **Woman, here is your son.**

N Then he said to the disciple,

J **Here is your mother.**

N And from that hour the disciple took her into his own home.

After this, when Jesus knew that all was now finished, in order to fulfill the Scripture, he said,

J **I am thirsty.**

N A jar full of sour wine was standing there. So they put a sponge full of the wine on a branch of hyssop and held it to his mouth.

When Jesus had received the wine, he said,

J **It is finished.**

N Then he bowed his head and gave up his spirit.

Here all kneel and pause for a short time.

N Since it was the day of Preparation, the Jews did not want the bodies left on the cross during the Sabbath, especially because that Sabbath was a day of great Solemnity. So they asked Pilate to have the legs of the crucified men broken and the bodies removed. Then the soldiers came and broke the legs of the first and of the other who had been crucified with him. But when they came to Jesus and saw that he was already dead, they did not break his legs. Instead, one of the soldiers pierced his side with a spear, and at once blood and water came out.

(He who saw this has testified so that you also may believe. His testimony is true, and he knows that he tells the truth.) These things occurred so that the Scripture might be fulfilled, "None of his bones shall be broken." And again another passage of Scripture says, "They will look on the one whom they have pierced."

After these things, Joseph of Arimathea, who was a disciple of Jesus, though a secret one because of his fear of the Jews, asked Pilate to let him take away the body of Jesus. Pilate gave him permission; so he came and removed his body.

Nicodemus, who had at first come to Jesus by night, also came, bringing a mixture of myrrh and aloes, weighing about a hundredweight. They took the body of Jesus and wrapped it with the spices in linen cloths, according to the burial custom of the Jews. Now there was a garden in the place where he was crucified, and in the garden there was a new tomb in which no one had ever been laid. And so, because it was the Jewish day of Preparation, and the tomb was nearby, they laid Jesus there.

The readers return to their places in silence.

THE SOLEMN INTERCESSIONS

For Holy Church

Let us pray, dearly beloved, for the holy Church of God, that our God and Lord be pleased to give her peace, to guard her and to unite her throughout the whole world and grant that, leading our life in tranquillity and quiet, we may glorify God the Father almighty. *(Pause)*

Almighty ever-living God, who in Christ revealed your glory to all the nations, watch over the works of your mercy, that your Church, spread throughout all the world, may persevere with steadfast faith in confessing your name. Through Christ our Lord. **Amen.**

For the Pope

Let us pray also for our most Holy Father Pope N., that our God and Lord, who chose him for the Order of Bishops, may keep him safe and unharmed for the Lord's holy Church, to govern the holy People of God. *(Pause)*

Almighty ever-living God, by whose decree all things are founded, look with favour on our prayers and in your kindness protect the Pope chosen for us, that, under him, the Christian people, governed by you their maker, may grow in merit by reason of their faith. Through Christ our Lord. **Amen.**

For all orders and degrees of the faithful
Let us pray also for our Bishop N., for all Bishops, Priests, and Deacons of the Church and for the whole of the faithful people. *(Pause)*

Almighty ever-living God, by whose Spirit the whole body of the Church is sanctified and governed, hear our humble prayer for your ministers, that, by the gift of your grace, all may serve you faithfully. Through Christ our Lord. **Amen.**

For catechumens
Let us pray also for (our) catechumens, that our God and Lord may open wide the ears of their inmost hearts and unlock the gates of his mercy, that, having received forgiveness of all their sins through the waters of rebirth, they, too, may be one with Christ Jesus our Lord. *(Pause)*

Almighty ever-living God, who make your Church ever fruitful with new offspring, increase the faith and understanding of (our) catechumens, that, reborn in the font of Baptism, they may be added to the number of your adopted children. Through Christ our Lord. **Amen.**

For the unity of Christians
Let us pray also for all our brothers and sisters who believe in Christ, that our God and Lord may

be pleased, as they live the truth, to gather them together and keep them in his one Church. *(Pause)*

Almighty ever-living God, who gather what is scattered and keep together what you have gathered, look kindly on the flock of your Son, that those whom one Baptism has consecrated may be joined together by integrity of faith and united in the bond of charity. Through Christ our Lord. **Amen.**

For the Jewish people
Let us pray also for the Jewish people, to whom the Lord our God spoke first, that he may grant them to advance in love of his name and in faithfulness to his covenant. *(Pause)*

Almighty ever-living God, who bestowed your promises on Abraham and his descendants, graciously hear the prayers of your Church, that the people you first made your own may attain the fullness of redemption. Through Christ our Lord. **Amen.**

For those who do not believe in Christ
Let us pray also for those who do not believe in Christ, that, enlightened by the Holy Spirit, they, too, may enter on the way of salvation. *(Pause)*

Almighty ever-living God, grant to those who do not confess Christ that, by walking before you with a sincere heart, they may find the truth and that we ourselves, being constant in mutual love and striving to understand more fully the mystery of your life, may be made more perfect witnesses to your love in the world. Through Christ our Lord. **Amen.**

277

For those who do not believe in God
Let us pray also for those who do not acknowledge God, that, following what is right in sincerity of heart, they may find the way to God himself. *(Pause)*

Almighty ever-living God, who created all people to seek you always by desiring you and, by finding you, come to rest, grant, we pray, that, despite every harmful obstacle, all may recognize the signs of your fatherly love and the witness of the good works done by those who believe in you, and so in gladness confess you, the one true God and Father of our human race. Through Christ our Lord. **Amen.**

For those in public office
Let us pray also for those in public office, that our God and Lord may direct their minds and hearts according to his will for the true peace and freedom of all. *(Pause)*

Almighty ever-living God, in whose hand lies every human heart and the rights of peoples, look with favour, we pray, on those who govern with authority over us, that throughout the whole world, the prosperity of peoples, the assurance of peace, and freedom of religion may through your gift be made secure. Through Christ our Lord. **Amen.**

For those in tribulation
Let us pray, dearly beloved, to God the Father almighty, that he may cleanse the world of all errors, banish disease, drive out hunger, unlock prisons, loosen fetters, granting to travellers safety, to pilgrims return, health to the sick, and salvation to the dying. *(Pause)*

Almighty ever-living God, comfort of mourners, strength of all who toil, may the prayers of those who cry out in any tribulation come before you, that all may rejoice, because in their hour of need your mercy was at hand. Through Christ our Lord. **Amen.**

ADORATION OF THE HOLY CROSS

Three times the priest or deacon invites the assembly to proclaim its faith:

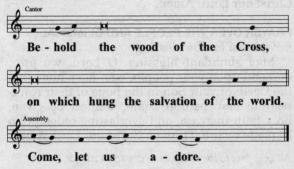

Behold the wood of the Cross, on which hung the salvation of the world. **Come, let us adore.**

After each response all adore the Cross briefly in silence. After the third response, the Cross and the candles are placed at the entrance to the sanctuary and the people approach, moving as in procession, to adore the Cross. They may make a simple genuflection or perform some other appropriate sign of reverence according to local custom.

During the adoration, suitable songs may be sung. All who have already adored the Cross remain seated. Where large numbers of people make individual adoration difficult, the priest may raise the Cross briefly for all to adore in silence.

HOLY COMMUNION

LORD'S PRAYER *(p. 68)*

PRAYER AFTER COMMUNION

Almighty ever-living God, who have restored us to life by the blessed Death and Resurrection of your Christ, preserve in us the work of your mercy, that, by partaking of this mystery, we may have a life unceasingly devoted to you. Through Christ our Lord. **Amen.**

PRAYER OVER THE PEOPLE AND DISMISSAL

Bow down for the blessing.

May abundant blessing, O Lord, we pray, descend upon your people, who have honoured the Death of your Son in the hope of their resurrection: may pardon come, comfort be given, holy faith increase, and everlasting redemption be made secure. Through Christ our Lord. **Amen.**

All genuflect to the Cross, then depart in silence.

April 15
Resurrection of the Lord

O truly blessed night, when things of heaven are wed to those of earth and divine to the human. (Exsultet)

A blessed night indeed, when God's love overcame the finality of death to raise Jesus to life. Jesus' humanity was defeated by hatred and fear and succumbed to the grip of death. But in an instant, that defeated humanity was suffused with divine Love and resurrected, because God's love is greater than hatred, fear, sin or even death. And now Jesus' resurrected humanity is forever integrated inseparably within the Divinity.

Thus we can take courage from the words of the Angel to the women at the tomb, "Do not be afraid." What is there to fear when our God has accepted our humanity as an integral element of the Divine? What can defeat us when God's love is so much more powerful than death? Surely the only legitimate response we can have is that of the women, filled with awe and great joy.

On this most blessed night, as we contemplate the empty tomb, let us allow ourselves to be overwhelmed with awe and joy at the extraordinary power of Love. Let us pray that the Lord will banish fear from our lives, so that we may live every day in the joy of the Resurrection!

Fr. Len Altilia, SJ, Winnipeg, MB

SOLEMN BEGINNING OF THE VIGIL
(Lucernarium)

GREETING

The priest and the ministers, one of whom carries the unlit paschal candle, approach the fire.

In the name of the Father, and of the Son, and of the Holy Spirit. **Amen.**

1   The grace of our Lord Jesus Christ, and the love of God, and the communion of the Holy Spirit be with you all.

2   Grace to you and peace from God our Father and the Lord Jesus Christ.

3   The Lord be with you.
And with your spirit.

BLESSING OF THE FIRE

Dear brothers and sisters, on this most sacred night, in which our Lord Jesus Christ passed over from death to life, the Church calls upon her sons and daughters, scattered throughout the world, to come together to watch and pray. If we keep the memorial of the Lord's paschal solemnity in this way, listening to his word and celebrating his mysteries, then we shall have the sure hope of sharing his triumph over death and living with him in God.

Let us pray. O God, who through your Son bestowed upon the faithful the fire of your glory, sanctify this new fire, we pray, and grant that, by these paschal celebrations, we may be so inflamed with heavenly desires, that with minds made pure we may attain festivities of unending splendour. Through Christ our Lord. **Amen.**

PREPARATION AND LIGHTING OF THE CANDLE

The priest cuts a cross in the paschal candle and traces the Greek letters alpha (A) and omega (Ω) and the numerals 2017, saying:

Christ yesterday and today, the Beginning and the End, the Alpha and the Omega. All time belongs to him, and all the ages. To him be glory and power, through every age and for ever. Amen.

When the marks have been made, the priest may insert five grains of incense into the candle in the form of a cross, saying:

By his holy and glorious wounds, may Christ our Lord guard us and protect us. Amen.

The priest lights the paschal candle from the new fire, saying:

May the light of Christ rising in glory dispel the darkness of our hearts and minds.

PROCESSION WITH THE PASCHAL CANDLE

The deacon or another suitable minister holds the paschal candle and, three times during the procession to the altar, lifts it high and sings.

Deacon/Cantor   Assembly

The Light of Christ.   **Thanks be to God.**

The Light of Christ. **Thanks be to God.**

After the first response, the priest lights his candle from the paschal candle.

After the second response, all the people light their candles from the flame of the paschal candle.

After the third response, all the lights in the church are lit, except for the altar candles.

EASTER PROCLAMATION *(EXSULTET)*

For the shorter version, omit the indented parts.
Exult, let them exult, the hosts of heaven,
exult, let Angel ministers of God exult,
let the trumpet of salvation
sound aloud our mighty King's triumph!
Be glad, let earth be glad, as glory floods her,
ablaze with light from her eternal King,
let all corners of the earth be glad,
knowing an end to gloom and darkness.
Rejoice, let Mother Church also rejoice,
arrayed with the lightning of his glory,
let this holy building shake with joy,
filled with the mighty voices of the peoples.

> (Therefore, dearest friends,
> standing in the awesome glory of this holy light,
> invoke with me, I ask you,
> the mercy of God almighty,
> that he, who has been pleased to number me,
> though unworthy, among the Levites,
> may pour into me his light unshadowed,
> that I may sing this candle's perfect praises.)

(The Lord be with you. **And with your spirit.**)
Lift up your hearts. **We lift them up to the Lord.**
Let us give thanks to the Lord our God. **It is right and just.**

It is truly right and just,
with ardent love of mind and heart
and with devoted service of our voice,
to acclaim our God invisible, the almighty Father,
and Jesus Christ, our Lord, his Son, his Only Begotten.
Who for our sake paid Adam's debt to the
eternal Father,

and, pouring out his own dear Blood,
wiped clean the record of our ancient sinfulness.

These, then, are the feasts of Passover,
in which is slain the Lamb, the one true Lamb,
whose Blood anoints the doorposts of believers.

This is the night
when once you led our forebears, Israel's children,
from slavery in Egypt
and made them pass dry-shod through the Red Sea.

This is the night
that with a pillar of fire
banished the darkness of sin.

This is the night
that even now, throughout the world,
sets Christian believers apart from worldly vices
and from the gloom of sin,
leading them to grace
and joining them to his holy ones.

This is the night
when Christ broke the prison-bars of death
and rose victorious from the underworld.

Our birth would have been no gain,
had we not been redeemed.

O wonder of your humble care for us!
O love, O charity beyond all telling,
to ransom a slave you gave away your Son!
O truly necessary sin of Adam,
destroyed completely by the Death of Christ!
O happy fault
that earned so great, so glorious a Redeemer!

longer version:

O truly blessed night,
worthy alone to know
the time and hour
when Christ rose from
the underworld!

This is the night of
which it is written:
The night shall be as
bright as day, dazzling
is the night for me,
and full of gladness.

The sanctifying
power of this night
dispels wickedness,
washes faults away,
restores innocence
to the fallen, and joy
to mourners, drives
out hatred, fosters
concord, and brings
down the mighty.

On this, your night of
grace, O holy Father,
accept this candle, a
solemn offering, the
work of bees and of
your servants' hands,
an evening sacrifice
of praise, this gift
from your most holy
Church.

shorter version:

The sanctifying
power of this night
dispels wickedness,
washes faults away,
restores innocence
to the fallen, and
joy to mourners.

O truly blessed night,
when things of heaven
are wed to those of
earth and divine to
the human.

On this, your night of
grace, O holy Father,
accept this candle, a
solemn offering, the
work of bees and of
your servants' hands,
an evening sacrifice of
praise, this gift from
your most holy Church.

But now we know the
praises of this pillar,
which glowing fire
ignites for God's
honour, a fire into
many flames divided,
yet never dimmed by
sharing of its light,
for it is fed by melting
wax, drawn out by
mother bees to build
a torch so precious.

O truly blessed night,
when things of heaven
are wed to those of
earth, and divine to
the human.

Therefore, O Lord,
we pray you that this candle,
hallowed to the honour of your name,
may persevere undimmed,
to overcome the darkness of this night.
Receive it as a pleasing fragrance,
and let it mingle with the lights of heaven.
May this flame be found still burning
by the Morning Star:
the one Morning Star who never sets,
Christ your Son,
who, coming back from death's domain,
has shed his peaceful light on humanity,
and lives and reigns for ever and ever.
Amen.

LITURGY OF THE WORD

Dear brothers and sisters, now that we have begun our solemn Vigil, let us listen with quiet hearts to the Word of God. Let us meditate on how God in times past saved his people and in these, the last days, has sent us his Son as our Redeemer. Let us pray that our God may complete this paschal work of salvation by the fullness of redemption.

FIRST READING *(Genesis 1.1 – 2.2)*

For the shorter version, omit the indented parts.

In the beginning when God created the heavens and the earth,

> the earth was a formless void and darkness covered the face of the deep, while the spirit of God swept over the face of the waters. Then God said, "Let there be light"; and there was light. And God saw that the light was good; and God separated the light from the darkness. God called the light "Day," and the darkness he called "Night." And there was evening and there was morning, the first day.

> And God said, "Let there be a dome in the midst of the waters, and let it separate the waters from the waters." So God made the dome and separated the waters that were under the dome from the waters that were above the dome. And it was so. God called the dome "Sky." And there was evening and there was morning, the second day.

> And God said, "Let the waters under the sky be gathered together into one place, and let the dry land appear." And it was so. God

called the dry land "Earth," and the waters that were gathered together he called "Seas." And God saw that it was good.

Then God said, "Let the earth put forth vegetation: plants yielding seed, and fruit trees of every kind on earth that bear fruit with the seed in it." And it was so. The earth brought forth vegetation: plants yielding seed of every kind, and trees of every kind bearing fruit with the seed in it. And God saw that it was good. And there was evening and there was morning, the third day.

And God said, "Let there be lights in the dome of the sky to separate the day from the night; and let them be for signs and for seasons and for days and years, and let them be lights in the dome of the sky to give light upon the earth." And it was so.

God made the two great lights — the greater light to rule the day and the lesser light to rule the night — and the stars. God set them in the dome of the sky to give light upon the earth, to rule over the day and over the night, and to separate the light from the darkness. And God saw that it was good. And there was evening and there was morning, the fourth day.

And God said, "Let the waters bring forth swarms of living creatures, and let birds fly above the earth across the dome of the sky." So God created the great sea monsters and every living creature that moves, of every kind, with which the waters swarm, and every winged bird of every kind. And God saw that it was good. God blessed them, saying, "Be fruitful and multiply and fill the waters in the seas, and let birds multiply on the earth." And there was evening and there was morning, the fifth day.

And God said, "Let the earth bring forth living creatures of every kind: cattle and creeping things and wild animals of the earth of every kind." And it was so. God made the wild animals of the earth of every kind, and the cattle of every kind, and everything that creeps upon the ground of every kind. And God saw that it was good. Then God said, "Let us make man in our image, according to our likeness; and let them have dominion over the fish of the sea, and over the birds of the air, and over the cattle, and over all the wild animals of the earth, and over every creeping thing that creeps upon the earth." So God created man in his image, in the image of God he created him; male and female he created them.

God blessed them, and God said to them, "Be fruitful and multiply, and fill the earth and subdue it; and have dominion over the fish of the sea and over the birds of the air and over every living thing that moves upon the earth."

God said, "See, I have given you every plant yielding seed that is upon the face of all the earth, and every tree with seed in its fruit; you shall have them for food. And to every beast of the earth, and to every bird of the air, and to everything that creeps on the earth, everything that has the breath of life, I have given every green plant for food." And it was so.

God saw everything that he had made, and indeed, it was very good. And there was evening and there was morning, the sixth day.

Thus the heavens and the earth were finished, and all their multitude. And on the seventh day God finished the work that he had done, and he rested on the seventh day from all the work that he had done.

The word of the Lord. **Thanks be to God.**

An alternate psalm follows.

RESPONSORIAL PSALM *(Psalm 104)*

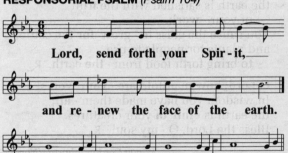

Lord, send forth your Spir-it,
and re-new the face of the earth.

℟. **Lord, send forth your Spirit,
and renew the face of the earth.**

Bless the Lord, O · **my** soul.
O Lord my God, you are very · **great.**
You are clothed with · **honour** and majesty,
wrapped in light as with · **a** garment. ℟.

You set the earth on its · **foun-**dations,
so that it shall never be · **shaken.**
You cover it with the deep as · **with** a garment;
the waters stood above · **the** mountains. R.

You make springs gush forth in · **the** valleys;
they flow between the · **hills.**
By the streams the birds of the air
    have their · **ha-**bi-tation;
they sing among · **the** branches. R.

From your lofty abode
    you water · **the** mountains;
the earth is satisfied with the fruit
    of your · **work.**
You cause the grass to · **grow_for** the cattle,
and plants for people to use,
    to bring forth food from · **the** earth. R.

O Lord, how manifold are · **your** works!
In wisdom you have made them · **all;**
the earth is · **full_of** your creatures.
Bless the Lord, O · **my** soul. R.

or

RESPONSORIAL PSALM *(Psalm 33)*

The earth is full of the stead-fast love of the Lord.

℟. **The earth is full of the steadfast love
of the Lord.**

The word of the Lord · **is** upright,
and all his work is done · **in** faithfulness.
He loves righteousness · **and** justice;
the earth is full of the steadfast love
of · **the** Lord. ℟.

By the word of the Lord
the heavens · **were** made,
and all their host by the breath of · **his** mouth.
He gathered the waters of the sea
as in · **a** bottle;
he put the deeps · **in** storehouses. ℟.

Blessed is the nation whose God is · **the** Lord,
the people whom he has chosen
as · **his** heritage.
The Lord looks down · **from** heaven;
he sees all · **human** beings. ℟.

Our soul waits for · **the** Lord;
he is our help · **and** shield.
Let your steadfast love, O Lord, be · **up-**on_us,
even as we hope · **in** you. R.

PRAYER

Let us pray. *(Pause)*

1 Almighty ever-living God, who are wonderful
in the ordering of all your works, may those
you have redeemed understand that there ex-
ists nothing more marvellous than the world's
creation in the beginning except that, at the
end of the ages, Christ our Passover has been
sacrificed. Who lives and reigns for ever and
ever. **Amen.**

2 O God, who wonderfully created human nature and still more wonderfully redeemed it,
grant us, we pray, to set our minds against the
enticements of sin, that we may merit to attain
eternal joys. Through Christ our Lord. **Amen.**

SECOND READING *(Genesis 22.1-18)*

For the shorter version, omit the indented parts.

God tested Abraham. He said to him, "Abraham!"
And Abraham said, "Here I am." God said, "Take
your son, your only son Isaac, whom you love,
and go to the land of Moriah, and offer him there
as a burnt offering on one of the mountains that
I shall show you."

> So Abraham rose early in the morning, sad-
> dled his donkey, and took two of his young

men with him, and his son Isaac; he cut the wood for the burnt offering, and set out and went to the place in the distance that God had shown him.

On the third day Abraham looked up and saw the place far away. Then Abraham said to his young men, "Stay here with the donkey; the boy and I will go over there; we will worship, and then we will come back to you." Abraham took the wood of the burnt offering and laid it on his son Isaac, and he himself carried the fire and the knife. So the two of them walked on together.

Isaac said to his father Abraham, "Father!" And Abraham said, "Here I am, my son." Isaac said, "The fire and the wood are here, but where is the lamb for a burnt offering?" Abraham said, "God himself will provide the lamb for a burnt offering, my son." So the two of them walked on together.

When Abraham and Isaac came to the place that God had shown him, Abraham built an altar there and laid the wood in order. He bound his son Isaac, and laid him on the altar, on top of the wood. Then Abraham reached out his hand and took the knife to kill his son.

But the Angel of the Lord called to him from heaven, and said, "Abraham, Abraham!" And he said, "Here I am." The Angel said, "Do not lay your hand on the boy or do anything to him; for now I know that you fear God, since you have not withheld your son, your only son, from me." And Abraham looked up and saw a ram, caught in a thicket by its horns. Abraham went and took the ram and offered it up as a burnt offering instead of his son.

So Abraham called that place "The Lord will provide"; as it is said to this day, "On the mount of the Lord it shall be provided."

The Angel of the Lord called to Abraham a second time from heaven, and said, "By myself I have sworn, says the Lord: Because you have done this, and have not withheld your son, your only son, I will indeed bless you, and I will make your offspring as numerous as the stars of heaven and as the sand that is on the seashore. And your offspring shall possess the gate of their enemies, and by your offspring shall all the nations of the earth gain blessing for themselves, because you have obeyed my voice."

The word of the Lord. **Thanks be to God.**

RESPONSORIAL PSALM *(Psalm 16)*

Pro - tect me, O God, — for in

you I take re - fuge.

℟. **Protect me, O God, for in you I take refuge.**

The Lord is my chosen portion · **and_my** cup;
you hold · **my** lot.
I keep the Lord always · **be**-fore_me;
because he is at my right hand,
 I shall · **not** be moved. ℟.

Therefore my heart is glad,
 and my soul · **re**-joices;
my body also rests · **se**-cure.
For you do not give me up · **to** Sheol,
or let your faithful one · **see** the Pit. ℟.

You show me the path · **of** life.
In your presence there is fullness · **of** joy;
in your right hand · **are** pleasures
for-·**ev**-er-more. ℟.

©2009 Gordon Johnston/Novalis

PRAYER
Let us pray. *(Pause)* O God, supreme Father of
the faithful, who increase the children of your
promise by pouring out the grace of adoption

throughout the whole world and who through the Paschal Mystery make your servant Abraham father of nations, as once you swore, grant, we pray, that your peoples may enter worthily into the grace to which you call them. Through Christ our Lord. **Amen.**

THIRD READING *(Exodus 14.15-31; 15.20, 1)*

The Lord said to Moses, "Why do you cry out to me? Tell the children of Israel to go forward. But you, lift up your staff, and stretch out your hand over the sea and divide it, that the children of Israel may go into the sea on dry ground. Then I will harden the hearts of the Egyptians so that they will go in after them; and so I will gain glory for myself over Pharaoh and all his army, his chariots, and his chariot drivers. And the Egyptians shall know that I am the Lord, when I have gained glory for myself over Pharaoh, his chariots, and his chariot drivers."

The Angel of God who was going before the Israelite army moved and went behind them; and the pillar of cloud moved from in front of them and took its place behind them. It came between the army of Egypt and the army of Israel. And so the cloud was there with the darkness, and it lit up the night; one did not come near the other all night. Then Moses stretched out his hand over the sea. The Lord drove the sea back by a strong east wind all night, and turned the sea into dry land; and the waters were divided. The children of Israel went into the sea on dry ground, the waters forming a wall for them on their right and on their left.

The Egyptians pursued, and went into the sea after them, all of Pharaoh's horses, chariots, and chariot drivers. At the morning watch, the Lord in the pillar of fire and cloud looked down upon the Egyptian army, and threw the Egyptian army into panic. He clogged their chariot wheels so that they turned with difficulty. The Egyptians said, "Let us flee from the children of Israel, for the Lord is fighting for them against Egypt."

Then the Lord said to Moses, "Stretch out your hand over the sea, so that the water may come back upon the Egyptians, upon their chariots and chariot drivers." So Moses stretched out his hand over the sea, and at dawn the sea returned to its normal depth. As the Egyptians fled before it, the Lord tossed the Egyptians into the sea. The waters returned and covered the chariots and the chariot drivers, the entire army of Pharaoh that had followed them into the sea; not one of them remained.

But the children of Israel walked on dry ground through the sea, the waters forming a wall for them on their right and on their left. Thus the Lord saved Israel that day from the Egyptians; and Israel saw the Egyptians dead on the seashore. Israel saw the great work that the Lord did against the Egyptians. So the people feared the Lord and believed in the Lord and in his servant Moses.

The Prophet Miriam, Aaron's sister, took a tambourine in her hand; and all the women went out after her with tambourines and with dancing. Moses and the children of Israel sang this song to the Lord:

RESPONSORIAL PSALM *(Exodus 15)*

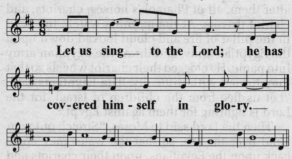

Let us sing___ to the Lord; he has
cov-ered him-self in glo-ry.___

R̰. **Let us sing to the Lord;**
he has covered himself in glory.

I will sing to the Lord,
for he has triumphed · **gloriously;**
horse and rider he has thrown into · **the** sea.
The Lord is my strength and my · **might,**
and he has become my · **sal**-vation;
this is my God, and I will · **praise_him,**
my father's God, and I will · **ex**-alt_him. R̰.

The Lord is a · **warrior;**
the Lord is · **his** name.
Pharaoh's chariots and his army
he cast into the · **sea;**
his picked officers were sunk in the · **Red** Sea.
The floods · **covered_them;**
they went down into the depths
· **like_a** stone. R̰.

Your right hand, O Lord, glorious in · **power;**
your right hand, O Lord, shattered · **the** enemy.
In the greatness of your · **majesty**
you overthrew · **your** adversaries;
you sent out your · **fury,**
it consumed them · **like** stubble. R̰

You brought your people · **in**
and plant·**-ed** them
on the mountain of your own pos·**-session,**
the place, O Lord, that you made your · **a-**bode,
the sanctuary, O Lord, that your hands
    have es·**-tablished.**
The Lord will reign forever · **and** ever. R̰

©*2009 Gordon Johnston/Novalis*

PRAYER

Let us pray. *(Pause)*

1 O God, whose ancient wonders remain undimmed in splendour even in our day, for
what you once bestowed on a single people,
freeing them from Pharaoh's persecution by
the power of your right hand, now you bring
about as the salvation of the nations through
the waters of rebirth, grant, we pray, that the
whole world may become children of Abraham and inherit the dignity of Israel's birth-
right. Through Christ our Lord. **Amen.**

2 O God, who by the light of the New Testament have unlocked the meaning of wonders
worked in former times, so that the Red Sea
prefigures the sacred font and the nation delivered from slavery foreshadows the Christian people, grant, we pray, that all nations,

obtaining the privilege of Israel by merit of faith, may be reborn by partaking of your Spirit. Through Christ our Lord. **Amen.**

FOURTH READING (Isaiah 54.5-14)

Thus says the Lord, the God of hosts. Your Maker is your husband, the Lord of hosts is his name; the Holy One of Israel is your Redeemer, the God of the whole earth he is called. For the Lord has called you like a wife forsaken and grieved in spirit, like the wife of a man's youth when she is cast off, says your God.

For a brief moment I abandoned you, but with great compassion I will gather you. In overflowing wrath for a moment I hid my face from you, but with everlasting love I will have compassion on you, says the Lord, your Redeemer.

This is like the days of Noah to me: Just as I swore that the waters of Noah would never again go over the earth, so I have sworn that I will not be angry with you and will not rebuke you. For the mountains may depart and the hills be removed, but my steadfast love shall not depart from you, and my covenant of peace shall not be removed, says the Lord, who has compassion on you.

O afflicted one, storm-tossed, and not comforted, I am about to set your stones in antimony, and lay your foundations with sapphires. I will make your pinnacles of rubies, your gates of jewels, and all your walls of precious stones.

All your children shall be taught by the Lord, and great shall be the prosperity of your children. In righteousness you shall be established; you

shall be far from oppression, for you shall not fear;
and from terror, for it shall not come near you.

The word of the Lord. **Thanks be to God.**

RESPONSORIAL PSALM *(Psalm 30)*

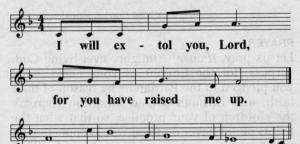

R. **I will extol you, Lord,**
for you have raised me up.

I will extol you, O Lord, for you have
drawn me · **up,**
and did not let my foes rejoice · **over_me.**
O Lord, you brought up my soul from · **Sheol,**
restored me to life from among those gone
down · **to_the** Pit. R.

Sing praises to the Lord,
O you his · **faithful_ones,**
and give thanks to his holy · **name.**
For his anger is but for a moment;
his favour is for a · **lifetime.**
Weeping may linger for the night,
but joy comes · **with_the** morning. R.

Hear, O Lord, and be gracious to · **me!**
O Lord, be my · **helper!**
You have turned my mourning into · **dancing.**
O Lord my God, I will give thanks
    to you · **for**-ever. ℟.

PRAYER

Let us pray. *(Pause)* Almighty ever-living God, surpass, for the honour of your name, what you pledged to the Patriarchs by reason of their faith, and through sacred adoption increase the children of your promise, so that what the Saints of old never doubted would come to pass your Church may now see in great part fulfilled. Through Christ our Lord. **Amen.**

FIFTH READING *(Isaiah 55.1-11)*

Thus says the Lord: "Everyone who thirsts, come to the waters; and you that have no money, come, buy and eat! Come, buy wine and milk without money and without price. Why do you spend your money for that which is not bread, and your labour for that which does not satisfy? Listen carefully to me, and eat what is good, and delight yourselves in rich food. Incline your ear, and come to me; listen, so that you may live. I will make with you an everlasting covenant, my steadfast, sure love for David.

"See, I made him a witness to the peoples, a leader and commander for the peoples. See, you shall call nations that you do not know, and nations that do not know you shall run to you, because of the Lord your God, the Holy One of Israel, for he has glorified you.

"Seek the Lord while he may be found, call upon him while he is near; let the wicked person forsake their way, and the unrighteous person their thoughts; let that person return to the Lord that he may have mercy on them, and to our God, for he will abundantly pardon.

"For my thoughts are not your thoughts, nor are your ways my ways, says the Lord. For as the heavens are higher than the earth, so are my ways higher than your ways and my thoughts than your thoughts. For as the rain and the snow come down from heaven, and do not return there until they have watered the earth, making it bring forth and sprout, giving seed to the sower and bread to the one who eats, so shall my word be that goes out from my mouth; it shall not return to me empty, but it shall accomplish that which I purpose, and succeed in the thing for which I sent it."

The word of the Lord. **Thanks be to God.**

RESPONSORIAL PSALM *(Isaiah 12)*

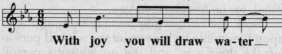

With joy you will draw wa-ter

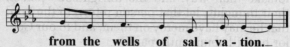

from the wells of sal-va-tion.

R. **With joy you will draw water**
from the wells of salvation.

Surely God is my salvation;
  I will trust, and will not · **be** a-fraid,
for the Lord God is my strength and my might;
  he has be--**come_my** sal-vation.
With joy · **you_will** draw water
from the wells · **of** sal-vation. R.

Give thanks · **to** the Lord,
call · **on** his name;
make known his deeds a--**mong** the nations;
proclaim that his · **name_is** ex-alted. R.

Sing praises to the Lord,
  for he · **has** done gloriously;
let this be known in · **all** the earth.
Shout aloud and sing for joy, O · **roy-**al Zion,
for great in your midst
  is the Holy · **One** of Israel. R.

To hear the Sunday Psalms, visit www.livingwithchrist.ca.

PRAYER

Let us pray. *(Pause)* Almighty ever-living God, sole hope of the world, who by the preaching of your Prophets unveiled the mysteries of this present age, graciously increase the longing of your people, for only at the prompting of your grace do the faithful progress in any kind of virtue. Through Christ our Lord. **Amen.**

SIXTH READING *(Baruch 3.9-15, 32 – 4.4)*

Hear the commandments of life, O Israel; give ear, and learn wisdom! Why is it, O Israel, why is it that you are in the land of your enemies, that you are growing old in a foreign country, that you are defiled with the dead, that you are counted among those in Hades? You have forsaken the fountain of wisdom. If you had walked in the way of God, you would be living in peace forever.

Learn where there is wisdom, where there is strength, where there is understanding, so that you may at the same time discern where there is length of days, and life, where there is light for the eyes, and peace. Who has found her place? And who has entered her storehouses?

But the one who knows all things knows her, he found her by his understanding. The one who prepared the earth for all time filled it with four-footed creatures; the one who sends forth the light, and it goes; he called it, and it obeyed him, trembling; the stars shone in their watches, and were glad; he called them, and they said, "Here we are!" They shone with gladness for him who made them.

This is our God; no other can be compared to him. He found the whole way to knowledge, and gave her to his servant Jacob and to Israel, whom he loved. Afterward she appeared on earth and lived with humanity. She is the book of the commandments of God, the law that endures forever. All who hold her fast will live, and those who forsake her will die. Turn, O Jacob, and take her; walk toward the shining of her light. Do not give your glory to another, or your advantages to an alien people.

Happy are we, O Israel, for we know what is pleasing to God.

The word of the Lord. **Thanks be to God.**

RESPONSORIAL PSALM *(Psalm 19)*

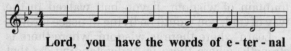

Lord, you have the words of e-ter-nal

life.

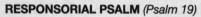

R. **Lord, you have the words of eternal life.**

The law of the Lord is · **perfect,**
reviving the · **soul;**
the decrees of the Lord are · **sure,**
making · **wise** the simple. R.

The precepts of the Lord are · **right,**
rejoicing the · **heart;**
the commandment of the Lord is · **clear,**
en-·**lightening** the eyes. R.

The fear of the Lord is · **pure,**
enduring for·-**ever;**
the ordinances of the Lord are · **true**
and righteous · **al-**to-gether. ℟

More to be desired are they than · **gold,**
even much fine · **gold;**
sweeter also than · **honey,**
and drippings · **of** the honeycomb. ℟

PRAYER
Let us pray. *(Pause)* O God, who constantly increase your Church by your call to the nations,
graciously grant to those you wash clean in the
waters of Baptism the assurance of your unfailing
protection. Through Christ our Lord. **Amen.**

SEVENTH READING *(Ezekiel 36.16-17a, 18-28)*
The word of the Lord came to me: Son of man,
when the house of Israel lived on their own soil,
they defiled it with their ways and their deeds;
their conduct in my sight was unclean. So I
poured out my wrath upon them for the blood
that they had shed upon the land, and for the
idols with which they had defiled it. I scattered
them among the nations, and they were dispersed
through the countries; in accordance with their
conduct and their deeds I judged them.

But when they came to the nations, wherever
they came, they profaned my holy name, in that
it was said of them, "These are the people of the
Lord, and yet they had to go out of his land."

But I had concern for my holy name, which the house of Israel had profaned among the nations to which they came. Therefore say to the house of Israel, Thus says the Lord God: It is not for your sake, O house of Israel, that I am about to act, but for the sake of my holy name, which you have profaned among the nations to which you came.

I will sanctify my great name, which has been profaned among the nations, and which you have profaned among them; and the nations shall know that I am the Lord, says the Lord God, when through you I display my holiness before their eyes.

I will take you from the nations, and gather you from all the countries, and bring you into your own land.

I will sprinkle clean water upon you, and you shall be clean from all your uncleanness, and from all your idols I will cleanse you.

A new heart I will give you, and a new spirit I will put within you; and I will remove from your body the heart of stone and give you a heart of flesh. I will put my spirit within you, and make you follow my statutes and be careful to observe my ordinances. Then you shall live in the land that I gave to your ancestors; and you shall be my people, and I will be your God.

The word of the Lord. **Thanks be to God.**

An alternate psalm follows. When baptism is celebrated, sing Isaiah 12 (p. 306).

RESPONSORIAL PSALM *(Psalm 42; 43)*

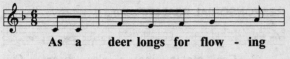

As a deer longs for flow - ing

streams, my soul longs for you, O God.

R. **As a deer longs for flowing streams,
my soul longs for you, O God.**

My soul thirsts for · **God,**
for the living · **God.**
When shall I · **come**
and behold the face · **of** God? R.

I went with the · **throng,**
and led them in procession
    to the house of · **God,**
with glad shouts and songs of · **thanksgiving,**
a multitude · **keeping** festival. R.

O send out your light and your · **truth;**
let them · **lead_me;**
let them bring me to your holy · **mountain**
and to · **your** dwelling. R.

Then I will go to the altar of · **God,**
to God my exceeding · **joy;**
and I will praise you with the · **harp,**
O God, · **my** God. R.

or

RESPONSORIAL PSALM *(Psalm 51)*

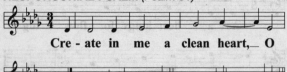

Cre - ate in me a clean heart,_ O

God.

R̸. **Create in me a clean heart, O God.**

Create in me a clean heart, · **O God,**
and put a new and right spirit · **with-**in_me.
Do not cast me away from · **your** presence,
and do not take your holy · **spirit** from me. R̸.

Restore to me the joy of your · **sal-**vation,
and sustain in me a will-**-ing** spirit.
Then I will teach transgressors · **your** ways,
and sinners will re--**turn** to you. R̸.

For you have no delight · **in** sacrifice;
if I were to give a burnt offering,
    you would not · **be** pleased.
The sacrifice acceptable to God
    is a bro--**ken** spirit;
a broken and contrite heart, O God,
    you will · **not** de-spise. R̸.

PRAYER

Let us pray. *(Pause)*

1 O God of unchanging power and eternal light, look with favour on the wondrous mystery of the whole Church and serenely accomplish the work of human salvation, which you planned from all eternity; may the whole world know and see that what was cast down is raised up, what had become old is made new, and all things are restored to integrity through Christ, just as by him they came into being. Who lives and reigns for ever and ever. **Amen**.

2 O God, who by the pages of both Testaments instruct and prepare us to celebrate the Paschal Mystery, grant that we may comprehend your mercy, so that the gifts we receive from you this night may confirm our hope of the gifts to come. Through Christ our Lord. **Amen**.

GLORY TO GOD *(p. 10)*

COLLECT

Let us pray. O God, who make this most sacred night radiant with the glory of the Lord's Resurrection, stir up in your Church a spirit of adoption, so that, renewed in body and mind, we may render you undivided service. Through our Lord Jesus Christ, your Son, who lives and reigns with you in the unity of the Holy Spirit, one God, for ever and ever. **Amen.**

EPISTLE *(Romans 6.3-11)*

Brothers and sisters: Do you not know that all of us who have been baptized into Christ Jesus were baptized into his death? Therefore we have been buried with him by baptism into death, so that, just as Christ was raised from the dead by the glory of the Father, so we too might walk in newness of life. For if we have been united with him in a death like his, we will certainly be united with him in a resurrection like his.

We know that our old self was crucified with him so that the body of sin might be destroyed, and we might no longer be enslaved to sin. For whoever has died is freed from sin. But if we have died with Christ, we believe that we will also live with him.

We know that Christ, being raised from the dead, will never die again; death no longer has dominion over him. The death he died, he died to sin, once for all; but the life he lives, he lives to God. So you also must consider yourselves dead to sin and alive to God in Christ Jesus.

The word of the Lord. **Thanks be to God.**

SOLEMN ALLELUIA *(Psalm 118)*

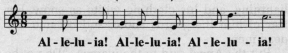

Al - le-lu - ia! Al-le-lu-ia! Al - le-lu - ia!

℟. **Alleluia! Alleluia! Alleluia!**

O give thanks to the Lord, for · **he** is good;
his steadfast love en-·**dures** for-ever.
Let Is-·**rael** say,
"His steadfast love en-·**dures** for-ever." ℟.

"The right hand of the Lord · **is** ex-alted;
the right hand of the · **Lord** does valiantly."
I shall not die, but · **I_shall** live,
and recount the · **deeds_of** the Lord. ℟.

The stone that the · **builders** re-jected
has become · **the** chief cornerstone.
This is the · **Lord's** doing;
it is marvellous · **in** our eyes. ℟.

©2009 Gordon Johnston/Novalis

GOSPEL *(Matthew 28.1-10)*

The Lord be with you. **And with your spirit.**
A reading from the holy Gospel according to Matthew. **Glory to you, O Lord.**

After the Sabbath, as the first day of the week was dawning, Mary Magdalene and the other Mary went to see the tomb. And suddenly there was a great earthquake; for an Angel of the Lord, descending from heaven, came and rolled back the stone and sat on it. His appearance was like lightning, and his clothing white as snow. For fear of him the guards shook and became like dead men.

But the Angel said to the women, "Do not be afraid; I know that you are looking for Jesus who was crucified. He is not here; for he has been raised, as he said. Come, see the place where he lay. Then go quickly and tell his disciples, 'He has been raised from the dead, and indeed he is going ahead of you to Galilee; there you will see him.' This is my message for you."

So they left the tomb quickly with fear and great joy, and ran to tell his disciples. Suddenly Jesus met them and said, "Greetings!" And they came to him, took hold of his feet, and worshipped him. Then Jesus said to them, "Do not be afraid; go and tell my brothers to go to Galilee; there they will see me."

The Gospel of the Lord. **Praise to you, Lord Jesus Christ.**

BAPTISMAL LITURGY

This celebration combines text from The Roman Missal
(2011) and the Rite of Christian Initiation of Adults *(1987),*
where appropriate.

INTRODUCTION

1   *If there are candidates for baptism:*
Dearly beloved, with one heart and one soul,
let us by our prayers come to the aid of these
our brothers and sisters in their blessed hope,
so that, as they approach the font of rebirth,
the almighty Father may bestow on them all
his merciful help.

2   *If there are no candidates for baptism:*
Dearly beloved, let us humbly invoke upon
this font the grace of God the almighty Father,
that those who from it are born anew may be
numbered among the children of adoption in
Christ.

3   *If there are no candidates for baptism and the font is not
to be blessed, proceed to the Blessing of Water, p. 325.*

LITANY OF THE SAINTS

Cantor   Assembly

Lord, have mer - cy.   Lord, have mer - cy.

Lord, have mercy. **Lord, have mercy.**
Christ, have mercy. **Christ, have mercy.**
Lord, have mercy. **Lord, have mercy.**

Holy Mary, Mother of God,   pray for us.

Holy Mary, Mother of God, **pray for us.**
Saint Michael,
Holy Angels of God,
Saint John the Baptist,
Saint Joseph,
Saint Peter and Saint Paul,
Saint Andrew,
Saint John,
Saint Mary Magdalene,
Saint Stephen,
Saint Ignatius of Antioch,
Saint Lawrence,
Saint Perpetua and Saint Felicity,
Saint Agnes,
Saint Gregory,
Saint Augustine,
Saint Athanasius,
Saint Basil,
Saint Martin,
Saint Benedict,
Saint Francis and Saint Dominic,
Saint Francis Xavier,
Saint John Vianney,
Saint Catherine of Siena,
Saint Teresa of Jesus,
(other saints)
All holy men and women, Saints of God,

Lord, be mer-ci-ful, Lord, de-liv-er us, we pray.

Lord, be merciful, **Lord, deliver us, we pray.**
From all evil,
From every sin,
From everlasting death,
By your Incarnation,
By your Death and Resurrection,
By the outpouring of the Holy Spirit,

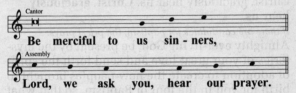

Be merciful to us sin-ners,

Lord, we ask you, hear our prayer.

Be merciful to us sinners, **Lord, we ask you, hear our prayer.**

1   *If there are candidates for baptism:*
    Bring these chosen ones to new birth through
    the grace of Baptism, **Lord, we ask you, hear
    our prayer.**

2   *If there are no candidates for baptism:*
    Make this font holy by your grace for the new
    birth of your children, **Lord, we ask you, hear
    our prayer.**

Jesus, Son of the living God, **Lord, we ask you,
hear our prayer.**

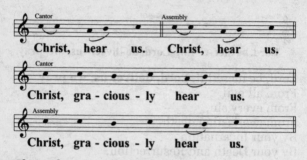

Christ, hear us. **Christ, hear us.**
Christ, graciously hear us. **Christ, graciously hear us.**

If there are candidates for baptism, the priest prays:

Almighty ever-living God, be present by the mysteries of your great love and send forth the spirit of adoption to create the new peoples brought to birth for you in the font of Baptism, so that what is to be carried out by our humble service may be brought to fulfillment by your mighty power. Through Christ our Lord. **Amen.**

BLESSING OF BAPTISMAL WATER

O God, who by invisible power accomplish a wondrous effect through sacramental signs and who in many ways have prepared water, your creation, to show forth the grace of Baptism;

O God, whose Spirit in the first moments of the world's creation hovered over the waters, so that the very substance of water would even then take to itself the power to sanctify;

O God, who by the outpouring of the flood foreshadowed regeneration, so that from the mystery of one and the same element of water would come an end to vice and a beginning of virtue;

O God, who caused the children of Abraham to pass dry-shod through the Red Sea, so that the chosen people, set free from slavery to Pharaoh, would prefigure the people of the baptized;

O God, whose Son, baptized by John in the waters of the Jordan, was anointed with the Holy Spirit, and, as he hung upon the Cross, gave forth water from his side along with blood, and after his Resurrection, commanded his disciples: "Go forth, teach all nations, baptizing them in the name of the Father and of the Son and of the Holy Spirit," look now, we pray, upon the face of your Church and graciously unseal for her the fountain of Baptism. May this water receive by the Holy Spirit the grace of your Only Begotten Son, so that human nature, created in your image and washed clean through the Sacrament of Baptism from all the squalor of the life of old, may be found worthy to rise to the life of newborn children through water and the Holy Spirit.

May the power of the Holy Spirit, O Lord, we pray, come down through your Son into the fullness of this font, so that all who have been buried with Christ by Baptism into death may rise again to life with him. Who lives and reigns with you in the unity of the Holy Spirit, one God, for ever and ever. **Amen.**

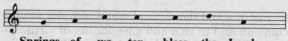

Springs of wa - ter, bless the Lord;

praise and exalt him above all for ev - er.

Springs of water, bless the Lord;
praise and exalt him above all for ever.

RENUNCIATION OF SIN

Using one of the following formularies, the priest questions
all the candidates together or individually.

1 Do you reject sin so as to live in the freedom
   of God's children? **I do.**
   Do you reject the glamour of evil, and refuse
   to be mastered by sin? **I do.**
   Do you reject Satan, father of sin and prince
   of darkness? **I do.**
2 Do you reject Satan, and all his works, and
   all his empty promises? **I do.**
3 Do you reject Satan? **I do.**
   And all his works? **I do.**
   And all his empty promises? **I do.**

Adult candidates may now be anointed with the Oil of
Catechumens.

We anoint you with the oil of salvation in the
name of Christ our Saviour. May he strengthen
you with his power. **Amen.**

PROFESSION OF FAITH

N., do you believe in God, the Father almighty,
creator of heaven and earth? **I do.**

Do you believe in Jesus Christ, his only Son, our Lord, who was born of the Virgin Mary, was crucified, died, and was buried, rose from the dead, and is now seated at the right hand of the Father? **I do.**

Do you believe in the Holy Spirit, the holy catholic Church, the communion of saints, the forgiveness of sins, the resurrection of the body, and the life everlasting? **I do.**

BAPTISM

The priest baptizes each candidate either by immersion or by the pouring of water.

N., I baptize you in the name of the Father, and of the Son, and of the Holy Spirit.

ANOINTING AFTER BAPTISM

Any newly baptized infants are anointed now with chrism.

The God of power and Father of our Lord Jesus Christ has freed you from sin and brought you to new life through water and the Holy Spirit.

He now anoints you with the chrism of salvation, so that, united with his people, you may remain for ever a member of Christ who is Priest, Prophet, and King. **Amen.**

CLOTHING WITH A BAPTISMAL GARMENT

All the newly baptized receive a white garment.

N. and N., you have become a new creation and have clothed yourselves in Christ. Receive this baptismal garment and bring it unstained to the judgment seat of our Lord Jesus Christ, so that you may have everlasting life. **Amen.**

PRESENTATION OF A LIGHTED CANDLE

Godparents, please come forward to give to the newly baptized the light of Christ.

A godparent of each of the newly baptized lights a candle from the paschal candle and presents it to the newly baptized.

You have been enlightened by Christ. Walk always as children of the light and keep the flame of faith alive in your hearts. When the Lord comes, may you go out to meet him with all the saints in the heavenly kingdom. **Amen.**

CONFIRMATION OF ADULTS

The newly baptized adults with their godparents stand before the priest.

My dear candidates for confirmation, by your baptism you have been born again in Christ and you have become members of Christ and of his priestly people. Now you are to share in the outpouring of the Holy Spirit among us, the Spirit sent by the Lord upon his apostles at Pentecost and given by them and their successors to the baptized.

The promised strength of the Holy Spirit, which you are to receive, will make you more like Christ and help you to be witnesses to his suffering, death, and resurrection. It will strengthen you to be active members of the Church and to build up the Body of Christ in faith and love.

My dear friends, let us pray to God our Father, that he will pour out the Holy Spirit on these candidates for confirmation to strengthen them with his gifts and anoint them to be more like Christ, the Son of God.

LAYING ON OF HANDS

All-powerful God, Father of our Lord Jesus Christ, by water and the Holy Spirit you freed your sons and daughters from sin and gave them new life.

Send your Holy Spirit upon them to be their helper and guide.

Give them the spirit of wisdom and understanding, the spirit of right judgment and courage, the spirit of knowledge and reverence. Fill them with the spirit of wonder and awe in your presence. We ask this through Christ our Lord. **Amen.**

ANOINTING WITH CHRISM

During the conferral of the sacrament an appropriate song may be sung.

N., be sealed with the Gift of the Holy Spirit. **Amen.**
Peace be with you. **And with your spirit.**

BLESSING OF WATER

(when no one is to be baptized)

Dear brothers and sisters, let us humbly beseech the Lord our God to bless this water he has created, which will be sprinkled upon us as a memorial of our Baptism. May he graciously renew us, that we may remain faithful to the Spirit whom we have received. *(Pause)*

Lord our God, in your mercy be present to your people who keep vigil on this most sacred night, and, for us who recall the wondrous work of our creation and the still greater work of our redemption, graciously bless this water. For you created water to make the fields fruitful and to refresh and cleanse our bodies. You also made water the instrument

325

of your mercy: for through water you freed your people from slavery and quenched their thirst in the desert; through water the Prophets proclaimed the new covenant you were to enter upon with the human race; and last of all, through water, which Christ made holy in the Jordan, you have renewed our corrupted nature in the bath of regeneration.

Therefore, may this water be for us a memorial of the Baptism we have received, and grant that we may share in the gladness of our brothers and sisters, who at Easter have received their Baptism. Through Christ our Lord. **Amen.**

RENEWAL OF BAPTISMAL PROMISES

While holding lit candles, the entire community renews its baptismal promises, if it has not already done so.

Dear brothers and sisters, through the Paschal Mystery we have been buried with Christ in Baptism, so that we may walk with him in newness of life. And so, now that our Lenten observance is concluded, let us renew the promises of Holy Baptism, by which we once renounced Satan and his works and promised to serve God in the holy Catholic Church.

And so I ask you:

1 Do you renounce Satan? **I do.**
   And all his works? **I do.**
   And all his empty show? **I do.**
2 Do you renounce sin, so as to live in the freedom of the children of God? **I do.**
   Do you renounce the lure of evil, so that sin may have no mastery over you? **I do.**

Do you renounce Satan, the author and prince of sin? **I do.**

3 Do you reject sin so as to live in the freedom of God's children? **I do.**

Do you reject the glamour of evil, and refuse to be mastered by sin? **I do.**

Do you reject Satan, father of sin and prince of darkness? **I do.**

The community professes its faith:

Do you believe in God, the Father almighty, Creator of heaven and earth? **I do.**

Do you believe in Jesus Christ, his only Son, our Lord, who was born of the Virgin Mary, suffered death and was buried, rose again from the dead and is seated at the right hand of the Father? **I do.**

Do you believe in the Holy Spirit, the holy catholic Church, the communion of saints, the forgiveness of sins, the resurrection of the body, and life everlasting? **I do.**

And may almighty God, the Father of our Lord Jesus Christ, who has given us new birth by water and the Holy Spirit and bestowed on us forgiveness of our sins, keep us by his grace, in Christ Jesus our Lord, for eternal life. **Amen.**

The priest sprinkles the people with blessed water, while an appropriate song is sung.

PRAYER OF THE FAITHFUL

The following intentions are suggestions only. There are more suggestions at www.livingwithchrist.ca

℟. **Lord, hear our prayer.**

For the Church, joyful witness to the resurrection of the Lord, we pray to the Lord: ℟.

For the world's nations and people, to whom Christ's resurrection offers the fullness of God's peace, we pray to the Lord: ℞.

For those baptized this night into Christ's death and resurrection, called as Christ's body to witness to the Good News, we pray to the Lord: ℞.

For Christian communities everywhere, embodying the triumph of life over death in their neighbourhoods and cities, we pray to the Lord: ℞.

LITURGY OF THE EUCHARIST

PREPARATION OF THE GIFTS (p. 14)

PRAYER OVER THE OFFERINGS
Accept, we ask, O Lord, the prayers of your people with the sacrificial offerings, that what has begun in the paschal mysteries may, by the working of your power, bring us to the healing of eternity. Through Christ our Lord. **Amen.**

PREFACE (Easter I, p. 22)

COMMUNION ANTIPHON (1 Corinthians 5.7-8)
Christ our Passover has been sacrificed; therefore let us keep the feast with the unleavened bread of purity and truth, alleluia.

PRAYER AFTER COMMUNION
Pour out on us, O Lord, the Spirit of your love, and in your kindness make those you have nour-

ished by this paschal Sacrament one in mind and heart. Through Christ our Lord. **Amen.**

SOLEMN BLESSING — EASTER

Bow down for the blessing.

May almighty God bless you through today's Easter Solemnity and, in his compassion, defend you from every assault of sin. **Amen.**

And may he, who restores you to eternal life in the Resurrection of his Only Begotten, endow you with the prize of immortality. **Amen.**

Now that the days of the Lord's Passion have drawn to a close, may you who celebrate the gladness of the Paschal Feast come with Christ's help, and exulting in spirit, to those feasts that are celebrated in eternal joy. **Amen.**

And may the blessing of almighty God, the Father, and the Son, and the Holy Spirit, come down on you and remain with you for ever. **Amen.**

DISMISSAL

1 Go forth, the Mass is ended, alleluia, alleluia!
2 Go in peace, alleluia, alleluia!

Thanks be to God, al - le - lu - ia, al - le - lu - ia!

℟. **Thanks be to God, alleluia, alleluia!**

April 16

Resurrection of the Lord

Today's gospel reading is one that never grows old or boring for me, because it is a story of such sharp contrasts. Dark becomes light; weeping turns to joy; despair changes into hope. If I were to sum up Easter in one word, it would be "transformation."

Just think about the disciples. In the weeks and months after the Resurrection, they found themselves doing things they could never have imagined. Take Peter in today's first reading: he was the one who a few days earlier had denied even knowing Jesus and was now fearlessly proclaiming his lordship. For all the disciples, life would never be the same again. Their encounter with the Risen Christ had changed them forever.

Each time we gather to celebrate the Eucharist, Jesus is in our midst, just as surely as he was for Mary Magdalene and the disciples on that first Easter morning. Our faith in the real presence assures us of this. And just as their encounter with the Risen Lord changed the disciples' lives forever, we too should never leave any celebration of the Eucharist unchanged. We receive his Body and Blood so that we might become his Body and Blood in a world much in need of God's presence. Nourished and transformed, we go forth to love and serve the Lord and one another. Alleluia! Alleluia!

Teresa Whalen Lux, Regina, SK

ENTRANCE ANTIPHON *(Cf. Psalm 138.18, 5-6)*
I have risen, and I am with you still, alleluia. You have laid your hand upon me, alleluia. Too wonderful for me, this knowledge, alleluia, alleluia.
   or (Luke 24.34; cf. Revelation 1.6)
The Lord is truly risen, alleluia. To him be glory and power for all the ages of eternity, alleluia, alleluia.

INTRODUCTORY RITES *(p. 5)*

COLLECT
O God, who on this day, through your Only Begotten Son, have conquered death and unlocked for us the path to eternity, grant, we pray, that we who keep the solemnity of the Lord's Resurrection may, through the renewal brought by your Spirit, rise up in the light of life. Through our Lord Jesus Christ, your Son, who lives and reigns with you in the unity of the Holy Spirit, one God, for ever and ever. **Amen.**

FIRST READING *(Acts 10.34a, 37-43)*
Peter began to speak: "You know the message that spread throughout Judea, beginning in Galilee after the baptism that John announced: how God anointed Jesus of Nazareth with the Holy Spirit and with power; how he went about doing good and healing all who were oppressed by the devil, for God was with him.

"We are witnesses to all that he did both in Judea and in Jerusalem. They put him to death by hanging him on a tree; but God raised him on the third day and allowed him to appear, not to all

331

the people but to us who were chosen by God as witnesses, and who ate and drank with him after he rose from the dead.

"He commanded us to preach to the people and to testify that he is the one ordained by God as judge of the living and the dead. All the Prophets testify about him that everyone who believes in him receives forgiveness of sins through his name."

The word of the Lord. **Thanks be to God.**

RESPONSORIAL PSALM *(Psalm 118)*

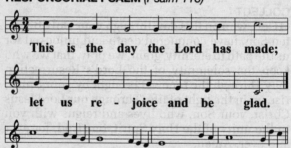

This is the day the Lord has made;

let us re - joice and be glad.

R. **This is the day the Lord has made;**
  let us rejoice and be glad.
or **Alleluia! Alleluia! Alleluia!**

O give thanks to the Lord, for · **he** is good;
his steadfast love en·-**dures** for-ever.
Let Is·-**rael** say,
"His steadfast love en·-**dures** for-ever." R.

"The right hand of the Lord · **is** ex-alted;
the right hand of the · **Lord** does valiantly."
I shall not die, but · **I_shall** live,
and recount the · **deeds_of** the Lord. R.

The stone that the · **builders** re-jected
has become · **the** chief cornerstone.
This is the · **Lord's** doing;
it is marvellous · **in** our eyes. R.

To hear the Sunday Psalms, visit www.livingwithchrist.ca.

An alternate reading follows.

SECOND READING *(Colossians 3.1-4)*

Brothers and sisters: If you have been raised with
Christ, seek the things that are above, where
Christ is, seated at the right hand of God. Set your
minds on things that are above, not on things
that are on earth, for you have died, and your
life is hidden with Christ in God. When Christ
who is your life is revealed, then you also will be
revealed with him in glory.

The word of the Lord. **Thanks be to God.**

or

SECOND READING *(1 Corinthians 5.6b-8)*

Do you not know that a little yeast leavens the
whole batch of dough? Clean out the old yeast
so that you may be a new batch, as you really
are unleavened. For our paschal lamb, Christ,
has been sacrificed. Therefore, let us celebrate
the festival, not with the old yeast, the yeast of
malice and evil, but with the unleavened bread
of sincerity and truth.

The word of the Lord. **Thanks be to God.**

EASTER SEQUENCE

On this day the following sequence is sung. An earlier version can be found at CBW II 202.

1. Christians, praise the paschal victim!
   Offer thankful sacrifice!

2. Christ the Lamb has saved the sheep,
   Christ the just one paid the price,
   Reconciling sinners to the Father.

3. Death and life fought bitterly
   For this wondrous victory;
   The Lord of life who died reigns glorified!

4. "O Mary, come and say
   what you saw at break of day."

5. "The empty tomb of my living Lord!
   I saw Christ Jesus risen and adored!

6. "Bright Angels testified,
   Shroud and grave clothes side by side!

7. "Yes, Christ my hope rose gloriously.
   He goes before you into Galilee."

8. Share the Good News, sing joyfully:
   His death is victory!
   Lord Jesus, Victor King, show us mercy.

Text: *Victimae Paschali Laudes;* tr. © 1983 *Peter J. Scagnelli.*
Tune: VICTIMAE PASCHALI LAUDES. **Music:** *CBW III 690*

GOSPEL ACCLAMATION *(1 Corinthians 5.7-8)*
Alleluia. Alleluia. Christ, our Paschal Lamb, has been sacrificed; let us feast with joy in the Lord. **Alleluia.**

The Gospel from the Easter Vigil (p. 315) may be read instead. For an afternoon or evening Mass, see p. 336.

GOSPEL *(John 20.1-18)*

The shorter version ends at the asterisks.

The Lord be with you. **And with your spirit.**
A reading from the holy Gospel according to John.
Glory to you, O Lord.

Early on the first day of the week, while it was still dark, Mary Magdalene came to the tomb and saw that the stone had been removed from the tomb. So she ran and went to Simon Peter and the other disciple, the one whom Jesus loved, and said to them, "They have taken the Lord out of the tomb, and we do not know where they have laid him."

Then Peter and the other disciple set out and went toward the tomb. The two were running together, but the other disciple outran Peter and reached the tomb first. He bent down to look in and saw the linen wrappings lying there, but he did not go in.

Then Simon Peter came, following him, and went into the tomb. He saw the linen wrappings lying there, and the cloth that had been on Jesus' head, not lying with the linen wrappings but rolled up in a place by itself. Then the other disciple, who reached the tomb first, also went in, and he saw and believed; for as yet they did not understand the Scripture, that he must rise from the dead.

* * *

Then the disciples returned to their homes. But Mary Magdalene stood weeping outside the tomb. As she wept, she bent over to look into the tomb; and she saw two Angels in white, sitting where the body of Jesus had been lying, one at the head and the other at the feet. They said to her, "Woman, why are you weeping?" She said to them, "They have taken away my Lord, and I do not know where they have laid him."

When she had said this, she turned around and saw Jesus standing there, but she did not know that it was Jesus. Jesus said to her, "Woman, why are you weeping? Whom are you looking for?" Supposing him to be the gardener, she said to him, "Sir, if you have carried him away, tell me where you have laid him, and I will take him away."

Jesus said to her, "Mary!" She turned and said to him in Hebrew, "Rabbouni!" which means Teacher. Jesus said to her, "Do not hold on to me, because I have not yet ascended to the Father. But go to my brothers and say to them, 'I am ascending to my Father and your Father, to my God and your God.'"

Mary Magdalene went and announced to the disciples, "I have seen the Lord," and she told them that he had said these things to her.

The Gospel of the Lord. **Praise to you, Lord Jesus Christ.**

Alternate Gospel for an afternoon or evening Mass:

GOSPEL *(Luke 24.13-35)*
The Lord be with you. **And with your spirit.**
A reading from the holy Gospel according to Luke. **Glory to you, O Lord.**

On the first day of the week, two of the disciples were going to a village called Emmaus, about eleven kilometres from Jerusalem, and talking with each other about all these things that had happened. While they were talking and discussing, Jesus himself came near and went with them, but their eyes were kept from recognizing him.

And he said to them, "What are you discussing with each other while you walk along?" They stood still, looking sad. Then one of them, whose name was Cleopas, answered him, "Are you the only stranger in Jerusalem who does not know the things that have taken place there in these days?"

He asked them, "What things?" They replied, "The things about Jesus of Nazareth, who was a Prophet mighty in deed and word before God and all the people, and how our chief priests and leaders handed him over to be condemned to death and crucified him. But we had hoped that he was the one to redeem Israel. Yes, and besides all this, it is now the third day since these things took place. Moreover, some women of our group astounded us. They were at the tomb early this morning, and when they did not find his body there, they came back and told us that they had indeed seen a vision of Angels who said that he was alive. Some of those who were with us went to the tomb and found it just as the women had said; but they did not see him."

Then he said to them, "Oh, how foolish you are, and how slow of heart to believe all that the Prophets have declared! Was it not necessary that the Christ should suffer these things and then enter into his glory?"

Then beginning with Moses and all the Prophets, he interpreted to them the things about himself in all the Scriptures. As they came near the village to which they were going, he walked ahead as if he were going on. But they urged him strongly, saying, "Stay with us, because it is almost evening and the day is now nearly over." So he went in to stay with them.

When he was at the table with them, he took bread, blessed and broke it, and gave it to them. Then their eyes were opened, and they recognized him; and he vanished from their sight.

They said to each other, "Were not our hearts burning within us while he was talking to us on the road, while he was opening the Scriptures to us?"

That same hour they got up and returned to Jerusalem; and they found the eleven and their companions gathered together. These were saying, "The Lord has risen indeed, and he has appeared to Simon!"

Then they told what had happened on the road, and how he had been made known to them in the breaking of the bread.

The Gospel of the Lord. **Praise to you, Lord Jesus Christ.**

RENEWAL OF BAPTISMAL PROMISES (p. 326)

PRAYER OF THE FAITHFUL

The following intentions are suggestions only. There are more suggestions at www.livingwithchrist.ca

R. **Lord, hear our prayer.**

For the Church, witness to Jesus risen and present among us in our daily lives, we pray to the Lord: R.

For peace among nations and between peoples, we pray to the Lord: R.

338

For those among us who lack caring and compassion, and for those who reach out to them, we pray to the Lord: R.

For us, God's people gathered here, called to be a community that recognizes and celebrates the presence of the risen Jesus, we pray to the Lord: R.

PREPARATION OF THE GIFTS (p. 14)

PRAYER OVER THE OFFERINGS
Exultant with paschal gladness, O Lord, we offer the sacrifice by which your Church is wondrously reborn and nourished. Through Christ our Lord. **Amen.**

PREFACE (Easter I, p. 22)

COMMUNION ANTIPHON (1 Corinthians 5.7-8)
Christ our Passover has been sacrificed, alleluia; therefore let us keep the feast with the unleavened bread of purity and truth, alleluia, alleluia.

PRAYER AFTER COMMUNION
Look upon your Church, O God, with unfailing love and favour, so that, renewed by the paschal mysteries, she may come to the glory of the resurrection. Through Christ our Lord. **Amen.**

SOLEMN BLESSING (Optional)
AND DISMISSAL (p. 329)

April 23
Divine Mercy Sunday

Today's gospel presents a very dramatic story, describing astonishing events. The resurrected Jesus somehow passes through locked doors and appears before his disciples. Later, Thomas the Doubter is invited to put his fingers right into the mortal wounds in Jesus' body to see for himself that the figure standing before them is truly their friend and teacher, who had been killed before their eyes just a few days earlier. These extraordinary moments offer important teachings, not just to the disciples, but to us, too.

But the most powerful teaching moment is also the quietest.

Jesus' followers are hiding in terror, their hopes crushed, their spirits defeated, afraid for their very lives. All seems lost. Then Jesus is somehow among them and says these simple words: "Peace be with you." Instantly their fear and dread are gone and in their place — joy.

Peace, inner peace, is the first gift the resurrected Jesus offers his disciples. Nourished by the peace of the Lord, this group of ordinary people will soon change the world.

And we, also ordinary women and men, also full of anxieties and disappointments, confused about the present and uncertain about the future, are offered the same gift. Right here, today, Jesus is saying to us, too, "Peace be with you." We need only to open our hearts to receive it.

Patrick Gallagher, Toronto, ON

ENTRANCE ANTIPHON *(1 Peter 2.2)*
Like newborn infants, you must long for the pure, spiritual milk, that in him you may grow to salvation, alleluia.

or (4 Esdras 2.36-37)
Receive the joy of your glory, giving thanks to God, who has called you into the heavenly kingdom, alleluia.

INTRODUCTORY RITES *(p. 5)*

COLLECT
God of everlasting mercy, who in the very recurrence of the paschal feast kindle the faith of the people you have made your own, increase, we pray, the grace you have bestowed, that all may grasp and rightly understand in what font they have been washed, by whose Spirit they have been reborn, by whose Blood they have been redeemed. Through our Lord Jesus Christ, your Son, who lives and reigns with you in the unity of the Holy Spirit, one God, for ever and ever. **Amen.**

FIRST READING *(Acts 2.42-47)*
They devoted themselves to the Apostles' teaching and fellowship, to the breaking of bread and the prayers. Awe came upon everyone, because many wonders and signs were being done by the Apostles.

All who believed were together and had all things in common; they would sell their possessions and goods and distribute the proceeds to all, as any had need. Day by day, as they spent much time together in the temple, they broke

bread in various houses and ate their food with
glad and generous hearts, praising God and having the goodwill of all the people. And day by
day the Lord added to their number those who
were being saved.

The word of the Lord. **Thanks be to God.**

RESPONSORIAL PSALM *(Psalm 118)*

Give thanks to the Lord for he   is good;

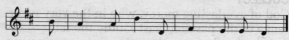

his stead-fast love en-dures for-ev-er.

R̷. **Give thanks to the Lord, for he is good;**
his steadfast love endures forever.
or **Alleluia!**

Let Israel · **say,**
"His steadfast love endures for--**ever.**"
Let the house of Aaron · **say,**
"His steadfast love endures for--**ever.**"
Let those who fear the Lord · **say,**
"His steadfast love endures for--**ever.**" R̷.

I was pushed hard, so that I was · **falling,**
but the Lord · **helped_me.**
The Lord is my strength and my · **might;**
he has become my sal--**vation.**

There are glad songs of · **victory**
in the tents of the · **righteous.** R.

The stone that the builders re--**jected**
has become the chief · **cornerstone.**
This is the Lord's · **doing;**
it is marvellous in our · **eyes.**
This is the day that the Lord has · **made;**
let us rejoice and be glad in · **it.** R.

©2010 Gordon Johnston/Novalis
To hear the Sunday Psalms, visit www.livingwithchrist.ca.

SECOND READING (1 Peter 1.3-9)

Blessed be the God and Father of our Lord Jesus Christ! By his great mercy he has given us a new birth into a living hope through the resurrection of Jesus Christ from the dead: a birth into an inheritance that is imperishable, undefiled, and unfading, kept in heaven for you, who are being protected by the power of God through faith for a salvation ready to be revealed in the last time.

In this you rejoice, even if now for a little while you have had to suffer various trials, so that the genuineness of your faith — being more precious than gold that, though perishable, is tested by fire — may be found to result in praise and glory and honour when Jesus Christ is revealed.

Although you have not seen him, you love him; and even though you do not see him now, you believe in him and rejoice with an indescribable and glorious joy, for you are receiving the outcome of your faith, the salvation of your souls.

The word of the Lord. **Thanks be to God.**

GOSPEL ACCLAMATION *(See John 20.29)*
Alleluia. Alleluia. You believed, Thomas, because you have seen me; blessed are those who have not seen, and yet believe. **Alleluia.**

GOSPEL *(John 20.19-31)*
The Lord be with you. **And with your spirit.**
A reading from the holy Gospel according to John.
Glory to you, O Lord.

It was evening on the day Jesus rose from the dead, the first day of the week, and the doors of the house where the disciples had met were locked for fear of the Jews. Jesus came and stood among them and said, "Peace be with you." After he said this, he showed them his hands and his side. Then the disciples rejoiced when they saw the Lord.

Jesus said to them again, "Peace be with you. As the Father has sent me, so I send you."

When he had said this, he breathed on them and said to them, "Receive the Holy Spirit. If you forgive the sins of any, they are forgiven them; if you retain the sins of any, they are retained."

But Thomas, who was called the Twin, one of the twelve, was not with them when Jesus came. So the other disciples told him, "We have seen the Lord." But he said to them, "Unless I see the mark of the nails in his hands, and put my finger in the mark of the nails and my hand in his side, I will not believe."

After eight days his disciples were again in the house, and Thomas was with them. Although the doors were shut, Jesus came and stood among them and said, "Peace be with you." Then he said to Thomas, "Put your finger here and see my hands. Reach out your hand and put it in my side. Do not doubt but believe." Thomas answered him, "My Lord and my God!"

Jesus said to him, "Have you believed because you have seen me? Blessed are those who have not seen and yet have come to believe."

Now Jesus did many other signs in the presence of his disciples, which are not written in this book. But these are written so that you may come to believe that Jesus is the Christ, the Son of God, and that through believing you may have life in his name.

The Gospel of the Lord. **Praise to you, Lord Jesus Christ.**

PROFESSION OF FAITH (p. 11)

PRAYER OF THE FAITHFUL

The following intentions are suggestions only. There are more suggestions at www.livingwithchrist.ca

R. **Lord, hear our prayer.**

For the Church throughout the world, witness to God's kingdom in daily life, we pray to the Lord: R.

For elected officials and leaders of nations, to whom their peoples look for justice, we pray to the Lord: R.

For those who are hungry, lonely, abused, sick and dying, especially those who are abandoned or destitute, we pray to the Lord: R.

For us, God's people gathered here, fed from God's table and called to feed all God's children, we pray to the Lord: R.

PREPARATION OF THE GIFTS (p. 14)

PRAYER OVER THE OFFERINGS
Accept, O Lord, we pray, the oblations of your people (and of those you have brought to new birth), that, renewed by confession of your name and by Baptism, they may attain unending happiness. Through Christ our Lord. **Amen.**

PREFACE (Easter I, p. 22)

COMMUNION ANTIPHON (Cf. John 20.27)
Bring your hand and feel the place of the nails, and do not be unbelieving but believing, alleluia.

PRAYER AFTER COMMUNION
Grant, we pray, almighty God, that our reception of this paschal Sacrament may have a continuing effect in our minds and hearts. Through Christ our Lord. **Amen.**

SOLEMN BLESSING — EASTER TIME (Optional)
Bow down for the blessing.

May God, who by the Resurrection of his Only Begotten Son was pleased to confer on you the gift of redemption and of adoption, give you gladness by his blessing. **Amen.**

May he, by whose redeeming work you have received the gift of everlasting freedom, make you heirs to an eternal inheritance. **Amen.**

And may you, who have already risen with Christ in Baptism through faith, by living in a right manner on this earth, be united with him in the homeland of heaven. **Amen.**

And may the blessing of almighty God, the Father, and the Son, and the Holy Spirit, come down on you and remain with you for ever. **Amen.**

DISMISSAL

1 Go forth, the Mass is ended, alleluia, alleluia!
2 Go in peace, alleluia, alleluia!

Thanks be to God, al - le - lu - ia,
al - le - lu - ia!

R. **Thanks be to God, alleluia, alleluia!**

April 30

In the Easter season we hear accounts of our risen Lord appearing to the disciples. Today's gospel is a well-told story and we are challenged to hear with new ears. The disciples are walking to Emmaus, upset and confused, when Jesus appears among them. It is after Jesus blesses and breaks the bread that their eyes are opened and they recognize who is in their midst.

Perhaps we are burdened by sadness or confusion, unable to see God in our midst. We may need to see through a new lens. The disciples recognized Jesus while at table sharing food and drink. Eastertime is filled with opportunities to gather at family tables. As we gather with family and friends, may we begin by thanking God for the gifts in our lives and ask for the wisdom and understanding to see God present in each day.

Today, may we be attentive to Christ present among us. May we recognize him in those we have gathered to pray with, in our presiding priest, in the proclaimed Word, and as we come to share in the Body and Blood of Christ. May the gospel remind us to ask the Holy Spirit to open our minds, hearts and eyes so that we will recognize Christ in our midst and be a sign of Christ's living presence in our world.

Catherine Ecker, Barrie, ON

ENTRANCE ANTIPHON *(Cf. Psalm 65.1-2)*

Cry out with joy to God, all the earth; O sing to the glory of his name. O render him glorious praise, alleluia.

INTRODUCTORY RITES *(p. 5)*

COLLECT

May your people exult for ever, O God, in renewed youthfulness of spirit, so that, rejoicing now in the restored glory of our adoption, we may look forward in confident hope to the rejoicing of the day of resurrection. Through our Lord Jesus Christ, your Son, who lives and reigns with you in the unity of the Holy Spirit, one God, for ever and ever. **Amen.**

FIRST READING *(Acts 2.14, 22b-28)*

When the day of Pentecost had come, Peter, standing with the eleven, raised his voice and addressed the crowd, "Men of Judea and all who live in Jerusalem, let this be known to you, and listen to what I say. Jesus of Nazareth, a man attested to you by God with deeds of power, wonders, and signs that God did through him among you, as you yourselves know — this man, handed over to you according to the definite plan and foreknowledge of God, you crucified and killed by the hands of those outside the law.

"But God raised him up, having freed him from death, because it was impossible for him to be held in its power. For David says concerning him, 'I saw the Lord always before me, for he is at my right hand so that I will not be shaken; therefore my heart was glad, and my tongue rejoiced; moreover my flesh will live in hope. For you will not abandon my soul to Hades, or let your Holy One experience corruption. You have made known to me the ways of life; you will make me full of gladness with your presence.'"

The word of the Lord. **Thanks be to God.**

RESPONSORIAL PSALM *(Psalm 16)*

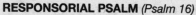

Lord, you will show me the path of

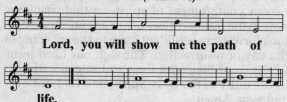

life.

R̰. **Lord, you will show me the path of life.**
or **Alleluia!**

Protect me, O God, for in you I · **take** refuge.
I say to the Lord, "You are · **my** Lord;
I have no good apart · **from** you."
The Lord is my chosen portion and my cup;
    you · **hold** my lot. R̰.

I bless the Lord who gives · **me** counsel;
in the night also my heart · **in**-structs_me.
I keep the Lord always · **be**-fore_me;
because he is at my right hand, I shall
    · **not** be moved. R̰.

Therefore my heart is glad, and my soul ·
    re-joices;
my body also rests · **se**-cure.

For you do not give me up · **to** Sheol,
or let your faithful one · **see** the Pit. R.

1 - You show me the path · **of** life.
2 - In your presence there is fullness · **of** joy;
4 - in your right hand are pleasures
  for--**ev**-er-more. R.

©2010 Gordon Johnston/Novalis
To hear the Sunday Psalms, visit www.livingwithchrist.ca.

SECOND READING *(1 Peter 1.17-21)*
Beloved: If you invoke as Father the one who
judges each person impartially according to each
one's deeds, live in reverent fear during the time
of your exile.

You know that you were ransomed from the
futile ways inherited from your ancestors, not
with perishable things like silver or gold, but with
the precious blood of Christ, like that of a lamb
without defect or blemish.

Christ was destined before the foundation of
the world, but was revealed at the end of the ages
for your sake. Through him you have come to
trust in God, who raised him from the dead and
gave him glory, so that your faith and hope are
set on God.

The word of the Lord. **Thanks be to God.**

GOSPEL ACCLAMATION *(See Luke 24.32)*
Alleluia. Alleluia. Lord Jesus, open the Scriptures to us; make our hearts burn with love when
you speak. **Alleluia.**

GOSPEL *(Luke 24.13-35)*

The Lord be with you. **And with your spirit.**
A reading from the holy Gospel according to
Luke. **Glory to you, O Lord.**

On the first day of the week, two of the disciples were going to a village called Emmaus, about eleven kilometres from Jerusalem, and talking with each other about all these things that had happened. While they were talking and discussing, Jesus himself came near and went with them, but their eyes were kept from recognizing him.

And he said to them, "What are you discussing with each other while you walk along?" They stood still, looking sad. Then one of them, whose name was Cleopas, answered him, "Are you the only stranger in Jerusalem who does not know the things that have taken place there in these days?"

He asked them, "What things?" They replied, "The things about Jesus of Nazareth, who was a Prophet mighty in deed and word before God and all the people, and how our chief priests and leaders handed him over to be condemned to death and crucified him. But we had hoped that he was the one to redeem Israel. Yes, and besides all this, it is now the third day since these things took place. Moreover, some women of our group astounded us. They were at the tomb early this morning, and when they did not find his body there, they came back and told us that they had indeed seen a vision of Angels who said that he was alive. Some of those who were with us went to the tomb and found it just as the women had said; but they did not see him."

Then he said to them, "Oh, how foolish you are, and how slow of heart to believe all that the Prophets have declared! Was it not necessary that the Christ should suffer these things and then enter into his glory?"

Then beginning with Moses and all the Prophets, he interpreted to them the things about himself in all the Scriptures. As they came near the village to which they were going, he walked ahead as if he were going on. But they urged him strongly, saying, "Stay with us, because it is almost evening and the day is now nearly over." So he went in to stay with them.

When he was at the table with them, he took bread, blessed and broke it, and gave it to them. Then their eyes were opened, and they recognized him; and he vanished from their sight.

They said to each other, "Were not our hearts burning within us while he was talking to us on the road, while he was opening the Scriptures to us?"

That same hour they got up and returned to Jerusalem; and they found the eleven and their companions gathered together. These were saying, "The Lord has risen indeed, and he has appeared to Simon!"

Then they told what had happened on the road, and how he had been made known to them in the breaking of the bread.

The Gospel of the Lord. **Praise to you, Lord Jesus Christ.**

PROFESSION OF FAITH *(p. 11)*

353

PRAYER OF THE FAITHFUL

The following intentions are suggestions only. There are more suggestions at www.livingwithchrist.ca

R̰. **Lord, hear our prayer.**

For the Church, sacrament of Christ in the midst of the world's struggles, we pray to the Lord: R̰.

For an end to ethnic and religious hatred, and the birth of understanding and peace among nations and peoples, we pray to the Lord: R̰.

For those among us who are poor, lonely, sick and dying, we pray to the Lord: R̰.

For us, God's holy people, embracing those who are nearing the end of life's journey, and supporting young people as they discover their life's direction, we pray to the Lord: R̰.

PREPARATION OF THE GIFTS *(p. 14)*

PRAYER OVER THE OFFERINGS

Receive, O Lord, we pray, these offerings of your exultant Church, and, as you have given her cause for such great gladness, grant also that the gifts we bring may bear fruit in perpetual happiness. Through Christ our Lord. **Amen.**

PREFACE *(Easter, p. 22)*

COMMUNION ANTIPHON *(Luke 24.35)*
The disciples recognized the Lord Jesus in the breaking of the bread, alleluia.

PRAYER AFTER COMMUNION
Look with kindness upon your people, O Lord, and grant, we pray, that those you were pleased to renew by eternal mysteries may attain in their flesh the incorruptible glory of the resurrection. Through Christ our Lord. **Amen.**

SOLEMN BLESSING (Optional, p. 346)

DISMISSAL (p. 70)

355

May Saints' Days

The following saints are traditionally remembered in May in Canada.

1   Saint Joseph the Worker
     Saint Pius V

2   Saint Athanasius

3   Saints Philip and James

4   Blessed Marie-Léonie Paradis

6   Saint François de Laval

8   Blessed Catherine of Saint Augustine

12   Saints Nereus and Achilleus
     Saint Pancras

13   Our Lady of Fatima

14   Saint Matthias

18   Saint John I

20   Saint Bernardine of Siena

21   Saint Christopher Magallanes and Companions
     Saint Eugène de Mazenod

22   Saint Rita of Cascia

24   Blessed Louis-Zéphirin Moreau

25   Saint Bede the Venerable
     Saint Gregory VII
     Saint Mary Magdalene de' Pazzi

26   Saint Philip Neri

27   Saint Augustine of Canterbury

May 7
World Day of Prayer for Vocations

He calls us by name.

After a long winter, spring finally arrives in the Yukon, sometime as late as May. When it comes, it is like a sudden revelation. First, a faint tinge of green sweeps across barren hillsides. In just days, trees burst out in full leaf. Long silent, held fast in a snow-covered land, life breaks free, filling the valleys and mountains to the brim.

Renewed by the increasing warmth of the sun, northerners deeply savour this abundance of creation. How many times have I climbed high to try to take in this majesty even more deeply from the vantage of some mountain pasture? In the words of the Bard of the Yukon, Robert Service, "It's the beauty that thrills me with wonder, it's the stillness that fills me with peace."

No matter what we have suffered or how much we have been asked to endure, the hope-filled offer of new life presents itself over and over again to us physically and spiritually. In the Acts of the Apostles, Peter called out to the "corrupt generation" of his day. "Repent, and be baptized," he urged. Do we hear the voice of Jesus, our Good Shepherd, calling today?

What does Jesus tell us of his vocation? "I came that they may have life, and have it abundantly." Green pastures await us if only we enter through his gate.

Michael Dougherty, Whitehorse, YT

ENTRANCE ANTIPHON *(Cf. Psalm 32.5-6)*
**The merciful love of the Lord fills the earth; by the
word of the Lord the heavens were made, alleluia.**

INTRODUCTORY RITES *(p. 5)*

COLLECT
Almighty ever-living God, lead us to a share in
the joys of heaven, so that the humble flock may
reach where the brave Shepherd has gone before.
Who lives and reigns with you in the unity of the
Holy Spirit, one God, for ever and ever. **Amen.**

FIRST READING *(Acts 2.14a, 36b-41)*
When the day of Pentecost had come, Peter,
standing with the eleven, raised his voice and addressed the crowd. "Let the entire house of Israel
know with certainty that God has made him both
Lord and Christ, this Jesus whom you crucified."

Now when the people heard this, they were
cut to the heart and said to Peter and to the other
Apostles, "Brothers, what should we do?" Peter
said to them, "Repent, and be baptized every one
of you in the name of Jesus Christ so that your
sins may be forgiven; and you will receive the
gift of the Holy Spirit. For the promise is for you,
for your children, and for all who are far away,
everyone whom the Lord our God calls to him."

And he testified with many other arguments
and exhorted them, saying, "Save yourselves
from this corrupt generation." So those who welcomed his message were baptized, and that day
were added about three thousand souls.

The word of the Lord. **Thanks be to God.**

RESPONSORIAL PSALM (Psalm 23)

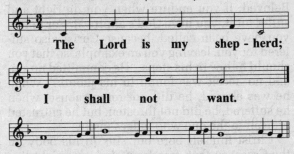

The Lord is my shep - herd;

I shall not want.

℟. **The Lord is my shepherd; I shall not want.**
or **Alleluia!**

The Lord is my shepherd, I shall · **not** want.
He makes me lie down in · **green** pastures;
he leads me be-·**side** still waters;
he re-·**stores** my soul. ℟.

He leads me in right paths for his · **name's** sake.
Even though I walk through the darkest valley,
    I fear · **no** evil;
for · **you** are with_me;
your rod and your · **staff** — they comfort_me. ℟.

You prepare a table · **be**-fore_me
in the presence · **of_my** enemies;
you anoint my · **head** with oil;
my · **cup** over-flows. ℟.

Surely goodness and mercy · **shall** follow_me
all the days of · **my** life,
and I shall dwell in the · **house_of** the Lord
my · **whole** life long. ℟.

©2009 Gordon Johnston/Novalis

SECOND READING *(1 Peter 2.20b-25)*

Beloved: If you endure when you do right and suffer for it, you have God's approval. For to this you have been called, because Christ also suffered for you, leaving you an example, so that you should follow in his steps. "He committed no sin, and no deceit was found in his mouth." When he was abused, he did not return abuse; when he suffered, he did not threaten; but he entrusted himself to the one who judges justly.

Christ himself bore our sins in his body on the Cross, so that, free from sins, we might live for righteousness; by his wounds you have been healed. For you were going astray like sheep, but now you have returned to the shepherd and guardian of your souls.

The word of the Lord. **Thanks be to God.**

GOSPEL ACCLAMATION *(John 10.14)*

Alleluia. Alleluia. I am the good shepherd, says the Lord; I know my sheep, and my own know me. **Alleluia.**

GOSPEL *(John 10.1-10)*

The Lord be with you. **And with your spirit.** A reading from the holy Gospel according to John. **Glory to you, O Lord.**

Jesus said: "Very truly, I tell you, anyone who does not enter the sheepfold by the gate but climbs in by another way is a thief and a bandit. The one who enters by the gate is the shepherd of the sheep. The gatekeeper opens the gate for him, and the sheep hear his voice. He calls his own sheep by name and leads them out. When he has brought out all his own, he goes ahead of them, and the sheep follow him because they know his voice. They will not follow a stranger, but they will run from him because they do not know the voice of strangers."

Jesus used this figure of speech with them, but they did not understand what he was saying to them. So again Jesus said to them, "Very truly, I tell you, I am the gate for the sheep. All who came before me are thieves and bandits; but the sheep did not listen to them. I am the gate. Whoever enters by me will be saved, and will come in and go out and find pasture. The thief comes only to steal and kill and destroy. I came that they may have life, and have it abundantly."

The Gospel of the Lord. **Praise to you, Lord Jesus Christ.**

PROFESSION OF FAITH (p. 11)

PRAYER OF THE FAITHFUL

The following intentions are suggestions only. There are more suggestions at www.livingwithchrist.ca

R. **Lord, hear our prayer.**

For all who hold positions of authority in the Church, called to model their leadership on that of the Good Shepherd, we pray to the Lord: R.

That the decisions and actions of political leaders may reflect God's wisdom and justice, we pray to the Lord: R.

For those who struggle to resist peer pressure and stand up for their convictions, we pray to the Lord: R.

For us, God's holy people, striving to live out the challenges of our vocations, we pray to the Lord: R.

PREPARATION OF THE GIFTS *(p. 14)*

PRAYER OVER THE OFFERINGS
Grant, we pray, O Lord, that we may always find delight in these paschal mysteries, so that the renewal constantly at work within us may be the cause of our unending joy. Through Christ our Lord. **Amen.**

PREFACE *(Easter, p. 22)*

COMMUNION ANTIPHON
The Good Shepherd has risen, who laid down his life for his sheep and willingly died for his flock, alleluia.

PRAYER AFTER COMMUNION
Look upon your flock, kind Shepherd, and be pleased to settle in eternal pastures the sheep you have redeemed by the Precious Blood of your Son. Who lives and reigns for ever and ever. **Amen.**

SOLEMN BLESSING *(Optional, p. 346)*

DISMISSAL *(p. 70)*

May 14

We are all familiar with that feeling of being at home. Sometimes this takes the form of feeling comfortable with someone, as if to say "I feel really at home being with you." At other times, it refers to the sense of comfort that we associate with the home in which we grew up. Consider for a moment how it would feel to be at home in a place in which we felt comfortable all the time.

During certain periods in our life, we may feel as though we do not know the best course of action to undertake. Christ invites us to believe and to reflect this belief in the work that we do. It is this work that allows the message of the gospel to be lived out in many different ways in today's world. If we ourselves believe, with God's help our work becomes an opportunity to illustrate to those around us the life that satisfies.

In the gospel today, Christ reminds us that an offer has been made to us that can be accepted at any time. This offer is to believe so much in God and the place that has been prepared for us, that we gently allow ourselves to be freed of our troubles by sharing them with Jesus. In so doing, we are indeed at home with our Creator.

John O'Brien, Oakville, ON

ENTRANCE ANTIPHON *(Cf. Psalm 97.1-2)*
O sing a new song to the Lord, for he has worked wonders; in the sight of the nations he has shown his deliverance, alleluia.

INTRODUCTORY RITES *(p. 5)*

COLLECT
Almighty ever-living God, constantly accomplish the Paschal Mystery within us, that those you were pleased to make new in Holy Baptism may, under your protective care, bear much fruit and come to the joys of life eternal. Through our Lord Jesus Christ, your Son, who lives and reigns with you in the unity of the Holy Spirit, one God, for ever and ever. **Amen.**

FIRST READING *(Acts 6.1-7)*
Now during those days, when the disciples were increasing in number, the Hellenists complained against the Hebrews because their widows were being neglected in the daily distribution of food. And the twelve called together the whole community of the disciples and said, "It is not right that we should neglect the word of God in order to wait on tables. Therefore, brothers, select from among yourselves seven men of good standing, full of the Spirit and of wisdom, whom we may appoint to this task, while we, for our part, will devote ourselves to prayer and to serving the word."

What they said pleased the whole community, and they chose Stephen, a man full of faith and the Holy Spirit, together with Philip, Prochorus, Nicanor, Timon, Parmenas, and Nicolaus, a convert of Antioch. They had these men stand before the Apostles, who prayed and laid their hands on them.

The word of God continued to spread; the number of the disciples increased greatly in Jerusalem, and a great many of the priests became obedient to the faith.

The word of the Lord. **Thanks be to God.**

RESPONSORIAL PSALM (*Psalm 33*)

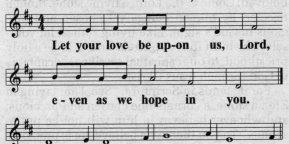

Let your love be up-on us, Lord, e-ven as we hope in you.

℟ **Let your love be upon us, Lord, even as we hope in you.**
or **Alleluia!**

Rejoice in the Lord, O you · **righteous.**
Praise befits the · **upright.**
Praise the Lord with the · **lyre;**
make melody to him with the harp of
    ten · **strings.** ℟

For the word of the Lord is · **upright,**
and all his work is done in · **faithfulness.**
He loves righteousness and · **justice;**
the earth is full of the steadfast love
    of the · **Lord.** ℟

Truly the eye of the Lord is on those
who · **fear_him,**
on those who hope in his steadfast · **love,**
to deliver their soul from · **death,**
and to keep them alive in · **famine.** R̲

©2010 Gordon Johnston/Novalis
To hear the Sunday Psalms, visit www.livingwithchrist.ca.

SECOND READING *(1 Peter 2.4-9)*

Beloved: Come to the Lord, a living stone, though rejected by human beings yet chosen and precious in God's sight. Like living stones, let yourselves be built into a spiritual house, to be a holy priesthood, to offer spiritual sacrifices acceptable to God through Jesus Christ.

For it stands in Scripture: "See, I am laying in Zion a stone, a cornerstone chosen and precious; and whoever believes in him will not be put to shame." To you then who believe, he is precious; but for those who do not believe, "The stone that the builders rejected has become the very head of the corner," and "A stone that makes them stumble, and a rock that makes them fall." They stumble because they disobey the word, as they were destined to do.

But you are a chosen race, a royal priesthood, a holy nation, God's own people, in order that you may proclaim the mighty acts of him who called you out of darkness into his marvellous light.

The word of the Lord. **Thanks be to God.**

GOSPEL ACCLAMATION *(John 14.6)*
Alleluia. Alleluia. I am the way, the truth, and the life, says the Lord; no one comes to the Father, except through me. **Alleluia.**

GOSPEL *(John 14.1-12)*
The Lord be with you. **And with your spirit.**
A reading from the holy Gospel according to John.
Glory to you, O Lord.

Jesus said to his disciples: "Do not let your hearts be troubled. Believe in God, believe also in me. In my Father's house there are many dwelling places. If it were not so, would I have told you that I go to prepare a place for you? And if I go and prepare a place for you, I will come again and will take you to myself, so that where I am, there you may be also. And you know the way to the place where I am going."

Thomas said to him, "Lord, we do not know where you are going. How can we know the way?"

Jesus said to him, "I am the way, and the truth, and the life. No one comes to the Father except through me. If you know me, you will know my Father also. From now on you do know him and have seen him."

Philip said to him, "Lord, show us the Father, and we will be satisfied." Jesus said to him, "Have I been with you all this time, Philip, and you still do not know me? Whoever has seen me has seen the Father. How can you say, 'Show us the Father'? Do you not believe that I am in the Father and the Father is in me? The words that I say to you I do not speak on my own; but the Father who dwells in me does his works. Believe

367

me that I am in the Father and the Father is in me; but if you do not, then believe me because of the works themselves. Very truly, I tell you, the one who believes in me will also do the works that I do and, in fact, will do greater works than these, because I am going to the Father."

The Gospel of the Lord. **Praise to you, Lord Jesus Christ.**

PROFESSION OF FAITH (p. 11)

PRAYER OF THE FAITHFUL

The following intentions are suggestions only. There are more suggestions at www.livingwithchrist.ca

R. **Lord, hear our prayer.**

For the Church, a community of young and old, called to firm faith and enduring love, we pray to the Lord: R.

For the end of persecution among nations and between peoples, we pray to the Lord: R.

For those among us who are poor, lonely and seeking God's consolation, we pray to the Lord: R.

For all mothers today, in gratitude for their loving witness, we pray to the Lord: R.

For us, God's people, called to manifest our discipleship by the love we have for one another, we pray to the Lord: R.

PREPARATION OF THE GIFTS (p. 11)

PRAYER OVER THE OFFERINGS

O God, who by the wonderful exchange effected in this sacrifice have made us partakers of the one supreme Godhead, grant, we pray, that, as we have come to know your truth, we may make it ours by a worthy way of life. Through Christ our Lord. **Amen.**

PREFACE (Easter, p. 22)

COMMUNION ANTIPHON (Cf. John 15.1, 5)

I am the true vine and you are the branches, says the Lord. Whoever remains in me, and I in him, bears fruit in plenty, alleluia.

PRAYER AFTER COMMUNION

Graciously be present to your people, we pray, O Lord, and lead those you have imbued with heavenly mysteries to pass from former ways to newness of life. Through Christ our Lord. **Amen.**

SOLEMN BLESSING (Optional, p. 346)

DISMISSAL (p. 70)

May 21

Do you ever feel alone? We all do at times, but in today's gospel we are reminded that we are never truly alone. The Advocate, the Spirit of truth, has been given to us by God and is abiding with us, inclining our hearts to make the right choice about where to go, what path to take, what decision to make at any given moment.

'Abide' is one of the most beautiful words in Scripture. With the noise of the world surrounding us, and perhaps an agitated spirit (which is not of the Spirit) circulating in us, it is not always easy to hear this abiding Spirit of truth. God is with me, and I am in God; what can be more beautiful or life-affirming?

How can we know this Spirit of truth? We need to ask the Holy Spirit to lead us to the deepest desire of our hearts, to show us where the Spirit dwells — and then the truth will be revealed.

The Spirit of truth is not temporary or passing — it is a promise forever. In these times where a commitment for "forever" is rare, it is comforting to know that we can count on the Holy Spirit in this ever-changing, ever-challenging world.

Let us give thanks for the gift of the Holy Spirit in our lives.

Sr. Nancy Sullivan, CSJ, Hamilton, ON

National Collection for the Pope's Pastoral Works

ENTRANCE ANTIPHON *(Cf. Isaiah 48.20)*
Proclaim a joyful sound and let it be heard; proclaim to the ends of the earth: The Lord has freed his people, alleluia.

INTRODUCTORY RITES *(p. 5)*

COLLECT
Grant, almighty God, that we may celebrate with heartfelt devotion these days of joy, which we keep in honour of the risen Lord, and that what we relive in remembrance we may always hold to in what we do. Through our Lord Jesus Christ, your Son, who lives and reigns with you in the unity of the Holy Spirit, one God, for ever and ever. **Amen.**

FIRST READING *(Acts 8.5-8, 14-17)*
In those days: Philip went down to the city of Samaria and proclaimed the Christ to them. The crowds with one accord listened eagerly to what was said by Philip, hearing and seeing the signs that he did, for unclean spirits, crying with loud shrieks, came out of many who were possessed; and many others who were paralysed or lame were cured. So there was great joy in that city.

Now when the Apostles at Jerusalem heard that Samaria had accepted the word of God, they sent Peter and John to them. The two went down and prayed for them that they might receive the Holy Spirit; (for as yet the Spirit had not come upon any of them; they had only been baptized in the name of the Lord Jesus). Then Peter and

John laid their hands on them, and they received the Holy Spirit.

The word of the Lord. **Thanks be to God.**

RESPONSORIAL PSALM (Psalm 66)

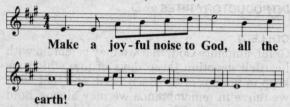

Make a joy-ful noise to God, all the earth!

R. **Make a joyful noise to God, all the earth!**
or **Alleluia!**

Make a joyful noise to God, all · **the** earth;
sing the glory · **of_his** name;
give to him · **glorious** praise.
Say to God, "How awesome are
    your · **deeds!**" R.

"All the earth · **worships** you;
they sing praises to you, sing praises
    · **to_your** name."
Come and see what God · **has** done:
he is awesome in his deeds among
    the children of · **Adam.** R.

He turned the sea into · **dry** land;
they passed through the river · **on** foot.
There we rejoiced · **in** him,
who rules by his might for--**ever.** R.

Come and hear, all you who · **fear** God,
and I will tell what he · **has** done_for_me.

Blessed be God, because he has not
rejected · **my** prayer
or removed his steadfast love from · **me.** R.

To hear the Sunday Psalms, visit www.livingwithchrist.ca.

SECOND READING *(1 Peter 3.15-18)*
Beloved: In your hearts sanctify Christ as Lord.
Always be ready to make your defence to anyone
who demands from you an accounting for the
hope that is in you; yet do it with gentleness and
reverence. Keep your conscience clear, so that,
when you are maligned, those who abuse you for
your good conduct in Christ may be put to shame.
For it is better to suffer for doing good, if suffering
should be God's will, than to suffer for doing evil.

For Christ also suffered for sins once for all, the
righteous for the unrighteous, in order to bring
you to God. He was put to death in the flesh, but
made alive in the spirit.

The word of the Lord. **Thanks be to God.**

GOSPEL ACCLAMATION *(John 14.23)*
Alleluia. Alleluia. All who love me will keep my
word, and my Father will love them, and we will
come to them. **Alleluia.**

GOSPEL *(John 14.15-21)*
The Lord be with you. **And with your spirit.**
A reading from the holy Gospel according to John.
Glory to you, O Lord.

Jesus said to his disciples: "If you love me, you
will keep my commandments. And I will ask the

373

Father, and he will give you another Advocate, to be with you forever. This is the Spirit of truth, whom the world cannot receive, because it neither sees him nor knows him. You know him, because he abides with you, and he will be in you.

"I will not leave you orphaned; I am coming to you. In a little while the world will no longer see me, but you will see me; because I live, you also will live. On that day you will know that I am in my Father, and you in me, and I in you.

"The one who has my commandments and keeps them is the one who loves me; and the one who loves me will be loved by my Father, and I will love them and reveal myself to them."

The Gospel of the Lord. **Praise to you, Lord Jesus Christ.**

PROFESSION OF FAITH (p. 11)

PRAYER OF THE FAITHFUL

The following intentions are suggestions only. There are more suggestions at www.livingwithchrist.ca

R. **Lord, hear our prayer.**

For the Church, temple of God's living word, we pray to the Lord: R.

For those who strive to make peace and justice part of everyday life in all nations, we pray to the Lord: R.

For those among us who do not recognize their worth as precious children fashioned in God's image, we pray to the Lord: R.

For us, the Body of Christ, as we minister to the sick, the lonely and those in need, we pray to the Lord: R.

PREPARATION OF THE GIFTS *(p. 14)*

PRAYER OVER THE OFFERINGS
May our prayers rise up to you, O Lord, together with the sacrificial offerings, so that, purified by your graciousness, we may be conformed to the mysteries of your mighty love. Through Christ our Lord. **Amen.**

PREFACE *(Easter, p. 22)*

COMMUNION ANTIPHON *(John 14.15-16)*
If you love me, keep my commandments, says the Lord, and I will ask the Father and he will send you another Paraclete, to abide with you for ever, alleluia.

PRAYER AFTER COMMUNION
Almighty ever-living God, who restore us to eternal life in the Resurrection of Christ, increase in us, we pray, the fruits of this paschal Sacrament and pour into our hearts the strength of this saving food. Through Christ our Lord. **Amen.**

SOLEMN BLESSING *(Optional, p. 346)*

DISMISSAL *(p. 70)*

May 28

World Communications Day

"Go," says Jesus to his confused followers, "make disciples of all nations... And remember, I am with you always." Witnesses of Jesus' words and acts, people transformed through close relationship with him, they are instructed to build a community that embraces the whole world. Go... do... assured of the Spirit's presence — this is their direction and ours.

The readings chosen today to mark Ascension are closely interwoven, focusing as they do on the post-resurrection role of Jesus' disciples. And they are timely. They invite us to reflect on how we are to live this command, on what making "disciples of all nations" might involve in our pluralistic world.

We painfully recall some past attempts at shaping disciples — forced baptisms and the condemnation of indigenous religious values and rituals, for example — that did not reflect Jesus' loving hospitality. And we have an increased awareness of and respect for the many paths to the divine discerned among the world's cultures. So, as disciples today, what are we to communicate?

Answers emerge from our dynamic relationship with Christ, Paul suggests. Through prayer, sacraments and our experience as individuals in community, we are transformed in love. Learning to see with the eyes of our heart enlightened, he suggests, allows us to experience resurrection and pass it on! As resurrection people, we witness to hope and love.

Ella Allen, Fredericton, NB

ENTRANCE ANTIPHON *(Acts 1.11)*

Men of Galilee, why gaze in wonder at the heavens? This Jesus whom you saw ascending into heaven will return as you saw him go, alleluia.

INTRODUCTORY RITES *(p. 5)*

COLLECT

Gladden us with holy joys, almighty God, and make us rejoice with devout thanksgiving, for the Ascension of Christ your Son is our exaltation, and, where the Head has gone before in glory, the Body is called to follow in hope. Through our Lord Jesus Christ, your Son, who lives and reigns with you in the unity of the Holy Spirit, one God, for ever and ever. **Amen.**

or

Grant, we pray, almighty God, that we, who believe that your Only Begotten Son, our Redeemer, ascended this day to the heavens, may in spirit dwell already in heavenly realms. Who lives and reigns with you in the unity of the Holy Spirit, one God, for ever and ever. **Amen.**

FIRST READING *(Acts 1.1-11)*

In the first book, Theophilus, I wrote about all that Jesus did and taught from the beginning until the day when he was taken up to heaven, after giving instructions through the Holy Spirit to the Apostles whom he had chosen. After his suffering he presented himself alive to them by many convincing proofs, appearing to them during forty days and speaking about the kingdom of God.

While staying with them, he ordered them not to leave Jerusalem, but to wait there for the promise of the Father. "This," he said, "is what you have heard from me; for John baptized with water, but you will be baptized with the Holy Spirit not many days from now."

So when they had come together, they asked him, "Lord, is this the time when you will restore the kingdom to Israel?" He replied, "It is not for you to know the times or periods that the Father has set by his own authority. But you will receive power when the Holy Spirit has come upon you; and you will be my witnesses in Jerusalem, in all Judea and Samaria, and to the ends of the earth."

When he had said this, as they were watching, he was lifted up, and a cloud took him out of their sight. While he was going and they were gazing up toward heaven, suddenly two men in white robes stood by them. They said, "Men of Galilee, why do you stand looking up toward heaven? This Jesus, who has been taken up from you into heaven, will come in the same way as you saw him go into heaven."

The word of the Lord. **Thanks be to God.**

RESPONSORIAL PSALM *(Psalm 47)*

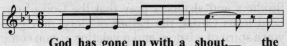

God has gone up with a shout,___ the

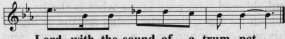

Lord with the sound of a trum‑pet.___

℟. **God has gone up with a shout,
the Lord with the sound of a trumpet.**
or **Alleluia!**

Clap your hands, all · **you** peoples;
shout to God with loud songs · **of** joy.
For the Lord, the Most High, · **is** awesome,
a great king over · **all** the earth. ℟.

God has gone up · **with_a** shout,
the Lord with the sound of · **a** trumpet.
Sing praises to God, · **sing** praises;
sing praises to our · **King,** sing praises. ℟.

For God is the king of all · **the** earth;
sing praises · **with_a** Psalm.
God is king over · **the** nations;
God sits on his · **ho**‑ly throne. ℟.

SECOND READING *(Ephesians 1.17-23)*

Brothers and sisters: I pray that the God of our Lord Jesus Christ, the Father of glory, may give you a spirit of wisdom and revelation as you come to know him, so that, with the eyes of your heart enlightened, you may know what is the hope to which he has called you, what are the riches of his glorious inheritance among the saints, and what is the immeasurable greatness of his power for us who believe, according to the working of his great power.

God put this power to work in Christ when he raised him from the dead and seated him at his right hand in the heavenly places, far above all rule and authority and power and dominion, and above every name that is named, not only in this age but also in the age to come.

And he has put all things under his feet and has made him the head over all things for the Church, which is his body, the fullness of him who fills all in all.

The word of the Lord. **Thanks be to God.**

GOSPEL ACCLAMATION *(Matthew 28.19, 20)*

Alleluia. Alleluia. Go make disciples of all nations; I am with you always, to the end of the age. **Alleluia.**

GOSPEL *(Matthew 28.16-20)*

The Lord be with you. **And with your spirit.** A reading from the holy Gospel according to Matthew. **Glory to you, O Lord.**

The eleven disciples went to Galilee, to the mountain to which Jesus had directed them. When they saw him, they worshipped him; but some doubted.

And Jesus came and said to them, "All authority in heaven and on earth has been given to me. Go therefore and make disciples of all nations, baptizing them in the name of the Father and of the Son and of the Holy Spirit, and teaching them to obey everything that I have commanded you. And remember, I am with you always, to the end of the age."

The Gospel of the Lord. **Praise to you, Lord Jesus Christ.**

PROFESSION OF FAITH *(p. 11)*

PRAYER OF THE FAITHFUL

The following intentions are suggestions only. There are more suggestions at www.livingwithchrist.ca

R. **Lord, hear our prayer.**

For the Church, community of disciples entrusted with authority and power to witness to the name of Jesus, we pray to the Lord: R.

For all leaders and teachers in the Church, we pray to the Lord: R.

For the poor and unemployed, at home and abroad, who need our encouragement and our help, we pray to the Lord: R.

For our parish community, called to act and speak courageously as we spread the Good News, we pray to the Lord: R.

PREPARATION OF THE GIFTS *(p. 14)*

PRAYER OVER THE OFFERINGS
We offer sacrifice now in supplication, O Lord, to honour the wondrous Ascension of your Son: grant, we pray, that through this most holy exchange we, too, may rise up to the heavenly realms. Through Christ our Lord. **Amen.**

PREFACE *(Ascension, p. 25)*

COMMUNION ANTIPHON *(Matthew 28.20)*
Behold, I am with you always, even to the end of the age, alleluia.

PRAYER AFTER COMMUNION
Almighty ever-living God, who allow those on earth to celebrate divine mysteries, grant, we pray, that Christian hope may draw us onward to where our nature is united with you. Through Christ our Lord. **Amen.**

SOLEMN BLESSING — ASCENSION *(Optional)*
Bow down for the blessing.

May almighty God bless you, for on this very day his Only Begotten Son pierced the heights of heaven and unlocked for you the way to ascend to where he is. **Amen.**

May he grant that, as Christ after his Resurrection was seen plainly by his disciples, so when he comes as Judge he may show himself merciful to you for all eternity. **Amen.**

And may you, who believe he is seated with the Father in his majesty, know with joy the fulfillment of his promise to stay with you until the end of time. **Amen.**

And may the blessing of almighty God, the Father, and the Son, and the Holy Spirit, come down on you and remain with you for ever. **Amen.**

DISMISSAL *(p. 70)*

June Saints' Days

The following saints are traditionally remembered in June in Canada.

1 Saint Justin

2 Saints Marcellinus and Peter

3 Saint Charles Lwanga and Companions

5 Saint Boniface

6 Saint Norbert

9 Saint Ephrem

11 Saint Barnabas

13 Saint Anthony of Padua

19 Saint Romuald

21 Saint Aloysius Gonzaga

22 Saint Paulinus of Nola
Saints John Fisher and Thomas More

24 The Nativity of John the Baptist

27 Blesseds Nykyta Budka and Vasyl Velychkowsky
Saint Cyril of Alexandria

28 Saint Irenaeus

29 Saints Peter and Paul

30 The First Martyrs of the Holy Roman Church

June 4

The meeting with the Risen Lord in John's account of Pentecost is the humble yet powerful beginning of a new age: fear is transformed into joy; pain is changed to peace and trust; flight and hiding become courage and mission. Division and hatred are vanquished by the gift of the Holy Spirit.

"Peace be with you" is the greeting and gift of the Risen Lord. The Hebrew word *shalom* means re-establishing the full meaning of things. Biblical peace is not only a pact that allows for a peaceful life, or indicates the opposite of a time of war. Rather, peace refers to the well-being of daily existence, to one's state of living in harmony with nature, with oneself and with God.

The gift of peace that Jesus entrusted to his first disciples becomes a promise and a prayer shared with the entire Christian community. The movement of the Spirit in people results in gifts and talents. This movement does not reach its end in individuals. Rather, it is supposed to have a ripple effect so that our unique abilities promote the common good. The Spirit's gifts are many: wisdom, understanding, counsel, knowledge, fortitude, piety and fear of the Lord. The Spirit will increase our gifts to the extent that we love Jesus and our brothers and sisters, obey the commandments and freely share with others what we have so lavishly received.

Fr. Thomas Rosica, CSB, Toronto, ON

ENTRANCE ANTIPHON *(Wisdom 1.7)*
The Spirit of the Lord has filled the whole world and that which contains all things understands what is said, alleluia.

or (Romans 5.5; cf. 8.11)
The love of God has been poured into our hearts through the Spirit of God dwelling within us, alleluia.

INTRODUCTORY RITES *(p. 5)*

COLLECT
O God, who by the mystery of today's great feast sanctify your whole Church in every people and nation, pour out, we pray, the gifts of the Holy Spirit across the face of the earth and, with the divine grace that was at work when the Gospel was first proclaimed, fill now once more the hearts of believers. Through our Lord Jesus Christ, your Son, who lives and reigns with you in the unity of the Holy Spirit, one God, for ever and ever. **Amen.**

FIRST READING *(Acts 2.1-11)*
When the day of Pentecost had come, they were all together in one place. And suddenly from heaven there came a sound like the rush of a violent wind, and it filled the entire house where they were sitting. Divided tongues, as of fire, appeared among them, and a tongue rested on each of them. All of them were filled with the Holy Spirit and began to speak in other languages, as the Spirit gave them ability.

Now there were devout Jews from every nation under heaven living in Jerusalem. And at this sound the crowd gathered and was bewildered, because each one heard them speaking in their own language. Amazed and astonished, they asked, "Are not all these who are speaking Galileans? And how is it that we hear, each of us, in our own language? Parthians, Medes, Elamites, and residents of Mesopotamia, Judea and Cappadocia, Pontus and Asia, Phrygia and Pamphylia, Egypt and the parts of Libya belonging to Cyrene, and visitors from Rome, both Jews and converts, Cretans and Arabs — in our own languages we hear them speaking about God's deeds of power."

The word of the Lord. **Thanks be to God.**

RESPONSORIAL PSALM (*Psalm 104*)

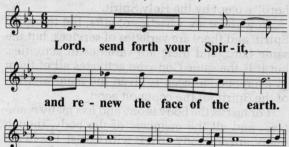

℞. **Lord, send forth your Spirit,**
   and renew the face of the earth.
or **Alleluia!**

Bless the Lord, O · **my** soul.
O Lord my God, you are very · **great.**
O Lord, how manifold · **are** your works!
The earth is full of · **your** creatures. ℞.

When you take away · **their** breath,
they die and return to their · **dust.**
When you send forth your spirit,
  they · **are** cre-ated;
and you renew the face of · **the** earth. R.

May the glory of the Lord endure · **for**-ever;
may the Lord rejoice in his · **works.**
May my meditation be · **pleasing** to him,
for I rejoice in · **the** Lord. R.

©2009 Gordon Johnston/Novalis
To hear the Sunday Psalms, visit www.livingwithchrist.ca.

SECOND READING *(1 Corinthians 12.3b-7, 12-13)*
Brothers and sisters: No one can say "Jesus is Lord" except by the Holy Spirit.

Now there are varieties of gifts, but the same Spirit; and there are varieties of services, but the same Lord; and there are varieties of activities, but it is the same God who activates all of them in everyone. To each is given the manifestation of the Spirit for the common good.

For just as the body is one and has many members, and all the members of the body, though many, are one body, so it is with Christ. For in the one Spirit we were all baptized into one body — Jews or Greeks, slaves or free — and we were all made to drink of one Spirit.

The word of the Lord. **Thanks be to God.**

SEQUENCE

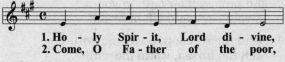

1. Ho - ly Spir - it, Lord di - vine,
2. Come, O Fa - ther of the poor,

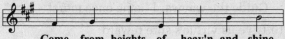

Come from heights of heav'n and shine,
Come, whose treas - ured gifts en - sure,

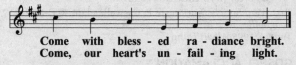

Come with bless - ed ra - diance bright.
Come, our heart's un - fail - ing light.

3. Of consolers, wisest, best,
   And our soul's most welcome guest,
   Sweet refreshment, sweet repose.

4. In our labour, rest most sweet,
   Pleasant coolness in the heat,
   Consolation in our woes.

5. Light most blessed, shine with grace
   In our heart's most secret place,
   Fill your faithful through and through.

6. Left without your presence here,
   Life itself would disappear,
   Nothing thrives apart from you!

7. Cleanse our soiled hearts of sin,
   Arid souls refresh within,
   Wounded lives to health restore.

8. On the faithful who are true
   and profess their faith in you,
   In your sev'nfold gift descend!

9. Bend the stubborn heart and will,
   Melt the frozen, warm the chill,
   Guide the wayward home once more!

10. Give us virtue's sure reward,
    Give us your salvation, Lord,
    Give us joys that never end!

Text: *Veni Sancte Spiritus;* tr. E. Caswell; adapt. © *Peter J. Scagnelli.*
Tune: ©*1995 Albert Dunn*

GOSPEL ACCLAMATION

Alleluia. Alleluia. Come, Holy Spirit, fill the hearts of your faithful and kindle in them the fire of your love. **Alleluia.**

GOSPEL *(John 20.19-23)*

The Lord be with you. **And with your spirit.**
A reading from the holy Gospel according to John.
Glory to you, O Lord.

It was evening on the day Jesus rose from the dead, the first day of the week, and the doors of the house where the disciples had met were locked for fear of the Jews. Jesus came and stood among them and said, "Peace be with you." After he said this, he showed them his hands and his side. Then the disciples rejoiced when they saw the Lord.

Jesus said to them again, "Peace be with you. As the Father has sent me, so I send you."

When he had said this, he breathed on them and said to them, "Receive the Holy Spirit. If you forgive the sins of any, they are forgiven them; if you retain the sins of any, they are retained."

The Gospel of the Lord. **Praise to you, Lord Jesus Christ.**

PROFESSION OF FAITH *(p. 11)*

PRAYER OF THE FAITHFUL

The following intentions are suggestions only. There are more suggestions at www.livingwithchrist.ca

R. **Send forth your Spirit, O Lord.**

For the Church, carrying on the ministry of Jesus by mediating the mercy and compassion of God, we pray to the Lord: R.

For people throughout the world, longing for God's peace and justice, we pray to the Lord: R.

For those among us who are sick, hungry, unemployed or suffering in any way, we pray to the Lord: R.

For the outpouring of God's Spirit on our parish community as we love and serve God and each other, we pray to the Lord: R.

PREPARATION OF THE GIFTS *(p. 14)*

PRAYER OVER THE OFFERINGS

Grant, we pray, O Lord, that, as promised by your Son, the Holy Spirit may reveal to us more abundantly the hidden mystery of this sacrifice and graciously lead us into all truth. Through Christ our Lord. **Amen.**

PREFACE *(Pentecost, p. 26)*

COMMUNION ANTIPHON *(Acts 2.4, 11)*
They were all filled with the Holy Spirit and spoke of the marvels of God, alleluia.

PRAYER AFTER COMMUNION
O God, who bestow heavenly gifts upon your Church, safeguard, we pray, the grace you have given, that the gift of the Holy Spirit poured out upon her may retain all its force and that this spiritual food may gain her abundance of eternal redemption. Through Christ our Lord. **Amen.**

SOLEMN BLESSING — THE HOLY SPIRIT *(Optional)*
Bow down for the blessing.

May God, the Father of lights, who was pleased to enlighten the disciples' minds by the outpouring of the Spirit, the Paraclete, grant you gladness by his blessing and make you always abound with the gifts of the same Spirit. **Amen.**

May the wondrous flame that appeared above the disciples powerfully cleanse your hearts from every evil and pervade them with its purifying light. **Amen.**

And may God, who has been pleased to unite many tongues in the profession of one faith, give you perseverance in that same faith and, by believing, may you journey from hope to clear vision. **Amen.**

And may the blessing of almighty God, the Father, and the Son, and the Holy Spirit, come down on you and remain with you for ever. **Amen.**

DISMISSAL

1 Go forth, the Mass is ended, alleluia, alleluia!
2 Go in peace, alleluia, alleluia!

Thanks be to God, al - le - lu - ia,

al - le - lu - ia!

R. **Thanks be to God, alleluia, alleluia!**

June 11

I smile when Trinity reflections begin with how hard it is to explain the Trinity and then try to do just that. I promise not to do that... well, maybe just a little bit.

I see today's readings being about my relationships with others, with God and in my own self. For me, this feast is about healthy relationships. Relationships God sees as healthy are not always what I recognize as healthy. God is in the cloud of my unknowing, merciful and gracious. God is in my moments of love and peace, in right relationship. And yes, God's promise to us of eternal life is made real in the clouds and the relationships.

How will I remember in moments of doubt and unknowing, and moments of peace and right relationship, that God is present? How do I draw my inner source of self from the core — from God — and reach out to those around me? Daily prayer, including the Eucharist, community and outreach are elements that help me to remember, and to re-direct my focus on relationships with those around me. I trust I am not alone on my spiritual journey, and maybe my journey may help others on theirs.

This week, may the moments that challenge and the ones that console help us recognize God in our midst. That could be the hardest part of all.

Sr. Susan Kidd, CND, Charlottetown, PE

ENTRANCE ANTIPHON
Blest be God the Father, and the Only Begotten Son of God, and also the Holy Spirit, for he has shown us his merciful love.

INTRODUCTORY RITES *(p. 5)*

COLLECT
God our Father, who by sending into the world the Word of truth and the Spirit of sanctification made known to the human race your wondrous mystery, grant us, we pray, that in professing the true faith, we may acknowledge the Trinity of eternal glory and adore your Unity, powerful in majesty. Through our Lord Jesus Christ, your Son, who lives and reigns with you in the unity of the Holy Spirit, one God, for ever and ever. **Amen.**

FIRST READING *(Exodus 34.4b-6, 8-9)*
Moses rose early in the morning and went up on Mount Sinai, as the Lord had commanded him, and took in his hand the two tablets of stone. The Lord descended in the cloud and stood with him there, and proclaimed the name, "The Lord." The Lord passed before Moses, and proclaimed, "The Lord, the Lord, a God merciful and gracious, slow to anger, and abounding in steadfast love and faithfulness."

And Moses quickly bowed his head toward the earth, and worshipped. He said, "If now I have found favour in your sight, O Lord, I pray, let the Lord go with us. Although this is a stiff-necked people, pardon our iniquity and our sin, and take us for your inheritance."

The word of the Lord. **Thanks be to God.**

RESPONSORIAL PSALM *(Daniel 3)*

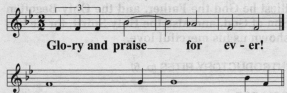

Glo-ry and praise___ for ev - er!

R̥. **Glory and praise for ever!**

Blessed are you, O Lord, God of our · **fathers**
and blessed is your glorious and
· **holy** name. R̥.

Blessed are you in the temple of your holy
· **glory,**
and to be extolled and highly glorified
· **for**-ever. R̥.

Blessed are you on the throne of your
· **kingdom,**
and to be extolled and highly exalted
· **for**-ever. R̥.

Blessed are you who look into the · **depths**
from your throne on · **the** cherubim. R̥.

Blessed are you in the firmament of · **heaven,**
to be sung and glorified · **for**-ever. R̥.

©2010 Gordon Johnston/Novalis
To hear the Sunday Psalms, visit www.livingwithchrist.ca.

SECOND READING *(2 Corinthians 13.11-13)*

Brothers and sisters, put things in order, listen to my appeal, agree with one another, live in peace; and the God of love and peace will be with you. Greet one another with a holy kiss. All the saints greet you.

The grace of the Lord Jesus Christ, the love of God, and the communion of the Holy Spirit be with all of you.

The word of the Lord. **Thanks be to God.**

GOSPEL ACCLAMATION *(See Revelation 1.8)*

Alleluia. Alleluia. Glory to the Father, the Son, and the Holy Spirit: to God who is, who was, and who is to come. **Alleluia.**

GOSPEL *(John 3.16-18)*

The Lord be with you. **And with your spirit.** A reading from the holy Gospel according to John. **Glory to you, O Lord.**

Jesus said to Nicodemus: "God so loved the world that he gave his only-begotten Son, so that everyone who believes in him may not perish but may have eternal life.

"Indeed, God did not send the Son into the world to condemn the world, but in order that the world might be saved through him. The one who believes in him is not condemned; but the one who does not believe is condemned already, for not having believed in the name of the only-begotten Son of God."

The Gospel of the Lord. **Praise to you, Lord Jesus Christ.**

PROFESSION OF FAITH (p. 11)

PRAYER OF THE FAITHFUL

The following intentions are suggestions only. There are more suggestions at www.livingwithchrist.ca

R. **Lord, hear our prayer.**

For the Church, called to deepen its understanding of the mystery of God, we pray to the Lord: R.

For our nation's leaders, seeking to learn the ways of peace and gentleness, we pray to the Lord: R.

For all who are oppressed because of race, gender or religion, and for those whose prejudice wounds them, we pray to the Lord: R.

For a deepening of our sense of gratitude expressed in the Eucharist, we pray to the Lord: R.

PREPARATION OF THE GIFTS (p. 14)

PRAYER OVER THE OFFERINGS

Sanctify by the invocation of your name, we pray, O Lord our God, this oblation of our service, and by it make of us an eternal offering to you. Through Christ our Lord. **Amen.**

PREFACE (Trinity, p. 26)

COMMUNION ANTIPHON (Galatians 4.6)

Since you are children of God, God has sent into your hearts the Spirit of his Son, the Spirit who cries out: Abba, Father.

PRAYER AFTER COMMUNION
May receiving this Sacrament, O Lord our God, bring us health of body and soul, as we confess your eternal holy Trinity and undivided Unity. Through Christ our Lord. **Amen.**

BLESSING AND DISMISSAL *(p. 70)*

June 18

I heard an expert on poetry remark recently that poetry is language that mirrors the soul. Jesus must have understood this, for he almost always turned to the language of poetry to convey to his listeners what was most important for them to understand: he is the gate of the sheepfold; he is the source of living water; he is the vine and they the branches — and in today's gospel, he says that to follow him it is essential to eat his body and drink his blood.

Jesus longs to convey to us just how profoundly we must remain in his love if we are going to understand his ministry and find strength to live out joyfully our own calling to be God's presence of loving compassion in our broken world. In the Eucharist we are invited to grasp the depth of the love of God for us and for our world, and to unite our own joy and pain with those of Christ.

Usually we receive the Eucharist with others. The Eucharist is a call to community. Together we draw strength and offer thanks, trusting in the wisdom of Pope Francis who has reminded us that the Eucharist is not "a prize for the perfect but... nourishment for the weak." *(Evangeli Gaudium, 47)*

Beth Porter, Richmond Hill, ON

ENTRANCE ANTIPHON *(Cf. Psalm 80.17)*
He fed them with the finest wheat and satisfied them with honey from the rock.

INTRODUCTORY RITES *(p. 5)*

COLLECT
O God, who in this wonderful Sacrament have left us a memorial of your Passion, grant us, we pray, so to revere the sacred mysteries of your Body and Blood that we may always experience in ourselves the fruits of your redemption. Who live and reign with God the Father in the unity of the Holy Spirit, one God, for ever and ever. **Amen.**

FIRST READING *(Deuteronomy 8.2-3, 14-16)*
Moses spoke to the people: "Remember the long way that the Lord your God has led you these forty years in the wilderness, in order to humble you, testing you to know what was in your heart, whether or not you would keep his commandments. He humbled you by letting you hunger, then by feeding you with manna, with which neither you nor your ancestors were acquainted, in order to make you understand that man does not live by bread alone, but by every word that comes from the mouth of the Lord.

"Do not exalt yourself, forgetting the Lord your God, who brought you out of the land of Egypt, out of the house of slavery, who led you through the great and terrible wilderness, an arid wasteland with poisonous snakes and scorpions. He made water flow for you from flint rock, and fed you in the wilderness with manna that your ancestors did not know, to humble you and to test you, and in the end to do you good."

The word of the Lord. **Thanks be to God.**

RESPONSORIAL PSALM *(Psalm 147)*

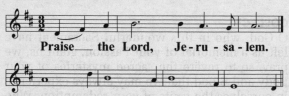

Praise— the Lord, Je-ru-sa-lem.

R̸. **Praise the Lord, Jerusalem.**
or **Alleluia!**

Praise the Lord, O Je· -**rusalem!**
Praise your God, O · **Zion!**
For he strengthens the bars of your · **gates;**
he blesses your children with-·**in_you.** R̸.

He grants peace within your · **borders;**
he fills you with the finest of · **wheat.**
He sends out his command to the · **earth;**
his word runs · **swiftly.** R̸.

He declares his word to · **Jacob,**
his statutes and ordinances to · **Israel.**
He has not dealt thus with any other · **nation;**
they do not know his · **ordinances.** R̸.

©2010 Gordon Johnston/Novalis
To hear the Sunday Psalms, visit www.livingwithchrist.ca.

SECOND READING *(1 Corinthians 10.16-17)*
Brothers and sisters: The cup of blessing that we bless, is it not a sharing in the Blood of Christ?

The bread that we break, is it not a sharing in the Body of Christ?

Because there is one bread, we who are many are one body, for we all partake of the one bread.

The word of the Lord. **Thanks be to God.**

SEQUENCE (Optional)

This sequence is to be sung. The shorter version begins at the asterisks (p. 405). An earlier version of this Sequence is set to music in CBW III 693.

1. Laud, O Sion, your salvation,
   laud with hymns of exultation
   Christ, your King and Shepherd true:
   Bring him all the praise you know,
   He is more than you bestow;
   never can you reach his due.

2. Wondrous theme for glad thanksgiving
   is the living and life-giving
   Bread today before you set,
   from his hands of old partaken,
   As we know, by faith unshaken,
   where the Twelve at supper met.

3. Full and clear ring out your chanting,
   let not joy nor grace be wanting.
   From your heart let praises burst.
   For this day the Feast is holden,
   When the institution olden
   of that Supper was rehearsed.

4. Here the new law's new oblation,
   by the new King's revelation,
   Ends the forms of ancient rite.
   Now the new the old effaces,

Substance now the shadow chases,
light of day dispels the night.

5. What he did at supper seated,
Christ ordained to be repeated,
His remembrance not to cease.
And his rule for guidance taking,
Bread and wine we hallow, making,
thus, our sacrifice of peace.

6. This the truth each Christian learns:
bread into his own flesh Christ turns,
To his precious Blood the wine.
Sight must fail, no thought conceives,
But a steadfast faith believes,
resting on a power divine.

7. Here beneath these signs are hidden
priceless things to sense forbidden.
Signs alone, not things, we see:
Blood and flesh as wine, bread broken;
Yet beneath each wondrous token,
Christ entire we know to be.

8. All who of this great food partake,
they sever not the Lord, nor break:
Christ is whole to all that taste.
Be one or be a thousand fed
They eat alike that living Bread,
eat of him who cannot waste.

9. Good and guilty likewise sharing,
though their different ends preparing:
timeless death, or blessed life.
Life to these, to those damnation,

Even like participation
is with unlike outcomes rife.

10. When the sacrament is broken,
doubt not, but believe as spoken,
That each severed outward token
does the very whole contain.
None that precious gift divides,
breaking but the sign betides.
Jesus still the same abides,
still unbroken he remains.

* * *

11. Hail, the food of Angels given
to the pilgrim who has striven,
to the child as bread from heaven,
food alone for spirit meant:
Now the former types fulfilling —
Isaac bound, a victim willing,
Paschal Lamb, its life-blood spilling,
manna to the ancients sent.

12. Bread yourself, good Shepherd, tend us;
Jesus, with your love befriend us.
You refresh us and defend us;
to your lasting goodness send us
That the land of life we see.
Lord, who all things both rule and know,
who on this earth such food bestow,
Grant that with your saints we follow
to that banquet ever hallow,
With them heirs and guests to be.

Text: translation ©2009 Concacan Inc.

GOSPEL ACCLAMATION *(John 6.51-52)*
Alleluia. Alleluia. I am the living bread that came down from heaven, says the Lord; whoever eats of this bread will live forever. **Alleluia.**

GOSPEL *(John 6.51-59)*
The Lord be with you. **And with your spirit.**
A reading from the holy Gospel according to John.
Glory to you, O Lord.

Jesus said to the people: "I am the living bread that came down from heaven. Whoever eats of this bread will live forever; and the bread that I will give for the life of the world is my flesh."

The people then disputed among themselves, saying, "How can this man give us his flesh to eat?"

So Jesus said to them, "Very truly, I tell you, unless you eat the flesh of the Son of Man and drink his blood, you have no life in you. Whoever eats my flesh and drinks my blood has eternal life, and I will raise them up on the last day; for my flesh is true food and my blood is true drink. Whoever eats my flesh and drinks my blood abides in me, and I in them.

"Just as the living Father sent me, and I live because of the Father, so whoever eats me will live because of me. This is the bread that came down from heaven, not like that which your ancestors ate, and they died. But the one who eats this bread will live forever."

Jesus said these things while he was teaching in the synagogue at Capernaum.

The Gospel of the Lord. **Praise to you, Lord Jesus Christ.**

PROFESSION OF FAITH (*p. 11*)

PRAYER OF THE FAITHFUL

The following intentions are suggestions only. There are more suggestions at www.livingwithchrist.ca

R̥. **Lord, hear our prayer.**

For the Church, the people of God, nourished by the real presence of Christ in the community, the word and the Eucharist, we pray to the Lord: R̥.

For governments searching for ways to ensure fair and equitable distribution of food and other resources, we pray to the Lord: R̥.

For the children in our own country who live in poverty, and for all the world's children whose parents and guardians lack the means to nourish them, we pray to the Lord: R̥.

For all fathers today: in gratitude for their love and care for their families, we pray to the Lord: R̥.

For the young people of our parish, in whose lives God is working, we pray to the Lord: R̥.

PREPARATION OF THE GIFTS (*p. 14*)

PRAYER OVER THE OFFERINGS
Grant your Church, O Lord, we pray, the gifts of unity and peace, whose signs are to be seen in mystery in the offerings we here present. Through Christ our Lord. **Amen.**

PREFACE (*Holy Eucharist, p. 27*)

COMMUNION ANTIPHON *(John 6.57)*
Whoever eats my flesh and drinks my blood remains in me and I in him, says the Lord.

PRAYER AFTER COMMUNION
Grant, O Lord, we pray, that we may delight for all eternity in that share in your divine life, which is foreshadowed in the present age by our reception of your precious Body and Blood. Who live and reign for ever and ever. **Amen.**

BLESSING AND DISMISSAL *(p. 70)*

June 25

We have all faced times when we have found it difficult to share our faith with others. We may be afraid of being criticized, teased or even losing our job. It is difficult to face these pressures and fears alone. The courage to face them comes only from trust in God's loving care.

In today's gospel, Jesus sends his disciples on a mission to proclaim his message publicly. He warns them that they will face opposition in the form of difficulties, persecution and humiliations, but tells them not to be afraid. He asks them and us to trust in God's faithful care and attention. God watches over the sparrow, the cheapest life sold at the market. He has also counted the hairs of our head, knowing whether they are many or few. If he cares for even the smallest creatures in nature and the smallest details of our lives, he will certainly not abandon anyone who follows the way of Christ. He will give us the strength and courage to defend our faith in Jesus.

Jesus is present to us in a special way in this eucharistic celebration. Let us ask him today for the strength and courage to give witness to our faith by our actions, our words and our choices, by the way we live our lives.

Nada Mazzei, Toronto, ON

ENTRANCE ANTIPHON *(Cf. Psalm 27.8-9)*
The Lord is the strength of his people, a saving refuge for the one he has anointed. Save your people, Lord, and bless your heritage, and govern them for ever.

INTRODUCTORY RITES *(p. 5)*

COLLECT
Grant, O Lord, that we may always revere and love your holy name, for you never deprive of your guidance those you set firm on the foundation of your love. Through our Lord Jesus Christ, your Son, who lives and reigns with you in the unity of the Holy Spirit, one God, for ever and ever. **Amen.**

FIRST READING *(Jeremiah 20.10-13)*
Jeremiah cried out: I hear many whispering: "Terror is all around! Denounce him! Let us denounce him!" All my close friends are watching for me to stumble. "Perhaps he can be enticed, and we can prevail against him, and take our revenge on him."

But the Lord is with me like a dread warrior; therefore my persecutors will stumble, and they will not prevail. They will be greatly shamed, for they will not succeed. Their eternal dishonour will never be forgotten.

O Lord of hosts, you test the righteous, you see the heart and the mind; let me see your retribution upon them, for to you I have committed my cause.

Sing to the Lord; praise the Lord! For he has delivered the life of the needy from the hands of evildoers.

The word of the Lord. **Thanks be to God.**

RESPONSORIAL PSALM (*Psalm 69*)

Lord, in your stead-fast love, an - swer me.

℟. **Lord, in your steadfast love, answer me.**

It is for your sake that I have borne
    re--**proach,**
that shame has covered · **my** face.
I have become a stranger to my · **kindred,**
an alien to my · **mother's** children.
It is zeal for your house that has
    con--**sumed_me;**
the insults of those who insult you have
    fallen · **on** me. ℟.

But as for me, my prayer is to you, O · **Lord.**
At an acceptable time, · **O God,**
in the abundance of your steadfast love,
    · **answer_me.**
With your steadfast · **help,** rescue_me.
Answer me, O Lord, for your steadfast love
    is · **good;**
according to your abundant mercy,
    turn · **to** me. ℟.

Let the oppressed see it and be · **glad;**
you who seek God, let your hearts · **re-**vive.
For the Lord hears the · **needy,**
and does not despise his own that are
    · **in bonds.**
Let heaven and earth · **praise_him,**
the seas and everything · **that**
    moves_in_them. R.

©2010 Gordon Johnston/Novalis
To hear the Sunday Psalms, visit www.livingwithchrist.ca.

SECOND READING *(Romans 5.12-15)*

Brothers and sisters: Just as sin came into the world through one man, and death came through sin, so death spread to all people because all have sinned. Sin was indeed in the world before the law, but sin is not reckoned when there is no law. Yet death exercised dominion from Adam to Moses, even those whose sins were not like the transgression of Adam, who is a type of the one who was to come.

But the free gift is not like the trespass. For if the many died through the one man's trespass, much more surely have the grace of God and the free gift in the grace of the one man, Jesus Christ, abounded for the many.

The word of the Lord. **Thanks be to God.**

GOSPEL ACCLAMATION *(See John 15.26, 27)*

Alleluia. Alleluia. The Spirit of truth will testify on my behalf, says the Lord, and you also are to testify. **Alleluia.**

GOSPEL *(Matthew 10.26-33)*

The Lord be with you. **And with your spirit.**
A reading from the holy Gospel according to Matthew. **Glory to you, O Lord.**

Jesus said to his Apostles: "Fear no one; for nothing is covered up that will not be uncovered, and nothing secret that will not become known. What I say to you in the dark, tell in the light; and what you hear whispered, proclaim from the housetops.

"Do not fear those who kill the body but cannot kill the soul; rather fear him who can destroy both soul and body in hell. Are not two sparrows sold for a penny? Yet not one of them will fall to the ground apart from your Father. And even the hairs of your head are all counted. So do not be afraid; you are of more value than many sparrows.

"Everyone therefore who acknowledges me before humans, I also will acknowledge before my Father in heaven; but whoever denies me before humans, I also will deny before my Father in heaven."

The Gospel of the Lord. **Praise to you, Lord Jesus Christ.**

PROFESSION OF FAITH *(p. 11)*

PRAYER OF THE FAITHFUL

The following intentions are suggestions only. There are more suggestions at www.livingwithchrist.ca

℟. **Lord, hear our prayer.**

For the Church, and for all who witness to Christ in the face of rejection, ridicule or danger, we pray to the Lord: ℟.

For a fairer distribution of the world's resources, we pray to the Lord: R.

For the chronically ill and all who suffer physical, emotional or mental pain, we pray to the Lord: R.

For our parish community, striving to bring God's love to those with whom we live and work, we pray to the Lord: R.

PREPARATION OF THE GIFTS *(p. 14)*

PRAYER OVER THE OFFERINGS
Receive, O Lord, the sacrifice of conciliation and praise and grant that, cleansed by its action, we may make offering of a heart pleasing to you. Through Christ our Lord. **Amen.**

PREFACE *(Sundays in Ordinary Time, p. 28)*

COMMUNION ANTIPHON *(Psalm 144.15)*
The eyes of all look to you, Lord, and you give them their food in due season.
   or (John 10.11, 15)
I am the Good Shepherd, and I lay down my life for my sheep, says the Lord.

PRAYER AFTER COMMUNION
Renewed and nourished by the Sacred Body and Precious Blood of your Son, we ask of your mercy, O Lord, that what we celebrate with constant devotion may be our sure pledge of redemption. Through Christ our Lord. **Amen.**

BLESSING AND DISMISSAL *(p. 70)*

July Saints' Days

The following saints are traditionally remembered in July in Canada.

3	Saint Thomas
4	Saint Elizabeth of Portugal
5	Saint Anthony Zaccaria
6	Saint Maria Goretti
9	Saint Augustine Zhao Rong and Companions
11	Saint Benedict
13	Saint Henry
14	Saint Camillus de Lellis
15	Saint Bonaventure
16	Our Lady of Mount Carmel
20	Saint Apollinaris
21	Saint Lawrence of Brindisi
22	Saint Mary Magdalene
23	Saint Bridget
24	Saint Sharbel Makhlûf
25	Saint James
26	Saint Anne and Saint Joachim
29	Saint Martha
30	Saint Peter Chrysologus
31	Saint Ignatius of Loyola

July 2

When I was an undergrad, I was told to read the Gospel of Matthew backwards, starting with the ending, the "Great Commission." Jesus' final words to his followers — "Go and make disciples of all nations" — resound in me and find a home in my heart, in the midst of the ordinariness of a Canadian mid-summer.

Today's gospel reading occurs after Jesus calls each of his disciples by name, these very ordinary people who had commonplace lives marked by birth, growing up, marriage, children, subsistence work and death, much like our own hidden lives. Jesus calls these people out of their everyday existence to a spectacular purpose: working with him to bring about the kingdom of justice, peace and love in this world and to prepare for the next.

In calling them, in calling us through the baptism that Paul refers to, Jesus affords each of us a dignity, a purpose and a value unique to our gifts and capacities.

For some of us, we may be called to welcome the stranger, as the Shunammite woman did, to listen with patience and openness to the prophets in our midst, no matter how unwelcome their message might be. Or maybe we are simply called to respond to someone's need for a cold cup of water to offset the heat of a blazing July sun.

Maureen Wicken, Vancouver, BC

ENTRANCE ANTIPHON *(Psalm 46.2)*
All peoples, clap your hands. Cry to God with shouts of joy!

INTRODUCTORY RITES *(p. 5)*

COLLECT
O God, who through the grace of adoption chose us to be children of light, grant, we pray, that we may not be wrapped in the darkness of error but always be seen to stand in the bright light of truth. Through our Lord Jesus Christ, your Son, who lives and reigns with you in the unity of the Holy Spirit, one God, for ever and ever. **Amen.**

FIRST READING *(2 Kings 4.8-12a, 14-16)*
One day Elisha was passing through Shunem, where a wealthy woman lived, who urged him to have a meal. So whenever he passed that way, he would stop there for a meal. She said to her husband, "Look, I am sure that this man who regularly passes our way is a holy man of God. Let us make a small roof chamber with walls, and put there for him a bed, a table, a chair, and a lamp, so that he can stay there whenever he comes to us."

One day when Elisha came there, he went up to the chamber and lay down there. He said to his servant Gehazi, "What then may be done for the woman?" Gehazi answered, "Well, she has no son, and her husband is old." Elisha said, "Call her." When the servant had called her, she stood at the door. Elisha said, "At this season, in due time, you shall embrace a son."

The word of the Lord. **Thanks be to God.**

RESPONSORIAL PSALM *(Psalm 89)*

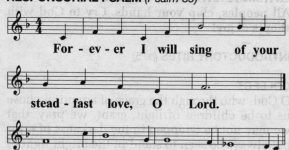

For - ev - er I will sing of your stead - fast love, O Lord.

℟. **Forever I will sing of your steadfast love, O Lord.**

I will sing of your steadfast love, O Lord,
    for-**ever**;
with my mouth I will proclaim your
    faithfulness to all gener-**ations.**
I declare that your steadfast love is established
    for-**ever**;
your faithfulness is as firm · **as_the** heavens. ℟.

Blessed are the people who know the festal
    · **shout,**
who walk, O Lord, in the light of your
    · **countenance;**
they exult in your name all day · **long,**
and extol · **your** righteousness. ℟.

For you are the glory of their · **strength;**
by your favour our horn is ex-**alted.**
For our shield belongs to the · **Lord,**
our king to the Holy One · **of** Israel. ℟.

©2010 Gordon Johnston/Novalis

SECOND READING *(Romans 6.3-4, 8-11)*

Brothers and sisters: All of us who have been baptized into Christ Jesus were baptized into his death. Therefore we have been buried with him by baptism into death, so that, just as Christ was raised from the dead by the glory of the Father, so we too might walk in newness of life.

But if we have died with Christ, we believe that we will also live with him. We know that Christ, being raised from the dead, will never die again; death no longer has dominion over him. The death he died, he died to sin, once for all; but the life he lives, he lives to God.

So you also must consider yourselves dead to sin and alive to God in Christ Jesus.

The word of the Lord. **Thanks be to God.**

GOSPEL ACCLAMATION *(See 1 Peter 2.9)*

Alleluia. Alleluia. You are a chosen race, a royal priesthood, a holy nation. Praise God who called you out of darkness into his marvellous light. **Alleluia.**

GOSPEL *(Matthew 10.37-42)*

The Lord be with you. **And with your spirit.** A reading from the holy Gospel according to Matthew. **Glory to you, O Lord.**

Jesus said to his Apostles: "Whoever loves father or mother more than me is not worthy of me; and whoever loves son or daughter more than me is not worthy of me; and whoever does not take up their cross and follow me is not worthy of me. Whoever finds their life will lose it, and whoever loses their life for my sake will find it.

"Whoever welcomes you welcomes me, and whoever welcomes me welcomes the one who sent me. Whoever welcomes a prophet in the name of a prophet will receive a prophet's reward; and whoever welcomes a righteous person in the name of a righteous person will receive the reward of the righteous; and whoever gives even a cup of cold water to one of these little ones in the name of a disciple — truly I tell you — that person will not lose their reward."

The Gospel of the Lord. **Praise to you, Lord Jesus Christ.**

PROFESSION OF FAITH (p. 11)

PRAYER OF THE FAITHFUL

The following intentions are suggestions only. There are more suggestions at www.livingwithchrist.ca

R. **Lord, hear our prayer.**

For the Church and its mission to the weary and the burdened, we pray to the Lord: R.

For world leaders committed to promoting the well-being of all citizens, we pray to the Lord: R.

For those who minister to the poor, the lonely and the vulnerable, we pray to the Lord: R.

For our community, dedicated to proclaiming the good news of a compassionate God, we pray to the Lord: R.

PREPARATION OF THE GIFTS (p. 14)

PRAYER OVER THE OFFERINGS

O God, who graciously accomplish the effects of your mysteries, grant, we pray, that the deeds by which we serve you may be worthy of these sacred gifts. Through Christ our Lord. **Amen.**

PREFACE *(Sundays in Ordinary Time, p. 28)*

COMMUNION ANTIPHON *(Cf. Psalm 102.1)*
Bless the Lord, O my soul, and all within me, his holy name.
   or (John 17.20-21)
O Father, I pray for them, that they may be one in us, that the world may believe that you have sent me, says the Lord.

PRAYER AFTER COMMUNION

May this divine sacrifice we have offered and received fill us with life, O Lord, we pray, so that, bound to you in lasting charity, we may bear fruit that lasts for ever. Through Christ our Lord. **Amen.**

BLESSING AND DISMISSAL *(p. 70)*

July 9

In our times of weariness and need, we can try to find some respite in our support system of close friends and family, in TV shows, shopping, social media and other pastimes. But we may discover that the people and material comforts we depend on cannot truly fill our emptiness and relieve our sufferings.

God alone has the boundless love, mercy and compassion to help us bear our crosses. In today's gospel, Jesus encourages those who are weary to come to him to find rest.

Though we cannot escape suffering, Jesus assures us that we are not alone in carrying our burdens if we take his yoke and learn from him. The metaphor of the yoke Jesus uses likely refers to a wooden crosspiece used on the necks of two animals as a means of pulling the plough or cart. In this sense, Jesus will carry our crosses with us, side by side, when we cannot bear the load of our sufferings on our own.

When the alternative is distress and despair, may we turn to our gracious and merciful God to help us find rest through living and learning Jesus' humble, gentle and compassionate way.

Christl Dabu, Hamilton, ON

ENTRANCE ANTIPHON *(Cf. Psalm 47.10-11)*
Your merciful love, O God, we have received in
the midst of your temple. Your praise, O God,
like your name, reaches the ends of the earth;
your right hand is filled with saving justice.

INTRODUCTORY RITES *(p. 5)*

COLLECT
O God, who in the abasement of your Son have
raised up a fallen world, fill your faithful with
holy joy, for on those you have rescued from slavery to sin you bestow eternal gladness. Through
our Lord Jesus Christ, your Son, who lives and
reigns with you in the unity of the Holy Spirit,
one God, for ever and ever. **Amen.**

FIRST READING *(Zechariah 9.9-10)*
Thus says the Lord:
Rejoice greatly, O daughter Zion!
Shout aloud, O daughter Jerusalem!
Lo, your king comes to you;
triumphant and victorious is he,
humble and riding on a donkey,
on a colt, the foal of a donkey.

He will cut off the chariot from Ephraim
and the war horse from Jerusalem;
and the warrior's bow shall be cut off,
and he shall command peace to the nations;
his dominion shall be from sea to sea,
and from the River to the ends of the earth.

The word of the Lord. **Thanks be to God.**

RESPONSORIAL PSALM *(Psalm 145)*

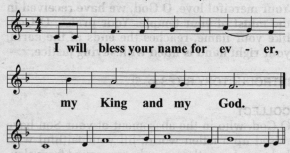

I will bless your name for ev - er,

my King and my God.

℟. **I will bless your name for ever,**
   my King and my God.
or **Alleluia!**

I will extol you, my God and · **King,**
and bless your name forever and · **ever.**
Every day I will · **bless_you,**
and praise your name forever · **and** ever. ℟.

The Lord is gracious and · **merciful,**
slow to anger and abounding in steadfast · **love.**
The Lord is good to · **all,**
and his compassion is over all that
   he · **has** made. ℟.

All your works shall give thanks to you,
   O · **Lord,**
and all your faithful shall · **bless_you.**
They shall speak of the glory of your
   · **kingdom,**
and tell of · **your** power. ℟.

The Lord is faithful in all his · **words,**
and gracious in all his · **deeds.**
The Lord upholds all who are · **falling,**
and raises up all who are · **bowed** down. R.

©2010 Gordon Johnston/Novalis

To hear the Sunday Psalms, visit www.livingwithchrist.ca.

SECOND READING *(Romans 8.9, 11-13)*
Brothers and sisters: You are not in the flesh; you
are in the Spirit, since the Spirit of God dwells
in you. Anyone who does not have the Spirit of
Christ does not belong to him.

If the Spirit of God who raised Jesus from the
dead dwells in you, he who raised Christ from
the dead will give life to your mortal bodies also
through his Spirit that dwells in you.

So then, brothers and sisters, we are debtors,
not to the flesh, to live according to the flesh — for
if you live according to the flesh, you will die; but
if by the Spirit you put to death the deeds of the
body, you will live.

The word of the Lord. **Thanks be to God.**

GOSPEL ACCLAMATION *(See Matthew 11.25)*
Alleluia. Alleluia. Blessed are you, Father, Lord
of heaven and earth; you have revealed to little
ones the mysteries of the kingdom. **Alleluia.**

GOSPEL *(Matthew 11.25-30)*
The Lord be with you. **And with your spirit.**
A reading from the holy Gospel according to Mat-
thew. **Glory to you, O Lord.**

425

At that time Jesus said, "I thank you, Father, Lord of heaven and earth, because you have hidden these things from the wise and the intelligent and have revealed them to infants; yes, Father, for such was your gracious will."

He continued: "All things have been handed over to me by my Father; and no one knows the Son except the Father, and no one knows the Father except the Son and anyone to whom the Son chooses to reveal him.

"Come to me, all you that are weary and are carrying heavy burdens, and I will give you rest. Take my yoke upon you, and learn from me; for I am gentle and humble in heart, and you will find rest for your souls. For my yoke is easy, and my burden is light."

The Gospel of the Lord. **Praise to you, Lord Jesus Christ.**

PROFESSION OF FAITH (p. 11)

PRAYER OF THE FAITHFUL

The following intentions are suggestions only. There are more suggestions at www.livingwithchrist.ca

R. **Lord, hear our prayer.**

For all in the Church who lead in the ways of simplicity and peace, we pray to the Lord: R.

For leaders of nations, from whom their people expect words and deeds rooted in peace, we pray to the Lord: R.

For those whose lives lack peace, and for those who reach out to them, we pray to the Lord: R.

For us, God's people gathered here, called to bring peace to the lives of others, we pray to the Lord: ℞

PREPARATION OF THE GIFTS *(p. 14)*

PRAYER OVER THE OFFERINGS
May this oblation dedicated to your name purify us, O Lord, and day by day bring our conduct closer to the life of heaven. Through Christ our Lord. **Amen.**

PREFACE *(Sundays in Ordinary Time, p. 28)*

COMMUNION ANTIPHON *(Psalm 33.9)*
Taste and see that the Lord is good; blessed the man who seeks refuge in him.
  or (Matthew 11.28)
Come to me, all who labour and are burdened, and I will refresh you, says the Lord.

PRAYER AFTER COMMUNION
Grant, we pray, O Lord, that, having been replenished by such great gifts, we may gain the prize of salvation and never cease to praise you. Through Christ our Lord. **Amen.**

BLESSING AND DISMISSAL *(p. 70)*

July 16

Today's gospel from Matthew — so familiar! — touches me in an unexpected new way. Jesus presents the Parable of the Sower to people familiar with farming techniques. He speaks of seeds being tossed upon varied qualities of soil and of the earth's response to their potential for growth. Seeds that fall above ground, on rocky soil or among thorns won't flourish, he says. Those absorbed into rich soil will reproduce... even a hundredfold!

I first learned about God as a non-Catholic five year old attending a convent close to my home. As my classmates prepared for the sacraments, I longed to receive Jesus. At age 21, my dream was realized. As an adult, the practice of my faith has been a source of intense joy. Yet when my beliefs are questioned or criticized, heartfelt prayer eludes me. Jesus likens the person who, rootless, falls away "when trouble or persecution arises on account of the word" to seed thrown on rocky soil. Do these words describe *me*? A disheartening thought!

Reflection, however, shows me that whenever I am lost, God in his mercy finds me. Today, Isaiah tells me that God's word will always accomplish the purpose for which it has been sent. The psalmist reassures me that whatever happens to the seed, God is blessing *my* growth. God's word offers comfort, understanding, encouragement and love.

Barbara K. d'Artois, Pierrefonds, QC

ENTRANCE ANTIPHON (Cf. Psalm 16.15)
As for me, in justice I shall behold your face; I
shall be filled with the vision of your glory.

INTRODUCTORY RITES (p. 5)

COLLECT
O God, who show the light of your truth to those
who go astray, so that they may return to the right
path, give all who for the faith they profess are
accounted Christians the grace to reject whatever
is contrary to the name of Christ and to strive after
all that does it honour. Through our Lord Jesus
Christ, your Son, who lives and reigns with you
in the unity of the Holy Spirit, one God, for ever
and ever. **Amen.**

FIRST READING (Isaiah 55.10-11)
Thus says the Lord: "As the rain and the snow
come down from heaven, and do not return there
until they have watered the earth, making it bring
forth and sprout, giving seed to the sower and
bread to the one who eats, so shall my word be
that goes out from my mouth; it shall not return
to me empty, but it shall accomplish that which
I purpose, and succeed in the thing for which I
sent it."

The word of the Lord. **Thanks be to God.**

RESPONSORIAL PSALM *(Psalm 65)*

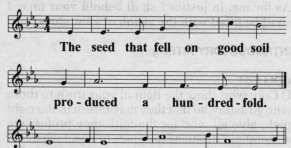

The seed that fell on good soil pro-duced a hun-dred-fold.

R. **The seed that fell on good soil
produced a hundredfold.**

You visit the earth and · **water_it,**
you greatly en--**rich_it;**
the river of God is full of · **water;**
you provide the people with · **grain.** R.

For so you have prepared the · **earth:**
you water its furrows a--**bundantly,**
settling its ridges, softening it with · **showers,**
and blessing its · **growth.** R.

You crown the year with your · **bounty;**
your pathways overflow with · **richness.**
The pastures of the wilderness over--**flow,**
the hills gird themselves with · **joy.** R.

1 - The meadows clothe themselves with ·
flocks,
3 - the valleys deck themselves with · **grain,**
4 - they shout and sing together for · **joy.** R.

SECOND READING *(Romans 8.18-23)*

Brothers and sisters: I consider that the sufferings of this present time are not worth comparing with the glory about to be revealed to us. For the creation waits with eager longing for the revealing of the children of God; for the creation was subjected to futility, not of its own will but by the will of the one who subjected it, in hope that the creation itself will be set free from its bondage to decay and will obtain the freedom of the glory of the children of God.

We know that the whole creation has been groaning in labour pains until now; and not only the creation, but we ourselves, who have the first fruits of the Spirit, groan inwardly while we wait for adoption to sonship, the redemption of our bodies.

The word of the Lord. **Thanks be to God.**

GOSPEL ACCLAMATION *(See Luke 8.11)*

Alleluia. Alleluia. The seed is the word of God, Christ is the sower; all who come to him will live for ever. **Alleluia.**

GOSPEL *(Matthew 13.1-23)*

The shorter reading ends at the asterisks.

The Lord be with you. **And with your spirit.** A reading from the holy Gospel according to Matthew. **Glory to you, O Lord.**

Jesus went out of the house and sat beside the sea. Such great crowds gathered around him that he got into a boat and sat there, while the whole crowd stood on the beach. And he told them many things in parables.

"Listen! A sower went out to sow. And as he sowed, some seeds fell on the path, and the birds came and ate them up. Other seeds fell on rocky ground, where they did not have much soil, and they sprang up quickly, since they had no depth of soil. But when the sun rose, they were scorched; and since they had no root, they withered away. Other seeds fell among thorns, and the thorns grew up and choked them. Other seeds fell on good soil and brought forth grain, some a hundredfold, some sixty, some thirty. Let anyone with ears listen!"

* * *

Then the disciples came and asked Jesus, "Why do you speak to them in parables?" He answered, "To you it has been given to know the secrets of the kingdom of heaven, but to them it has not been given. For to those who have, more will be given, and they will have an abundance; but from those who have nothing, even what they have will be taken away.

"The reason I speak to them in parables is that 'seeing they do not perceive, and hearing they do not listen, nor do they understand.' With them indeed is fulfilled the prophecy of Isaiah that says: 'You will indeed listen, but never understand, and you will indeed look, but never perceive. For this people's heart has grown dull, and their ears are hard of hearing, and they have shut their eyes; so that they might not look with their eyes, and listen with their ears, and understand with their heart and turn — and I would heal them.'

"But blessed are your eyes, for they see, and your ears, for they hear. Truly I tell you, many Prophets and righteous people longed to see what you see, but did not see it, and to hear what you hear, but did not hear it.

"Hear then the parable of the sower. When anyone hears the word of the kingdom and does not understand it, the evil one comes and snatches away what is sown in the heart; this is what was sown on the path. As for what was sown on rocky ground, this is the one who hears the word and immediately receives it with joy; yet such a person has no root, but endures only for a while, and when trouble or persecution arises on account of the word, that person immediately falls away. As for what was sown among thorns, this is the one who hears the word, but the cares of the world and the lure of wealth choke the word, and it yields nothing.

"But as for what was sown on good soil, this is the one who hears the word and understands it, who indeed bears fruit and yields, in one case a hundredfold, in another sixty, and in another thirty."

The Gospel of the Lord. **Praise to you, Lord Jesus Christ.**

PROFESSION OF FAITH *(p. 11)*

PRAYER OF THE FAITHFUL

The following intentions are suggestions only. There are more suggestions at www.livingwithchrist.ca

R. **Lord, hear our prayer.**

For the Church, healer and refuge as Jesus was, we pray to the Lord: R.

For leaders of nations who try to respond to cries for help, locally and globally, we pray to the Lord: R.

For the wounded, the alienated, the hungry who turn to us for help, we pray to the Lord: R.

For us, God's people, wounded and in need, looking to each other for sustenance, we pray to the Lord: R.

PREPARATION OF THE GIFTS *(p. 14)*

PRAYER OVER THE OFFERINGS

Look upon the offerings of the Church, O Lord, as she makes her prayer to you, and grant that, when consumed by those who believe, they may bring ever greater holiness. Through Christ our Lord. **Amen.**

PREFACE *(Sundays in Ordinary Time, p. 28)*

COMMUNION ANTIPHON *(Cf. Psalm 83.4-5)*
The sparrow finds a home, and the swallow a nest for her young: by your altars, O Lord of hosts, my King and my God. Blessed are they who dwell in your house, for ever singing your praise.

or (John 6.57)

Whoever eats my flesh and drinks my blood remains in me and I in him, says the Lord.

PRAYER AFTER COMMUNION

Having consumed these gifts, we pray, O Lord, that, by our participation in this mystery, its saving effects upon us may grow. Through Christ our Lord. **Amen.**

BLESSING AND DISMISSAL *(p. 70)*

July 23

One of the most frustrating yet consoling things about God is his patience. We can see many problems in the world: problems between nations, problems in the culture, problems in our families, and, if we're honest, problems in ourselves. How long, O Lord, will you allow this to continue?

Jesus' parables of the wheat, mustard seed and yeast remind us that our perspective on these things is limited. We know from our own experience that we rarely understand what God is doing until long after God has done it. But it is hard to trust the slow work of God. It is often easier to want to destroy evil without thinking about collateral damage.

But the truth is that evil and good are often entangled. This is as true on the grand scale of world history as it is in the lives of each one of us. Perhaps when we grow frustrated with the world and wonder why God doesn't seem to be acting — at least not in the way we would have him act — we can reflect on his patience with us.

And, if we do that, perhaps we will be able to cooperate more deeply in the slow work of God that will make all things right — in God's own time.

Brett Salkeld, Wilcox, SK

ENTRANCE ANTIPHON *(Psalm 53.6, 8)*
**See, I have God for my help. The Lord sustains
my soul. I will sacrifice to you with willing heart,
and praise your name, O Lord, for it is good.**

INTRODUCTORY RITES *(p. 5)*

COLLECT
Show favour, O Lord, to your servants and mercifully increase the gifts of your grace, that, made
fervent in hope, faith and charity, they may
be ever watchful in keeping your commands.
Through our Lord Jesus Christ, your Son, who
lives and reigns with you in the unity of the Holy
Spirit, one God, for ever and ever. **Amen.**

FIRST READING *(Wisdom 12.13, 16-19)*
There is no god besides you, Lord,
whose care is for all people,
to whom you should prove that you have not
    judged unjustly.

For your strength is the source of righteousness,
and your sovereignty over all causes you
    to spare all.
For you show your strength
when people doubt the completeness
    of your power,
and you rebuke any insolence among those
    who know it.
Although you are sovereign in strength,
you judge with mildness,
and with great forbearance you govern us;
for you have power to act whenever you choose.

437

Through such works you have taught your people
that the righteous must be kind,
and you have filled your children with good hope,
because you give repentance for sins.

The word of the Lord. **Thanks be to God.**

RESPONSORIAL PSALM (Psalm 86)

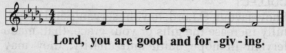

R. **Lord, you are good and forgiving.**

You, O Lord, are good and for·-**giving,**
abounding in steadfast love to all who
    call · **on** you.
Give ear, O Lord, to my · **prayer;**
listen to my cry of · **suppli**-cation. R.

All the nations you have made shall come
    and bow down before you, O · **Lord,**
and shall glorify · **your** name.
For you are great and do wondrous · **things;**
you alone · **are** God. R.

But you, O Lord, are a God merciful
    and · **gracious,**
slow to anger and abounding in steadfast
    love · **and** faithfulness.
Turn to me and be · **gracious_to_me.**
Give your strength to · **your** servant. R.

©2010 Gordon Johnston/Novalis

SECOND READING *(Romans 8.26-27)*
Brothers and sisters: The Spirit helps us in our weakness; for we do not know how to pray as we ought, but that very Spirit intercedes with sighs too deep for words.

And God, who searches the heart, knows what is the mind of the Spirit, because the Spirit intercedes for the saints according to the will of God.

The word of the Lord. **Thanks be to God.**

GOSPEL ACCLAMATION *(See Matthew 11.25)*
Alleluia. Alleluia. Blessed are you, Father, Lord of heaven and earth; you have revealed to little ones the mysteries of the kingdom. **Alleluia.**

GOSPEL *(Matthew 13.24-43)*
The shorter reading ends at the asterisks.
The Lord be with you. **And with your spirit.** A reading from the holy Gospel according to Matthew. **Glory to you, O Lord.**

Jesus put before the crowds a parable: "The kingdom of heaven may be compared to someone who sowed good seed in his field; but while everybody was asleep, an enemy came and sowed weeds among the wheat, and then went away.

"So when the plants came up and bore grain, then the weeds appeared as well. And the slaves of the householder came and said to him, 'Master, did you not sow good seed in your field? Where, then, did these weeds come from?' He answered, 'An enemy has done this.' The slaves said to him, 'Then do you want us to go and gather them?' But he replied, 'No; for in gathering the weeds you would uproot the wheat along with them.

439

Let both of them grow together until the harvest; and at harvest time I will tell the reapers, Collect the weeds first and bind them in bundles to be burned, but gather the wheat into my barn.'"

Jesus put before them another parable: "The kingdom of heaven is like a mustard seed that someone took and sowed in his field; it is the smallest of all the seeds, but when it has grown it is the greatest of shrubs and becomes a tree, so that the birds of the air come and make nests in its branches."

He told them another parable: "The kingdom of heaven is like yeast that a woman took and mixed in with three measures of flour until all of it was leavened."

* * *

Jesus told the crowds all these things in parables; without a parable he told them nothing. This was to fulfill what had been spoken through the Prophet: "I will open my mouth to speak in parables; I will proclaim what has been hidden from the foundation of the world."

Then Jesus left the crowds and went into the house. And his disciples approached him, saying, "Explain to us the parable of the weeds of the field." He answered, "The one who sows the good seed is the Son of Man; the field is the world, and the good seed are the children of the kingdom; the weeds are the children of the evil one, and the enemy who sowed them is the devil; the harvest is the end of the age, and the reapers are Angels. Just as the weeds are collected and burned up with fire, so will it be at the end of the age. The

Son of Man will send his Angels, and they will collect out of his kingdom all causes of sin and all evildoers, and they will throw them into the furnace of fire, where there will be weeping and gnashing of teeth. Then the righteous will shine like the sun in the kingdom of their Father. Let anyone with ears listen!"

The Gospel of the Lord. **Praise to you, Lord Jesus Christ.**

PROFESSION OF FAITH *(p. 11)*

PRAYER OF THE FAITHFUL

The following intentions are suggestions only. There are more suggestions at www.livingwithchrist.ca

R. **Lord, hear our prayer.**

For the Church, striving to live in openness to God's word revealed in our day, we pray to the Lord: R.

For the wisdom that inspires governments to support the weakest members of society, we pray to the Lord: R.

For busy people seeking stillness in order to listen to God in their own hearts, we pray to the Lord: R.

For this Christian community, called to put God's words of love into action every day, we pray to the Lord: R.

PREPARATION OF THE GIFTS *(p. 14)*

PRAYER OVER THE OFFERINGS

O God, who in the one perfect sacrifice brought to completion varied offerings of the law, accept, we pray, this sacrifice from your faithful servants and make it holy, as you blessed the gifts of Abel, so that what each has offered to the honour of your majesty may benefit the salvation of all. Through Christ our Lord. **Amen.**

PREFACE (Sundays in Ordinary Time, p. 28)

COMMUNION ANTIPHON (Psalm 110.4-5)

The Lord, the gracious, the merciful, has made a memorial of his wonders; he gives food to those who fear him.

or (Revelation 3.20)

Behold, I stand at the door and knock, says the Lord. If anyone hears my voice and opens the door to me, I will enter his house and dine with him, and he with me.

PRAYER AFTER COMMUNION

Graciously be present to your people, we pray, O Lord, and lead those you have imbued with heavenly mysteries to pass from former ways to newness of life. Through Christ our Lord. **Amen.**

BLESSING AND DISMISSAL (p. 70)

July 30

When I feel overwhelmed by the prospect of doing God's will, I find comfort in knowing that God is in that moment with me. I am not being asked to move mountains alone. I am being offered more love and grace than I could ever fathom. Like David, Solomon, Paul and the disciples, I am only being asked to open myself up to that love. God invites us into his love and prepares us to love; and by grace we come to love God's commands.

Solomon is keenly aware of God's love; filled with grace, he desires to govern well and care for God's people. Turning to God, Solomon offers himself as God's servant — wishing to discern between good and evil.

As Paul explains in his letter to the Romans, we are all "predestined to be conformed to the image of his Son." God's grace is always operative in us so that we come to share in God's purpose. God is the first mover and we are invited to be partners in mission. When God calls, will I say "YES!"?

The joy of responding to God's call is more wonderful than a hidden treasure or a fine pearl. By grace may we sell the things that are holding us back from saying YES! For those who love God are called, justified and glorified.

Michael and Vanessa Nicholas-Schmidt, Toronto, ON

ENTRANCE ANTIPHON (Cf. Psalm 67.6-7, 36)
God is in his holy place, God who unites those who dwell in his house; he himself gives might and strength to his people.

INTRODUCTORY RITES (p. 5)

COLLECT
O God, protector of those who hope in you, without whom nothing has firm foundation, nothing is holy, bestow in abundance your mercy upon us and grant that, with you as our ruler and guide, we may use the good things that pass in such a way as to hold fast even now to those that ever endure. Through our Lord Jesus Christ, your Son, who lives and reigns with you in the unity of the Holy Spirit, one God, for ever and ever. **Amen.**

FIRST READING (1 Kings 3.5-12)
At Gibeon the Lord appeared to Solomon in a dream by night; and God said, "Ask what I should give you." And Solomon said, "You have shown great and steadfast love to your servant my father David, because he walked before you in faithfulness, in righteousness, and in uprightness of heart toward you; and you have kept for him this great and steadfast love, and have given him a son to sit on his throne today.

"And now, O Lord my God, you have made your servant king in place of my father David, although I am only a little child; I do not know how to go out or come in. And your servant is in the midst of the people whom you have chosen, a great people, so numerous they cannot be numbered or counted. Give your servant therefore an understanding mind to govern your people, able to discern between good and evil; for who can govern this, your great people?"

It pleased the Lord that Solomon had asked this. God said to him, "Because you have asked this, and have not asked for yourself long life or riches, or for the life of your enemies, but have asked for yourself understanding to discern what is right, I now do according to your word. Indeed I give you a wise and discerning mind; no one like you has been before you and no one like you shall arise after you."

The word of the Lord. **Thanks be to God.**

RESPONSORIAL PSALM *(Psalm 119)*

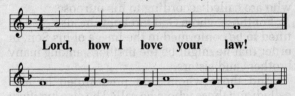

R. **Lord, how I love your law!**

The Lord is my · **portion;**
I promise to keep · **your** words.
The law of your mouth is better · **to** me
than thousands of gold and · **sil**-ver pieces. R.

Let your steadfast love become my · **comfort**
according to your promise · **to_your** servant.
Let your mercy come to me, that I · **may** live;
for your law is · **my** de-light. R.

Truly I love your commandments more
than · **gold,**
more than · **fine** gold.
Truly I direct my steps by all · **your** precepts;
I hate · **every** false way. R.

Your decrees are · **wonderful;**
therefore my · **soul** keeps_them.
The unfolding of your words · **gives** light;
it imparts understanding · **to** the simple. R.

©2010 Gordon Johnston/Novalis
To hear the Sunday Psalms, visit www.livingwithchrist.ca.

SECOND READING *(Romans 8.28-30)*

Brothers and sisters: We know that all things
work together for good for those who love God,
who are called according to his purpose.

For those whom God foreknew he also predestined to be conformed to the image of his Son, in
order that he might be the firstborn among many
brothers and sisters.

And those whom God predestined he also
called; and those whom he called he also justified;
and those whom he justified he also glorified.

The word of the Lord. **Thanks be to God.**

GOSPEL ACCLAMATION *(See Matthew 11.25)*

Alleluia. Alleluia. Blessed are you, Father, Lord
of heaven and earth; you have revealed to little
ones the mysteries of the kingdom. **Alleluia.**

GOSPEL *(Matthew 13.44-52)*

The shorter reading ends at the asterisks.

The Lord be with you. **And with your spirit.**
A reading from the holy Gospel according to Matthew. **Glory to you, O Lord.**

Jesus spoke to the crowds: "The kingdom of heaven is like treasure hidden in a field, which someone found and hid; then in his joy he goes and sells all that he has and buys that field.

"Again, the kingdom of heaven is like a merchant in search of fine pearls; on finding one pearl of great value, he went and sold all that he had and bought it.

"Again, the kingdom of heaven is like a net that was thrown into the sea and caught fish of every kind; when it was full, they drew it ashore, sat down, and put the good into baskets but threw out the bad.

* * *

"So it will be at the end of the age. The Angels will come out and separate the evil from the righteous and throw them into the furnace of fire, where there will be weeping and gnashing of teeth.

"Have you understood all this?" They answered, "Yes." And he said to them, "Therefore every scribe who has been trained for the kingdom of heaven is like the master of a household who brings out of his treasure what is new and what is old."

The Gospel of the Lord. **Praise to you, Lord Jesus Christ.**

447

PROFESSION OF FAITH *(p. 11)*

PRAYER OF THE FAITHFUL

The following intentions are suggestions only. There are more suggestions at www.livingwithchrist.ca

R. **Lord, hear our prayer.**

For the Church, people of prayer and praise, we pray to the Lord: R.

For the healing of nations, and for the dawning of peace and justice in lands torn by strife, we pray to the Lord: R.

For the poor and the suffering, and for those who are hurt and wounded, we pray to the Lord: R.

For us, God's people, seeking strength in our common prayer and our desire to do God's will, we pray to the Lord: R.

PREPARATION OF THE GIFTS *(p. 14)*

PRAYER OVER THE OFFERINGS

Accept, O Lord, we pray, the offerings which we bring from the abundance of your gifts, that through the powerful working of your grace these most sacred mysteries may sanctify our present way of life and lead us to eternal gladness. Through Christ our Lord. **Amen.**

PREFACE *(Sundays in Ordinary Time, p. 28)*

COMMUNION ANTIPHON *(Psalm 102.2)*
Bless the Lord, O my soul, and never forget all
his benefits.

or (Matthew 5.7-8)
Blessed are the merciful, for they shall receive
mercy. Blessed are the clean of heart, for they
shall see God.

PRAYER AFTER COMMUNION
We have consumed, O Lord, this divine Sacrament, the perpetual memorial of the Passion of
your Son; grant, we pray, that this gift, which he
himself gave us with love beyond all telling, may
profit us for salvation. Through Christ our Lord.
Amen.

BLESSING AND DISMISSAL *(p. 70)*

August Saints' Days

The following saints are traditionally remembered in August in Canada.

1   Saint Alphonsus Liguori

2   Saint Eusebius of Vercelli
     Saint Peter Julian Eymard

4   Saint John Mary Vianney

5   Blessed Frédéric Janssoone

7   Saint Sixtus II and Companions
     Saint Cajetan

8   Saint Dominic

9   Saint Teresa Benedicta of the Cross

10   Saint Lawrence

11   Saint Clare

12   Saint Jane Frances de Chantal

13   Saints Pontian and Hippolytus

14   Saint Maximilian Kolbe

16   Saint Stephen of Hungary

17   Blessed Élisabeth Turgeon

19   Saint John Eudes

20   Saint Bernard

21   Saint Pius X

23   Saint Rose of Lima

24   Saint Bartholomew

25   Saint Louis
     Saint Joseph Calasanz

27   Saint Monica

28   Saint Augustine

August 6

Today's readings erupt with images of a God whose immensity is beyond our understanding. They take us from Daniel's dream vision of a fiery "Ancient One," to the psalm's evocation of God's all-encompassing power, to the disciples' mountaintop experience of the transfigured Jesus bathed in light and flanked by the prophets. It is little wonder that Peter, James and John cower in fear at the voice of this terrifying and overwhelming God!

How can we dare to even think about, let alone approach, such awesome immensity? For Christians, the answer is found in Jesus himself. See what happens next in the Transfiguration scene. What does Jesus do when the three disciples fall to the ground in terror? Bending down to *touch* them, he says the words that he repeats so often in the gospel narratives: "Do not be afraid." And after the swirling maelstrom of light and sound and heart-stopping majesty, suddenly they see only "Jesus himself alone."

To echo Peter's words in his eyewitness account of the gospel event, we would "do well to be attentive to this as to a lamp shining in a dark place." The transcendent God who is beyond our wildest imaginings is the same God who tenderly invites each of us into an intimate relationship of love. This is a profound mystery and a priceless gift.

Krystyna Higgins, Guelph, ON

ENTRANCE ANTIPHON *(Cf. Matthew 17.5)*
In a resplendent cloud the Holy Spirit appeared.
The Father's voice was heard: This is my beloved
Son, with whom I am well pleased. Listen to him.

INTRODUCTORY RITES *(p. 5)*

COLLECT
O God, who in the glorious Transfiguration of
your Only Begotten Son confirmed the mysteries
of faith by the witness of the Fathers and wonderfully prefigured our full adoption to sonship,
grant, we pray, to your servants, that, listening to
the voice of your beloved Son, we may merit to
become co-heirs with him. Who lives and reigns
with you in the unity of the Holy Spirit, one God,
for ever and ever. **Amen.**

FIRST READING *(Daniel 7.9-10, 13-14)*
As I watched, thrones were set in place, and the
One who is Ancient of Days took his throne. His
clothing was white as snow, and the hair of his
head like pure wool. His throne was fiery flames,
and its wheels were burning fire. A stream of
fire issued and flowed out from his presence. A
thousand thousands served him, and ten thousand times ten thousand stood attending him.
The court sat in judgment, and the books were
opened.

As I watched in the night visions, I saw one
like a son of man coming with the clouds of
heaven. And he came to the One who is Ancient
of Days and was presented before him.

To him was given dominion and glory and kingship, that all peoples, nations, and languages should serve him. His dominion is an everlasting dominion that shall not pass away, and his kingship is one that shall never be destroyed.

The word of the Lord. **Thanks be to God.**

RESPONSORIAL PSALM *(Psalm 97)*

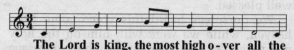

The Lord is king, the most high o-ver all the

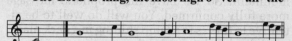

earth.

R. **The Lord is king, the most high over all the earth.**

The Lord is king! Let the earth re-·**joice;**
let the many coastlands · **be** glad!
Clouds and thick darkness are · **all** around him;
righteousness and justice are the foundation
· **of** his throne. R.

The mountains melt like wax before the · **Lord,**
before the Lord of · **all_the** earth.
The heavens pro-·**claim** his righteousness;
and all the peoples be-·**hold** his glory. R.

1 - For you, O Lord, are most high over all
the · **earth;**
4 - you are exalted far a-·**bove** all gods. R.

©2009 Gordon Johnston/Novalis
To hear the Sunday Psalms, visit www.livingwithchrist.ca.

SECOND READING *(2 Peter 1.16-19)*

We did not follow cleverly devised myths when we made known to you the power and coming of our Lord Jesus Christ, but we had been eyewitnesses of his majesty. For he received honour and glory from God the Father when that voice was conveyed to him by the Majestic Glory, saying, "This is my Son, the Beloved. With him I am well pleased."

We ourselves heard this voice come from heaven, while we were with him on the holy mountain. So we have the prophetic message more fully confirmed. You will do well to be attentive to this as to a lamp shining in a dark place, until the day dawns and the morning star rises in your hearts.

The word of the Lord. **Thanks be to God.**

GOSPEL ACCLAMATION *(Matthew 17.5)*
Alleluia. Alleluia. This is my Son, the Beloved; with him I am well pleased; listen to him! **Alleluia.**

GOSPEL *(Matthew 17.1-9)*
The Lord be with you. **And with your spirit.**
A reading from the holy Gospel according to Matthew. **Glory to you, O Lord.**

Jesus took with him Peter and James and his brother John and led them up a high mountain, by themselves. And he was transfigured before them, and his face shone like the sun, and his clothes became dazzling white. Suddenly there appeared to them Moses and Elijah, talking with him.

Then Peter said to Jesus, "Lord, it is good for us to be here; if you wish, I will make dwellings here, one for you, one for Moses, and one for Elijah."

While he was still speaking, suddenly a bright cloud overshadowed them, and from the cloud a voice said, "This is my Son, the Beloved; with him I am well pleased; listen to him!"

When the disciples heard this, they fell to the ground and were overcome by fear. But Jesus came and touched them, saying, "Get up and do not be afraid." And when they looked up, they saw no one except Jesus himself alone.

As they were coming down the mountain, Jesus ordered them, "Tell no one about the vision until after the Son of Man has been raised from the dead."

The Gospel of the Lord. **Praise to you, Lord Jesus Christ.**

PROFESSION OF FAITH (p. 11)

PRAYER OF THE FAITHFUL

The following intentions are suggestions only. There are more suggestions at www.livingwithchrist.ca

℟. **Lord, hear our prayer.**

For the Church, joyful witness to the resurrection of our Saviour and Redeemer, we pray to the Lord: ℟.

For leaders of nations working towards peace, we pray to the Lord: ℟.

For those now living with the realities of war and destruction, we pray to the Lord: ℟.

For Christian communities everywhere, embodying the triumph of life over death, we pray to the Lord: R.

PREPARATION OF THE GIFTS *(p. 14)*

PRAYER OVER THE OFFERINGS
Sanctify, O Lord, we pray, these offerings here made to celebrate the glorious Transfiguration of your Only Begotten Son, and by his radiant splendour cleanse us from the stains of sin. Through Christ our Lord. **Amen.**

PREFACE *(Transfiguration, p. 28)*

COMMUNION ANTIPHON *(Cf. 1 John 3.2)*
When Christ appears, we shall be like him, for we shall see him as he is.

PRAYER AFTER COMMUNION
May the heavenly nourishment we have received, O Lord, we pray, transform us into the likeness of your Son, whose radiant splendour you willed to make manifest in his glorious Transfiguration. Who lives and reigns for ever and ever. **Amen.**

BLESSING AND DISMISSAL *(p. 70)*

August 13

Several years ago, I was teaching today's gospel to a group of five year olds and one asked the question, "Why didn't his friends wear life-jackets?" To a five year old, this question makes sense; to a believer it takes a different thrust. Today's gospel speaks to us of the power of faith and truth, revealed to us through a deepening relationship between Jesus and his disciples.

After feeding more than five thousand people, Jesus sends his disciples into the lake. The waves become strong and the disciples are afraid. Jesus appears to them but they do not recognize him. Again Peter doubts him: "If it is you, command me to come to you on the water." Finally, the disciples recognize Jesus with the words, "Truly you are the Son of God."

In this passage we go from the unknown to the known, from darkness to light. Our faith is nourished through our relationship with Jesus. We should strive to better know Jesus, not to know *about* Jesus. To better know Jesus is the spiritual path of prayer and reflection.

Each of us has had a time in our lives when we have been frightened because of some unknown. How did we react? Was our faith strong enough to speak the assuring words, "Truly you are the Son of God"?

Sr. Johanna D'Agostino, IBVM, Toronto, ON

ENTRANCE ANTIPHON *(Cf. Psalm 73.20, 19, 22, 23)*
Look to your covenant, O Lord, and forget not
the life of your poor ones for ever. Arise, O God,
and defend your cause, and forget not the cries
of those who seek you.

INTRODUCTORY RITES *(p. 5)*

COLLECT
Almighty ever-living God, whom, taught by the
Holy Spirit, we dare to call our Father, bring,
we pray, to perfection in our hearts the spirit of
adoption as your sons and daughters, that we may
merit to enter into the inheritance which you have
promised. Through our Lord Jesus Christ, your
Son, who lives and reigns with you in the unity of
the Holy Spirit, one God, for ever and ever. **Amen.**

FIRST READING *(1 Kings 19.9, 11-13)*
When Elijah reached Horeb, the mountain of God,
he came to a cave, and spent the night there. Then
the word of the Lord came to him, saying, "Go out
and stand on the mountain before the Lord, for
the Lord is about to pass by."

Now there was a great wind, so strong that it
was splitting mountains and breaking rocks in
pieces before the Lord, but the Lord was not in
the wind; and after the wind an earthquake, but
the Lord was not in the earthquake; and after the
earthquake a fire, but the Lord was not in the fire;
and after the fire a sound of sheer silence.

When Elijah heard it, he wrapped his face in
his mantle and went out and stood at the entrance
of the cave.

The word of the Lord. **Thanks be to God.**

RESPONSORIAL PSALM *(Psalm 85)*

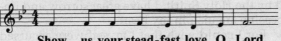

Show us your stead-fast love, O Lord,

and grant us your sal - va - tion.

℟. **Show us your steadfast love, O Lord,
and grant us your salvation.**

Let me hear what God the Lord will · **speak,**
for he will speak peace to his · **people.**
Surely his salvation is at hand for those
    who · **fear_him,**
that his glory may dwell · **in_our** land. ℟.

Steadfast love and faithfulness will · **meet;**
righteousness and peace will
    · **kiss_each_other.**
Faithfulness will spring up from the · **ground,**
and righteousness will look down
    · **from_the** sky. ℟.

The Lord will give what is · **good,**
and our land will yield its · **increase.**
Righteousness will go be-·**fore_him,**
and will make a path · **for_his** steps. ℟.

©2010 Gordon Johnston/Novalis

SECOND READING *(Romans 9.1-5)*
Brothers and sisters: I am speaking the truth in Christ. I am not lying; my conscience confirms it by the Holy Spirit. I have great sorrow and unceasing anguish in my heart.

For I could wish that I myself were accursed and cut off from Christ for the sake of my own people, my kindred according to the flesh. They are children of Israel, and to them belong the adoption, the glory, the covenants, the giving of the law, the worship, and the promises; to them belong the patriarchs, and from them, according to the flesh, comes the Christ, who is over all, God be blessed forever. Amen.

The word of the Lord. **Thanks be to God.**

GOSPEL ACCLAMATION *(Psalm 130.5)*
Alleluia. Alleluia. I wait for the Lord; I hope in his word. **Alleluia.**

GOSPEL *(Matthew 14.22-33)*
The Lord be with you. **And with your spirit.**
A reading from the holy Gospel according to Matthew. **Glory to you, O Lord.**

Immediately after feeding the crowd with the five loaves and two fish, Jesus made the disciples get into the boat and go on ahead to the other side, while he dismissed the crowds. And after he had dismissed the crowds, he went up the mountain by himself to pray.

When evening came, he was there alone, but by this time the boat, battered by the waves, was far from the land, for the wind was against them.

And early in the morning Jesus came walking toward them on the sea. But when the disciples saw him walking on the sea, they were terrified, saying, "It is a ghost!" And they cried out in fear. But immediately Jesus spoke to them and said, "Take heart, it is I; do not be afraid."

Peter answered him, "Lord, if it is you, command me to come to you on the water." Jesus said, "Come." So Peter got out of the boat, started walking on the water, and came toward Jesus. But when he noticed the strong wind, he became frightened, and beginning to sink, he cried out, "Lord, save me!"

Jesus immediately reached out his hand and caught him, saying to him, "You of little faith, why did you doubt?" When they got into the boat, the wind ceased. And those in the boat worshipped him, saying, "Truly you are the Son of God."

The Gospel of the Lord. **Praise to you, Lord Jesus Christ.**

PROFESSION OF FAITH (p. 11)

PRAYER OF THE FAITHFUL

The following intentions are suggestions only. There are more suggestions at www.livingwithchrist.ca

R. **Lord, hear our prayer.**

For the Church, faithful and steadfast sign of the love and trust between God and humanity, we pray to the Lord: R.

For world leaders, called to be just and caring stewards of the world's material wealth, we pray to the Lord: R.

For the poor, and all who search in hope for relief from their troubles, we pray to the Lord: R.

For this parish community, striving to live as God's holy people, we pray to the Lord: R.

PREPARATION OF THE GIFTS *(p. 14)*

PRAYER OVER THE OFFERINGS
Be pleased, O Lord, to accept the offerings of your Church, for in your mercy you have given them to be offered and by your power you transform them into the mystery of our salvation. Through Christ our Lord. **Amen.**

PREFACE *(Sundays in Ordinary Time, p. 28)*

COMMUNION ANTIPHON *(Psalm 147.12, 14)*
O Jerusalem, glorify the Lord, who gives you your fill of finest wheat.
or (Cf. John 6.51)
The bread that I will give, says the Lord, is my flesh for the life of the world.

PRAYER AFTER COMMUNION
May the communion in your Sacrament that we have consumed, save us, O Lord, and confirm us in the light of your truth. Through Christ our Lord. **Amen.**

BLESSING AND DISMISSAL *(p. 70)*

August 20

Holy Eucharist is distributed in such small portions; how can it be so full of mercy?

One answer is that even a little *good* food goes a long way. Ask any pup that waits around the table! The image of my dog cleaning up crumbs is a study in faithfulness, contentment and trust. Faithfulness because he always shows up; contentment because he doesn't complain about the size, flavour or quality of the crumbs; and trust because any dog knows that even the tiniest morsel is worth the effort of pursuit.

Clearly the Canaanite woman in today's gospel had similarly observed the persistence of hungry dogs. So it was that when her daughter was beset by a demon, she did not hesitate to seek out Jesus of Nazareth, Jewish though he was. Recognizing that even a crumb of his mercy contained more than enough grace to heal her daughter, she persevered in approaching Jesus, stating that even the smallest portion of food can satisfy one who trusts in a Master's goodness. This Gentile woman's unquenchable faith in God's mercy resulted in the instant healing of her daughter.

As we approach the table of the Lord today, let us with similar faithfulness, contentment and trust come to Christ Jesus for refreshment, sustenance and healing. Even one crumb of his mercy is more than enough!

Beverly Illauq, Kemptville, ON

ENTRANCE ANTIPHON *(Psalm 83.10-11)*
Turn your eyes, O God, our shield; and look on the face of your anointed one; one day within your courts is better than a thousand elsewhere.

INTRODUCTORY RITES *(p. 5)*

COLLECT
O God, who have prepared for those who love you good things which no eye can see, fill our hearts, we pray, with the warmth of your love, so that, loving you in all things and above all things, we may attain your promises, which surpass every human desire. Through our Lord Jesus Christ, your Son, who lives and reigns with you in the unity of the Holy Spirit, one God, for ever and ever. **Amen.**

FIRST READING *(Isaiah 56.1, 6-7)*
Thus says the Lord: "Maintain justice, and do what is right, for soon my salvation will come, and my deliverance be revealed.

"And the foreigners who join themselves to the Lord, to minister to him, to love the name of the Lord, and to be his servants, all who keep the Sabbath, and do not profane it, and hold fast my covenant — these I will bring to my holy mountain, and make them joyful in my house of prayer; their burnt offerings and their sacrifices will be accepted on my altar; for my house shall be called a house of prayer for all peoples."

The word of the Lord. **Thanks be to God.**

RESPONSORIAL PSALM *(Psalm 67)*

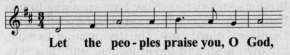

Let the peo-ples praise you, O God,

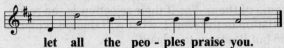

let all the peo - ples praise you.

℟. **Let the peoples praise you, O God,
let all the peoples praise you!**

May God be gracious to us · **and** bless_us
and make his face to shine · **up**-on_us,
that your way may be known up-·**on** earth,
your saving power a-·**mong** all nations. ℟.

Let the nations be glad and sing · **for** joy,
for you judge the peoples with equity and
    guide the nations · **upon** earth.
Let the peoples praise you, · **O** God;
let all the · **peo**-ples praise_you. ℟.

The earth has yielded · **its** increase;
God, our God, · **has** blessed_us.
May God continue · **to** bless_us;
let all the ends of the · **earth** re-vere_him. ℟.

©2010 Gordon Johnston/Novalis
To hear the Sunday Psalms, visit www.livingwithchrist.ca.

SECOND READING *(Romans 11.13-15, 29-32)*

Brothers and sisters: Now I am speaking to you Gentiles. Inasmuch then as I am an Apostle to the Gentiles, I glorify my ministry in order to make my own flesh and blood jealous, and thus save some of them. For if their rejection is the reconciliation of the world, what will their acceptance be but life from the dead!

The gifts and the calling of God are irrevocable. Just as you were once disobedient to God but have now received mercy because of their disobedience, so they have now been disobedient in order that, by the mercy shown to you, they too may now receive mercy. For God has imprisoned all in disobedience so that he may be merciful to all.

The word of the Lord. **Thanks be to God.**

GOSPEL ACCLAMATION *(See Matthew 4.23)*

Alleluia. Alleluia. Jesus proclaimed the good news of the kingdom and cured every sickness. **Alleluia.**

GOSPEL *(Matthew 15.21-28)*

The Lord be with you. **And with your spirit.** A reading from the holy Gospel according to Matthew. **Glory to you, O Lord.**

Jesus went away to the district of Tyre and Sidon. A Canaanite woman from that region came out, and started shouting, "Have mercy on me, Lord, Son of David; my daughter is tormented by a demon." But he did not answer her at all.

And his disciples came and urged him, saying, "Send her away, for she keeps shouting after us."

He answered, "I was sent only to the lost sheep of the house of Israel."

But the woman came and knelt before him, saying, "Lord, help me." He answered, "It is not fair to take the children's food and throw it to the dogs." She said, "Yes, Lord, yet even the dogs eat the crumbs that fall from their masters' table."

Then Jesus answered her, "Woman, great is your faith! Let it be done for you as you wish." And her daughter was healed instantly.

The Gospel of the Lord. **Praise to you, Lord Jesus Christ.**

PROFESSION OF FAITH *(p. 11)*

PRAYER OF THE FAITHFUL

The following intentions are suggestions only. There are more suggestions at www.livingwithchrist.ca

R. **Lord, hear our prayer.**

For the Church and its leaders, called to hear and to proclaim the words of the prophets, we pray to the Lord: R.

For leaders of nations willing to risk the prophetic task of establishing peace and justice, we pray to the Lord: R.

For those who are poor, sick and persecuted, and for all who minister to them, we pray to the Lord: R.

For this community, called in baptism to be a people of prophetic words and actions, we pray to the Lord: R.

PREPARATION OF THE GIFTS (p. 14)

PRAYER OVER THE OFFERINGS

Receive our oblation, O Lord, by which is brought about a glorious exchange, that, by offering what you have given, we may merit to receive your very self. Through Christ our Lord. **Amen.**

PREFACE (Sundays in Ordinary Time, p. 28)

COMMUNION ANTIPHON (Psalm 129.7)

With the Lord there is mercy; in him is plentiful redemption.

or (John 6.51-52)

I am the living bread that came down from heaven, says the Lord. Whoever eats of this bread will live for ever.

PRAYER AFTER COMMUNION

Made partakers of Christ through these Sacraments, we humbly implore your mercy, Lord, that, conformed to his image on earth, we may merit also to be his co-heirs in heaven. Who lives and reigns for ever and ever. **Amen.**

BLESSING AND DISMISSAL (p. 70)

August 27

In today's gospel, Jesus gives Peter the keys of the kingdom of heaven. He chooses Peter as the rock on which to build his Church, and the gates of Hades will not prevail against it.

This constant battle between good and evil — between angels and demons, and between God and Satan — for our souls is not an easy one and requires much prayer and perseverance. We must not get discouraged or give up, but rather surround ourselves with others and pray with them.

In *The Lord of the Rings*, Froddo Baggins is chosen to destroy evil by destroying the ring, but he constantly gets tempted by it. He fights orcs and hides with his fellow companions in order to stay alive and keep the ring from getting into the wrong hands and thus destroying the world. Even those who start out wanting to protect him are influenced by the evil of the ring and want to take it from him.

Peter, as the head of the Church, also suffered to protect the Church and to bring Jesus to others in the Blessed Sacrament, especially in the early Church when Christians were being killed. In today's eucharistic celebration, let us give thanks and praise for God's protection of our Holy Catholic Church — the Bride of Christ — and for our first Pope, Saint Peter.

Sarah Escobar (Du Broy), Ottawa, ON

ENTRANCE ANTIPHON *(Cf. Psalm 85.1-3)*
Turn your ear, O Lord, and answer me; save the servant who trusts in you, my God. Have mercy on me, O Lord, for I cry to you all the day long.

INTRODUCTORY RITES *(p. 5)*

COLLECT
O God, who cause the minds of the faithful to unite in a single purpose, grant your people to love what you command and to desire what you promise, that, amid the uncertainties of this world, our hearts may be fixed on that place where true gladness is found. Through our Lord Jesus Christ, your Son, who lives and reigns with you in the unity of the Holy Spirit, one God, for ever and ever. **Amen.**

FIRST READING *(Isaiah 22.15, 19-23)*
Thus says the Lord God of hosts: Go to the steward, to Shebna, who is master of the household, and say to him:

"I will thrust you from your office, and you will be pulled down from your post. On that day I will call my servant Eliakim son of Hilkiah, and will clothe him with your robe and bind your sash on him. I will commit your authority to his hand, and he shall be a father to the inhabitants of Jerusalem and to the house of Judah.

"I will place on his shoulder the key of the house of David; he shall open, and no one shall shut; he shall shut, and no one shall open. I will fasten him like a peg in a secure place, and he

will become a throne of honour to the house of
his ancestors."

The word of the Lord. **Thanks be to God.**

RESPONSORIAL PSALM *(Psalm 138)*

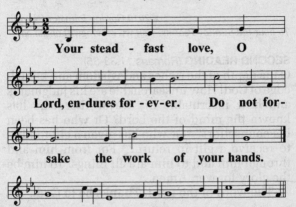

Your stead - fast love, O Lord, en-dures for - ev-er. Do not for-sake the work of your hands.

℟. **Your steadfast love, O Lord, endures forever.
Do not forsake the work of your hands.**

I give you thanks, O Lord, with my · **whole**
    heart;
before the Angels I sing · **your** praise;
I bow down toward your holy temple, and
    give thanks to · **your** name
for your steadfast · **love_and** your
    faithfulness. ℟.

For you have exalted · **your** name
and your word a--**bove** everything.
On the day I called, · **you** answered_me,
you increased my · **strength** of soul. ℟.

For though the Lord is high, he regards
· **the** lowly;
but the haughty he perceives from · **far_a**-way.
Your steadfast love, O Lord, endures · **for**-ever.
Do not forsake the · **work_of** your hands. ℞.

To hear the Sunday Psalms, visit www.livingwithchrist.ca.

SECOND READING *(Romans 11.33-36)*
O the depth of the riches and wisdom and knowledge of God! How unsearchable are his judgments
and how inscrutable his ways! "For who has
known the mind of the Lord? Or who has been
his counsellor?" "Or who has given a gift to him,
to receive a gift in return?" For from him and
through him and to him are all things. To him be
the glory forever. Amen.

The word of the Lord. **Thanks be to God.**

GOSPEL ACCLAMATION *(Matthew 16.18)*
Alleluia. Alleluia. You are Peter, and on this rock
I will build my Church; the gates of Hades will
not prevail against it. **Alleluia.**

GOSPEL *(Matthew 16.13-20)*
The Lord be with you. **And with your spirit.**
A reading from the holy Gospel according to Mat-
thew. **Glory to you, O Lord.**

When Jesus came into the district of Caesarea
Philippi, he asked his disciples, "Who do people
say that the Son of Man is?" And they said, "Some
say John the Baptist, but others Elijah, and still
others Jeremiah or one of the Prophets."

He said to them, "But who do you say that I am?" Simon Peter answered, "You are the Christ, the Son of the living God."

And Jesus answered him, "Blessed are you, Simon son of Jonah! For flesh and blood has not revealed this to you, but my Father in heaven. And I tell you, you are Peter, and on this rock I will build my Church, and the gates of Hades will not prevail against it. I will give you the keys of the kingdom of heaven, and whatever you bind on earth will be bound in heaven, and whatever you loose on earth will be loosed in heaven."

Then Jesus sternly ordered the disciples not to tell anyone that he was the Christ.

The Gospel of the Lord. **Praise to you, Lord Jesus Christ.**

PROFESSION OF FAITH (p. 11)

PRAYER OF THE FAITHFUL

The following intentions are suggestions only. There are more suggestions at www.livingwithchrist.ca

R̲. **Lord, hear our prayer.**

For all Christians, and all people of faith, sharing in the work of building up the kingdom of God, we pray to the Lord: R̲

For those who work, publicly and privately, to end unjust structures that oppress the poor and the powerless, we pray to the Lord: R̲

For those who feel excluded or unwelcome in our communities, we pray to the Lord: R̲

For us, called in baptism to welcome all in God's name, we pray to the Lord: R.

PREPARATION OF THE GIFTS *(p. 14)*

PRAYER OVER THE OFFERINGS

O Lord, who gained for yourself a people by adoption through the one sacrifice offered once for all, bestow graciously on us, we pray, the gifts of unity and peace in your Church. Through Christ our Lord. **Amen.**

PREFACE *(Sundays in Ordinary Time, p. 28)*

COMMUNION ANTIPHON *(Cf. Psalm 103.13-15)*
The earth is replete with the fruits of your work, O Lord; you bring forth bread from the earth and wine to cheer the heart.
or (Cf. John 6.54)
Whoever eats my flesh and drinks my blood has eternal life, says the Lord, and I will raise him up on the last day.

PRAYER AFTER COMMUNION

Complete within us, O Lord, we pray, the healing work of your mercy and graciously perfect and sustain us, so that in all things we may please you. Through Christ our Lord. **Amen.**

BLESSING AND DISMISSAL *(p. 70)*

September Saints' Days

The following saints are traditionally remembered in September in Canada.

2   Blessed André Grasset

3   Saint Gregory the Great

4   Blessed Dina Bélanger

9   Saint Peter Claver

13 Saint John Chrysostom

15 Our Lady of Sorrows

16 Saints Cornelius and Cyprian

17 Saint Robert Bellarmine

19 Saint Januarius

20 Saints Andrew Kim Tae-gon, Paul Chong
    Ha-sang and Companions

21 Saint Matthew

23 Saint Pius of Pietrelcina

24 Blessed Émilie Tavernier-Gamelin

25 Saints Cosmas and Damian

26 Saints John de Brébeuf, Isaac Jogues and
    Companions, Secondary Patrons of Canada

27 Saint Vincent de Paul

28 Saint Wenceslaus
    Saint Lawrence Ruiz and Companions

29 Saints Michael, Gabriel and Raphael

30 Saint Jerome

September 3

It is natural for us to make plans. As human beings, we anticipate what is next. But can we become too rigid about our expectations of God's plans for us? When we become set on one particular plan, especially when we think it is God's plan, it can get us into a lot of trouble.

In this gospel, Jesus begins to reveal a part of God's plan to the disciples, but it does not match their expectations of what should happen. Peter's response is to reject the idea that Jesus will be killed. For the disciples, suffering and death would mean defeat. God is powerful; the Messiah will triumph over adversity and oppression. Suffering and death don't make any sense. Where is the victory? They do not realize that this is the way God will save humanity and triumph for our sake over death itself.

Jesus tells the disciples who were having trouble moving beyond their own expectations of God's plan, "If anyone wants to become my follower, let him deny himself." To follow Jesus, we must let go of the idea that we know everything that should happen, and let grace lead our way. Let us find ways to remain open to plans bigger than our own.

Kelly Bourke, Victoria, BC

ENTRANCE ANTIPHON *(Cf. Psalm 85.3, 5)*
Have mercy on me, O Lord, for I cry to you all
the day long. O Lord, you are good and forgiving,
full of mercy to all who call to you.

INTRODUCTORY RITES *(p. 5)*

COLLECT
God of might, giver of every good gift, put into our
hearts the love of your name, so that, by deepening our sense of reverence, you may nurture in
us what is good and, by your watchful care, keep
safe what you have nurtured. Through our Lord
Jesus Christ, your Son, who lives and reigns with
you in the unity of the Holy Spirit, one God, for
ever and ever. **Amen.**

FIRST READING *(Jeremiah 20.7-9)*
O Lord, you have enticed me, and I was enticed;
you have overpowered me, and you have pre-
vailed. I have become a laughingstock all day
long; everyone mocks me. For whenever I speak,
I must cry out, I must shout, "Violence and destruction!" For the word of the Lord has become
for me a reproach and derision all day long.

If I say, "I will not mention him, or speak any
more in his name," then within me there is something like a burning fire shut up in my bones; I am
weary with holding it in, and I cannot.

The word of the Lord. **Thanks be to God.**

RESPONSORIAL PSALM *(Psalm 63)*

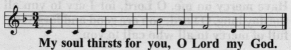

My soul thirsts for you, O Lord my God.

R. **My soul thirsts for you, O Lord my God.**

O God, you are my God, I · **seek_you,**
my soul · **thirsts_for_you;**
my flesh · **faints_for_you,**
as in a dry and weary land where there
   · **is** no water. R.

So I have looked upon you in the · **sanctuary,**
beholding your power and · **glory.**
Because your steadfast love is better than · **life,**
my · **lips** will praise_you. R.

So I will bless you as long as I · **live;**
I will lift up my hands and call on
   your · **name.**
My soul is satisfied as with a rich · **feast,**
and my mouth praises you with
   · **joy**-ful lips. R.

For you have been my · **help,**
and in the shadow of your wings I sing
   for · **joy.**
My soul · **clings_to_you;**
your right · **hand** up-holds_me. R.

©2010 Gordon Johnston/Novalis
To hear the Sunday Psalms, visit www.livingwithchrist.ca.

SECOND READING *(Romans 12.1-2)*

I appeal to you, brothers and sisters, by the mercies of God, to present your bodies as a living sacrifice, holy and acceptable to God, which is your spiritual worship. Do not be conformed to this world, but be transformed by the renewing of your minds, so that you may discern what is the will of God — what is good and acceptable and perfect.

The word of the Lord. **Thanks be to God.**

GOSPEL ACCLAMATION *(See Ephesians 1.17-18)*

Alleluia. Alleluia. May the Father of our Lord Jesus Christ enlighten the eyes of our heart, that we might know the hope to which we are called. **Alleluia.**

GOSPEL *(Matthew 16.21-27)*

The Lord be with you. **And with your spirit.** A reading from the holy Gospel according to Matthew. **Glory to you, O Lord.**

Jesus began to show his disciples that he must go to Jerusalem and undergo great suffering at the hands of the elders and chief priests and scribes, and be killed, and on the third day be raised.

And Peter took Jesus aside and began to rebuke him, saying, "God forbid it, Lord! This must never happen to you." But he turned and said to Peter, "Get behind me, Satan! You are a stumbling block to me; for you are thinking not as God does, but as humans do."

Then Jesus told his disciples, "If anyone wants to become my follower, let him deny himself and take up his cross and follow me. For whoever wants to save their life will lose it, and whoever loses their life for my sake will find it. For what will it profit anyone to gain the whole world but forfeit their life? Or what will anyone give in return for their life?

"For the Son of Man is to come with his Angels in the glory of his Father, and then he will repay each according to their work."

The Gospel of the Lord. **Praise to you, Lord Jesus Christ.**

PROFESSION OF FAITH *(p. 11)*

PRAYER OF THE FAITHFUL

The following intentions are suggestions only. There are more suggestions at www.livingwithchrist.ca

R. **Lord, hear our prayer.**

For the Church, witness in Christ's name to the dignity and equality of all people, we pray to the Lord: R.

For leaders of countries who work together to protect the environment, a fragile gift of God's creation, we pray to the Lord: R.

For those among us excluded from society for whatever reason, we pray to the Lord: R.

For us, called in baptism to make room at God's table for all people, we pray to the Lord: R.

PREPARATION OF THE GIFTS *(p. 14)*

PRAYER OVER THE OFFERINGS

May this sacred offering, O Lord, confer on us always the blessing of salvation, that what it celebrates in mystery it may accomplish in power. Through Christ our Lord. **Amen.**

PREFACE *(Sundays in Ordinary Time, p. 28)*

COMMUNION ANTIPHON *(Psalm 30.20)*

How great is the goodness, Lord, that you keep for those who fear you.

or (Matthew 5.9-10)

Blessed are the peacemakers, for they shall be called children of God. Blessed are they who are persecuted for the sake of righteousness, for theirs is the Kingdom of Heaven.

PRAYER AFTER COMMUNION

Renewed by this bread from the heavenly table, we beseech you, Lord, that, being the food of charity, it may confirm our hearts and stir us to serve you in our neighbour. Through Christ our Lord. **Amen.**

BLESSING AND DISMISSAL *(p. 70)*

September 10

The readings today focus on relationships and care of the other. These are not just any relationships, but the difficult and complex ones. Ezekiel cautions us not to give up on the wicked but rather warn them that their behaviour is unacceptable. However, if they do not heed our warning, then at least we will know that we tried to enlighten them.

The gospel today is very specific on how to deal with issues of conflict or disagreement. The scenario Jesus paints could apply to any family, community, workplace or environment which breeds conflict or confusion. It takes courage for us to be persistent and confront contentious issues first in private, then with witnesses, and finally in front of the assembly — to provide evidence of injustice or wrongdoing. If after all these measures have been taken and still there is no resolution, we must turn away and move on, knowing that we have done everything humanly possible to rectify the situation.

This is true love of self and neighbour. It in no way means we give up or are passive; rather, it shows us when to let go and let God. Sometimes this kind of integrity comes at a great cost. Yet is the price too great for the sake of building up the kingdom of God?

Marilyn Elphick, Mississauga, ON

ENTRANCE ANTIPHON *(Psalm 118.137, 124)*
You are just, O Lord, and your judgment is right;
treat your servant in accord with your merciful
love.

INTRODUCTORY RITES *(p. 5)*

COLLECT
O God, by whom we are redeemed and receive
adoption, look graciously upon your beloved
sons and daughters, that those who believe in
Christ may receive true freedom and an everlasting inheritance. Through our Lord Jesus Christ,
your Son, who lives and reigns with you in the
unity of the Holy Spirit, one God, for ever and
ever. **Amen.**

FIRST READING *(Ezekiel 33.7-9)*
Thus says the Lord: "So you, O son of man, I have
made a watchman for the house of Israel; whenever you hear a word from my mouth, you shall give
them warning from me. "If I say to the wicked, 'O
wicked one, you shall surely die,' and you do not
speak to warn the wicked to turn from their ways,
the wicked person shall die in their iniquity, but
their blood I will require at your hand.

"But if you warn the wicked person to turn
from their ways, and they do not turn from their
ways, they shall die in their iniquity, but you will
have saved your life."

The word of the Lord. **Thanks be to God.**

RESPONSORIAL PSALM *(Psalm 95)*

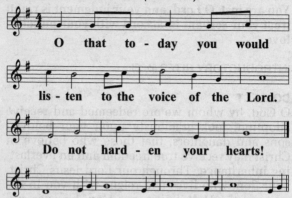

O that to-day you would lis-ten to the voice of the Lord. Do not hard-en your hearts!

℟. **O that today you would listen
to the voice of the Lord.
Do not harden your hearts!**

O come, let us sing to · **the** Lord.
Let us make a joyful noise to the rock of our
· **sal**-vation!
Let us come into his presence with · **thanks**-giving;
let us make a joyful noise to him with
songs · **of** praise! ℟.

O come, let us worship and · **bow** down,
let us kneel before the Lord, · **our** Maker!
For he is our God, and we are the people
of · **his** pasture,
and the sheep of · **his** hand. ℟.

O that today you would listen to · **his** voice!
Do not harden your hearts, as at Meribah,
as on the day at Massah in · **the** wilderness,

when your ancestors tested me, and put me
to · **the** proof,
though they had seen · **my** work. R̶

©*2010 Gordon Johnston/Novalis*

SECOND READING *(Romans 13.8-10)*
Brothers and sisters: Owe no one anything, except to love one another; for the one who loves
another has fulfilled the law.

The commandments, "You shall not commit
adultery; You shall not murder; You shall not
steal; You shall not covet"; and any other commandment, are summed up in this word, "Love
your neighbour as yourself."

Love does no wrong to a neighbour; therefore,
love is the fulfilling of the law.

The word of the Lord. **Thanks be to God.**

GOSPEL ACCLAMATION *(See 2 Corinthians 5.19)*
Alleluia. Alleluia. In Christ, God was reconciling
the world to himself, and entrusting the message
of reconciliation to us. **Alleluia.**

GOSPEL *(Matthew 18.15-20)*
The Lord be with you. **And with your spirit.**
A reading from the holy Gospel according to Mat-
thew. **Glory to you, O Lord.**

Jesus spoke to his disciples. "If your brother
or sister sins against you, go and point out the
fault when the two of you are alone. If he or she
listens to you, you have regained your brother or
sister. But if the person does not listen, take one
or two others along with you, so that every word

485

may be confirmed by the evidence of two or three witnesses. If the person refuses to listen to them, tell it to the Church; and if that person refuses to listen even to the Church, let such a one be to you as a Gentile and a tax collector.

"Truly I tell you, whatever you bind on earth will be bound in heaven, and whatever you loose on earth will be loosed in heaven. Again, truly I tell you, if two of you agree on earth about anything you ask, it will be done for you by my Father in heaven. For where two or three are gathered in my name, I am there among them."

The Gospel of the Lord. **Praise to you, Lord Jesus Christ.**

PROFESSION OF FAITH (p. 11)

PRAYER OF THE FAITHFUL

The following intentions are suggestions only. There are more suggestions at www.livingwithchrist.ca

R̰. **Lord, hear our prayer.**

For the Church and all its ministers, on whom the Spirit pours out the gift of wisdom, we pray to the Lord: R̰.

For world leaders, standing in need of wisdom, prudence and a passion for justice, we pray to the Lord: R̰.

For the needy and suffering, reaching out for God's healing strength, peace and joy, we pray to the Lord: R̰.

For us, God's people gathered here, on whom God pours out wisdom and love, we pray to the Lord: R̰.

PREPARATION OF THE GIFTS *(p. 14)*

PRAYER OVER THE OFFERINGS
O God, who give us the gift of true prayer and of
peace, graciously grant that, through this offering,
we may do fitting homage to your divine majesty
and, by partaking of the sacred mystery, we may
be faithfully united in mind and heart. Through
Christ our Lord. **Amen.**

PREFACE *(Sundays in Ordinary Time, p. 28)*

COMMUNION ANTIPHON *(Cf. Psalm 41.2-3)*
Like the deer that yearns for running streams, so
my soul is yearning for you, my God; my soul is
thirsting for God, the living God.
   or (John 8.12)
I am the light of the world, says the Lord; whoever follows me will not walk in darkness, but
will have the light of life.

PRAYER AFTER COMMUNION
Grant that your faithful, O Lord, whom you nourish and endow with life through the food of your
Word and heavenly Sacrament, may so benefit
from your beloved Son's great gifts that we may
merit an eternal share in his life. Who lives and
reigns for ever and ever. **Amen.**

BLESSING AND DISMISSAL *(p. 70)*

September 17

Forgiveness can be both the easiest and the most difficult thing a person is asked to give. Daily life is filled with moments in which we ask for forgiveness. Often a simple pardon is granted without much thought: "Don't worry about it" or "No problem" brushes off a minor transgression.

But this may not always be the case, since some moments are not so easily forgotten. Even though forgiveness may be spoken, a person may continue to harbour anger within their heart. In this case, forgiveness has not truly been granted. Some experiences may lead a person to feel so violated that they could never possibly grant a full pardon, even if they so desire it.

Sirach reminds us of the damaging effects that anger and vengeance can bring to our soul. If anger and vengeance are harboured, they violate our covenant with God. In his letter to the Romans, Paul examines the Lord's sacrifice through which we can all be pardoned. We are subsequently called to do as Christ has done, to forgive those who have trespassed against us.

Finally, in Matthew's gospel we learn that forgiveness is not finite and should never run dry. If it is perpetually poured from all people as it does from the Lord, then the cycle of anger, vengeance and hate will come to an end.

Dana Kenny, Charlottetown, PE

ENTRANCE ANTIPHON *(Cf. Sirach 36.18)*
Give peace, O Lord, to those who wait for you,
that your prophets be found true. Hear the prayers
of your servant, and of your people Israel.

INTRODUCTORY RITES *(p. 5)*

COLLECT
Look upon us, O God, Creator and ruler of all
things, and, that we may feel the working of your
mercy, grant that we may serve you with all our
heart. Through our Lord Jesus Christ, your Son,
who lives and reigns with you in the unity of the
Holy Spirit, one God, for ever and ever. **Amen.**

FIRST READING *(Sirach 27.30 – 28.7)*
Anger and wrath, these are abominations, yet a
sinner holds on to them. The vengeful person will
face the Lord's vengeance, for he keeps a strict
account of their sins. Forgive your neighbour the
wrong that is done, and then your sins will be
pardoned when you pray.

Does anyone harbour anger against another,
and expect healing from the Lord? If one has no
mercy toward another like oneself, can one then
seek pardon for one's own sins? If one who is but
flesh harbours wrath, who will make an atoning
sacrifice for that person's sins?

Remember the end of your life, and set enmity
aside; remember corruption and death, and be true to
the commandments. Remember the commandments,
and do not be angry with your neighbour; remember
the covenant of the Most High, and overlook faults.

The word of the Lord. **Thanks be to God.**

RESPONSORIAL PSALM *(Psalm 103)*

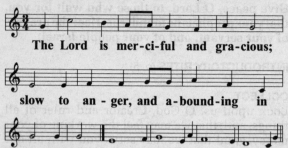

The Lord is mer-ci-ful and gra-cious;
slow to an-ger, and a-bound-ing in
stead-fast love.

℟. **The Lord is merciful and gracious;**
   slow to anger,
   and abounding in steadfast love.

Bless the Lord, O my · **soul,**
and all that is within me, bless his
   · **holy** name.
Bless the Lord, O my · **soul,**
and do not forget all · **his** benefits. ℟.

It is the Lord who forgives all your in-·**iquity,**
who heals all your · **dis-**eases,
who redeems your life from the · **Pit,**
who crowns you with steadfast love
   · **and** mercy. ℟.

He will not always ac-·**cuse,**
nor will he keep his anger · **for-**ever.
He does not deal with us according
   to our · **sins,**
nor repay us according to our · **in-**iquities. ℟.

For as the heavens are high above the · **earth,**
so great is his steadfast love toward those
  · **who** fear_him;
as far as the east is from the · **west,**
so far he removes our transgressions
  · **from** us. R.

To hear the Sunday Psalms, visit www.livingwithchrist.ca.

SECOND READING *(Romans 14.7-9)*

Brothers and sisters: We do not live to ourselves,
and we do not die to ourselves. If we live, we live
to the Lord, and if we die, we die to the Lord; so
then, whether we live or whether we die, we are
the Lord's. For to this end Christ died and lived
again, so that he might be Lord of both the dead
and the living.

The word of the Lord. **Thanks be to God.**

GOSPEL ACCLAMATION *(John 13.34)*

Alleluia. Alleluia. I give you a new commandment: love one another just as I have loved you.
Alleluia.

GOSPEL *(Matthew 18.21-35)*

The Lord be with you. **And with your spirit.**
A reading from the holy Gospel according to Matthew. **Glory to you, O Lord.**

Peter came and said to Jesus, "Lord, how often
should I forgive my brother or sister if they sin
against me? As many as seven times?" Jesus said
to him, "Not seven times, but, I tell you, seventy-
seven times.

"For this reason the kingdom of heaven may be compared to a king who wished to settle accounts with his slaves. When he began the reckoning, one who owed him ten thousand talents was brought to him; and, as he could not pay, his lord ordered him to be sold, together with his wife and children and all his possessions, and payment to be made. So the slave fell on his knees before him, saying, 'Have patience with me, and I will pay you everything.' The lord of that slave released him and forgave him the debt.

"But that same slave, as he went out, came upon one of his fellow slaves who owed him a hundred denarii; and seizing him by the throat, he said, 'Pay what you owe.' Then his fellow slave fell down and pleaded with him, 'Have patience with me, and I will pay you.' But he refused; then he went and threw him into prison until he would pay the debt.

"When his fellow slaves saw what had happened, they were greatly distressed, and they went and reported to their lord all that had taken place. Then his lord summoned him and said to him, 'You wicked slave! I forgave you all that debt because you pleaded with me. Should you not have had mercy on your fellow slave, as I had mercy on you?' And in anger his lord handed him over to be tortured until he would pay his entire debt.

"So my heavenly Father will also do to every one of you, if you do not forgive your brother or sister from your heart."

The Gospel of the Lord. **Praise to you, Lord Jesus Christ.**

PROFESSION OF FAITH *(p. 11)*

PRAYER OF THE FAITHFUL

The following intentions are suggestions only. There are more suggestions at www.livingwithchrist.ca

R. **Lord, hear our prayer.**

For the reconciliation of all Christians, called to be sacrament of God's unconditional love and infinite compassion, we pray to the Lord: R.

For the leaders of all nations and their peoples, entrusted as stewards of God's creation, we pray to the Lord: R.

For those whose anger, resentment and bitterness have caused them to withdraw, and for those who await their return, we pray to the Lord: R.

For us, God's people, called to stretch out our arms to all, we pray to the Lord: R.

PREPARATION OF THE GIFTS *(p. 14)*

PRAYER OVER THE OFFERINGS
Look with favour on our supplications, O Lord, and in your kindness accept these, your servants' offerings, that what each has offered to the honour of your name may serve the salvation of all. Through Christ our Lord. **Amen.**

PREFACE *(Sundays in Ordinary Time, p. 28)*

COMMUNION ANTIPHON *(Cf. Psalm 35.8)*

How precious is your mercy, O God! The children of men seek shelter in the shadow of your wings.

or (Cf. 1 Corinthians 10.16)

The chalice of blessing that we bless is a communion in the Blood of Christ; and the bread that we break is a sharing in the Body of the Lord.

PRAYER AFTER COMMUNION

May the working of this heavenly gift, O Lord, we pray, take possession of our minds and bodies, so that its effects, and not our own desires, may always prevail in us. Through Christ our Lord. **Amen.**

BLESSING AND DISMISSAL *(p. 70)*

September 24

We live in a culture that wants us to believe that our personal wealth, influence or possessions are what make us valuable. We are encouraged to compete, to measure ourselves against our friends, loved ones and neighbours. Who has more money? Who has a nicer car? Who works harder? We are greedy and fearful because it is a precarious way to live — at any given moment we could lose our place to someone who has hoarded more.

In today's parable of the wealthy landowner, we are shown a different kind of life. God's generosity offers all labourers the same share in the kingdom of heaven. Boundless, infinite, overflowing — the ability of God to give is beyond our ability to understand. Through his love, we are not measured on scales, but rather we are invited to live humbly, to take what we have earned and share what we can with others, all for the glory of the kingdom.

Each of us has a decision to make. Do we spend our lives competing and living with the fear of being found wanting? Or do we choose a life of generosity, service and humility, taking our fair share and holding out our hands to help those marginalized by society? Let us choose generosity, following the example found in today's gospel.

Fr. Matthew Durham, CSB, Windsor, ON

National Collection for the Needs of the Church in Canada

ENTRANCE ANTIPHON

I am the salvation of the people, says the Lord. Should they cry to me in any distress, I will hear them, and I will be their Lord for ever.

INTRODUCTORY RITES *(p. 5)*

COLLECT

O God, who founded all the commands of your sacred Law upon love of you and of our neighbour, grant that, by keeping your precepts, we may merit to attain eternal life. Through our Lord Jesus Christ, your Son, who lives and reigns with you in the unity of the Holy Spirit, one God, for ever and ever. **Amen.**

FIRST READING *(Isaiah 55.6-9)*

Seek the Lord while he may be found,
call upon him while he is near;
let the wicked person forsake their way,
and the unrighteous person their thoughts;
let that person return to the Lord that he may have
    mercy on them,
and to our God, for he will abundantly pardon.

For my thoughts are not your thoughts,
nor are your ways my ways, says the Lord.
For as the heavens are higher than the earth,
so are my ways higher than your ways
and my thoughts than your thoughts.

The word of the Lord. **Thanks be to God.**

RESPONSORIAL PSALM (*Psalm 145*)

The Lord is near to all who call on him.

R. **The Lord is near to all who call on him.**

Every day I will · **bless_you,**
and praise your name forever and · **ever.**
Great is the Lord, and greatly to be · **praised;**
his greatness is · **un**-searchable. R.

The Lord is gracious and · **merciful,**
slow to anger and abounding in steadfast · **love.**
The Lord is good to · **all,**
and his compassion is over all that
he · **has** made. R.

The Lord is just in all his · **ways,**
and kind in all his · **doings.**
The Lord is near to all who · **call_on_him,**
to all who call on him · **in** truth. R.

©2010 Gordon Johnston/Novalis
To hear the Sunday Psalms, visit www.livingwithchrist.ca.

SECOND READING (*Philippians 1.20-24, 27*)
Brothers and sisters: Christ will be exalted now as
always in my body, whether by life or by death.
For to me, living is Christ and dying is gain. If I
am to live in the flesh, that means fruitful labour
for me; and I do not know which I prefer. I am
hard pressed between the two: my desire is to

depart and be with Christ, for that is far better; but to remain in the flesh is more necessary for you. Live your life in a manner worthy of the Gospel of Christ.

The word of the Lord. **Thanks be to God.**

GOSPEL ACCLAMATION *(See Acts 16.14)*
Alleluia. Alleluia. Open our hearts, O Lord, to listen to the words of your Son. **Alleluia.**

GOSPEL *(Matthew 20.1-16)*
The Lord be with you. **And with your spirit.** A reading from the holy Gospel according to Matthew. **Glory to you, O Lord.**

Jesus spoke this parable to his disciples: "The kingdom of heaven is like a landowner who went out early in the morning to hire labourers for his vineyard. After agreeing with the labourers for the usual daily wage, he sent them into his vineyard. When he went out about nine o'clock, he saw others standing idle in the marketplace; and he said to them, 'You also go into the vineyard, and I will pay you whatever is right.' So they went.

"When he went out again about noon and about three o'clock, he did the same. And about five o'clock he went out and found others standing around; and he said to them, 'Why are you standing here idle all day?' They said to him, 'Because no one has hired us.' He said to them, 'You also go into the vineyard.'

"When evening came, the owner of the vineyard said to his manager, 'Call the labourers and give them their pay, beginning with the last and then going to the first.' When those hired about five o'clock came, each of them received the usual daily wage.

"Now when the first came, they thought they would receive more; but each of them also received the usual daily wage. And when they received it, they grumbled against the landowner, saying, 'These last worked only one hour, and you have made them equal to us who have borne the burden of the day and the scorching heat.' But he replied to one of them, 'Friend, I am doing you no wrong; did you not agree with me for the usual daily wage? Take what belongs to you and go; I choose to give to this last the same as I give to you. Am I not allowed to do what I choose with what belongs to me? Or are you envious because I am generous?'

"So the last will be first, and the first will be last."

The Gospel of the Lord. **Praise to you, Lord Jesus Christ.**

PROFESSION OF FAITH (p. 11)

PRAYER OF THE FAITHFUL

The following intentions are suggestions only. There are more suggestions at www.livingwithchrist.ca

R̰ **Lord, hear our prayer.**

For the Church, entrusted with the riches of the Gospel of life, we pray to the Lord: R̰

For those who govern nations and hold positions of authority, called to serve their people and the common good, we pray to the Lord: R̰

For the poor and needy of the world, defenceless against those who oppress them, we pray to the Lord: ℞.

For a generous spirit, as we are asked to give from our abundance to support the Church in Canada, we pray to the Lord: ℞.

PREPARATION OF THE GIFTS *(p. 14)*

PRAYER OVER THE OFFERINGS
Receive with favour, O Lord, we pray, the offerings of your people, that what they profess with devotion and faith may be theirs through these heavenly mysteries. Through Christ our Lord. **Amen.**

PREFACE *(Sundays in Ordinary Time, p. 28)*

COMMUNION ANTIPHON *(Psalm 118.4-5)*
You have laid down your precepts to be carefully kept; may my ways be firm in keeping your statutes.
or (John 10.14)
I am the Good Shepherd, says the Lord; I know my sheep, and mine know me.

PRAYER AFTER COMMUNION
Graciously raise up, O Lord, those you renew with this Sacrament, that we may come to possess your redemption both in mystery and in the manner of our life. Through Christ our Lord. **Amen.**

BLESSING AND DISMISSAL *(p. 70)*

October Saints' Days

The following saints are traditionally remembered in October in Canada.

1   Saint Thérèse of the Child Jesus

2   The Holy Guardian Angels

4   Saint Francis of Assisi

6   Blessed Marie-Rose Durocher
    Saint Bruno

7   Our Lady of the Rosary

9   Saint Denis and Companions
    Saint John Leonardi

11   Saint John XXIII

14   Saint Callistus I

15   Saint Teresa of Jesus

16   Saint Marguerite d'Youville

17   Saint Ignatius of Antioch

18   Saint Luke

19   Saint Paul of the Cross

20   Saint Hedwig
    Saint Margaret Mary Alacoque

22   Saint John Paul II

23   Saint John of Capistrano

24   Saint Anthony Mary Claret

28   Saints Simon and Jude

October 1

Today's Gospel Acclamation verse puts the meaning of this Sunday's readings succinctly. Christian life is about maintaining an intimate and trusting relationship with the Good Shepherd. Such a bond shapes hearts, determines actions, and reveals our shortcomings in such a way that we can regard them as failures and yet turn to, and rely on, God's mercy.

Ezekiel's words are meant to inspire rather than threaten, promising that God has a single, dependable criterion for judgment applicable to, and within the power of, each individual: righteousness. God takes no pleasure in the destruction of anyone but desires and offers life to each one.

A testimony to this truth can be found in Jesus Christ who, in his selfless act of sharing our human existence, his forgiveness of sinners and his acceptance of crucifixion, showed the extent of God's steadfast love. He liberated people from what bound them, restored them to community and called them to life. If we know *this* Shepherd, then we can willingly respond in obedient faith. Even when we fall short, though, we are not left without a remedy before God. The unrighteous tax collectors and prostitutes gained the kingdom through sincere repentance. We, too, growing in the kind of humble and open attitude towards God and others exemplified by Jesus, can also share the mind of Christ and his final victory.

Christine Mader, Waverley, NS

ENTRANCE ANTIPHON *(Daniel 3.31, 29, 30, 43, 42)*
All that you have done to us, O Lord, you have done with true judgment, for we have sinned against you and not obeyed your commandments. But give glory to your name and deal with us according to the bounty of your mercy.

INTRODUCTORY RITES *(p. 5)*

COLLECT
O God, who manifest your almighty power above all by pardoning and showing mercy, bestow, we pray, your grace abundantly upon us and make those hastening to attain your promises heirs to the treasures of heaven. Through our Lord Jesus Christ, your Son, who lives and reigns with you in the unity of the Holy Spirit, one God, for ever and ever. **Amen.**

FIRST READING *(Ezekiel 18.25-28)*
Thus says the Lord: "You object, O House of Israel! You say, 'The way of the Lord is unfair.' Hear now, O house of Israel: Is my way unfair? Is it not your ways that are unfair?

"When the righteous person turns away from their righteousness and commits iniquity, they shall die for it; for the iniquity that they have committed they shall die.

"Again, when the wicked person turns away from the wickedness they have committed and does what is lawful and right, they shall save their life. Because that person considered and turned away from all the transgressions that

503

they had committed, they shall surely live; they shall not die."

The word of the Lord. **Thanks be to God.**

RESPONSORIAL PSALM *(Psalm 25)*

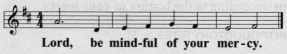

Lord, be mind-ful of your mer-cy.

℟. **Lord, be mindful of your mercy.**

Make me to know your ways, · **O** Lord;
teach · **me** your paths.
Lead me in your · **truth,** and teach_me,
for you are the God of · **my** sal-vation. ℟.

Be mindful of your mercy, O Lord,
  and of your stead·-**fast** love,
for they have been · **from** of old.
According to your steadfast · **love**
  re-member_me,
for the sake of your · **goodness,** O Lord! ℟.

Good and upright · **is_the** Lord;
therefore he instructs sinners · **in** the way.
He leads the humble in · **what** is right,
and teaches the · **humble** his way. ℟.

©2010 Gordon Johnston/Novalis
To hear the Sunday Psalms, visit www.livingwithchrist.ca.

SECOND READING *(Philippians 2.1-11)*

The shorter version ends at the asterisks.

Brothers and sisters: If there is any encouragement in Christ, any consolation from love, any sharing in the Spirit, any compassion and sympathy, then make my joy complete: be of the same mind, having the same love, being in full accord and of one mind. Do nothing from selfish ambition or conceit, but in humility regard others as better than yourselves. Let each of you look not to your own interests, but to the interests of others.

Let the same mind be in you that was in Christ Jesus.

* * *

who, though he was in the form of God,
did not regard equality with God as something
　to be exploited,
but emptied himself, taking the form of a slave,
being born in human likeness.
And being found in human form,
he humbled himself
and became obedient to the point of death —
even death on a cross.

Therefore God highly exalted him
and gave him the name that is above every name,
so that at the name of Jesus every knee should
　bend,
in heaven and on earth and under the earth,
and every tongue should confess that Jesus Christ
　is Lord,
to the glory of God the Father.

The word of the Lord. **Thanks be to God.**

GOSPEL ACCLAMATION *(See John 10.27)*
Alleluia. Alleluia. My sheep hear my voice,
says the Lord; I know them, and they follow me.
Alleluia.

GOSPEL *(Matthew 21.28-32)*
The Lord be with you. **And with your spirit.**
A reading from the holy Gospel according to Matthew. **Glory to you, O Lord.**

Jesus said to the chief priests and the elders of
the people: "What do you think? A man had two
sons; he went to the first and said, 'Son, go and
work in the vineyard today.' He answered, 'I will
not'; but later he changed his mind and went. The
father went to the second and said the same; and
he answered, 'I am going, sir'; but he did not go.
Which of the two did the will of his father?" They
said, "The first."

Jesus said to them, "Truly I tell you, the tax
collectors and the prostitutes are going into the
kingdom of God ahead of you. For John came to
you in the way of righteousness and you did not
believe him, but the tax collectors and the prostitutes believed him; and even after you saw it,
you did not change your minds and believe him."

The Gospel of the Lord. **Praise to you, Lord
Jesus Christ.**

PROFESSION OF FAITH *(p. 11)*

PRAYER OF THE FAITHFUL

The following intentions are suggestions only. There are more suggestions at www.livingwithchrist.ca

R̰. **Lord, hear our prayer.**

For the Church, called to give up everything that separates us from each other, we pray to the Lord: R̰.

For civic leaders, working for the true good of all their people, we pray to the Lord: R̰.

For all who hunger and thirst for acceptance, we pray to the Lord: R̰.

For us, God's people gathered here today, called to nurture true justice and resist the temptation to exploit the disadvantaged, we pray to the Lord: R̰.

PREPARATION OF THE GIFTS *(p. 14)*

PRAYER OVER THE OFFERINGS

Grant us, O merciful God, that this our offering may find acceptance with you and that through it the wellspring of all blessing may be laid open before us. Through Christ our Lord. **Amen.**

PREFACE *(Sundays in Ordinary Time, p. 28)*

COMMUNION ANTIPHON *(Cf. Psalm 118.49-50)*
Remember your word to your servant, O Lord, by which you have given me hope. This is my comfort when I am brought low.

or (1 John 3.16)

By this we came to know the love of God: that Christ laid down his life for us; so we ought to lay down our lives for one another.

PRAYER AFTER COMMUNION

May this heavenly mystery, O Lord, restore us in mind and body, that we may be co-heirs in glory with Christ, to whose suffering we are united whenever we proclaim his Death. Who lives and reigns for ever and ever. **Amen.**

BLESSING AND DISMISSAL *(p. 70)*

October 8

Most of us would agree that we have been given much in our lives for which to be thankful. If we're honest with ourselves, we would also agree that despite that abundance, we often do not use what we receive as well as we should. The earth was given to all, yet we often abuse it, hurting society's most vulnerable. We can see this in the tragic rise in migrants fleeing poverty caused by environmental degradation and economic exploitation, as Pope Francis points out in *Laudato Sí.*

In the reading from Isaiah, the Lord gives us a beautiful vineyard — our talents, earth's abundance, companionship of others — yet we take these things for granted. God expects to see justice, but there is bloodshed, suffering and injustice. The Lord's vineyard is not exclusive; it is open to all. The vineyard's bounty goes to those who, as Paul says, do what they have learned, received and heard in Christ Jesus.

In Psalm 80 we ask God to restore us to live out God's plan for us. Recognizing our weakness, we turn to God for strength and to realize the peace Paul says we can expect. The gospel strikes a similar chord. As with Christ himself, we know that, through God's help, even a rejected stone cannot simply be another foundation piece of our lives, but the cornerstone itself.

Jack Panozzo, Toronto, ON

ENTRANCE ANTIPHON *(Cf. Esther 4.17)*
Within your will, O Lord, all things are established, and there is none that can resist your will.
For you have made all things, the heaven and
the earth, and all that is held within the circle of
heaven; you are the Lord of all.

INTRODUCTORY RITES *(p. 5)*

COLLECT
Almighty ever-living God, who in the abundance
of your kindness surpass the merits and the
desires of those who entreat you, pour out your
mercy upon us to pardon what conscience dreads
and to give what prayer does not dare to ask.
Through our Lord Jesus Christ, your Son, who
lives and reigns with you in the unity of the Holy
Spirit, one God, for ever and ever. **Amen.**

FIRST READING *(Isaiah 5.1-7)*
Let me sing for my beloved my love song concerning his vineyard:

"My beloved had a vineyard on a very fertile
hill. He dug it and cleared it of stones, and planted
it with choice vines; he built a watchtower in the
midst of it, and hewed out a wine vat in it; he expected it to yield grapes, but it yielded wild grapes.

"And now, inhabitants of Jerusalem and people of Judah, judge between me and my vineyard.
What more was there to do for my vineyard that
I have not done in it? When I expected it to yield
grapes, why did it yield wild grapes?

"And now I will tell you what I will do to my
vineyard. I will remove its hedge, and it shall be

devoured; I will break down its wall, and it shall be trampled down. I will make it a waste; it shall not be pruned or hoed, and it shall be overgrown with briers and thorns; I will also command the clouds that they rain no rain upon it. For the vineyard of the Lord of hosts is the house of Israel, and the people of Judah are his pleasant planting; he expected justice, but saw bloodshed; righteousness, but heard a cry!"

The word of the Lord. **Thanks be to God.**

RESPONSORIAL PSALM *(Psalm 80)*

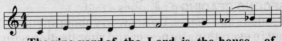

The vine-yard of the Lord is the house of

Is - ra - el.

R. **The vineyard of the Lord
is the house of Israel.**

You brought a vine out of · **Egypt;**
you drove out the nations and · **planted_it.**
It sent out its branches to the · **sea,**
and its shoots to · **the River.** R.

Why then have you broken down its · **walls,**
so that all who pass along the way pluck
its · **fruit?**
The boar from the forest · **ravages_it,**
and all that move in the · **field** feed_on_it. R.

Turn again, O God of · **hosts;**
look down from heaven, and · **see;**
have regard for this · **vine,**
the stock that your right · **hand** planted. R.

Then we will never turn back from · **you;**
give us life, and we will call on your · **name.**
Restore us, O Lord God of · **hosts;**
let your face shine, that we may · **be** saved. R.

©2010 Gordon Johnston/Novalis
To hear the Sunday Psalms, visit www.livingwithchrist.ca.

SECOND READING *(Philippians 4.6-9)*
Brothers and sisters: Do not worry about anything,
but in everything by prayer and supplication with
thanksgiving let your requests be made known to
God. And the peace of God, which surpasses all
understanding, will guard your hearts and your
minds in Christ Jesus.

Finally, brothers and sisters, whatever is true,
whatever is honourable, whatever is just, whatever is pure, whatever is pleasing, whatever is
commendable, if there is any excellence and if
there is anything worthy of praise, think about
these things. Keep on doing the things that you
have learned and received and heard and seen in
me, and the God of peace will be with you.

The word of the Lord. **Thanks be to God.**

GOSPEL ACCLAMATION *(See John 15.16)*
Alleluia. Alleluia. I have chosen you from the
world, says the Lord, to go and bear fruit that will
last. **Alleluia.**

GOSPEL *(Matthew 21.33-43)*

The Lord be with you. **And with your spirit.**
A reading from the holy Gospel according to Matthew. **Glory to you, O Lord.**

Jesus said to the chief priests and the elders of the people: "Listen to another parable. There was a landowner who planted a vineyard, put a fence around it, dug a wine press in it, and built a watchtower. Then he leased it to tenants and went to another country.

"When the harvest time had come, he sent his slaves to the tenants to collect his produce. But the tenants seized his slaves and beat one, killed another, and stoned another. Again he sent other slaves, more than the first; and they treated them in the same way.

"Finally he sent his son to them, saying, 'They will respect my son.' But when the tenants saw the son, they said to themselves, 'This is the heir; come, let us kill him and get his inheritance.' So they seized him, threw him out of the vineyard, and killed him.

"Now when the owner of the vineyard comes, what will he do to those tenants?" They said to him, "He will put those wretches to a miserable death, and lease the vineyard to other tenants who will give him the produce at the harvest time."

Jesus said to them, "Have you never read in the Scriptures:

'The stone that the builders rejected
has become the cornerstone;
this was the Lord's doing,
and it is amazing in our eyes'?

"Therefore I tell you, the kingdom of God will be taken away from you and given to a people that produces the fruits of the kingdom."

The Gospel of the Lord. **Praise to you, Lord Jesus Christ.**

PROFESSION OF FAITH (p. 11)

PRAYER OF THE FAITHFUL

The following intentions are suggestions only. There are more suggestions at www.livingwithchrist.ca

R. **Lord, hear our prayer.**

For the Church, people of God, entrusted with offering the gift of faith to the world, we pray to the Lord: R.

For leaders of the world's peoples, called to help their people grow to the fullness of their human dignity, we pray to the Lord: R.

For those who struggle for a share in the bounty of God's creation, we pray to the Lord: R.

For us, gathered here, a community of faith called to recognize the power entrusted to us, we pray to the Lord: R.

PREPARATION OF THE GIFTS (p. 14)

PRAYER OVER THE OFFERINGS

Accept, O Lord, we pray, the sacrifices instituted by your commands and, through the sacred mysteries, which we celebrate with dutiful service, graciously complete the sanctifying work by which you are pleased to redeem us. Through Christ our Lord. **Amen.**

PREFACE *(Sundays in Ordinary Time, p. 28)*

COMMUNION ANTIPHON *(Lamentations 3.25)*
The Lord is good to those who hope in him, to the soul that seeks him.
or (Cf. 1 Corinthians 10.17)
Though many, we are one bread, one body, for we all partake of the one Bread and one Chalice.

PRAYER AFTER COMMUNION
Grant us, almighty God, that we may be refreshed and nourished by the Sacrament which we have received, so as to be transformed into what we consume. Through Christ our Lord. **Amen.**

BLESSING AND DISMISSAL *(p. 70)*

October 15

Wedding feasts are celebrations of joy. The one in today's gospel, however, turns ugly. The guests refuse to attend; they attack the king's slaves. The king retaliates with murder and destruction. But the feast must go ahead. Just when things seem to be improving, the king notices a man without a wedding robe and casts him out into the darkness.

This parable is scary and makes me squirm. I recognize myself in those who ignored the king's invitation and in the man wearing the wrong outfit.

The parable challenges us to critique our friendship with God. God desires our friendship, inviting us time and time again into relationship. We sometimes fail in our response. Like those who rejected the invitation, we get busy with our own agendas; we ignore God. Or, like the man who shows up improperly attired, we have the wrong attitude. We may be smug, indifferent or insincere. We cast ourselves into the darkness when we refuse God's offer of friendship.

The Mass is a transitional time between the present and eternity. It is God's standing invitation to enter more deeply into relationship with God and others. Our presence here expresses our willingness to put on the robe of Christ so that we may stand confidently and joyfully in the light of God's friendship.

Louise McEwan, Trail, BC

ENTRANCE ANTIPHON *(Psalm 129.3-4)*
If you, O Lord, should mark iniquities, Lord, who could stand? But with you is found forgiveness, O God of Israel.

INTRODUCTORY RITES *(p. 5)*

COLLECT
May your grace, O Lord, we pray, at all times go before us and follow after and make us always determined to carry out good works. Through our Lord Jesus Christ, your Son, who lives and reigns with you in the unity of the Holy Spirit, one God, for ever and ever. **Amen.**

FIRST READING *(Isaiah 25.6-10a)*
On this mountain the Lord of hosts will make for all peoples a feast of rich food, a feast of well-aged wines, of rich food filled with marrow, of well-aged wines strained clear.

And he will destroy on this mountain the shroud that is cast over all peoples, the sheet that is spread over all nations; he will swallow up death forever. Then the Lord God will wipe away the tears from all faces, and the disgrace of his people he will take away from all the earth, for the Lord has spoken.

It will be said on that day, "Lo, this is our God; we have waited for him, so that he might save us. This is the Lord for whom we have waited; let us be glad and rejoice in his salvation. For the hand of the Lord will rest on this mountain."

The word of the Lord. **Thanks be to God.**

RESPONSORIAL PSALM *(Psalm 23)*

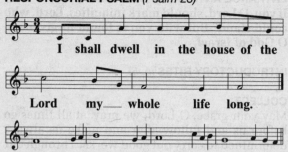

I shall dwell in the house of the Lord my whole life long.

℟. **I shall dwell in the house of the Lord my whole life long.**

The Lord is my shepherd, I shall · **not** want.
He makes me lie down in · **green** pastures;
he leads me be-·**side** still waters;
he re-·**stores** my soul. ℟.

He leads me in right paths for his · **name's** sake.
Even though I walk through the darkest
    valley, I fear · **no** evil;
for · **you** are with_me;
your rod and your · **staff** — they comfort_me. ℟.

You prepare a table · **be**-fore_me
in the presence · **of_my** enemies;
you anoint my · **head** with oil;
my · **cup** over-flows. ℟.

Surely goodness and mercy · **shall** follow_me
all the days of · **my** life,
and I shall dwell in the · **house_of** the Lord
my · **whole** life long. ℟.

SECOND READING *(Philippians 4.12-14, 19-20)*
Brothers and sisters: I know what it is to have little, and I know what it is to have plenty. In any and all circumstances I have learned the secret of being well-fed and of going hungry, of having plenty and of being in need. I can do all things through him who strengthens me. In any case, it was kind of you to share my distress.

My God will fully satisfy every need of yours according to his riches in glory in Christ Jesus. To our God and Father be glory forever and ever. Amen.

The word of the Lord. **Thanks be to God.**

GOSPEL ACCLAMATION *(See Ephesians 1.17-18)*
Alleluia. Alleluia. May the Father of our Lord Jesus Christ enlighten the eyes of our heart, that we might know the hope to which we are called. **Alleluia.**

GOSPEL *(Matthew 22.1-14)*
The shorter version ends with the asterisks.
The Lord be with you. **And with your spirit.**
A reading from the holy Gospel according to Matthew. **Glory to you, O Lord.**

Once more Jesus spoke to the chief priests and Pharisees in parables: "The kingdom of heaven may be compared to a king who gave a wedding banquet for his son. He sent his slaves to call those who had been invited to the wedding banquet, but they would not come.

"Again he sent other slaves, saying, 'Tell those who have been invited: "Look, I have prepared my dinner, my oxen and my fat calves have been

519

slaughtered, and everything is ready; come to the wedding banquet.'" But they made light of it and went away, one to his farm, another to his business, while the rest seized his slaves, mistreated them, and killed them. The king was enraged. He sent his troops, destroyed those murderers, and burned their city.

"Then he said to his slaves, 'The wedding is ready, but those invited were not worthy. Go therefore into the main streets, and invite everyone you find to the wedding banquet.' Those slaves went out into the streets and gathered all whom they found, both good and bad; so the wedding hall was filled with guests.

* * *

"But when the king came in to see the guests, he noticed a man there who was not wearing a wedding robe, and he said to him, 'Friend, how did you get in here without a wedding robe?' And he was speechless. Then the king said to the attendants, 'Bind him hand and foot, and throw him into the outer darkness, where there will be weeping and gnashing of teeth.' For many are called, but few are chosen."

The Gospel of the Lord. **Praise to you, Lord Jesus Christ.**

PROFESSION OF FAITH (p. 11)

PRAYER OF THE FAITHFUL

The following intentions are suggestions only. There are more suggestions at www.livingwithchrist.ca

℟. **Lord, hear our prayer.**

For the Church, a community committed to faith and justice, we pray to the Lord: ℟.

For the leaders of nations, called to effective action on behalf of the poor, we pray to the Lord: ℟.

For people uprooted by war or natural disaster, we pray to the Lord: ℟.

For this community, called as a parish to act justly and lovingly, we pray to the Lord: ℟.

PREPARATION OF THE GIFTS *(p. 14)*

PRAYER OVER THE OFFERINGS

Accept, O Lord, the prayers of your faithful with the sacrificial offerings, that, through these acts of devotedness, we may pass over to the glory of heaven. Through Christ our Lord. **Amen.**

PREFACE *(Sundays in Ordinary Time, p. 28)*

COMMUNION ANTIPHON *(Cf. Psalm 33.11)*
The rich suffer want and go hungry, but those who seek the Lord lack no blessing.

or (1 John 3.2)

When the Lord appears, we shall be like him, for we shall see him as he is.

PRAYER AFTER COMMUNION
We entreat your majesty most humbly, O Lord, that, as you feed us with the nourishment which comes from the most holy Body and Blood of your Son, so you may make us sharers of his divine nature. Who lives and reigns for ever and ever. **Amen.**

BLESSING AND DISMISSAL *(p. 70)*

October 22
World Mission Sunday

This gospel passage recounts the first of four challenges to Jesus from Jewish leaders. The message Jesus preached had reached them and threatened the détente they had attained with the Romans who had mandated that taxes had to be paid. Tragically, this made the Jewish people complicit in their own oppression. Jesus' retort challenges the Pharisees and us to look beyond the obvious and remain focused on what belongs to God.

Although paying taxes still rankles us, we recognize that they provide education, health care, a standard of living and more that could not be sustained otherwise. The common good, a principle of Catholic social teaching, can only be achieved and maintained if we come together in concern for one another.

Today is World Mission Sunday. Through our generosity, we can extend our concern beyond our borders to our brothers and sisters who are in need in every corner of the world. Our contributions testify to the fact that we believe that all of humanity is from God and worthy of our care.

Jesus counters the Pharisees by asking whose image was stamped on their coin. For us, the important question goes beyond image. We are challenged to declare that it is Jesus, the son of the living God, who lives in our hearts, so that we might place love above all else.

Connie Paré, London, ON

ENTRANCE ANTIPHON (Cf. Psalm 16.6, 8)

To you I call; for you will surely heed me, O God; turn your ear to me; hear my words. Guard me as the apple of your eye; in the shadow of your wings protect me.

INTRODUCTORY RITES (p. 5)

COLLECT

Almighty ever-living God, grant that we may always conform our will to yours and serve your majesty in sincerity of heart. Through our Lord Jesus Christ, your Son, who lives and reigns with you in the unity of the Holy Spirit, one God, for ever and ever. **Amen.**

FIRST READING (Isaiah 45.1, 4-6)

Thus says the Lord to his anointed, to Cyrus, whose right hand I have grasped to subdue nations before him and strip kings of their robes, to open doors before him — and the gates shall not be closed:

"For the sake of my servant Jacob, and Israel my chosen, I call you by your name, I surname you, though you do not know me. I am the Lord, and there is no other; besides me there is no god. I arm you, though you do not know me, so that all may know, from the rising of the sun and from the west, that there is no one besides me; I am the Lord, and there is no other."

The word of the Lord. **Thanks be to God.**

RESPONSORIAL PSALM *(Psalm 96)*

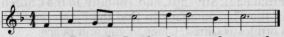

As-cribe to the Lord glo-ry and strength.

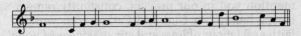

R̂. **Ascribe to the Lord glory and strength.**

O sing to the Lord · **a** new song;
sing to the Lord, · **all** the earth.
Declare his glory a-**mong** the nations,
his marvellous works a-**mong_all**
    the peoples. R̂.

For great is the Lord, and greatly · **to** be praised;
he is to be revered a-**bove** all gods.
For all the gods of the · **peoples** are idols,
but the · **Lord_made** the heavens. R̂.

Ascribe to the Lord, O families · **of** the peoples,
ascribe to the Lord · **glory** and strength.
Ascribe to the Lord the glory · **due** his name;
bring an offering, and come · **into** his courts. R̂.

Worship the Lord in · **ho**-ly splendour;
tremble before him, · **all** the earth.
Say among the nations, "The · **Lord** is king!
He will judge the · **peoples** with equity." R̂.

©2010 Gordon Johnston/Novalis
To hear the Sunday Psalms, visit www.livingwithchrist.ca.

SECOND READING *(1 Thessalonians 1.1-5ab)*
From Paul, Silvanus, and Timothy, to the Church
of the Thessalonians in God the Father and the
Lord Jesus Christ: Grace to you and peace.

We always give thanks to God for all of you and
mention you in our prayers, constantly remem-
bering before our God and Father your work of
faith and labour of love and steadfastness of hope
in our Lord Jesus Christ. For we know, brothers
and sisters beloved by God, that he has chosen
you, because our message of the Gospel came to
you not in word only, but also in power and in
the Holy Spirit and with full conviction.

The word of the Lord. **Thanks be to God.**

GOSPEL ACCLAMATION *(See Philippians 2.15-16)*
Alleluia. Alleluia. Shine like stars in the world,
holding fast to the word of life. **Alleluia.**

GOSPEL *(Matthew 22.15-21)*
The Lord be with you. **And with your spirit.**
A reading from the holy Gospel according to Mat-
thew. **Glory to you, O Lord.**

The Pharisees went and plotted to entrap Jesus
in what he said. So they sent their disciples to
him, along with the Herodians, saying, "Teacher,
we know that you are sincere, and teach the way
of God in accordance with truth, and show defer-
ence to no one; for you do not regard people with
partiality. Tell us, then, what you think. Is it lawful to pay taxes to the emperor, or not?"

But Jesus, aware of their malice, said, "Why
are you putting me to the test, you hypocrites?

Show me the coin used for the tax." And they brought him a denarius.

Then he said to them, "Whose head is this, and whose title?" They answered, "Caesar's." Then he said to them, "Give therefore to Caesar the things that are Caesar's, and to God the things that are God's."

The Gospel of the Lord. **Praise to you, Lord Jesus Christ.**

PROFESSION OF FAITH (p. 11)

PRAYER OF THE FAITHFUL

The following intentions are suggestions only. There are more suggestions at www.livingwithchrist.ca

R. **Lord, hear our prayer.**

For the Church and its leaders, called to proclaim Jesus Christ in today's world, we pray to the Lord: R.

For all who seek God through different paths, enriching our human community by their spiritual values, we pray to the Lord: R.

For missionaries, men and women of faith who model Christ for others, we pray to the Lord: R.

For us, a community of faith, entrusted by our baptism to witness to Jesus Christ, we pray to the Lord: R.

PREPARATION OF THE GIFTS (p. 14)

PRAYER OVER THE OFFERINGS

Grant us, Lord, we pray, a sincere respect for your gifts, that, through the purifying action of your grace, we may be cleansed by the very mysteries we serve. Through Christ our Lord. **Amen.**

PREFACE (Sundays in Ordinary Time, p. 28)

COMMUNION ANTIPHON (Cf. Psalm 32.18-19)

Behold, the eyes of the Lord are on those who fear him, who hope in his merciful love, to rescue their souls from death, to keep them alive in famine.

or (Mark 10.45)

The Son of Man has come to give his life as a ransom for many.

PRAYER AFTER COMMUNION

Grant, O Lord, we pray, that, benefiting from participation in heavenly things, we may be helped by what you give in this present age and prepared for the gifts that are eternal. Through Christ our Lord. **Amen.**

BLESSING AND DISMISSAL (p. 70)

October 29

Silenced. Through the stunning simplicity of his message, Jesus sometimes left his listeners absolutely speechless. The truth of his message could not be argued. It simply stood there as fact.

Light-heartedly, we might chuckle as we note that they chose a lawyer to question him. Their spokesperson was someone accustomed to winning arguments. They were represented by someone skilled in the art of asking questions that were often intended to intimidate. Jesus was not cowed, but responded with confidence.

With pinpoint accuracy, Jesus focuses on the heart of the matter: *love*. Love of God, love of self and love of neighbour. He cuts through the multitude of rules and regulations that direct and dictate our words and actions. Jesus simply silences all the confusing questions.

In the midst of our own confounding and confusing times, it might be helpful if we simply stop and quietly ask ourselves: What is the most loving thing to do — right now — for myself and for the other? Imagine how quickly anger, sarcasm, hatred and violence could be transformed into words and actions that are loving.

In the end, that is all that is asked of us. Quiet and prayerful, we might imagine the simplicity of a face-to-face conversation. As we listen, God gently inquires: Did you love?

Brenda Merk Hildebrand, Campbell River, BC

ENTRANCE ANTIPHON *(Cf. Psalm 104.3-4)*
Let the hearts that seek the Lord rejoice; turn to the Lord and his strength; constantly seek his face.

INTRODUCTORY RITES *(p. 5)*

COLLECT
Almighty ever-living God, increase our faith, hope and charity, and make us love what you command, so that we may merit what you promise. Through our Lord Jesus Christ, your Son, who lives and reigns with you in the unity of the Holy Spirit, one God, for ever and ever. **Amen.**

FIRST READING *(Exodus 22.21-27)*
Thus says the Lord: "You shall not wrong or oppress a resident alien, for you were aliens in the land of Egypt. You shall not abuse any widow or orphan. If you do abuse them, when they cry out to me, I will surely heed their cry; my wrath will burn, and I will kill you with the sword, and your wives shall become widows and your children orphans.

"If you lend money to my people, to the poor one among you, you shall not deal with them as a creditor; you shall not exact interest from them. If you take your neighbour's cloak in pawn, you shall restore it to that person before the sun goes down; for it may be their only clothing to use as cover; in what else shall that person sleep? And if that person cries out to me, I will listen, for I am compassionate."

The word of the Lord. **Thanks be to God.**

RESPONSORIAL PSALM (Psalm 18)

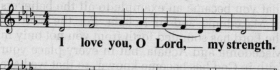

I love you, O Lord, ___ my strength.

℟. **I love you, O Lord, my strength.**

I love you, O Lord, my · **strength.**
The Lord is my rock, my fortress,
    and my de·-**liverer.**
My God, my rock in whom I take · **refuge,**
my shield, and the source of my salvation,
· **my** stronghold. ℟.

I call upon the Lord, who is worthy
    to be · **praised,**
so I shall be saved from my · **enemies.**
From his temple he heard my · **voice,**
and my cry to him reached · **his** ears. ℟.

The Lord lives! Blessed be my · **rock,**
and exalted be the God of my sal·-**vation,**
Great triumphs he gives to his · **king,**
and shows steadfast love to · **his_a**-nointed. ℟.

©2010 Gordon Johnston/Novalis
To hear the Sunday Psalms, visit www.livingwithchrist.ca.

SECOND READING (1 Thessalonians 1.5c-10)
Brothers and sisters: You know what kind of persons we proved to be among you for your sake. And you became imitators of us and of the Lord, for in spite of persecution you received

the word with joy inspired by the Holy Spirit, so that you became an example to all the believers in Macedonia and in Achaia. For the word of the Lord has sounded forth from you not only in Macedonia and Achaia, but in every place your faith in God has become known, so that we have no need to speak about it. For the people of those regions report about us what kind of welcome we had among you, and how you turned to God from idols, to serve a living and true God, and to wait for his Son from heaven, whom he raised from the dead — Jesus, who rescues us from the wrath that is coming.

The word of the Lord. **Thanks be to God.**

GOSPEL ACCLAMATION (*John 14.23*)
Alleluia. Alleluia. The one who loves me will keep my word and my Father will love him and we will come to him. **Alleluia.**

GOSPEL (*Matthew 22.34-40*)
The Lord be with you. **And with your spirit.**
A reading from the holy Gospel according to Matthew. **Glory to you, O Lord.**

When the Pharisees heard that Jesus had silenced the Sadducees, they gathered together, and one of them, a lawyer, asked him a question to test him. "Teacher, which commandment in the Law is the greatest?"

Jesus said to him, "'You shall love the Lord your God with all your heart, and with all your soul, and with all your mind.' This is the greatest and first commandment.

"And a second is like it: 'You shall love your neighbour as yourself.' On these two commandments hang all the Law and the Prophets."

The Gospel of the Lord. **Praise to you, Lord Jesus Christ.**

PROFESSION OF FAITH (p. 11)

PRAYER OF THE FAITHFUL

The following intentions are suggestions only. There are more suggestions at www.livingwithchrist.ca

R. **Lord, hear our prayer.**

For the Church, sacrament of God's forgiveness in word and action, we pray to the Lord: R.

For leaders, entrusted with the protection and promotion of the common good, we pray to the Lord: R.

For all who search for forgiveness and for those who reach out to them, we pray to the Lord: R.

For us, God's holy people, called to offer each other God's mercy and forgiveness, we pray to the Lord: R.

PREPARATION OF THE GIFTS (p. 14)

PRAYER OVER THE OFFERINGS

Look, we pray, O Lord, on the offerings we make to your majesty, that whatever is done by us in your service may be directed above all to your glory. Through Christ our Lord. **Amen.**

PREFACE *(Sundays in Ordinary Time, p. 28)*

COMMUNION ANTIPHON *(Cf. Psalm 19.6)*
We will ring out our joy at your saving help and
exult in the name of our God.

or (Ephesians 5.2)
Christ loved us and gave himself up for us, as a
fragrant offering to God.

PRAYER AFTER COMMUNION
May your Sacraments, O Lord, we pray, perfect in
us what lies within them, that what we now celebrate in signs we may one day possess in truth.
Through Christ our Lord. **Amen.**

BLESSING AND DISMISSAL *(p. 70)*

November Saints' Days

The following saints are traditionally remembered in November in Canada.

1   All Saints

2   All Souls' Day

3   Saint Martin de Porres

4   Saint Charles Borromeo

10 Saint Leo the Great

11 Saint Martin of Tours

12 Saint Josaphat

15 Saint Albert the Great

16 Saint Margaret of Scotland
    Saint Gertrude

17 Saint Elizabeth of Hungary

22 Saint Cecilia

23 Saint Clement I
    Saint Columban

24 Saint Andrew Düng-Lac and Companions

25 Saint Catherine of Alexandria

30 Saint Andrew

November 5

In today's gospel Jesus denounces the Pharisees and scribes for practising a superficial faith that is overly concerned with how they are seen by others. Although this passage from Matthew's Gospel is a strong critique of the religious leaders of his day, Christ's sharp admonishment cuts to the heart of us all.

For whom do we make our displays of faith? Do we practise our piety out of joy at what the Lord has done for us? Or out of fear of social rejection; a desire to win the praise and good opinion of others; or merely to attract attention? Are we people-pleasers or God-pleasers?

In asking us to examine the motivations behind our actions, God helps us to realize more deeply who the object of our worship is: others, ourselves or God? Today, God invites us to free ourselves from our pride and make him the object of our worship.

So, when we feel the temptation to keep one eye open during the prayers at Mass to spy which of our friends bothered to show up, or recite the Creed a little louder than the person sitting next to us, let us remember that today's celebration of Mass is about honouring our Lord.

Cheridan Sanders, Toronto, ON

ENTRANCE ANTIPHON *(Cf. Psalm 37.22-23)*
Forsake me not, O Lord, my God; be not far from me! Make haste and come to my help, O Lord, my strong salvation!

INTRODUCTORY RITES *(p. 5)*

COLLECT
Almighty and merciful God, by whose gift your faithful offer you right and praiseworthy service, grant, we pray, that we may hasten without stumbling to receive the things you have promised. Through our Lord Jesus Christ, your Son, who lives and reigns with you in the unity of the Holy Spirit, one God, for ever and ever. **Amen.**

FIRST READING *(Malachi 1.14 – 2.2, 8-10)*
"I am a great King," says the Lord of hosts, "and my name is reverenced among the nations.

"And now, O priests, this command is for you. If you will not listen, if you will not lay it to heart to give glory to my name," says the Lord of hosts, "then I will send the curse on you and I will curse your blessings; indeed I have already cursed them, because you do not lay it to heart.

"You have turned aside from the way; you have caused many to stumble by your instruction; you have corrupted the covenant of Levi," says the Lord of hosts, "and so I make you despised and abased before all the people, inasmuch as you have not kept my ways but have shown partiality in your instruction."

Have we not all one father? Has not one God created us? Why then are we faithless to one another, profaning the covenant of our ancestors?

The word of the Lord. **Thanks be to God.**

RESPONSORIAL PSALM *(Psalm 131)*

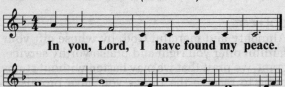

In you, Lord, I have found my peace.

℟. **In you, Lord, I have found my peace.**

O Lord, my heart is not lifted · **up,**
my eyes are not raised · **too** high;
I do not occupy myself · **with** things
too great and too · **marvellous** for me. ℟.

But I have calmed and quieted my · **soul,**
like a weaned child with · **its** mother;
my soul is like the · **weaned** child
that · **is** with me. ℟.

1 - O Israel, hope in the · **Lord**
4 - from this time on and for--**ev**-er-more. ℟.

©2010 Gordon Johnston/Novalis
To hear the Sunday Psalms, visit www.livingwithchrist.ca.

SECOND READING *(1 Thessalonians 2.7-9, 13)*
Brothers and sisters: Though we might have made demands as Apostles of Christ, we were gentle among you, like a nurse tenderly caring for her own children. So deeply do we care for you that

we are determined to share with you not only the Gospel of God but also our own selves, because you have become very dear to us. You remember our labour and toil, brothers and sisters; we worked night and day, so that we might not burden any of you while we proclaimed to you the Gospel of God.

We also constantly give thanks to God for this, that when you received the word of God that you heard from us, you accepted it not as a human word but as what it really is, the word of God, which is also at work in you believers.

The word of the Lord. **Thanks be to God.**

GOSPEL ACCLAMATION (See Matthew 23.9, 10)
Alleluia. Alleluia. You have one Father, your Father in heaven; you have one teacher, the Lord Jesus Christ! **Alleluia.**

GOSPEL (Matthew 23.1-12)
The Lord be with you. **And with your spirit.**
A reading from the holy Gospel according to Matthew. **Glory to you, O Lord.**

Then Jesus said to the crowds and to his disciples, "The scribes and the Pharisees sit in Moses' chair; therefore, do whatever they teach you and follow it; but do not do as they do, for they do not practise what they teach. They tie up heavy burdens, hard to bear, and lay them on the shoulders of others; but they themselves are unwilling to lift a finger to move them. They do all their deeds to be seen by others; for they make their phylacteries broad and their fringes long. They love to have the place of honour at banquets

539

and the best seats in the synagogues, and to be greeted with respect in the marketplaces, and to have people call them rabbi.

"But you are not to be called rabbi, for you have one teacher, and you are all brothers and sisters. And call no one your father on earth, for you have one Father — the one in heaven. Nor are you to be called instructors, for you have one instructor, the Christ. The greatest among you will be your servant. Whoever exalts himself will be humbled, and whoever humbles himself will be exalted."

The Gospel of the Lord. **Praise to you, Lord Jesus Christ.**

PROFESSION OF FAITH *(p. 11)*

PRAYER OF THE FAITHFUL

The following intentions are suggestions only. There are more suggestions at www.livingwithchrist.ca

R. **Lord, hear our prayer.**

For the Church, sacrament of Christ's salvation offered to all, we pray to the Lord: R.

For all leaders, called to serve others through their leadership, we pray to the Lord: R.

For the sick and elderly who struggle to maintain dignity, and for those who care for them, we pray to the Lord: R.

For us, God's priestly people gathered here, called to pray daily, we pray to the Lord: R.

PREPARATION OF THE GIFTS *(p. 14)*

PRAYER OVER THE OFFERINGS
May these sacrificial offerings, O Lord, become for you a pure oblation, and for us a holy outpouring of your mercy. Through Christ our Lord. **Amen.**

PREFACE *(Sundays in Ordinary Time, p. 28)*

COMMUNION ANTIPHON *(Cf. Psalm 15.11)*
You will show me the path of life, the fullness of joy in your presence, O Lord.
or (John 6.58)
Just as the living Father sent me and I have life because of the Father, so whoever feeds on me shall have life because of me, says the Lord.

PRAYER AFTER COMMUNION
May the working of your power, O Lord, increase in us, we pray, so that, renewed by these heavenly Sacraments, we may be prepared by your gift for receiving what they promise. Through Christ our Lord. **Amen.**

BLESSING AND DISMISSAL *(p. 70)*

November 12

The parable of the ten bridesmaids used to strike me as unreasonably harsh. Why, I wondered, were the "wise" ones so unhelpful to their "foolish" sisters? Could they not have simply shared their oil? Further reflection, however, brings to light some other aspects of the story.

In some respects the ten are all the same. All of them fall asleep. Later on, all are called to accompany the bridegroom into the wedding banquet.

What distinguishes five of them as wise, however, is that they have come *prepared*. When the call is heard, therefore, they are the ones who are ready and able to respond. The others are foolish because, though they hear the same call, they are not in a state of readiness to answer that summons.

Note the importance of the words "wise," "ready" and "awake." We hear in them echoes of the first reading's description of wisdom: she is given to those "who desire her," who "rise early to seek her," who are "vigilant."

In our efforts to be faithful disciples we need to be *available*, to be always open to God's call whenever it comes, even — or especially — in places of darkness and unexpectedness. God understands our weaknesses and our failings. The disposition of our hearts is what makes all the difference.

Krystyna Higgins, Guelph, ON

ENTRANCE ANTIPHON *(Cf. Psalm 87.3)*
Let my prayer come into your presence. Incline your ear to my cry for help, O Lord.

INTRODUCTORY RITES *(p. 5)*

COLLECT
Almighty and merciful God, graciously keep from us all adversity, so that, unhindered in mind and body alike, we may pursue in freedom of heart the things that are yours. Through our Lord Jesus Christ, your Son, who lives and reigns with you in the unity of the Holy Spirit, one God, for ever and ever. **Amen.**

FIRST READING *(Wisdom 6.12-16)*
Wisdom is radiant and unfading,
and she is easily discerned by those who love her,
and is found by those who seek her.
She hastens to make herself known to those
    who desire her.
One who rises early to seek her will have no
    difficulty,
for she will be found sitting at the gate.

To fix one's thought on her is perfect
    understanding,
and one who is vigilant on her account will
    soon be free from care,
because she goes about seeking those worthy of her,
and she graciously appears to them in their paths,
and meets them in every thought.

The word of the Lord. **Thanks be to God.**

RESPONSORIAL PSALM *(Psalm 63)*

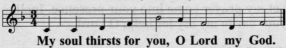

My soul thirsts for you, O Lord my God.

R. My soul thirsts for you, O Lord my God.

O God, you are my God, I · **seek_you**,
my soul · **thirsts_for_you**;
my flesh · **faints_for_you**,
as in a dry and weary land where there
· **is** no water. R.

So I have looked upon you in the · **sanctuary**,
beholding your power and · **glory**.
Because your steadfast love is better than · **life**,
my · **lips** will praise_you. R.

So I will bless you as long as I · **live**;
I will lift up my hands and call on
your · **name**.
My soul is satisfied as with a rich · **feast**,
and my mouth praises you with
· **joy**-ful lips. R.

I think of you on my · **bed**,
and meditate on you in the watches
of the · **night**;
for you have been my · **help**,
and in the shadow of your wings I · **sing**
for joy. R.

©2010 Gordon Johnston/Novalis
To hear the Sunday Psalms, visit www.livingwithchrist.ca.

SECOND READING *(1 Thessalonians 4.13-18)*

We do not want you to be uninformed, brothers and sisters, about those who have died, so that you may not grieve as others do who have no hope. For since we believe that Jesus died and rose again, even so, through Jesus, God will bring with him those who have died. For this we declare to you by the word of the Lord, that we who are alive, who are left until the coming of the Lord, will by no means precede those who have died.

For the Lord himself, with a cry of command, with the Archangel's call and with the sound of God's trumpet, will descend from heaven, and the dead in Christ will rise first. Then we who are alive, who are left, will be caught up in the clouds together with them to meet the Lord in the air; and so we will be with the Lord forever. Therefore encourage one another with these words.

The word of the Lord. **Thanks be to God.**

GOSPEL ACCLAMATION *(See Matthew 24.42, 44)*
Alleluia. Alleluia. Keep awake and be ready: you do not know when the Son of Man is coming. **Alleluia.**

GOSPEL *(Matthew 25.1-13)*
The Lord be with you. **And with your spirit.**
A reading from the holy Gospel according to Matthew. **Glory to you, O Lord.**

Jesus spoke this parable to the disciples: "The kingdom of heaven will be like this. Ten bridesmaids took their lamps and went to meet the bridegroom. Five of them were foolish, and five were wise. When the foolish took their lamps, they took no oil with them; but the wise took flasks of oil with their lamps. As the bridegroom was delayed, all of them became drowsy and slept.

"But at midnight there was a shout, 'Look! Here is the bridegroom! Come out to meet him.' Then all those bridesmaids got up and trimmed their lamps. The foolish said to the wise, 'Give us some of your oil, for our lamps are going out.' But the wise replied, 'No! There will not be enough for you and for us; you had better go to the dealers and buy some for yourselves.' And while they went to buy it, the bridegroom came, and those who were ready went with him into the wedding banquet; and the door was shut.

"Later the other bridesmaids came also, saying, 'Lord, lord, open to us.' But he replied, 'Truly I tell you, I do not know you.' Keep awake therefore, for you know neither the day nor the hour."

The Gospel of the Lord. **Praise to you, Lord Jesus Christ.**

PROFESSION OF FAITH *(p. 11)*

PRAYER OF THE FAITHFUL

The following intentions are suggestions only. There are more suggestions at www.livingwithchrist.ca

R. **Lord, hear our prayer.**

For the Church, instrument of God's gracious hospitality, we pray to the Lord: R.

For peaceful understanding in troubled areas of the world, we pray to the Lord: R.

For the needs of the forgotten in our midst, we pray to the Lord: R.

For parish communities proclaiming the gospel of mercy and love for all, we pray to the Lord: R.

PREPARATION OF THE GIFTS (p. 14)

PRAYER OVER THE OFFERINGS
Look with favour, we pray, O Lord, upon the sacrificial gifts offered here, that, celebrating in mystery the Passion of your Son, we may honour it with loving devotion. Through Christ our Lord. **Amen.**

PREFACE (Sundays in Ordinary Time, p. 28)

COMMUNION ANTIPHON (Cf. Psalm 22.1-2)
The Lord is my shepherd; there is nothing I shall want. Fresh and green are the pastures where he gives me repose, near restful waters he leads me.
or (Cf. Luke 24.35)
The disciples recognized the Lord Jesus in the breaking of bread.

PRAYER AFTER COMMUNION
Nourished by this sacred gift, O Lord, we give you thanks and beseech your mercy, that, by the pouring forth of your Spirit, the grace of integrity may endure in those your heavenly power has entered. Through Christ our Lord. **Amen.**

BLESSING AND DISMISSAL (p. 70)

November 19

The talents in this week's gospel can be interpreted as money, gifts and even a crown, but we are to continue to use them and not save them. We are given these talents through God's great mercy and favour. We are in God's favour.

Recently, I felt as though my talent had been taken from me as I found myself on a very hard path. As I look at my everyday life, I often find that, not only has my talent not been taken from me, but it is revealed in how I choose to live each day. I have realized that through the gift of God's mercy, I am able to continue to use my talents each and every day.

Every one of us has a crown to wear, not a crutch to carry. Many will try and knock that crown off of our heads, but through perseverance and faith, we must continue to wear our crowns and to use our talents. If we do not, our crowns will become rusty and worthless. God's light shines on us when we use our talents, no matter how they manifest themselves.

Through reflection on this important gospel, let us ask ourselves how we are using our talents. Are we allowing the mercy and grace of God to shine each and every day?

Jacki Lavigne, Kitchener, ON

ENTRANCE ANTIPHON *(Jeremiah 29.11, 12, 14)*

The Lord said: I think thoughts of peace and not of affliction. You will call upon me, and I will answer you, and I will lead back your captives from every place.

INTRODUCTORY RITES *(p. 5)*

COLLECT

Grant us, we pray, O Lord our God, the constant gladness of being devoted to you, for it is full and lasting happiness to serve with constancy the author of all that is good. Through our Lord Jesus Christ, your Son, who lives and reigns with you in the unity of the Holy Spirit, one God, for ever and ever. **Amen.**

FIRST READING

(Proverbs 31.10-13, 16-18, 20, 26, 28-31)
A capable wife, who can find her?
She is far more precious than jewels.
The heart of her husband trusts in her,
and he will have no lack of gain.
She does him good, and not harm,
all the days of her life.
She seeks wool and flax,
and works with willing hands.

She considers a field and buys it;
with the fruit of her hands she plants a vineyard.
She girds herself with strength,
and makes her arms strong.
She perceives that her merchandise is profitable.
Her lamp does not go out at night.

She opens her hand to the poor,
and reaches out her hands to the needy.

She opens her mouth with wisdom,
and the teaching of kindness is on her tongue.

Her children rise up and call her happy;
her husband too, and he praises her:
"Many women have done excellently,
but you surpass them all."
Charm is deceitful, and beauty is vain,
but a woman who fears the Lord is to be praised.
Give her a share in the fruit of her hands,
and let her works praise her in the city gates.

The word of the Lord. **Thanks be to God.**

RESPONSORIAL PSALM *(Psalm 128)*

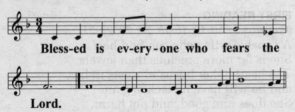

R. **Blessed is everyone who fears the Lord.**

Blessed is everyone who fears · **the** Lord,
who walks in · **his** ways.
You shall eat the fruit of the labour of · **your**
hands;
you shall be happy, and it shall go well
· **with** you. R.

Your wife will be like a fruit-**ful** vine
within · **your** house;
your children will be · **like** olive_shoots
around · **your** table. R.

Thus shall the man be blessed who
    fears · **the** Lord.
The Lord bless you · **from** Zion.
May you see the prosperity of · **Je**-rusalem
all the days of · **your** life. R.

To hear the Sunday Psalms, visit www.livingwithchrist.ca.

SECOND READING *(1 Thessalonians 5.1-6)*
Now concerning the times and the seasons, brothers and sisters, you do not need to have anything
written to you. For you yourselves know very
well that the day of the Lord will come like a
thief in the night. When they say, "There is peace
and security," then sudden destruction will come
upon them, as labour pains come upon a pregnant
woman, and there will be no escape!

But you, beloved, are not in darkness for that
day to surprise you like a thief. You are all children of light and children of the day; we are not
of the night or of darkness. So then let us not fall
asleep as others do, but let us keep awake and
be sober.

The word of the Lord. **Thanks be to God.**

GOSPEL ACCLAMATION *(See John 15.4, 5)*
Alleluia. Alleluia. Abide in me as I in you, says
the Lord; my branches bear much fruit. **Alleluia.**

GOSPEL *(Matthew 25.14-30)*

For the shorter version, omit the indented parts.

The Lord be with you. **And with your spirit.** A reading from the holy Gospel according to Matthew. **Glory to you, O Lord.**

Jesus spoke this parable to his disciples: "For it is as if a man, going on a journey, summoned his slaves and entrusted his property to them; to one he gave five talents, to another two, to another one, to each according to his ability. Then he went away.

"The one who had received the five talents went off at once and traded with them, and made five more talents. In the same way, the one who had the two talents made two more talents. But the one who had received the one talent went off and dug a hole in the ground and hid his master's money.

"After a long time the master of those slaves came and settled accounts with them. Then the one who had received the five talents came forward, bringing five more talents, saying, 'Master, you handed over to me five talents; see, I have made five more talents.' His master said to him, 'Well done, good and trustworthy slave; you have been trustworthy in a few things, I will put you in charge of many things; enter into the joy of your master.'

"And the one with the two talents also came forward, saying, 'Master, you handed over to me two talents; see, I have made two more talents. His master said to him, 'Well done, good and trustworthy slave; you have been trustworthy in a few things, I will put you in charge of many things; enter into the joy of your master.'

"Then the one who had received the one talent also came forward, saying, 'Master, I knew that you were a harsh man, reaping where you did not sow, and gathering where you did not scatter seed; so I was afraid, and I went and hid your talent in the ground. Here you have what is yours.'

"But his master replied, 'You wicked and lazy slave! You knew, did you, that I reap where I did not sow, and gather where I did not scatter? Then you ought to have invested my money with the bankers, and on my return I would have received what was my own with interest. So take the talent from him, and give it to the one with the ten talents. For to all those who have, more will be given, and they will have an abundance; but from those who have nothing, even what they have will be taken away. As for this worthless slave, throw him into the outer darkness, where there will be weeping and gnashing of teeth.'"

The Gospel of the Lord. **Praise to you, Lord Jesus Christ.**

PROFESSION OF FAITH *(p. 11)*

PRAYER OF THE FAITHFUL

The following intentions are suggestions only. There are more suggestions at www.livingwithchrist.ca

R. **Lord, hear our prayer.**

For the Church, working to establish peace and justice as we await the coming of God's kingdom, we pray to the Lord: R.

For world leaders, inspired to work together to make peace a reality in the world, we pray to the Lord: R.

For those among us who suffer from depression and despair, we pray to the Lord: R.

For us, God's holy people, called to witness to God's presence in our daily lives, we pray to the Lord: R.

PREPARATION OF THE GIFTS *(p. 14)*

PRAYER OVER THE OFFERINGS

Grant, O Lord, we pray, that what we offer in the sight of your majesty may obtain for us the grace of being devoted to you and gain us the prize of everlasting happiness. Through Christ our Lord. **Amen.**

PREFACE *(Sundays in Ordinary Time, p. 28)*

COMMUNION ANTIPHON *(Psalm 72.28)*
To be near God is my happiness, to place my hope in God the Lord.
or (Mark 11.23-24)
Amen, I say to you: Whatever you ask in prayer, believe that you will receive, and it shall be given to you, says the Lord.

PRAYER AFTER COMMUNION
We have partaken of the gifts of this sacred mystery, humbly imploring, O Lord, that what your Son commanded us to do in memory of him may bring us growth in charity. Through Christ our Lord. **Amen.**

BLESSING AND DISMISSAL *(p. 70)*

November 26

We live in a 'humpty-dumpty world,' a broken world. Millions slaughtered by their own kind, mass migration of refugees across the globe, disease ravaging continents, and the ever-widening gap between the rich and the poor are some signs of the cruel joke. 'All the king's men' — the kings of science, technology, economics, politics and even religion — 'could not put Humpty together again.'

There is only one King who can bring fulfillment and that is Christ the King, raised from the dead. He will rescue his sheep from all the places where they have been scattered: by disease, starvation, war and oppressive authority. Those baptized into the life and death of Christ are called to share kingship with Jesus the Good Shepherd who seeks and rescues the lost sheep.

We are called to be kings of a 'humpty-dumpty' world. We are the King's men and women putting Humpty together again, restoring life not as the kings and queens of illusion would have it, but as Christ the King would have it. "Truly I tell you, just as you did it to one of the least of these brothers and sisters of mine, you did it to me."

With the new liturgical year soon upon us — a time of new beginnings — let us make a stronger commitment to respond with care and compassion to those around us and work for a more just world.

Anthony Chezzi, Sudbury, ON

ENTRANCE ANTIPHON *(Revelation 5.12; 1.6)*
How worthy is the Lamb who was slain, to receive power and divinity, and wisdom and strength and honour. To him belong glory and power for ever and ever.

INTRODUCTORY RITES *(p. 5)*

COLLECT
Almighty ever-living God, whose will is to restore all things in your beloved Son, the King of the universe, grant, we pray, that the whole creation, set free from slavery, may render your majesty service and ceaselessly proclaim your praise. Through our Lord Jesus Christ, your Son, who lives and reigns with you in the unity of the Holy Spirit, one God, for ever and ever. **Amen.**

FIRST READING *(Ezekiel 34.11-12, 15-17)*
Thus says the Lord God:
"I myself will search for my sheep,
and will seek them out.
As a shepherd seeks out his flock
when he is among his scattered sheep,
so I will seek out my sheep.
I will rescue them from all the places
to which they have been scattered
on a day of clouds and thick darkness.

"I myself will be the shepherd of my sheep,
and I will make them lie down,"
says the Lord God.
"I will seek the lost,
and I will bring back the strayed,

and I will bind up the injured,
and I will strengthen the weak,
but the fat and the strong I will destroy.
I will feed my sheep with justice.

"As for you, my flock," thus says the Lord God:
"I shall judge between one sheep and another,
between rams and goats."

The word of the Lord. **Thanks be to God.**

RESPONSORIAL PSALM *(Psalm 23)*

℟. **The Lord is my shepherd; I shall not want.**

The Lord is my shepherd, I shall · **not** want.
He makes me lie down in · **green** pastures;
he leads me be-**side** still waters;
he re-**stores** my soul. ℟.

He leads me in right paths for his · **name's** sake.
Even though I walk through the darkest valley,
    I fear · **no** evil;
for · **you** are with_me;
your rod and your · **staff** — they comfort_me. ℟.

You prepare a table · **be**-fore_me
in the presence · **of_my** enemies;
you anoint my · **head** with oil;
my · **cup** over-flows. ℞

Surely goodness and mercy · **shall** follow_me
all the days of · **my** life,
and I shall dwell in the · **house_of** the Lord
my · **whole** life long. ℞

To hear the Sunday Psalms, visit www.livingwithchrist.ca.

SECOND READING *(1 Corinthians 15.20-26, 28)*
Brothers and sisters: Christ has been raised from
the dead, the first fruits of those who have fallen
asleep. For since death came through a man, the
resurrection of the dead has also come through a
man; for as all die in Adam, so all will be made
alive in Christ. But each in his own order: Christ
the first fruits, then at his coming those who belong to Christ.

Then comes the end, when he hands over the
kingdom to God the Father, after he has destroyed
every ruler and every authority and power. For he
must reign until he has put all his enemies under
his feet. The last enemy to be destroyed is death.

When all things are subjected to him, then the
Son himself will also be subjected to the one who
put all things in subjection under him, so that
God may be all in all.

The word of the Lord. **Thanks be to God.**

GOSPEL ACCLAMATION *(Mark 11.9, 10)*
Alleluia. Alleluia. Blessed is the one who comes in the name of the Lord. Blessed is the coming kingdom of our father David. **Alleluia.**

GOSPEL *(Matthew 25.31-46)*
The Lord be with you. **And with your spirit.**
A reading from the holy Gospel according to Matthew. **Glory to you, O Lord.**

Jesus said to his disciples: "When the Son of Man comes in his glory, and all the Angels with him, then he will sit on the throne of his glory. All the nations will be gathered before him, and he will separate people one from another as a shepherd separates the sheep from the goats, and he will put the sheep at his right hand and the goats at the left.

"Then the king will say to those at his right hand, 'Come, you that are blessed by my Father, inherit the kingdom prepared for you from the foundation of the world; for I was hungry and you gave me food, I was thirsty and you gave me something to drink, I was a stranger and you welcomed me, I was naked and you gave me clothing, I was sick and you took care of me, I was in prison and you visited me.'

"Then the righteous will answer him, 'Lord, when was it that we saw you hungry and gave you food, or thirsty and gave you something to drink? And when was it that we saw you a stranger and welcomed you, or naked and gave you clothing? And when was it that we saw you sick or in prison and visited you?' And the king will answer them, 'Truly I tell you, just as you did it to one of the least of these brothers and sisters of mine, you did it to me.'

"Then he will say to those at his left hand, 'You that are accursed, depart from me into the eternal fire prepared for the devil and his angels; for I was hungry and you gave me no food, I was thirsty and you gave me nothing to drink, I was a stranger and you did not welcome me, naked and you did not give me clothing, sick and in prison and you did not visit me.'

"Then they also will answer, 'Lord, when was it that we saw you hungry or thirsty or a stranger or naked or sick or in prison, and did not take care of you?' Then he will answer them, 'Truly I tell you, just as you did not do it to one of the least of these, you did not do it to me.' And these will go away into eternal punishment, but the righteous into eternal life."

The Gospel of the Lord. **Praise to you, Lord Jesus Christ.**

PROFESSION OF FAITH *(p. 11)*

PRAYER OF THE FAITHFUL

The following intentions are suggestions only. There are more suggestions at www.livingwithchrist.ca

℟ **Lord, hear our prayer.**

For the Church, instrument of unity and salvation, we pray to the Lord: ℟

For the triumph of peace, harmony and hope in the world community, we pray to the Lord: ℟

For those among us who are poor, persecuted or alone, we pray to the Lord: **R.**

For us, God's people, called as a parish to witness to Christ and his salvation, we pray to the Lord: **R.**

PREPARATION OF THE GIFTS *(p. 14)*

PRAYER OVER THE OFFERINGS
As we offer you, O Lord, the sacrifice by which the human race is reconciled to you, we humbly pray that your Son himself may bestow on all nations the gifts of unity and peace. Through Christ our Lord. **Amen.**

PREFACE *(Christ the King, p. 32)*

COMMUNION ANTIPHON *(Psalm 28.10-11)*
The Lord sits as King for ever. The Lord will bless his people with peace.

PRAYER AFTER COMMUNION
Having received the food of immortality, we ask, O Lord, that, glorying in obedience to the commands of Christ, the King of the universe, we may live with him eternally in his heavenly Kingdom. Who lives and reigns for ever and ever. **Amen.**

BLESSING AND DISMISSAL *(p. 70)*

THE POPE'S PRAYER INTENTIONS FOR 2016-2017

DECEMBER 2016

Universal: That the scandal of child-soldiers may be eliminated the world over.

Evangelization: That the peoples of Europe may rediscover the beauty, goodness and truth of the Gospel which gives joy and hope to life.

JANUARY 2017*

Evangelization: Christian Unity.

That all Christians may be faithful to the Lord's teaching by striving with prayer and fraternal charity to restore ecclesial communion and by collaborating to meet the challenges facing humanity.

FEBRUARY 2017

Universal: Comfort for the Afflicted.

That all those who are afflicted, especially the poor, refugees, and marginalized, may find welcome and comfort in our communities.

Starting in 2017, The Pope's Worldwide Prayer Network (apostleshipofprayer.org) will release one Prayer Intention per month ahead of time (see above), and one Urgent Prayer Intention at the beginning of each month. Visit livingwithchrist.ca each month to see the Pope's Urgent Prayer Intention.

MARCH 2017
Evangelization: Support for Persecuted Christians.

That persecuted Christians may be supported by the prayers and material help of the whole Church.

APRIL 2017
Universal: Young People.

That young people may respond generously to their vocations and seriously consider offering themselves to God in the priesthood or consecrated life.

MAY 2017
Evangelization: Christians in Africa.

That Christians in Africa, in imitation of the Merciful Jesus, may give prophetic witness to reconciliation, justice, and peace.

JUNE 2017
Universal: National Leaders.

That national leaders may firmly commit themselves to ending the arms trade, which victimizes so many innocent people.

JULY 2017
Evangelization: Lapsed Christians.

That our brothers and sisters who have strayed from the faith, through our prayer and witness to the Gospel, may rediscover the merciful closeness of the Lord and the beauty of the Christian life.

AUGUST 2017
Universal: Artists.

That artists of our time, through their ingenuity, may help everyone discover the beauty of creation.

SEPTEMBER 2017
Evangelization: Parishes.

That our parishes, animated by a missionary spirit, may be places where faith is communicated and charity is seen.

OCTOBER 2017
Universal: Workers and the Unemployed.

That all workers may receive respect and protection of their rights, and that the unemployed may receive the opportunity to contribute to the common good.

NOVEMBER 2017
Evangelization: Christians in Asia.

That Christians in Asia, bearing witness to the Gospel in word and deed, may promote dialogue, peace, and mutual understanding, especially with those of other religions.

DECEMBER 2017
Universal: The Elderly.

That the elderly, sustained by families and Christian communities, may apply their wisdom and experience to spreading the faith and forming the new generations.

YEAR A: THE GOSPEL OF MATTHEW

Scholars remain undecided about several aspects concerning this longest of the gospels which for centuries held pride of place in the Church's teaching and life.

Mainstream scriptural interpreters place this gospel's composition towards the end of the first century (80–90 AD), possibly in a mixed Jewish-Gentile community such as was found at Antioch in Syria.

Matthew's gospel stresses that Jesus is the Son of God who fulfills what the Old Testament foretold of the Messiah (for example, "This was to fulfill what had been spoken by the Lord through the prophet, 'Out of Egypt I have called my son'" [2.15]).

Inviting the follower of Jesus to confess in both word and deed that Jesus is Lord (cf. Matthew 7.21), Matthew depicts Jesus as a prophet powerful in word and deed (4.23; 9.35).

To underline this emphasis on Jesus' words and deeds, the evangelist intersperses narrative blocks depicting Jesus' healings and miracles with five major speeches.

The Sermon on the Mount constitutes the first of the five great addresses Jesus gives (chapters 5–7). Later, Jesus shares instructions with his apostles as he sends them out on mission (chapter 10), then proclaims to them the parables of the kingdom of heaven and their meaning (chapter 13).

In chapter 18, Jesus describes how life should be lived in the Church, focusing on the need to care for vulnerable "little ones"– who are easily led astray by bad example – and on the enduring need for forgiveness among his disciples.

The climax to Jesus' instructions are found in his eschatological parables and teaching, which culminate in the Last Judgment (chapters 24–25). At the end of the ages, as the glorious Son of Man, Jesus uncovers the criterion for inheriting the Father's kingdom: what was done or not done "for the least of my brethren" (25.40, 45) was given or refused to Jesus. All will be judged on their deeds.

This gospel emphasis on "doing" has often coloured the way people interpret the message of the Beatitudes. Some people are led to think that only when they have conformed their lives to the program Jesus enunciates will they become pleasing to God. There is a risk here of getting Jesus' message backwards.

Jesus proclaims good news from God to the poor in spirit, the mourning, those who hunger and thirst for righteousness (right relations between God and humanity and among members of the human family).

Jesus declares that God has chosen to give humans, who struggle in their yearnings, the free gift of the kingdom. In this vein, one "dynamic equivalence" translation—one that attempts to give the sense of the passage rather than word-for-word equivalence—rendered the "poor in spirit" of the first beatitude as "those who know their need for God" (J.B. Phillips).

In beginning with God, all is grace, all is gift. Then comes the challenge to every person who would remain a charter member of God's household: Be what you are! Live the life of the kingdom!

The message of the Sermon on the Mount constantly oscillates between the call God makes possible ("You are the light of the world") and the challenge to live it out ("Let your light shine before others"). Putting all the onus on oneself could lead to frustration or to self-righteousness.

Yet, to do nothing but wait on God would be to fall into the error of spiritual passivity. Life in the kingdom is a partnership begun and sustained by God, but which his children rejoice in making their own. They go so far as to rejoice in suffering willingly for Jesus' sake (when people "utter all kinds of evil against you falsely on my account" [5.11]).

Matthew's is the gospel of the risen, cosmic Christ. The Messiah, son of Abraham, son of David, Son of Man, Son of God, who fulfills all messianic expectations through the cosmic event of his death and resurrection, is present in the reading or proclamation of the gospel ("for where two or three are gathered in my name, I am there among them" [18.20]).

Jesus is God's chosen, powerful in word and deed, who calls others to have a consistency between what they say and do. All disciples are moving towards the last judgment, but need not fear this occurrence, for the Lord who is to come is already with his Church ("remember, I am with you always until the end of the age" [28.20]).

Archbishop Terence Prendergast, SJ, *Living God's Word: Reflections on the Sunday Readings for Year A* (Toronto: Novalis, 2010), pp. 14-16.

EUCHARISTIC PRAYERS AND CREATION

The Greek word *eucharistia* (εὐχαριστία) means "thanksgiving" – not only for our own life, but also for the presence of God in the life of the community and for the life that God breathes into his Creation.

The Eucharistic liturgy is, surprisingly, a fertile source of environmental awareness. The liturgy has its roots in the ancient Greek and Semitic cultures, which saw their environment as the result of the creative work of God. This is evident in two commonly used parts of the Eucharistic Prayers: the prayer for the preparation of the gifts, and the prayer immediately following the Sanctus in Eucharistic prayer III.

PRAYER FOR THE PREPARATION OF THE GIFTS

"Blessed are you, Lord God of all creation,
for through your goodness we have received
    the bread we offer you;
fruit of the earth and work of human hands,
it will become for us the bread of life.

Blessed are you, Lord God of all creation,
for through your goodness we have received
    the wine we offer you;
fruit of the vine and work of human hands,
it will become our spiritual drink."

These two prayers stem from the Jewish prayer of blessing for the bread that has been sung for centuries during the Sabbath and the Passover supper: "Blessed are You, Lord out God, King of the universe, who brings forth bread from the earth."

That this ritual meal is organized every year in spring, when nature is reborn, makes the need to give thanks to God even more meaningful. If God no longer provided for us, we could not eat bread, "fruit of the earth," and drink wine, "fruit of the vine." Both are also the result of human labour, a sign that human beings are co-creators with God. Holding the bread in our hands, we marvel that humankind is able to care for the earth and make it even more bountiful.

Knowing that this blessing is so essential, can we just turn our backs and not be mindful of the ecological crisis? God can give us bread and wine, provided there is an ecological balance. But if the soil is impoverished and climate change threatens the harvest, soon nothing will grow and the responsibility will be ours.

BREAD

For the apostles sitting around the table with Jesus at the Last Supper, brad was the product of the land (wheat), the result of human labour and their daily food. Jesus added another level of meaning to the bread: his body given for us.

Can we, as Christians, allow the bread of which we partake, the body of Christ, to be made of wheat grown with the use of pesticides and chemical fertilizers? Pesticides can cause cancer, and the run-off from chemical fertilizers upsets the chemical balance in many lakes, causing blue-green algae, for example. But there is good news: more and more parishes and dioceses insist that the hosts they use are made from organic-ally grown wheat. In 2012, the Sisters of Saint Clare in Valleyfield, Quebec, agreed to use only organic flour in the making of altar breads, a first in Canada!

WINE

For the apostles sitting around the table with Jesus, the wine made from grapes was the product of the vine, the result of human labour, and a drink for celebrations. Jesus added another level of meaning to the wine: his blood shed for us.

So, Jesus took the daily food of bread, and he took the drink reserved for special occasions: wine. This wine, in all likelihood, was produced locally or regionally. It was transported to market in a cart pulled by a donkey. Today, wine can travel great distances before arriving at our table. In eastern Canada, almost all parishes use an altar wine from California, 4,000 kilometres away. The farther it travels, the more greenhouse gases are emitted by the trucks carrying it, which traps heat in the atmosphere and leads to radical changes in climate. The place of origin of the wine we buy has an impact on the quality of life of future generations. Parishes and dioceses can consider buying wine from local or regional vineyards. The *Côtes d'Ardoise* vineyard in Durham, Quebec, for example, offers both a red and a white wine that were officially approved as sacramental wine by the bishop of Saint-Hyacinthe in May 2011.

Norman Lévesque, *Greening Your Church: A Practical Guide to Creation Care Ministry for Parishes, Dioceses and Religious Communities* (Novalis: Toronto, 2014), pp. 47-49.

HOLY COMMUNION: RECEIVED BY ALL OUR SENSES

Whether it has been a month or decades since our First Communion, it is good to remember that when we receive Christ in Communion, it should involve our whole person and all our senses.

Cyril, a fourth-century patriarch of Jerusalem, gave great advice to the newly baptized on how to receive the sacrament: "In approaching therefore, come not with your wrists extended, or your fingers spread; but make your left hand a throne for the right, so as to receive a King." He then described how we are made holy by the touch of the sacred species on our hands and by looking at it with our eyes. He also talked about receiving from the cup: "Draw near also to the cup of his Blood; not stretching forth your hands, but bending, and saying with an air of worship and reverence, Amen." The key is that Communion is something received by all of our senses.

What does this mean? First, our whole person should be focused, with an attitude of reception. When we do something repeatedly, it becomes easy to think of it as a given. Even with something as special as Communion, we need to work to ensure that Communion is not taken for granted. Here are some specific suggestions.

During the week, we should spend time preparing for Communion: praying, being reconciled – including sacramental reconciliation – and doing works of justice. We also prepare by fasting for at least an hour before receiving Communion.

During Mass, we should keep Communion in mind throughout the celebration. The Introductory Rites are there in part to prepare us for Communion. So, too, the readings, the Homily, the Creed, the intercessions and the Eucharistic Prayer. We should pay special attention to the elements of the Communion Rite. This includes everything from the Lord's Prayer to the Communion Antiphon, offering moments that encourage us to prepare both with the community and in personal prayer.

Once Communion begins, we praise God for the Eucharist by singing. The Communion Chant starts as the priest receives Communion and should last until the end of Communion. The Communion procession engages our whole person in an attitude of reception, in union with the whole Church in the great parade that will one day end in the heavenly banquet. Once we reach the altar area, some form of reverence, such as a small bow, is required. This varies from diocese to diocese.

Receiving Communion should engage our heart and mind, but also our senses. Think about what is happening. If you receive in the hand, offer both hands, with the one that will lift the host to your lips supporting the hand where the host is placed. It is important that you not wear gloves, both for practical reasons and because part of the experience of receiving the sacrament is the sense of touch. Reverently consume the sacred species. If you receive on the tongue, make sure there is no danger of the host falling. Should the host fall to the ground, the minister of Communion will know to set it aside and see that it is dealt with in an appropriate manner. Should the precious Blood fall to the floor, the floor is to be rinsed with water, which is then disposed of in an appropriate manner. To avoid this, when receiving from the chalice, take the cup in your hands. The minister of Communion may also keep hold. It is important not to let reverent fear keep us from the full experience of Communion.

Those not receiving Communion – for whatever reason – are not mentioned in the ritual. In some places they are encouraged to come forward for a blessing, indicating this by crossing their hands across their chests.

After Communion, we can of course kneel in personal prayer, but in many places people are now encouraged to stand and sing until everyone has received Communion. Being called to this assembly and to receive Communion, again, as Cyril tells us, is having been "deemed worthy by the Holy Spirit." As the holy family of chosen ones, we stand and praise God.

For the rest of Sunday and during the week, we should pause from time to time in our prayer to remember that we have been fed by Jesus, our God. Whether in adoration in church or being aware of this before we have lunch, we can better see that God is reaching out to us every day, feeding us and guiding us home.

Novalis Staff

MUSIC DURING THE LITURGY

*The General Instruction of the Roman Missal
(GIRM) is the set of instructions that governs the
celebration of the Eucharist. It was updated in 2001,
as a result of reflection on the 40 years of experience
since Vatican II, and came into force in Canada
with the coming of the new translation of the missal.*

*Perhaps one of the most interesting and least
known contributions of the new GIRM is its reflection on the role of singing in the liturgy. It offers a
genuine theology of music at mass, with insights
into the role of the choir, the ministry of the cantor,
and the meaning of various chants in the liturgy.*

*The GIRM places the singing of the assembly
at the very centre of its reflection. All musical
choices are at the service of helping the assembly
to sing. In this short article, I offer some commen-
tary on the three major moments of singing and
on the closing moments of the mass.*

THE ENTRANCE CHANT

When the people are gathered, and as the Priest
enters with the Deacon and ministers, the Entrance Chant begins. Its purpose is to:

1. open the celebration,

2. foster the unity of those who have been gathered,

3. introduce their thoughts to the mystery of the
   liturgical time or festivity, and

4. accompany the procession of the Priest and
   ministers.

This chant is sung

- alternately by the choir and the people or
- similarly by a cantor and the people, or
- entirely by the people,
- or by the choir alone.

In the dioceses of Canada the Entrance Chant may be chosen from among the following:

- the antiphon with its Psalm from the Graduale Romanum or the Graduale Simplex, or
- another chant that is suited to the sacred action, the day, or the time of year, and whose text has been approved by the Conference of Bishops of Canada.

The Entrance chant's most important function is to open the celebration. Thus, the singing of the assembly is the genuine beginning of the mass (as opposed to the priest's sign of the cross) This beginning has the further ritual purpose of fostering unity and focusing attention. Only as a function of all these things does it accompany the procession.

How to foster unity and focus attention? The manner of singing proposed by the GIRM offers some significant clues: the preferred manner is call and response (i.e. dialogue) between choir/ cantor and assembly. This use of dialogue singing creates a dynamic of ritual interaction that brings participants together into one body; dialogical singing is also more engaging and dramatic while being easy on the people, since they need only remember a refrain or response, which also allows them to be attentive to what is going on. This dynamic of practical community building and fostering attentiveness can also be achieved by having the entire group sing together, but then attention ought to be paid to how the musical quality of the chant awakens feelings of presence and joy. Only as a last resort ought the choir to sing alone, and even then the musical selection ought to foster unity and focus attention rather than promoting the passivity of the assembly.

The GIRM mentions here the Graduale Romanum and the Graduale Simplex; these are collections of antiphons for the Church year which are to be used with seasonal psalms. The entrance and communion antiphons we see in our missals come from the Graduale Romanum. This focus reflects the GIRM's overall concern for singing TEXTS. This can provide a helpful clue for the selection of appropriate music. The idea is to choose music not according to a unifying "theme" for the whole liturgy, but to express the various texts of the liturgy. For example:

- when trying to find an appropriate processional chant to open the liturgy, and assuming that one is not looking to sing the antiphon with a seasonal psalm, one might ask: does this antiphon text remind me of a hymn, or are its images reminiscent of a particular song?

- *rather than think of how all the songs express the same theme, think of reproducing the way in which the collect, antiphons, scripture texts and so on "bounce off" each other with contrasting or complementary images and musical ideas.*

THE OFFERTORY CHANT

The procession bringing the gifts is accompanied by the Offertory Chant, which continues at least until the gifts have been placed on the altar. The norms on the manner of singing are the same as for the Entrance Chant. Singing may always accompany the rite at the Offertory, even when there is no procession with the gifts.

The question to ask here is: what is the mystery to which the thoughts of the assembly ought to be introduced, even as the song fosters their unity and opens a new time in the celebration? The mystery in question is that of the Eucharist about to be celebrated. So a chant or hymn that helps people focus on the mystery of the Eucharist as meal and sacrifice of thanksgiving, and opens the people up to offering themselves to God with the gifts, in light of the Word's proclamation in this liturgy, is most appropriate here.

Note that the GIRM refers back to the manner of singing outlined for the Entrance Chant: first in order of preference, dialogue between assembly and cantor/choir, then people as one, and lastly choir alone.

AT COMMUNION TIME

While the Priest is receiving the Sacrament, the Communion Chant is begun, its purpose being

- to express the spiritual union of the communicants by means of the unity of their voices,

- to show gladness of heart, and

- to bring out more clearly the "communitarian" character of the procession to receive the Eucharist.

The singing is prolonged for as long as the Sacrament is being administered to the faithful. However, if there is to be a hymn after Communion, the Communion Chant should be ended in a timely manner.

Care should be taken that singers, too, can receive Communion with ease.

In the dioceses of Canada singing at Communion may be chosen from among the following: the antiphon from the Graduale Romanum, with or without the Psalm, or the antiphon with Psalm from the Graduale Simplex, or some other suitable liturgical chant approved by the Conference of Bishops of Canada. This is sung either

- by the choir alone or

- by the choir or a cantor with the people.

Notice the shift in the purpose and role of singing during the Communion procession.

Notice also that this is the only place where the choir is given preference over the assembly as the main ministers of singing, although the most important purpose is still to express the union of the communicants by the unity of their voices.

Notice, finally, that the singing is tightly linked to the procession, and should end when the procession ends. A second chant or hymn is envisaged as a possibility, but as we see below, it has a different purpose and should be clearly separated from the processional chant by a short time of silence.

When the distribution of Communion is over, if appropriate, the Priest and faithful pray quietly for some time. If desired, a Psalm or other canticle of praise or a hymn may also be sung by the whole congregation.

The psalm or canticle of praise is a time for the assembly to give thanks WITH ONE VOICE, as is indicated by the reference to the whole congregation. Keep in mind the importance given to silence in the liturgy; there needn't always be a thanksgiving after Communion, and certainly, people should have the opportunity to pray silently between the Communion processional and the thanksgiving chant.

AT THE END OF THE MASS

To the Concluding Rites belong the following:

a) brief announcements, should they be necessary;

b) the Priest's Greeting and Blessing, which on certain days and occasions is expanded and expressed by the Prayer over the People or another more solemn formula;

c) the Dismissal of the people by the Deacon or the Priest, so that each may go back to doing good works, praising and blessing God;

d) the kissing of the altar by the Priest and the Deacon, followed by a profound bow to the altar by the Priest, the Deacon, and the other ministers.

There is no rubric for a song of sending forth; in Canada, the custom has been to have such a song, and the suggestion is that this song should be in the spirit of the dismissal over the people: "going out to do good works, praising and blessing God." The song should be short and should end just as the procession leaves the Church proper. This ensures that the energy of the dismissal and sending out is not lost.

Alternatively, this would be a good time to feature an organ piece or a more complex choir piece, something that is energetic and helps people go forth in the spirit of the dismissal.

Fr. Gilles Mongeau, SJ
Contributing Editor, *Living with Christ*

TRADITIONAL PRAYERS

HAIL MARY
Hail Mary, full of grace, the Lord is with thee. Blessed art thou among women and blessed is the fruit of thy womb, Jesus.

Holy Mary, Mother of God, pray for us sinners, now and at the hour of our death. Amen.

GLORY BE TO THE FATHER
Glory be to the Father, and to the Son, and to the Holy Spirit. As it was in the beginning, is now, and ever shall be, world without end. Amen.

COME, HOLY SPIRIT
Come, Holy Spirit, fill the hearts of your faithful and kindle in them the fire of your love. Send forth your Spirit, O Lord, and renew the face of the earth. Amen.

ACT OF FAITH
O my God, I firmly believe that you are one God in three divine Persons, Father, Son, and Holy Spirit. I believe that your divine Son became man, died for our sins, and that he will come to judge the living and the dead. I believe these and all the truths which the holy Catholic Church teaches, because you have revealed them, who can neither deceive nor be deceived. Amen.

ACT OF HOPE

O my God, relying on your almighty power and infinite mercy and promises, I hope to obtain pardon of my sins, the help of your grace, and life everlasting through the merits of Jesus Christ, my Lord and Redeemer. Amen.

ACT OF LOVE

O my God, I love you above all things, with my whole heart and soul, because you are all good and worthy of all love. I love my neighbour as myself for the love of you. I forgive all who have injured me, and ask pardon of all whom I have injured. Amen.

DIVINE PRAISES

Blessed be God.
Blessed be his holy name.

Blessed be Jesus Christ, true God and true man.
Blessed be the name of Jesus.
Blessed be his most sacred heart.
Blessed be his most precious blood.
Blessed be Jesus in the sacrament of the altar.

Blessed be the Holy Spirit, the Paraclete.

Blessed be the Mother of God, Mary most holy.
Blessed be her holy and immaculate conception.
Blessed be her glorious assumption.
Blessed be the name of Mary, virgin and mother.

Blessed be Saint Joseph, her most chaste spouse.
Blessed be God in his angels and in his saints.

ANGELUS

The angel of the Lord declared unto Mary, and she conceived of the Holy Spirit. *Hail Mary...*

Behold, the handmaid of the Lord; be it done to me according to your word. *Hail Mary...*

And the word was made flesh, and dwelt among us. *Hail Mary...*

Pray for us, O holy Mother of God; that we may be made worthy of the promises of Christ.

Pour forth, we beseech you, O Lord, your grace into our hearts that we, to whom the incarnation of your Son was made known by the message of an angel, may by his passion and cross be brought to the glory of his resurrection. We ask this through the same Christ, our Lord. Amen.

REGINA CAELI

O Queen of heaven, rejoice, alleluia!
For he whom you chose to bear, alleluia!
Is risen as he said, alleluia!
Pray for us to God, alleluia!
Rejoice and be glad, O Virgin Mary, alleluia!
For the Lord is truly risen, alleluia!

O God, by the resurrection of your Son, our Lord, you were pleased to make glad the whole world. Grant, we beseech you, that through the intercession of the Virgin Mary, his mother, we may attain the joys of everlasting life, through the same Christ our Lord. Amen.

HAIL, HOLY QUEEN

Hail, holy Queen, mother of mercy, our life, our sweetness and our hope. To you we cry, poor banished children of Eve. To you we send up our sighs, mourning and weeping in this valley of tears. Turn then, most gracious advocate, your eyes of mercy upon us, and after this, our exile, show unto us the blessed fruit of your womb, Jesus. O clement, O loving, O kind Virgin Mary.

MEMORARE

Remember, O most gracious Virgin Mary, that never was it known that anyone who fled to thy protection, implored thy help or sought thy intercession, was left unaided. Inspired with this confidence, I fly unto thee, O Virgin of virgins my Mother; to thee I come, before thee I stand, sinful and sorrowful; O Mother of the Word Incarnate, despise not my petitions, but in thy mercy hear and answer me. Amen.

MAGNIFICAT

My soul proclaims the greatness of the Lord, my spirit rejoices in God my Saviour; for he has looked with favour on his lowly servant.

From this day all generations will call me blessed: the Almighty has done great things for me, and holy is his Name.

He has mercy on those who fear him in every generation. He has shown the strength of his arm, he has scattered the proud in their conceit.

He has cast down the mighty from their thrones, and has lifted up the lowly. He has filled the hungry with good things, and the rich he has sent away empty.

He has come to the help of his servant Israel for he has remembered his promise of mercy, the promise he made to our fathers, to Abraham and his children forever.

ICEL

PRAYER TO SAINT JOSEPH

O Saint Joseph, whose protection is so great, so strong, so prompt before the throne of God, I place in thee all my interests and desires. O Saint Joseph, assist me by thy powerful intercessions and obtain for me all spiritual blessings through thy foster Son, Jesus Christ Our Lord, so that, having engaged here below thy heavenly power, I may offer my thanksgiving and homage.

O Saint Joseph, I never weary contemplating thee and Jesus asleep in thine arms. I dare not approach while he reposes near thy heart. Press him in my name and kiss his fine head for me, and ask him to return the kiss when I draw my dying breath.

Saint Joseph, patron of departing souls, pray for me. Amen.

THE ROSARY

In the Rosary we focus on 20 events or mysteries in the life and death of Jesus and meditate on how we share with Mary in the redemptive work of Christ. Reading a pertinent passage from the Bible helps to deepen meditation on a particular mystery. The scriptural references given here are not exhaustive. In many instances, other biblical texts are equally suitable for meditation.

~ Begin the Rosary at the crucifix by praying the Apostles' Creed (p. 13)
~ At each large bead, pray the Lord's Prayer
~ At each small bead, pray the Hail Mary
~ At the first three beads it is customary to pray a Hail Mary for each of the gifts of faith, hope, and love
~ For each mystery, begin with the Lord's Prayer, then recite the Hail Mary ten times, and end with Glory Be to the Father.

The Five Joyful Mysteries:

The Annunciation (Luke 1.26-38)
The Visitation (Luke 1.39-56)
The Nativity (Luke 2.1-20)
The Presentation (Luke 2.22-38)
The Finding in the Temple (Luke 2.41-52)

The Five Mysteries of Light:

The Baptism in the Jordan (Matthew 3.13-17)
The Wedding at Cana (John 2.1-12)
The Proclamation of the Kingdom (Mark 1.15)
The Transfiguration (Luke 9.28-36)
The First Eucharist (Matthew 26.26-29)

The Five Sorrowful Mysteries:

The Agony in the Garden (Matthew 26.36-56)
The Scourging at the Pillar (Matthew 27.20-26)
The Crowning with Thorns (Matthew 27.27-30)
The Carrying of the Cross (Matthew 27.31-33)
The Crucifixion (Matthew 27.34-60)

The Five Glorious Mysteries:

The Resurrection (John 20.1-18)
The Ascension (Acts 1.9-11)
The Descent of the Holy Spirit (John 20.19-23)
The Assumption of Mary (John 11.26)
The Crowning of Mary (Philippians 2.1-11)

THE STATIONS OF THE CROSS
(Traditional version)

PRAYER BEFORE EACH STATION:
We adore you, O Christ, and we praise you, because by your holy cross you have redeemed the world.

1. JESUS IS CONDEMNED TO DEATH

Consider how Jesus, having been scourged and crowned with thorns, is unjustly condemned by Pilate to death on a cross.

2. JESUS TAKES UP HIS CROSS

Consider how Jesus, bearing this cross on his shoulders, offers his suffering to the Father for us.

3. JESUS FALLS FOR THE FIRST TIME

Consider this first fall. Jesus, bleeding, crowned with thorns, so weak he can hardly walk, yet forced to carry this heavy burden. The soldiers strike him and he falls.

4. JESUS MEETS HIS MOTHER

Consider this meeting between mother and son... their tender love for one another, their hearts torn asunder.

5. SIMON HELPS JESUS CARRY THE CROSS

Consider how the torturers force the bystander Simon to carry Jesus' cross. They want Jesus to stay alive long enough to die crucified.

6. VERONICA WIPES JESUS' FACE

Consider how Veronica recognizes Jesus' pain and attempts to lessen his suffering.

7. JESUS FALLS FOR THE SECOND TIME

Consider this second fall. It reopens his wounds, hurts his head, pains his whole body.

8. THE WOMEN OF JERUSALEM WEEP FOR JESUS

Consider how these compassionate women wept at the sight of the tortured Jesus.

9. JESUS FALLS FOR THE THIRD TIME

Consider this third fall. Though extremely weak, Jesus is urged on by the soldiers.

10. JESUS IS STRIPPED OF HIS GARMENTS

Consider the violence with which the soldiers tear off the bloody garments which cling to his broken skin and start the wounds bleeding again.

11. JESUS IS NAILED TO THE CROSS

Consider how Jesus, arms extended on the cross, offers to his Father the ultimate sacrifice for our salvation.

12. JESUS DIES ON THE CROSS

Consider how Jesus, after hours of agony and anguish on the cross, abandons himself to the Father and dies.

13. JESUS IS REMOVED FROM THE CROSS

Consider how two disciples take the broken body down from the cross and place Jesus in his grieving mother's arms.

14. JESUS IS PLACED IN THE TOMB

Consider how the disciples, filled with grief, carry the body to the burial place. They close the tomb and come away confused and sorrowful.

THE WAY OF THE CROSS

(Revised version: The Sacred Congregation for Divine Worship recommends that the traditional Stations be revised to emphasize that the sufferings and resurrection of Christ are one redemptive mystery.)

OPENING PRAYER

Lord Jesus, all of your life led up to the Way of the Cross. In this final journey you lay down your life for your friends.

Jesus, you consider us your friends. You walk side by side with us on the journey of life. You know its joys and hopes, its suffering and pain. Today we want to walk side by side with you on your way to the Cross. Your suffering, your death, your rising from the dead give meaning to our lives. The way of the Cross is the way of life.

Lord, as you took the bread, your body, take us, bless us, break us, give us to others, so that in you we may be instruments of salvation for the world. **Amen.**

1. THE LAST SUPPER

Jesus said to them, "I have wanted so much to eat this Passover meal with you before I suffer! For I tell you, I will never eat it until it is given its full meaning in the Kingdom of God."

Then Jesus took a cup, gave thanks to God, and said, "Take this and share it among yourselves. I tell you that from now on I will not drink this wine until the Kingdom of God comes."

Then he took a loaf of bread, gave thanks to God, broke it, and gave it to them, saying, "This is my body, which is given for you. Do this in memory of me." In the same way, he gave them the cup after supper, saying, "This cup is God's new covenant sealed with my blood, which is poured out for you." *(Luke 22.15-20)*

Jesus, you love us. Make us realize we are a covenant people, make our Eucharists moments when we feel your friendship, so that we may live this out for all humankind.

2. IN THE GARDEN OF GETHSEMANE

Then Jesus went with his disciples to a place called Gethsemane, and said to them, "Sit here while I go over there and pray." He took with him Peter and the two sons of Zebedee. Grief and anguish came over him, and he said to them, "The sorrow in my heart is so great that it almost crushes me. Stay here and keep watch with me." *(Matthew 26.36-38)*

Jesus, you love us. Comfort us in times of distress. Help us to see beyond ourselves; help us to overcome the feeling of senseless chaos; help us to see the joy and hope of those who truly suffer and who truly believe. Remind us of your covenant of friendship with us.

3. BEFORE THE SANHEDRIN

Jesus was taken to the High Priest's house, where the chief priests, the elders, and the teachers of the Law were gathering. Peter followed at a distance and went into the courtyard, where he sat down with the guards, keeping himself warm by the fire. The chief priests and the whole Council tried to find some evidence against Jesus in order to put him to death, but they could not find any. *(Mark 14.53-55)*

594

Jesus, you love us. Help us live out your covenant of friendship; give us strength to stand against authorities who exercise power for evil. Make us nonviolent, but strong in this struggle for humankind. Jesus, strengthen us.

4. BEFORE PONTIUS PILATE

Early in the morning Jesus was taken from Caiaphas' house to the governor's palace. The Jewish authorities did not go inside the palace, for they wanted to keep themselves ritually clean in order to be able to eat the Passover meal. So Pilate went outside to them and asked, "What do you accuse this man of?" Their answer was, "We would not have brought him to you if he had not committed a crime." *(John 18.28-30)*

Jesus, you love us. You stand with the victims in this world. Is that one meaning of the covenant for us: that we too should side with the oppressed against the oppressor? Lord, this is hard for us, teach us how to side with the oppressed, with the victims.

5. THE WHIPPING AND CROWNING WITH THORNS

Then Pilate took Jesus and had him whipped. The soldiers made a crown of thorny branches, put it on his head, then put a purple robe on him. They came to him and said, "Long live the King of the Jews!" and slapped him. *(John 19.1-3)*

Jesus, you love us. Turn our sympathies to the poor victims of desperate soldiers all over the world. Empower us to stop the sale of arms to ruthless armies. Show us the way to curb sense-

less attacks by states against their own people. Jesus, teach us how to resist evil.

6. THE CARRYING OF THE CROSS

So they took charge of Jesus. He went out, carrying his cross, and came to the 'Place of the Skull,' as it is called. (In Hebrew it is called 'Golgotha.') *(John 19.16-17)*

Jesus, you love us. Your love for us affirms the goodness of our humanity. We are the friends for whom you suffered. Teach us to respect others, not to dismiss or diminish them as less human.

7. SIMON OF CYRENE

On the way they met a man named Simon, who was coming into the city from the country. The soldiers forced him to carry Jesus' cross. *(Mark 15.21)*

Jesus, you love us. We don't like carrying crosses, but many times our cross is of our own making. It is a self-centred cross. Help us find the true cross in the lives of the poor. Help us to help carry their burden. Jesus, help us!

8. THE WOMEN OF JERUSALEM

A large crowd of people followed him; among them were some women who were weeping and wailing for him. Jesus turned to them and said, "Women of Jerusalem! Do not cry for me, but for yourselves and your children. For the days are coming when people will say, 'How lucky are the women who never had children, who never bore babies, who never nursed them!' " *(Luke 23.27-31)*

Jesus, you love us. Allow us to comfort the grieving women of our time. But even more, enable us to prevent their grief, which so often could be avoided. Help us to break down the human systems which starve and kill. Jesus, make us angry about this unnecessary grief and suffering. Teach us to weep, knowing all the time that tears are never enough.

9. THE STRIPPING AND CRUCIFIXION

They came to a place called Golgotha, which means 'Place of the Skull.' There they offered Jesus wine mixed with a bitter substance; but after tasting it, he would not drink it.

They crucified him and then divided his clothes among them by throwing dice. *(Matthew 27.33-35)*

Jesus, you love us. Stripped naked, nailed to the cross, you have given your all for us. Jesus, help us break the bonds of our selfishness and materialism. Show us how we can give our life for others, in your covenant.

10. THE SECOND THIEF

One of the criminals hanging there hurled insults at him: "Aren't you the Messiah? Save yourself and us!"

The other one, however, rebuked him, saying, "Don't you fear God? You received the same sentence he did. Ours, however, is only right because we are getting what we deserve; but he has done no wrong." And he said to Jesus, "Remember me, Jesus, when you come as King!"

Jesus said to him, "I promise you that today you will be in Paradise with me." *(Luke 23.39-43)*

Jesus, you love us. Impress on us that the lives we live, the work we do, have consequences for others. Awaken our awareness to real evil and real faith. Help us honour your covenant of friendship in our lives.

11. MARY AND JOHN

Standing close to Jesus' cross were his mother, his mother's sister, Mary the wife of Clopas, and Mary Magdalene. Jesus saw his mother and the disciple he loved standing there; so he said to his mother, "He is your son."

Then he said to the disciple, "She is your mother." From that time the disciple took her to live in his home. *(John 19.25-27)*

Jesus, you love us. You gave us your mother Mary as our own mother. Touch our hearts with her sorrow at your death. Lift our eyes so we may see in her the beauty of your covenant; the beauty of her gift of herself to you and to us.

12. DEATH ON THE CROSS

But when they came to Jesus, they saw that he was already dead, so they did not break his legs. One of the soldiers, however, plunged his spear into Jesus' side, and at once blood and water poured out. *(John 19.33-34)*

Jesus, you love us. Teach us your way. Give us the wisdom to recognize evil. Give us the courage to confront it, to struggle against it, so that we may truly be your friends.

13. THE NEW SEPULCHRE

When it was evening, a rich man from Arimathea arrived; his name was Joseph, and he also was a disciple of Jesus. He went to Pilate and asked for the body of Jesus. Pilate gave orders for the body to be given to Joseph. So Joseph took it, wrapped it in a new linen sheet, and placed it in his own tomb which he had just recently dug out of solid rock. Then he rolled a large stone across the entrance to the tomb and went away. *(Matthew 27.57-60)*

Jesus, you love us. Help us to distinguish justice and charity. Sometimes it is easier to do charity than to do justice. Let us know which should be our response and when, in our lives. Give us the grace to act charitably and justly.

14. THE RESURRECTION

Very early on Sunday morning the women went to the tomb, carrying the spices they had prepared. They found the stone rolled away from the entrance to the tomb, so they went in; but they did not find the body of the Lord Jesus. *(Luke 24.1-3)*

Jesus, you love us. You have returned from the dead to be with us. Be our promise, our hope that all evil will be overcome. Bless us with full life for all humankind, under your covenant.

FINAL PRAYER

We know that Christ has been raised from death and will never die again — death will no longer rule over him. And so, because he died, sin has no power over him; and now he lives his life in fellowship with God. In the same way, you are to think of yourselves as dead, so far as sin is concerned, but living in fellowship with God through Christ Jesus. *(Romans 6.9-11)*

Father, your only Son gave up his life for us, his friends. Help us understand the meaning of that friendship. Help us grow in that friendship.

We are a weak and distracted people. Often we neglect you, but you never abandon us. You love us. Make us a less selfish and a more caring people. Help us to share the crosses of others, as Simon did. Show us how to live your covenant of friendship day by day with the victims and the poor of this world. Father, we depend on you.

We pray this through Jesus, the Christ, your Son who has risen from the dead. Amen.

PRAYING WITH THE EUCHARIST

ANIMA CHRISTI

Soul of Christ, be my sanctification;
Body of Christ, be my salvation;
Blood of Christ, fill all my veins;
Water of Christ's side, wash out my stains;
Passion of Christ, my comfort be;
O good Jesus, listen to me;
In Thy wounds I fain would hide;
Ne'er to be parted from Thy side;
Guard me, should the foe assail me;
Call me when my life shall fail me;
Bid me come to Thee above,
With Thy saints to sing Thy love,
World without end. Amen.

* * *

My Lord, I offer Thee myself in turn as a sacrifice of thanksgiving. Thou hast died for me, and I in turn make myself over to Thee. I am not my own. Thou hast bought me; I will by my own act and deed complete the purchase. My wish is to be separated from everything of this world; to cleanse myself simply from sin; to put away from me even what is innocent, if used for its own sake, and not for Thine. I put away reputation and honour, and influence, and power, for my praise and strength shall be in Thee. Enable me to carry on what I profess. Amen.

Blessed John Henry Newman

I believe Thou art present in the Blessed Sacrament, O Jesus. I love Thee and desire Thee. Come into my heart. I embrace Thee, O never leave me. I beseech Thee, O Lord Jesus, may the burning and most sweet power of Thy love absorb my mind, that I may die through love of Thy love, Who wast graciously pleased to die through love of my love.

Saint Francis of Assisi

***

Lord Jesus, Who in the Eucharist make your dwelling among us and become our traveling companion, sustain our Christian communities so that they may be ever more open to listening and accepting your Word. May they draw from the Eucharist a renewed commitment to spreading in society, by the proclamation of your Gospel, the signs and deeds of an attentive and active charity.

Saint John Paul II

AN ACT OF SPIRITUAL COMMUNION
My Jesus, I believe that you are present in the most Blessed Sacrament. I love You above all things and I desire to receive You into my soul. Since I cannot now receive You sacramentally, come at least spiritually into my heart. I embrace You as if You have already come, and unite myself wholly to You. Never permit me to be separated from You. Amen.

Saint Alphonsus Liguori

INSPIRATION FROM THE SAINTS

LIVING HOPE

Consult not your fears but your hopes and your dreams. Think not about your frustrations, but about your unfulfilled potential. Concern yourself not with what you tried and failed in, but with what it is still possible for you to do.

Saint John XXIII

SEEKING JESUS

It is Jesus that you seek when you dream of happiness; He is waiting for you when nothing else you find satisfies you; He is the beauty to which you are so attracted; it is He who provoked you with that thirst for fullness that will not let you settle for compromise; it is He who urges you to shed the masks of a false life; it is He who reads in your heart your most genuine choices, the choices that others try to stifle.

It is Jesus who stirs in you the desire to do something great with your lives, the will to follow an ideal, the refusal to allow yourselves to be ground down by mediocrity, the courage to commit yourselves humbly and patiently to improving yourselves and society, making the world more human.

Saint John Paul II, World Youth Day, August 19, 2000

GOD'S HANDIWORK

It is with the smallest brushes that the artist paints the most exquisitely beautiful pictures.

Saint André Bessette

PRAYER OF ST. THOMAS AQUINAS

Grant me, O Lord my God,
a mind to know you,
a heart to seek you,
wisdom to find you,
conduct pleasing to you,
faithful perseverance in waiting for you,
and a hope of finally embracing you.

Saint Thomas Aquinas

DOING GOD'S WILL

Lord Jesus, teach me to be generous;
teach me to serve you as you deserve;
to give and not count the cost,
to fight and not heed the wounds,
to toil and not seek for rest,
to labour and not to seek reward,
except that of knowing that I do your will.

Saint Ignatius Loyola

* * *

Give me, Lord, a full faith, a firm hope and a fervent love, a love for you incomparably above the love of myself. These things, good Lord, that I pray for, give me your grace also to labour for.

Saint Thomas More

THE PEACE PRAYER OF ST. FRANCIS

Lord, make me an instrument of your peace.
Where there is hatred let me sow love;
where there is injury, pardon;
where there is doubt, faith;
where there is despair, hope;
where there is darkness, light;
and where there is sadness, joy.

Divine Master,
grant that I may not so much seek
to be consoled as to console,
to be understood as to understand,
to be loved as to love.

For it is in giving that we receive,
in pardoning that we are pardoned,
and in dying that we are brought to eternal life.

Unknown, ca. 1915

IN SERVICE TO GOD

Govern everything by your wisdom, O Lord,
so that my soul may always be serving you
in the way you will
and not as I choose.
Let me die to myself so that I may serve you;
let me live to you who are life itself.

Saint Teresa of Avila

God doesn't ask for the impossible, but wants everyone to offer their good intentions, their day's work, and some prayers: that will help them a lot. The best Way of the Cross is when people accept willingly the crosses that are sent to them.

Saint André Bessette

The lover gives her life gladly for the beloved. She does not know her own interests or even her own needs. Sickness and health, prosperity and adversity, life and death, consolation and desolation are alike to her.

Saint Marguerite Bourgeoys

Give something, however small, to the one in need. For it is not small to one who has nothing. Neither is it small to God, if we have given what we could.

Saint Gregory Nazianzen

The Eucharist is the heart of the Christian religion. It is an ineffable mystery that embraces the untold depths of divine love, and in which God bestows upon us all blessings and graces.

Saint Francis de Sales

PRAYERS FOR CEMETERY VISITS

PSALM 23 — THE DIVINE SHEPHERD

The Lord is my shepherd, I shall not want.
He makes me lie down in green pastures;
he leads me beside still waters;
he restores my soul.
He leads me in right paths
for his name's sake.

Even though I walk through the darkest valley,
I fear no evil;
for you are with me;
your rod and your staff —
they comfort me.

You prepare a table before me
in the presence of my enemies;
you anoint my head with oil;
my cup overflows.

Surely goodness and mercy shall follow me
all the days of my life,
and I shall dwell in the house of the Lord
my whole life long.

ETERNAL REST

Eternal rest grant unto them, O Lord,
and let perpetual light shine upon them.
May the souls of the faithful departed,
through the mercy of God,
rest in peace. Amen.

DE PROFUNDIS *(Psalm 130)*
Out of the depths I cry to You, O Lord;
Lord, hear my voice.
Let Your ears be attentive
to my voice in supplication.
If You, O Lord, mark iniquities,
Lord, who can stand?
But with You is forgiveness,
that You may be revered.

I trust in the Lord;
my soul trusts in His word.
My soul waits for the Lord
more than sentinels wait for the dawn.
More than sentinels wait for the dawn,
let Israel wait for the Lord,

For with the Lord is kindness
and with Him is plenteous redemption;
And He will redeem Israel
from all their iniquities.

* * *

Lord, support us all the day long,
until the shadows lengthen
    and the evening comes,
and the busy world is hushed
and the fever of life is over
and our work is done.
Then in thy mercy grant us
a safe lodging,
and a holy rest,
and peace at the last.

Blessed John Henry Newman

PRAYER IN THE MORNING

INVITATION TO PRAYER

Lord, open our lips.
And we shall proclaim your praise.
Glory to God in the highest.
And peace to God's people on earth.

HYMN OF PRAISE (Optional)

PSALM OF PRAISE

Psalm 63 and/or another psalm of praise, followed by a moment of silence.

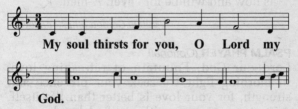

My soul thirsts for you, O Lord my God.

℟. **My soul thirsts for you, O Lord my God.**

O God, you are my God, I · **seek_you**,
my soul · **thirsts_for_you;**
my flesh · **faints_for_you,**
as in a dry and weary land
   where there · **is** no water. ℟.

So I have looked upon you in the · **sanctuary,**
beholding your power and · **glory.**
Because your steadfast love is better than · **life,**
my · **lips** will praise_you. ℟.

So I will bless you as long as I · **live;**
I will lift up my hands and call on your · **name.**
My soul is satisfied as with a rich · **feast,**
and my mouth praises you
 with · **joy**-ful lips. R

For you have been my · **help**,
and in the shadow of your wings I sing for · **joy**.
My soul · **clings_to_you;**
your right · **hand** up-holds_me. R

Glory to the Father, and to the · **Son,**
and to the Holy · **Spirit.**
As it was in the be--**ginning,**
is now and will be for · **ever.** A-men. R

PSALM PRAYER *(Optional)*
Lord our God, Fountain of refreshing love,
in morning light we seek your presence and
strength, for your love is better than life itself.
Accept our prayers with uplifted hands as we
proclaim your praise in songs of joy. Satisfy our
longing hearts and renew our thirsting spirits that
our worship may give you glory and our lives be
poured out in loving service.

Glory and praise to you, loving God, through
our Lord Jesus Christ, your Son, who lives and
reigns with you in the unity of the Holy Spirit,
God for ever and ever. **Amen.**

WORD OF GOD
*Appropriate verse(s) selected beforehand from the readings
of the day, followed by a moment of silence.*

CANTICLE OF ZECHARIAH

1. Blessed be the God of Israel,
   Who comes to set us free,
   Who visits and redeems us,
   And grants us liberty.
   The prophets spoke of mercy,
   Of freedom and release;
   God shall fulfill the promise
   To bring our people peace.

2. Now from the house of David
   A child of grace is giv'n;
   A Saviour comes among us
   To raise us up to heaven.
   Before him goes the herald,
   Forerunner in the way:
   The prophet of salvation,
   The messenger of Day.

3. Where once were fear and darkness
   The sun begins to rise,
   The dawning of forgiveness
   Upon the sinners' eyes,
   To guide the feet of pilgrims
   Along the paths of peace:
   O bless our God and Saviour
   With songs that never cease!

Text: Michael Perry, ©*1973 Hope Publishing Co.*
Tune: MERLE'S TUNE, *76.76.D.;* ©*1983 Hope Publishing Co.*
Used by per mission. All rights reserved.
Music: *CBW III* 13E

PETITIONS

These reflect the needs of the Church, the world, the suffering, and the local community. Weekly suggestions are available at www.livingwithchrist.ca

OUR FATHER...

CONCLUDING PRAYER

God of glory and compassion, at your touch the wilderness blossoms, broken lives are made whole, and fearful hearts grow strong in faith. Open our eyes to your presence and awaken our hearts to sing your praise. To all who long for your Son's return grant perseverance and patience, that we may announce in word and deed the good news of the kingdom.

We ask this through our Lord Jesus Christ, your Son, who lives and reigns with you in the unity of the Holy Spirit, God for ever and ever. **Amen.**

BLESSING

May the Lord almighty order our days and our deeds in lasting peace. **Amen.**

Let us offer each other a sign of Christ's peace.

The celebration ends with the exchange of peace.

* * *

For a fuller version of the Liturgy of the Hours, consult the Living with Christ *missalette.*

PRAYER IN THE EVENING

The paschal candle is lit and carried in procession. During Advent, the Advent wreath may be lit instead. If you plan to use Psalm 141, prepare the thurible beforehand so that incense may be burned during the singing of the psalm.

INVITATION TO PRAYER

God, come to our assistance.
Lord, make haste to help us.
Glory to the Father, and to the Son, and to the Holy Spirit.
As it was in the beginning, is now, and will be forever. Amen.

HYMN OF PRAISE *(Optional)*

PSALM OF PRAISE

Psalm 141 and/or another psalm of praise, followed by a moment of silence.

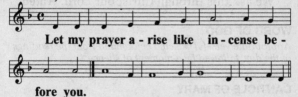

Let my prayer a-rise like in-cense be-fore you.

℟. **Let my prayer arise like incense before you.**

I call upon you, O Lord: come quickly to · **me;**
give ear to my voice when I call to · **you.**
Let my prayer be counted as incense be-**fore_you.**
and the lifting up of my hands as
an eve-**ning** sacrifice. ℟.

Set a guard over my mouth, O · **Lord;**
keep watch over the door of my · **lips.**
But my eyes are turned toward you,
    O God, my · **Lord;**
in you I seek refuge; do not leave me
  · **de**-fenceless. ℟

Glory to the Father, and to the · **Son,**
and to the Holy · **Spirit.**
As it was in the be-·-**ginning,**
is now and will be for ever. · **A**-men. ℟

©2008 Gordon Johnston/Novalis

PSALM PRAYER *(Optional)*

Loving God, creator of light and life, may our prayers ascend to you like the fragrance of incense. Purify our hearts to sing your praise in the company of your saints in glory.

We ask this through Christ our Lord. **Amen.**

WORD OF GOD

Appropriate verse(s) selected beforehand from the readings of the day, followed by a moment of silence.

CANTICLE OF MARY

1. My soul proclaims the Lord my God.
   My spirit sings God's praise,
   Who looks on me and lifts me up,
   That gladness fill my days.
2. All nations now will share my joy,
   For gifts God has outpoured.
   This lowly one has been made great
   I magnify the Lord.

3. For those who fear the Holy One,
   God's mercy will not die,
   Whose strong right arm puts down the proud,
   And lifts the lowly high.
4. God fills the hungry with good things,
   And sends the rich away.
   The promise made to Abraham,
   Is filled to endless day.
5. Then let all nations praise our God,
   The Father and the Son,
   The Spirit blest who lives in us,
   While endless ages run.

Text: Anne Carter, ©1988 Religious of the Sacred Heart.
Tune: HEATHER DEW **Music:** CBW III 592, 617; CBW II 74, 589

PETITIONS

These reflect the needs of the Church, the world, the suffering, and the local community. Weekly suggestions are available at www.livingwithchrist.ca

OUR FATHER...

CONCLUDING PRAYER

Creator of the universe, watch over us and keep us in the light of your presence. May our praise continually blend with that of all creation, until we come together to the eternal joys which you promise in your love.

We ask this through our Lord Jesus Christ, your Son, who lives and reigns with you in the unity of the Holy Spirit, God for ever and ever. **Amen.**

BLESSING

May God the Father almighty bless and keep us. **Amen.**

May Jesus Christ, his only Son, our Lord, graciously smile upon us. **Amen.**

May the Holy Spirit, the Lord and giver of life, grant us peace. **Amen.**

Let us offer each other a sign of Christ's peace.

The celebration ends with the exchange of peace.

* * *

For a fuller version of the Liturgy of the Hours, consult the Living with Christ missalette.

CELEBRATING THE SACRAMENT OF RECONCILIATION

When ready to celebrate the sacrament of Reconciliation (Confession), the following steps are involved.

BEFOREHAND
Examination of Conscience:
Pray to the Holy Spirit for light and strength, examine your conscience in the light of the Scriptures and the Commandments since your last confession and become truly sorry for your sins.

GOING TO CONFESSION
Welcome:
The priest welcomes you, the penitent. It is helpful if you indicate the time of your last Confession and anything else that will help the priest hearing your confession.

Scripture:
A short passage of Scripture may be read.

Confession:
Confess your sins and listen to the advice of the priest.

Penance:
The priest proposes a good action or prayer to help make up for sin and deepen virtue.

Prayer of Sorrow (Act of Contrition):
Pray expressing personal sorrow and asking for forgiveness.

Absolution:
The priest grants absolution in the name of God and the Church.

617

Praise of God and Dismissal:
The priest invites you to praise God and dismisses
you with the command to go in peace.

AFTERWARD
Spend some time in thanking God for forgiving us
and restoring us to full life in Christ.

EXAMINATION OF CONSCIENCE

Do I centre my life on God, on fidelity to the Gospel and the Commandments? Do I set aside time
for personal prayer?

Do I keep Sunday by participating in the Eucharist?

Is Sunday a day of prayer and rest? Do I observe
the penitential practices of the Church? Do I keep
Lent as a time of prayer and sacrifice?

Do I behave as a Christian in daily and public life?
Is my faith reflected in my employment?

Have I taken property of others including my
employer?

Am I envious of what others have? Do I share my
goods and time with those in need? Do I respect
the reputation of others?

Do I care for my family? Do I model Christian life
for my family: parents, wife, husband, children?

Do I exercise authority with genuine concern and
responsibility? Do I give others the same respect
that I expect for myself?

Have I dishonoured my body by thoughts or actions incompatible with Christian life? Am I faithful to my marriage? Do I set an example of committed single living?

Do I live out my commitments to my spouse and my children to the best of my ability and reflect God's love and faithfulness?

How do I deal with the difficulties, failures and disappointments of life?

Do I tend to the spiritual, physical and medical needs of my body? Can others see the grace of Baptism at work in my life?

ACT OF CONTRITION

My God,
I am sorry for my sins with all my heart.
In choosing to do wrong
and failing to do good,
I have sinned against you
whom I should love above all things.
I firmly intend, with your help,
to do penance,
to sin no more,
and to avoid whatever leads me to sin.
Our Saviour Jesus Christ
suffered and died for us.
In his name, my God, have mercy.

Excerpted from *Celebrating Reconciliation*
(Ottawa: Concacan Inc., 2006).

KYRIE – PENITENTIAL ACT, FORM 1

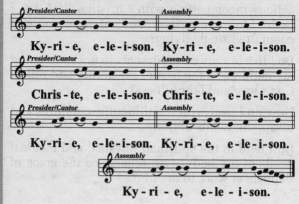

Presider/Cantor *Assembly*
Ky-ri-e, e-le-i-son. Ky-ri-e, e-le-i-son.

Presider/Cantor *Assembly*
Chris-te, e-le-i-son. Chris-te, e-le-i-son.

Presider/Cantor *Assembly*
Ky-ri-e, e-le-i-son. Ky-ri-e, e-le-i-son.

Assembly
Ky-ri-e, e-le-i-son.

or

Presider/Cantor *Assembly*
Lord, have mer-cy. Lord, have mer-cy.

Presider/Cantor *Assembly*
Christ, have mer-cy. Christ, have mer-cy.

Presider/Cantor *Assembly*
Lord, have mer-cy. Lord, have mer-cy.

Text and setting: *Excerpts from Chants of the Roman Missal* © 2010 ICEL. Used with permission.

KYRIE – PENITENTIAL ACT, FORM 2

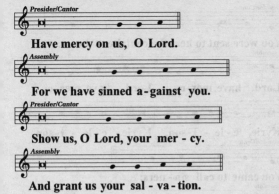

Presider/Cantor

Have mercy on us, O Lord.

Assembly

For we have sinned a-gainst you.

Presider/Cantor

Show us, O Lord, your mer-cy.

Assembly

And grant us your sal-va-tion.

Text and setting: *Excerpts from Chants of the Roman Missal © 2010 ICEL. Used with permission.*

KYRIE – PENITENTIAL ACT, FORM 3

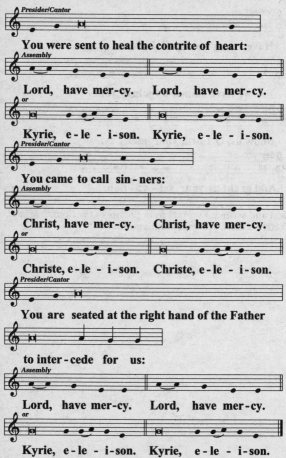

Presider/Cantor

You were sent to heal the contrite of heart:

Assembly

Lord, have mer-cy. Lord, have mer-cy.

or

Kyrie, e - le - i-son. Kyrie, e - le - i-son.

Presider/Cantor

You came to call sin-ners:

Assembly

Christ, have mer-cy. Christ, have mer-cy.

or

Christe, e - le - i-son. Christe, e - le - i-son.

Presider/Cantor

You are seated at the right hand of the Father

to inter-cede for us:

Assembly

Lord, have mer-cy. Lord, have mer-cy.

or

Kyrie, e - le - i-son. Kyrie, e - le - i-son.

Text and setting: *Excerpts from Chants of the Roman Missal* © 2010 ICEL. Used with permission.

GLORIA

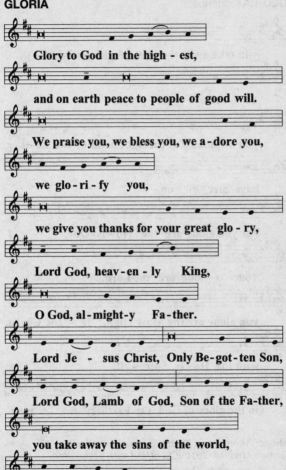

Glory to God in the high - est,

and on earth peace to people of good will.

We praise you, we bless you, we a - dore you,

we glo - ri - fy you,

we give you thanks for your great glo - ry,

Lord God, heav - en - ly King,

O God, al - might - y Fa - ther.

Lord Je - sus Christ, Only Be - got - ten Son,

Lord God, Lamb of God, Son of the Fa - ther,

you take away the sins of the world,

have mer - cy on us;

623

GLORIA *(continue)*

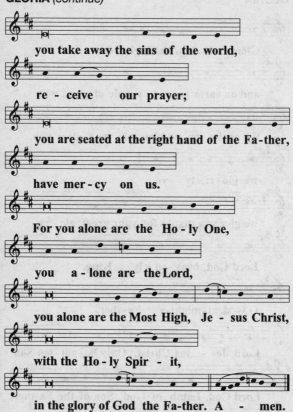

you take away the sins of the world,

re - ceive our prayer;

you are seated at the right hand of the Fa-ther,

have mer - cy on us.

For you alone are the Ho - ly One,

you a - lone are the Lord,

you alone are the Most High, Je - sus Christ,

with the Ho - ly Spir - it,

in the glory of God the Fa-ther. A - men.

Music: *Anonymous.* **Text:** *Excerpts from Chants of the Roman Missal © 2010 ICEL. Used with permission.*

HOLY, HOLY, HOLY

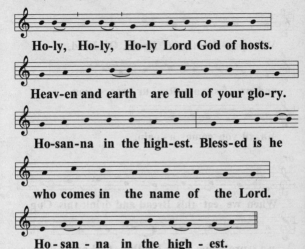

Ho-ly, Ho-ly, Ho-ly Lord God of hosts.

Heav-en and earth are full of your glo-ry.

Ho-san-na in the high-est. Bless-ed is he

who comes in the name of the Lord.

Ho - san - na in the high - est.

Text and setting: *Excerpts from Chants of the Roman Missal*
© 2010 ICEL. Used with permission.

MEMORIAL ACCLAMATIONS

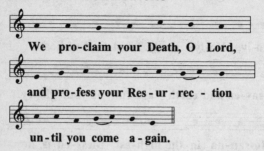

We pro-claim your Death, O Lord,

and pro-fess your Res - ur - rec - tion

un-til you come a - gain.

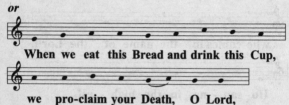

or

When we eat this Bread and drink this Cup,

we pro-claim your Death, O Lord,

un-til you come a - gain.

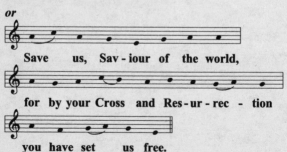

or

Save us, Sav - iour of the world,

for by your Cross and Res - ur - rec - tion

you have set us free.

Text and setting: *Excerpts from Chants of the Roman Missal*
© *2010 ICEL. Used with permission.*

LAMB OF GOD

Lamb of God,

you take a - way the sins of the world,

have mer - cy on us.

Lamb of God,

you take a - way the sins of the world,

have mer - cy on us.

Lamb of God,

you take a - way the sins of the world,

Grant us peace.

Text and setting: *Excerpts from Chants of the Roman Missal* © 2010, ICEL. Used with permission.

Hymns

ON JORDAN'S BANK

1. On Jordan's bank the Baptist's cry
   Announces that the Lord is nigh;
   Awake and hearken, for he brings
   Glad tidings of the King of kings!

2. Then cleansed be ev'ry life from sin;
   Make straight the way for God within;
   And let us all our hearts prepare
   For Christ to come and enter there.

3. We hail you as our Saviour, Lord,
   Our refuge and our great reward;
   Without your grace we waste away
   Like flow'rs that wither and decay.

4. Stretch forth your hand, our health restore,
   And make us rise to fall no more;
   O, let your face upon us shine
   And fill the world with love divine.

Text: *Jordanis oras praevis,* Charles Coffin, 1676-1749; tr. st. 1-3 John Chandler, 1806-76; st. 4 unknown; alt.
Tune: WINCHESTER NEW, LM **Music:** CBW II 443; CBW III 350

O COME, O COME EMMANUEL

1. O come, O come, Emmanuel,
   And ransom captive Israel
   That mourns in lonely exile here
   Until the Son of God appear.

Ref: Rejoice! Rejoice! Emmanuel
   shall come to you, O Israel.

2. O come, O Wisdom from on high,
   Who order all things mightily;
   To us the path of knowledge show,
   And teach us in your ways to go.

3. O come, O come, great Lord of might,
   Who to your tribes on Sinai's height
   In ancient times once gave the law,
   In cloud, and majesty, and awe.

4. O come, O rod of Jesse's stem,
   From ev'ry foe deliver them
   That trust your mighty pow'r to save,
   and give them vict'ry o'er the grave.

5. O come, O key of David, come
   And open wide our heav'nly home;
   Make safe the way that leads on high,
   And close the path to misery.

6. O come, O Dayspring from on high,
   And cheer us by your drawing nigh;
   Disperse the gloomy clouds of night,
   And death's dark shadow put to flight.

7. O come, Desire of nations, bind
   In one the hearts of humankind;
   O bid our sad divisions cease,
   And be for us our king of peace.

Text: *Veni, veni Emmanuel;* Latin 9th c.; tr. by John Mason
Neale, 1818-1866, alt. **Tune:** VENI, VENI EMMANUEL
Music: CBW II 440; CBW III 312

O COME, DIVINE MESSIAH!

1. O come, divine Messiah!
   The world in silence waits the day
   When hope shall sing its triumph,
   And sadness flee away.

Ref: Sweet Saviour, haste;
   Come, come to earth:
   Dispel the night, and show thy face,
   And bid us hail the dawn of grace.
   O come, divine Messiah,
   The world in silence waits the day
   When hope shall sing its triumph,
   And sadness flee away.

2. O thou, whom nations sighed for,
   Whom priests and prophets long foretold,
   Wilt break the captive fetters,
   Redeem the long-lost fold.

3. Shalt come in peace and meekness,
   And lowly will your cradle be:
   All clothed in human weakness
   Shall we thy God-head see.

Text: Abbé Pellegrin, 1663-1745; tr. Sr. Mary of St. Philip
Tune: VENEZ DIVIN MESSIE, 78.76.888 **Music:** CBW II 441;
CBW III 310

THE FIRST NOWELL

1. The first Nowell the angel did say
   Was to certain poor shepherds in fields as they lay;
   In fields where they lay, keeping their sheep,
   On a cold winter's night that was so deep.

Ref: Nowell, Nowell, Nowell, Nowell,
   born is the King of Israel.

2. They lookéd up and saw a star
   Shining in the east, beyond them far,
   And to the earth it gave great light
   And so it continued both day and night.

3. And by the light of that same star
   Three wise men came from country far;
   To seek for a king was their intent,
   And to follow the star wherever it went.

4. This star drew nigh to the northwest,
   O'er Bethlehem it took its rest,
   And there it did both stop and stay
   Right over the place where Jesus lay.

5. Then entered in those wise men three,
   Full reverently upon their knee,
   And offered there in his presence,
   Their gold and myrrh and frankincense.

6. Then let us all with one accord
   Sing praises to our heav'nly Lord:
   Who with the Father we adore
   And Spirit blest for evermore.

Text: English Carol, 17th c. **Tune:** THE FIRST NOWELL,
Irregular **Music:** CBW II 460; CBW III 344

WHAT CHILD IS THIS

1. What Child is this, who laid to rest,
   On Mary's lap is sleeping?
   Whom angels greet with anthems sweet,
   While shepherds watch are keeping?

Ref: This, this is Christ the King,
   Whom shepherds guard and angels sing:
   Haste, haste to bring him laud,
   The babe, the son of Mary.

2. Why lies he in such mean estate
   Where ox and ass are feeding?
   Good Christian, fear: for sinners here
   The silent Word is pleading.

3. So bring him incense, gold, and myrrh,
   Come, peasant, king to own him,
   The King of kings salvation brings,
   Let loving hearts enthrone him.

Text: William Chatterton Dix, 1837-1898 **Tune:** GREENSLEEVES,
87 87 with refrain **Music:** CBW II 461; CBW III 338

GOOD CHRISTIAN FRIENDS, REJOICE

Good Christian friends, rejoice
With heart and soul and voice;

1. O give heed to what we say:
   Jesus Christ was born today!
   Ox and ass before him bow,
   and he is in the manger now.
   Christ is born today!
   Christ is born today!

2. Now you hear of endless bliss:
   Jesus Christ was born for this!
   He has opened heaven's door,
   And we are blest for ever more.
   Christ was born for this!
   Christ was born for this!

3. Now you need not fear the grave:
   Jesus Christ was born to save!
   Calls you one and calls you all
   To gain his everlasting hall.
   Christ was born to save!
   Christ was born to save!

Text: *In dulci jubilo;* Latin and German, 14th c., tr. John
Mason Neale, 1818-1866, alt. **Tune:** IN DULCI JUBILO; 66 77
77 55 **Music:** *CBW II 465; CBW III 322*

O COME, ALL YE FAITHFUL

1. O come, all ye faithful, joyful and triumphant,
   O come ye, o come ye to Bethlehem;
   Come and behold him, born the king of angels.

Ref: O come, let us adore him,
   O come, let us adore him,
   O come, let us adore him, Christ, the Lord!

2. Sing, choirs of angels, sing in exultation,
   Sing, all ye citizens of heav'n above!
   Glory to God in the highest.

3. Yea, Lord, we greet thee, born this happy morning,
   Jesus, to thee be glory giv'n;
   Word of the Father, now in flesh appearing.

Text: *Adeste, fideles;* John F. Wade, c. 1711-1786; tr.
Frederick Oakley, 1802-80, alt. **Tune:** ADESTE, FIDELES,
Irregular with refrain; John F. Wade, c. 1711-1786
Music: CBW II 458; CBW III 329

TAKE UP YOUR CROSS

1. Take up your cross, the Saviour said,
   If you would my disciple be;
   Take up your cross with willing heart,
   And humbly follow after me.

2. Take up your cross, let not its weight
   Fill your weak spirit with alarm;
   His strength shall bear your spirit up,
   And brace your heart and nerve your arm.

3. Take up your cross, heed not the shame,
   And let your foolish heart be still;
   The Lord for you accepted death
   Upon a cross, on Calvary's hill.

4. Take up your cross, then, in his strength,
   And calmly every danger brave:
   It guides you to abundant life,
   And leads to vict'ry o'er the grave.

5. Take up your cross, and follow Christ,
   Nor think till death to lay it down;
   For only those who bear the cross
   May hope to wear the glorious crown.

Text: Charles W. Everest, 1814-1877, alt. **Tune:** ERHALT UNS, HERR, LM **Music:** CBW II 481; CBW III 352

O SACRED HEAD SURROUNDED

1. O sacred head surrounded
   By crown of piercing thorn.
   O bleeding head, so wounded
   Reviled and put to scorn.
   The pow'r of death comes o'er you,
   The glow of life decays,
   Yet angel hosts adore you,
   And tremble as they gaze.

2. In this your bitter passion,
   Good Shepherd, think of me
   With your most sweet compassion,
   Unworthy though I be:
   Beneath your cross abiding
   For ever would I rest,
   In your dear love confiding,
   And with your presence blest.

3. Christ Jesus, we adore you,
   Our thorn-crowned Lord and King.
   We bow our heads before you,
   And to your cross we cling.
   Lord, give us strength to bear it
   With patience and with love,
   That we may truly merit
   A glorious crown above.

Text: Bernard of Clairvaux, v. 1, tr. Henry W. Baker, 1821-77;
v. 2 & 3, tr. Arthur T. Russell, 1806-74, alt. **Tune:** PASSION
CHORALE; 76 76 D; Hans Leo Hassler, 1564-1612
Music: CBW 11 491; CBW III 377

LORD, WHO THROUGHOUT THESE FORTY DAYS

1. Lord, who throughout these forty days
   For us did fast and pray,
   Teach us to overcome our sins
   And close by you to stay.

2. As you with Satan did contend
   And did the vict'ry win,
   O give us strength in you to fight,
   In you to conquer sin.

3. As you did hunger and did thirst,
   So teach us, gracious Lord,
   To die to self and so to live
   By your most holy word.

4. And through these days of penitence,
   and through your passion-tide,
   For evermore, in life and death,
   O Lord, with us abide.

5. Abide with us, that through this life
   Of doubts and hopes and pain
   An Easter of unending joy
   We may at last attain.

Text: Claudia F. Hernaman, 1838-98, in her *A Child's Book of Praise*, 1873, alt. **Tune:** ST. FLAVIAN, CM; adapted from Day's Psalter, 1562 **Music:** CBW II 482; CBW III 367

WHEN I BEHOLD THE WONDROUS CROSS

1. When I behold the wondrous cross
   On which the prince of glory died,
   My richest gain I count but loss
   And pour contempt on all my pride.

2. Forbid it, Lord, that I should boast
   Save in the death of Christ, my God;
   The vain things that attract me most,
   I sacrifice them to his blood.

3. See, from his head, his hands, his feet,
    Sorrow and love flow mingled down.
    Did e'er such love and sorrow meet,
    Or thorns compose so rich a crown?

4. Were all the realms of nature mine,
    It would be off'ring far too small;
    Love so amazing, so divine,
    Demands my soul, my life, my all!

Text: Isaac Watts, 1674-1748, alt. **Tune:** ROCKINGHAM, LM
Music: CBW II 489; CBW III 382

O SONS AND DAUGHTERS

Ref: Alleluia, alleluia, alleluia!

1. O sons and daughters, let us sing!
    The king of heav'n, our glorious king,
    From death today rose triumphing. Alleluia!

2. That Easter morn, at break of day,
    The faithful women went their way,
    To seek the tomb where Jesus lay. Alleluia!

3. An angel clothed in white they see,
    Who sat and spoke unto the three,
    "Your Lord has gone to Galilee." Alleluia!

4. That night th'apostles met in fear;
    And Christ did in their midst appear,
    And said, "My peace be with you here." Alleluia!

5. How blest are they who have not seen,
    And yet whose faith has constant been,
    For they eternal life shall win. Alleluia!

6. On this most holy day of days,
    To God your hearts and voices raise,
    In laud and jubilee and praise. Alleluia!

Text: Jean Tisserand, †1494; tr. John Mason Neale, 1818-66, alt.
Tune: O FILII ET FILIAE 8 8 8 4 with Alleluias
Music: CBW II 506; CBW III 404

JESUS CHRIST IS RIS'N TODAY

1. Jesus Christ is ris'n today, Alleluia!
   Our triumphant holy day, Alleluia!
   Who did once upon the cross, Alleluia!
   Suffer to redeem our loss. Alleluia!

2. Hymns of praise then let us sing, Alleluia!
   Unto Christ our heav'nly king, Alleluia!
   Who endured the cross and grave, Alleluia!
   Sinners to redeem and save. Alleluia!

3. But the pains which he endured, Alleluia!
   Our salvation have procured; Alleluia!
   Now above the sky he's king, Alleluia!
   Where the angels ever sing. Alleluia!

4. Sing we to our God above, Alleluia!
   Praise eternal as his love, Alleluia!
   Praise him, now his might confess, Alleluia!
   Father, Son and Spirit bless. Alleluia!

Text: Lyra Davidica, 1708, alt. & others **Tune:** EASTER HYMN;
77 77 with Alleluias **Music:** CBW II 500; CBW III 389

SING WITH ALL THE SAINTS IN GLORY

1. Sing with all the saints in glory,
   Sing the resurrection song!
   Death and sorrow, earth's dark story,
   To the former days belong.
   All around the clouds are breaking,
   Soon the storms of time shall cease;
   In God's likeness we awaken,
   Knowing everlasting peace.

2. O what glory, far exceeding
   All that eye has yet perceived!
   Holiest hearts for ages pleading,
   Never that full joy conceived.

God has promised, Christ prepares it,
There on high our welcome waits;
Ev'ry humble spirit shares it,
Christ has passed th'eternal gates.

3. Life eternal! heav'n rejoices:
   Jesus lives who once was dead;
   Shout with joy, O deathless voices!
   Child of God, lift up your head!
   Patriarchs from distant ages,
   Saints all longing for their heaven,
   Prophets, psalmists, seers, and sages,
   All await the glory giv'n.

Text: 1 Cor 15.20; William J. Irons, 1812-1883, alt.
Tune: HYMN TO JOY, 87 87 D **Music:** CBW III 406

THE STRIFE IS O'ER

Ref: Alleluia, alleluia, alleluia!

1. The strife is o'er, the battle done;
   Now is the victor's triumph won;
   O let the song of praise be sung! Alleluia!

2. The pow'rs of sin have done their worst;
   But Jesus has his foes dispersed;
   Let shouts of joy and praise out-burst! Alleluia!

3. Lord, by the stripes which wounded you,
   From death's sting free your servants too,
   That we may live and sing to you. Alleluia!

4. On the third morn you rose again,
   Glorious in majesty to reign;
   O let us swell the joyful strain! Alleluia!

Text: *Finita iam sunt praelia*, Latin 12th c.; *Symphonia Sirenum Selectarum*, Cologne, 1695; tr. Francis Pott, 1832-1909, alt. **Tune:** VICTORY, 8 8 8 with Alleluias **Music:** CBW II 503; CBW III 395

THAT EASTER DAY WITH JOY WAS BRIGHT

1. That Easter day with joy was bright,
   The sun shone out with fairer light,
   Alleluia, alleluia!
   When to their longing eyes restored,
   The glad apostles saw their Lord.

Ref: Alleluia, alleluia, alleluia, alleluia, alleluia!

2. His risen flesh with radiance glowed;
   His wounded hands and feet he showed;
   Alleluia, alleluia!
   Those scars their solemn witness gave
   That Christ was risen from the grave.

3. O Jesus, in your gentleness,
   With constant love our hearts possess;
   Alleluia, alleluia!
   To you our lips will ever raise
   The tribute of our grateful praise.

4. O Lord of all, with us abide
   In this our joyful Eastertide;
   Alleluia, alleluia!
   From ev'ry weapon death can wield
   Your own redeemed for ever shield.

5. All praise to you, O risen Lord,
   Now by both heav'n and earth adored;
   Alleluia, alleluia!
   To God the Father equal praise,
   And Spirit blest our songs we raise.

Text: *Claro paschali gaudio;* Latin 5th c; tr. By John Mason Neal, 1818-1866; alt. **Tune:** LASST UNS ERFREUEN, LM with Alleluias **Music:** CBW II 507; CBW III 392

HAIL, HOLY QUEEN, ENTHRONED ABOVE

1. Hail, holy Queen, enthroned above, O Maria!
   Hail, Queen of mercy and of love, O Maria!

Ref: Triumph, all you cherubim,
   sing with us, you seraphim,
   Heav'n and earth resound the hymn:
   Salve, salve, salve, Regina!

2. Our life, our sweetness here below, O Maria!
   Our hope in sorrow and in woe, O Maria!

3. We honour you for Christ, your son, O Maria!
   Who has for us redemption won, O Maria!

Text: *Salve, Regina, mater misericordiae,* c. 1080; tr. from
the *Roman Hymnal,* 1884 **Tune:** SALVE, REGINA COELITUM,
84 84 with refrain **Music:** CBW II 610; CBW III 457

IMMACULATE MARY

1. Immaculate Mary, your praises we sing,
   You reign now in heaven with Jesus our king.

Ref: Ave, Ave, Ave, Maria!
   Ave, Ave, Ave, Maria!

2. In heaven, the blessed your glory proclaim;
   On earth, we your children invoke your fair
   name.

3. Your name is our power, your virtues our light;
   Your love is our comfort, your pleading our might.

4. We pray for our mother the Church upon earth,
   And bless, dearest lady, the land of our birth.

Text: Anon., in *Parochial Hymn Book,* Boston, 1897, rev.
version of "Hail, Virgin of Virgins," by Jeremiah Cummings,
1814-1866, in his *Songs for Catholic Schools,* 1860, alt.
Tune: LOURDES HYMN, 11 11 **Music:** CBW II 611: CBW III 463A

HOLY GOD, WE PRAISE YOUR NAME

1. Holy God, we praise your name;
   Lord of all, we bow before you.
   All on earth your sceptre claim;
   All in heav'n above adore you.
   Infinite your vast domain;
   Everlasting is your reign.

2. Hark, the glad celestial hymn
   Angel choirs above are raising:
   Cherubim and seraphim,
   In unceasing chorus praising,
   Fill the heav'ns with sweet accord:
   "Holy, holy, holy Lord!"

3. Lo, the apostolic train
   Joins your sacred name to hallow;
   Prophets swell the glad refrain,
   And the white-robed martyrs follow;
   And from morn to set of sun,
   Through the church the song goes on.

4. Holy Father, holy Son,
   Holy Spirit, three we name you,
   Though in essence only one;
   Undivided God, we claim you,
   And, adoring, bend the knee
   While we own the mystery.

Text: *Te Deum laudamus; tr.* Clarence Walworth, 1820-1900, in *Catholic Psalmist*, 1858, alt. **Tune:** GROSSER GOTT, 7 8 7 8 77 **Music:** CBW II 631; CBW III 555

ALL PEOPLE THAT ON EARTH DO DWELL

1. All people that on earth do dwell,
   Sing to the Lord with cheerful voice;
   Him serve with mirth, his praise forth tell,
   Come we before him and rejoice.

2. Know that the Lord is God indeed;
   Without our aid he did us make;
   We are his folk, he does us feed,
   And for his sheep he does us take.

3. O enter then his gates with praise;
   Approach with joy his courts unto;
   Praise, laud, and bless his name always,
   For it is seemly so to do.

4. For why? The Lord our God is good:
   His mercy is for ever sure;
   His truth at all times firmly stood,
   And shall from age to age endure.

5. To Father, Son, and Holy Ghost,
   The God whom heav'n and earth adore,
   From us and from the angel host
   Be praise and glory evermore.

6. Praise God, from whom all blessings flow,
   Praise him, all creatures here below;
   Praise him above, you heav'nly host;
   Praise Father, Son, and Holy Ghost.

Text: Psalm 100; William Kethe, d. c. 1594; v. 6: Thomas
Ken, 1637-1711 **Tune:** OLD HUNDREDTH, LM 8 8 8 8
Music: CBW II 621; CBW III 578

O GOD, OUR HELP IN AGES PAST

1. Our God, our help in ages past,
   Our hope for years to come,
   Our shelter from the stormy blast,
   And our eternal home.

2. Beneath the shadow of your throne,
   Your saints have dwelt secure;
   Sufficient is your arm alone,
   And our defence is sure.

3. Before the hills in order stood,
   Or earth received its frame,
   From everlasting you are God,
   To endless years the same.

4. A thousand ages in your sight
   Are like an ev'ning gone,
   Short as the watch that ends the night
   Before the rising sun.

5. Time, like an ever-rolling stream,
   Bears all our lives away;
   Thy fly, forgotten, as a dream
   Dies at the op'ning day.

6. O God, our help in ages past,
   Our hope for years to come,
   Be now our guide while life shall last,
   And our eternal home.

Text: Psalm 90; Isaac Watts, 1674-1748, alt.
Tune: ST. ANNE, CM **Music:** CBW II 640; CBW III 644

COME, HOLY SPIRIT

1. Come, Holy Spirit, Creator blest,
   And in our hearts take up your rest;
   Come with your grace and heav'nly aid
   To fill the hearts which you have made.

2. O Comforter, to you we cry,
   The heav'nly gift of God most high;
   The fount of life and fire of love,
   And sweet anointing from above.

3. To ev'ry sense your light impart,
   And shed your love in ev'ry heart.
   To our weak flesh your strength supply:
   Unfailing courage from on high.

4. O grant that we through you may come
   To know the Father and the Son,
   And hold with firm, unchanging faith
   That you are Spirit of them both.

5. Now let us praise Father and Son,
   And Holy Spirit, with them one;
   And may the Son on us bestow
   The gifts that from the Spirit flow.

Text: *Veni, Creator Spiritus,* anon., 9th c.; tr. by Edward
Caswall, 1814-1878, et al.; alt. **Tune:** LAMBILLOTTE, LM
Music: CBW II 516; CBW III 416

ALLELUIA! SING TO JESUS!

1. Alleluia! Sing to Jesus!
   His the sceptre, his the throne;
   Alleluia! His the triumph,
   His the victory alone;
   Hark! The songs of peaceful Sion
   Thunder like a mighty flood;
   Jesus out of ev'ry nation
   Has redeemed us by his blood.

2. Alleluia! Not as orphans
   Are we left in sorrow now;
   Alleluia! He is near us,
   Faith believes, nor questions how:
   Though the cloud from sight received him
   When the forty days were o'er,
   Shall our hearts forget his promise,
   "I am with you evermore"?

3. Alleluia! Bread of heaven,
   Here on earth our food and stay;
   Alleluia! Here the sinful
   Turn to you from day to day:
   Intercessor, friend of sinners,
   Earth's Redeemer, plead for us
   Where the voices of the blessed
   Join the chant victorious.

4. Alleluia! King eternal,
   you are Lord of lords alone.
   Alleluia! Born of Mary,
   Earth your footstool, heav'n your throne:
   You within the veil have entered,
   Robed in flesh, our great high priest;
   You on earth, both priest and victim.
   In the eucharistic feast.

Text: William Chatteron Dix, 1837-1898; alt.
Tune: HYFRYDOL, 87 87 D **Music:** CBW II 536; CBW III 426

FOR ALL THE SAINTS

1. For all the saints,
   Who from their labours rest,
   Who their great faith
   To all the world confessed,
   Your name, O Jesus,
   Be forever blest. Alleluia, alleluia.

2. You were their rock,
   Their fortress and their might,
   Their strength and solace
   In the well-fought fight,
   And in the darkness
   their unfailing light. Alleluia, alleluia.

3. O blest communion,
   Family divine,
   We live and struggle,
   You in glory shine;
   Yet all are one
   within God's great design. Alleluia, alleluia.

4. And when the strife
   Is fierce, the conflict long,
   Then from the distance
   Sounds the trumpet song,
   And hearts are bold again,
   And courage strong. Alleluia, alleluia.

Text: William How, 1823-1897 **Tune:** SINE NOMINE, 10 10 10 with Alleluias **Music:** CBW II 617; CBW III 449.

Music Index

SERVICE MUSIC

HYMNS